THE ART OF THE SONNET

THE ART OF THE Sonnet

STEPHEN BURT

DAVID MIKICS

THE BELKNAP PRESS OF
HARVARD UNIVERSITY PRESS

Cambridge, Massachusetts
London, England

2010

Additional copyright notices appear
on pages 437–441, which constitute
an extension of the copyright page.

Designed by Annamarie McMahon Why

Library of Congress Cataloging-in-Publication Data

Burt, Stephen, 1971–

   The art of the sonnet / Stephen Burt and David Mikics.

      p.   cm.

   Includes bibliographical references and index.

   ISBN 978-0-674-04814-0 (alk. paper)

      1. Sonnets, English.   2. Sonnets, English—History and criticism.   3. Sonnets, Italian—
History and criticism.   I. Mikics, David, 1961–   II. Title.

   PR1195.S5B87   2010

   821'.04209—dc22   2009049069

To Jessie and Nathan
and to Victoria

Contents

Contents

How To Use These Sonnets

THIS BOOK presents and examines one hundred sonnets that repay sustained attention, memorable poems from the English Renaissance to the present day. Brief accompanying essays show how you might read a particular sonnet, and what you might hear or find in it: we explain what each sonnet does as an arrangement of language, an event in literary history, an embodiment of human emotion, an exploration of form, a work of art. Each essay also makes available information that the poem demands: we gloss unusual words, for example, and explain historical references. We have chosen the sonnets and written the introduction jointly; each essay about a sonnet, however, has one and only one author, either David Mikics or Stephen Burt. (We divided the poems, each taking fifty.) We imagine, as our reader, anyone with a serious interest in poetry; while we hope that some of our essays will bring news and insight even for academics, we do not write for experts alone.

We do not expect you to read this book straight through. The sonnets, and the essays about them, may be read in any order, or in none, with or without help from our introduction. You might start with the Romantics, or with the Victorians, or with a favorite author, such as Yeats or Frost. You might even read all hundred sonnets, sans commentary, then start again on the essays. Each pair (sonnet plus essay) makes up a self-sufficient unit; those units, taken together, make up a partial history of the sonnet form.

We have made our selection with range in mind. Some poems come from famous sequences of sonnets, starting with Philip Sidney's *Astrophel and Stella*. Some poems represent major writers, such as William Shakespeare and William Wordsworth, who both mastered and altered the form. A few are translations or adaptations from French, Spanish, and German, from writers who strongly influenced English-language poets (such as Petrarch, Baudelaire, and Rilke). And some poems are here for no reason other than our admiration, our belief that they are worth repeated rereading. We have omitted some major poets whose sonnets are not their best work, such as Alfred, Lord Tennyson and Robert Browning. Several poems, especially toward the end of the volume, show what the sonnet has meant, and how it has changed, for nations and groups of people far from the European and courtly origins of the form. We regret the omission of translations from other languages with sonnet traditions, among them Portuguese, Russian, Hebrew, Polish, and Dutch; we are delighted, on the other hand, to include fine recent sonnets that belong to the traditions of global English, with words and scenes from Newfoundland, New Zealand, the West Indies, Karnataka in India (by way of Chicago), and Australia.

We have chosen only poems we admire, though we do not mean to claim equal stature for every one. We have also left out some sonnets that stand—by modern consensus and by our own estimates—among the finest in the language (for example, Shakespeare's Sonnet 73, "That time of year thou mayst in me behold"), because those sonnets have been discussed so often, and so well, elsewhere, and because we have sought to mix the very well known and the not yet famous. We give just three sonnets by Shakespeare, and no more than two by any other hand. Some famous poets are represented by some of their most famous sonnets (Wyatt, Herbert, Shakespeare, Wordsworth, Shelley, Frost, and Yeats, for example); others, by relatively neglected gems (Spenser, Shakespeare, Keats, Millay, and Robert Lowell).

Our desire to display the unfamiliar, to add to what other anthologists have not done, also led us to make generous selections from contemporary work: to err, within reason, on the side of poets and poems that reflect our own time. There are, simply, many more poets at work now in English than ever, and we have tried to do justice to the many kinds of transformation those poets have worked on the venerable form. (A book like ours, compiled a hundred years hence, would surely give less space than we do to the period from 1960 to 2010, just as we give less space than Victorian editors did to their own era.) Readers who want more than we are able to give on the major poets of the sixteenth, seventeenth, and nineteenth centuries may turn to other anthologies and to a multitude of critical works, including those quoted in our own essays. We give our sources, along with suggestions for further critical reading, at the back of this book.

Many of our essays note allusions, connecting one sonnet to its precursors or to other poems. Until the late twentieth century, almost all poets who wrote memorably in English knew the King James Bible well; so did most of their readers. If you are not used to reading older poetry—or to reading it with commentaries—you may be surprised at how often we find sources for one or another line in the Hebrew scriptures (later incorporated by Christianity as the Old Testament) or in the New Testament, even for poets, and poems, with no pious or orthodox intent. We also take care to point out recurring themes in the history of the sonnet, themes that tie some of our hundred essays together. The first well-known sonnets in English, like the best-known sonnets in Italian and French, concern romantic or erotic love; you will find erotic love, both returned and unreturned, among the sonnets here. We have also chosen more than a handful of elegies, poems that mourn or commemorate a dead person; some remember a dead beloved. Other sonnets draw on the pastoral tradition, which depicts (and fantasizes about) the lives of shepherds— one of several connections between the sonnet and the classical past.

The clearest modern definition of "sonnet" specifies a poem of fourteen lines in iambic pentameter (da-*da* da-*da* da-*da* da-*da* da-*da*), divided by its rhymes, and by its internal logic, in one of two ways. A sonnet with a group of eight lines (the octave) and then a group of six (the sestet) is called Italian, since the most famous sonnets in Italian, those of Petrarch and Dante, rhyme in that way. A sonnet with three groups of four lines (three quatrains) and then a group of two (a couplet) is called English, or Shakespearean. Many of our hundred sonnets qualify as Italian or as Shakespearean; some rhyme according to other patterns, and some from the twentieth and twenty-first centuries do not rhyme at all. Poets and critics have argued for centuries about how to define the sonnet, and where to locate the borders of the form. We have admitted as sonnets contemporary poems of fourteen lines with no rhyme and no meter if we believe they use sonnet structure well. Often we identify a sonnet as Italianate, or as Shakespearean, even if the poet plays a variation on the pattern (for example, if the sestet comes first). We often discuss the volta (or turn) in the sonnet, which normally comes at the end of the octave, and the further twist that Shakespearean form often puts in the last two lines. These and other aspects of sonnet structure—which writers of sonnets learn, preeminently, from earlier writers of sonnets—will, we hope, grow on you, and become more familiar as you make your way through our hundred essays and our hundred poems.

The Art of the Sonnet does not and could not contain nearly as many sonnets as some existing anthologies of sonnets in English and in English translation. Some recent and comprehensive anthologies are John Fuller's *Oxford Book of Sonnets* (2000), Phillis Levin's *Penguin Book of the Sonnet* (2001), and *The Making of a Sonnet: A Norton Anthology,* edited by Eavan Boland and Edward Hirsch (2008). We have consulted them, and their many precursors, as we made our own selection, though we are proud to offer some sonnets that none of these books contains. Our texts are not always the same as theirs. For the most part, we have modernized Renaissance spellings and punctuation; we have, with only a few modifications, followed the editions listed at the end of this volume, although we have consulted others.

Our aim in this book is not only to show which sonnets have stood out, and which ones deserve further notice, but how, and why. We hope that our commentaries illuminate these writers' inventions, and that, in offering a hundred sonnets together, we can show how even the strangest contemporary sonnet draws on, and works with, the form in all its variety, with all its available ties to the past.

Introduction

FEW POETIC forms have found more uses than the sonnet, and none is now more recognizable. Imported from Italy to England in the sixteenth century, the compact sonnet suited private contemplation, introspection, guilt, and fruitless love; it also (especially after John Milton) gave verdicts on public events. The sonnet could be serious, or satirical, or self-mocking; it could set the standard for a national language, or revel in idiosyncrasy; could exult, or cast itself down. Sonnets made poets' reputations, in the Renaissance and again in the Romantic era and the centuries that followed. Some talented poets, such as Charles Tennyson Turner and Jones Very, wrote almost nothing else. The sonnet attracted amateurs in eras when the writing, and the reading, of lyric poetry was customary among people who pursued other professions. President John Quincy Adams wrote well-crafted sonnets; so did King James I of England (James VI of Scotland), the British prime minister William Gladstone, the American abolitionist William Lloyd Garrison, and the novelist Edith Wharton, who called the sonnet a "pure form . . . like some chalice of old time." Today, journals, anthologies, websites, and even exhibitions (the New York Public Library played host to one in 2003) dedicate themselves exclusively to the form. The sonnet has more varieties, and more readers, today than ever before. Some of its contemporary versions are self-consciously traditional; others, decidedly impure.

The sonnet is one of the longest-lived of verse forms, and one of the briefest. A mere fourteen lines, laced together by intricate rhymes, it is, as Dante Gabriel Rossetti called it, "a moment's monument." Often, the sonnet makes an occasion crucial, and fixes it to the page. It is predictable yet supple in its application of rules. This formal strength makes something as seemingly slight as a lyric poem a work for the ages. Rapturous praise, bitter exclamation, and step-by-step reasoning frequently intertwine in its concise shape. The poem's form contains and focuses its author's passions, and very often expresses a drive toward idealization: emotion achieves clarity and substantial life under the lamp of art. Obsessive care and fascination mark the sonnet from its beginnings.

The rest of this book gives one hundred exemplary sonnets, with commentaries on the inner workings, and the historical contexts, for each one. This introduction complements those essays with a short history of the form. We begin with some detail about the sonnet in Italy, where it originated, and with its greatest Italian practitioners, Petrarch and Dante, since their achievements lie behind so many of the English-language sonnets we discuss in this book. We then describe the sonnet in the English Renaissance. A story with some unity about the use and meaning of the sonnet before 1800 (in its Petrarchan and English or Shakespearean varieties) becomes, in the nineteenth century, a much more complicated set of stories about how different poets have used the form. What counts as a sonnet, we shall see, changes over time. After tracing the sonnet through the Renaissance in several languages, our introduction follows sonnets in English. The profusion of developments within that set, its relative independence from Continental languages, and the fact that our book is in English dictate this approach.

The sonnet was born in early thirteenth-century Sicily, at the court of a cultivated, cosmopolitan ruler, Frederick II. Sicily was a crossroads: it had absorbed the scientific advances of Islamic North Africa, along with the chivalric habits and troubadour poetry of southern France. Both of these currents contributed to the making of the early Sicilian sonnet, which incorporated courtly sophistication as well as a taste for argument and precise form. No stranger to exoticism, Frederick (who ruled from 1205 to 1250) had a menagerie consisting of camels, hawks, horned owls, panthers, doves, giraffes, and an elephant. But he was also a serious scholar and student of the arts. Frederick's passions were falconry, Roman law, and the classics, and he was a poet himself.

About sixty sonnets survive from the *scuola siciliana*. The Sicilian poets looked back to the Provençal troubadours of the twelfth century, who celebrated a form of eros both illicit and glorious: their love for their (usually married) ladies. The troubadours prided themselves on a refined understanding of love's torments, its harsh disappointments and its joys. This was *fin amors,* a higher eros. The poet, swayed from patience to wild frustration and back, became the student of his own emotions. The troubadour was sometimes discouraged, sometimes ecstatic, all-dependent on his lady's response to his amorous plea. He served his beloved as a knight of desire waiting on her every wish and gesture. The troubadour poet, often separated from his lady, spoke of love at a distance *(amor de longh)*. This emphasis on the removed, even inaccessible, position of the beloved carries over into the sonnet tradition.

The Sicilian poets gave the Italianate sonnet the formal properties it still has today: fourteen lines divided into an octave (the opening eight lines) and a sestet (the closing six lines), the division between the two sections being marked with a volta, or turn of thought ("volta" means "turn" in Italian). The Sicilian school borrowed the octave from the *strambotto,* a peasant song. The sonnet, however, was no song. It was asymmetrical, suited to meditative logic rather than music. The troubadours sang their poems; the sonneteer composed his for private enjoyment. Intensely contemplative, sonnet writers rejected the repetitive ease of the ballad, along with the vocal flourishes of troubadour lyric. Already the sonnet was moving "close . . . to aria and aphorism, close to syllogism, close to prayer" (as the critic David Bromwich remarks about the sonnet form). The sonnet summarizes, begs, proves, and experiments; it calculates its effects, and turns in on itself with patient intent.

The most prominent of the early Sicilian sonneteers, and perhaps the inventor of the form, was Giacomo da Lentini (ca. 1210–ca. 1260), one of Frederick's notaries (court officials). The balanced clarity of Giacomo's poetry rejects the troubadours' uneven bravado, their blend of crude impulse and courtly finesse. The lucid fire of Giacomo's verses seems at home in the sun-drenched landscape of Sicily. His poems are bright and hard, but they also feature a profoundly introspective quiet, and a somber manipulation of words.

The arrival of the sonnet marks an inward turn in Italian poetry: lyric purifies itself, and becomes a reflection on reflection. The sonnet form thrives on, and fosters, debate within the self, a thorny internal monologue. But it also reins in, and rounds off, thinking, and so makes inwardness complete.

The Sicilian poets were followed, in the thirteenth century, by the *stilnovisti* of northern Italy, among them Guido Guinizelli and Guido Cavalcanti. The *stilnovisti* practiced the *dolce stil nuovo* ("sweet new style"). Clear and introspective, they avoided the Sicilian poets' use of riddling wordplay. Their sonnets make a case, arguing the author's love in stately measures. The patient, incantatory character of *stilnovist* verse comes across even in translation, as does its fervor. The *stilnovist* poet centers his poem on a magnificent apparition: the radiant, quasi-divine lady. He strives not to seduce or persuade, but simply to honor her.

Italy's greatest poet, Dante Alighieri, employed the sonnet in his ravishing accounts of love's trials: the *Vita nuova* (New Life; ca. 1294) and the *Rime petrose* (Stony Rhymes; 1296). The *Vita nuova,* a prose story with several dozen sonnets (and other lyric forms) embedded in it, narrates Dante's violent initiation into love. The *Vita* begins when Dante, at age nine, first glimpses Beatrice, also nine years old: in a dream, the god of love feeds the poet's burning heart to the unwilling Beatrice.

In the *Vita nuova,* Dante makes the sonnet embody the crucial moments of the inner life. In his hands, the sonnet gives voice to the suffering lover, and charts the plot of his passion. He melds praise of his lady, the same Beatrice who will guide him in the later *Divina commedia* (Divine Comedy; written 1308–1321), with reflection on his own sharp-edged mood. The *Vita nuova* narrates the education of the lover at the hands of Beatrice. In the course of the autobiographical story, Dante comes to understand that Beatrice offers a revelation from another world; and so his desire proves spiritual.

Francesco Petrarca (1304–1374), known as Petrarch, follows in the enormous wake of Dante. Petrarch is the most influential sonnet writer in history. He put his impress on a whole tradition of writing and thinking; we still speak of "Petrarchan love poetry." The Petrarchan sonnet consists of an octave, rhyming *abbaabba* (two "closed" quatrains, as opposed to the "open" *abab*), and a sestet, often rhyming *cdecde, cdcdcd,* or *cdedce.* With Petrarch, the lyric poem, now a coordinated, perfectly smooth action, completes its journey: once a token of chivalric loyalty or a gesture of affection, lyric verse has become a way of talking to oneself.

Petrarchan love is ideal, yet earthbound. Dante elevated his beloved into a force of divine harmony; she presides over the intricate cosmos of the *Divine Comedy,* leading the poet-pilgrim from mere earthly desire to godly illumination. Petrarch, by contrast, continues to wander among the torments and pleasures of the erotic life we all know. He refines his consciousness, and casts his weary mind back over his long history of frustrated love.

Petrarch's famous beloved, Laura, may not have existed; so one of Petrarch's own contemporaries charged. Perhaps she was more a symbol than a reality. But Petrarch asserts that he glimpsed her when he was twenty-two at a church in Avignon, the cosmopolitan city in southern France where he spent his youth; and that she died in 1348, a victim of the Black Plague that was sweeping through Europe. Laura, "illustrious through her own virtues, and long famed through my verses" (Petrarch writes), haunts like an ethereal phantom his vast collection, *Rime sparse* (Scattered Rhymes; 1374). She is seen from a distance, or in memory, for more than three hundred poems (sonnets and canzoni, irregular long poems on the Provençal model). Petrarch remains obsessed with the image of the lady. His fixation drives him—so he claims—nearly to madness.

In Petrarch's *Rime,* the beloved's image, like the poet's own mind, proves unreliable, and adept at deception. She has the inconstancy of a dream. The poet wanders, meditative and intense, through the landscape of his own hopes and fears. He longs for a brief sight of happiness, a favorable sign from his Laura. Laura is also, punningly, the laurel, the wreath that adorns the poet's head (in a ceremony of his own devising, Petrarch got himself crowned poet laureate in Rome in 1341).

Driven by perpetual change, always incomplete and questing, the Petrarchan self knows no calm. The poet suffers; the heart sighs. Petrarch returns again and again to the remembered sight of Laura. He finds himself manipulated by opposites: "I fear, and hope, and burn and freeze," he writes (*Rime* 134). He argues with love, and love argues back (*Rime* 35). The self is fragile, reduced to helpless desire; its satisfaction, in moments of fantasy or dream, remains a brief illusion. Miserable, he weeps, yet fluently composes his copious verses. There is no end to his troubles—or his desire to record them.

Poem 190 from the *Rime sparse,* "Una candida cerva," demonstrates Petrarch's reliance on a troubled, visionary moment. The sonnet would be imitated by Sir Thomas Wyatt in 1557 as "Whoso list to hunt," one of the most influential English Renaissance poems (we discuss Wyatt's version immediately after this introduction). Here is the poem, in David Mikics' English version and then in Petrarch's Italian:

A shining doe on the green grass
Appeared to me, with two horns of gold,
Between two streams, in the shade of a laurel,
When the sun was rising in the unripe season.

Her air was so sweetly proud
That I left all labor to pursue her,
Like the miser who, in his search for treasure,
Relieves his trouble with delight.

"No one touch me": around her beautiful neck
this was written in diamond and topaz.
"It pleased my Caesar to set me free."

And the sun had turned at midday,
My eyes were tired with gazing, not satisfied . . .
When I fell in the water and she vanished.

Una candida cerva sopra l'erba
Verde m'apparve con duo corna d'oro,
Fra due riviere all'ombra d'un alloro,
Levando 'l sole a la stagione acerba.

Era sua vista sì dolce superba
Ch'i' lasciai per seguirla ogni lavoro,
Come l'avaro che'n cercar tesoro
Con diletto l'affanno disacerba.

"Nessun mi tocchi," al bel collo d'intorno
scritto avea di diamanti et di topazi.
"Libera farmi al mio Cesare parve."

Et era 'l sol già vòlto al mezzo giorno,
Gli occhi miei stanchi di mirar, non sazi,
Quand'io caddi ne l'acqua et ella sparve.

Petrarch begins with a symbol: the doe, sacred to Diana, goddess of chastity. The animal represents his beloved Laura, seen in "la stagione acerba," the bitter or unripe season of youth. She is shaded by the laurel, sign of the poetic fame that Petrarch desires. The landscape is dreamlike, abstract. Symmetry and stillness frame the vision: two streams, two golden horns. The rest of the octave, lines 5–8, engages in paradox. The doe's expression is "sì dolce superba," "so sweetly proud." Like the miser who delights in hoarding his money, the poet cherishes his bitter erotic pursuit, and makes it sweet.

But the sestet brings him up short. The poet finds himself stopped by an injunction: don't touch. The risen Jesus spoke this line to Mary Magdalene, warning her, "Noli me tangere" (Petrarch translates the Latin of the Vulgate into Italian). Petrarch also alludes to a secular legend: that centuries after Augustus Caesar's death, white stags were found with collars bearing the inscription, "Noli me tangere, Caesaris sum"—"Touch me not, for I am Caesar's." Who owns this doe? Apparently no one; she has been set free, independent and wild. Yet she remains forever inaccessible. (The diamond and topaz symbolize chastity.)

Petrarch trades in hallucinatory unclarity. He hints at the quasi-sacred aura that surrounds Laura (or the doe), and stays distant from her. Yet he also suggests that her image exists purely within his own mind. Weary, still unsatisfied, he falls into the water, breaking the spell. The poet implies that, like Narcissus, he has been staring at his own reflection, which he cannot grasp because it eludes recognition. Like the miser, Narcissus is really a poor man. Fooled by desire, he wants what seems present and graspable, but this immediacy proves a mere illusion. And so it is with the poet, deceived by appearance and the sound of words. Laura represents the laurel wreath destined for his own brow, sign of his poetic fame. Entranced by her, he remains in bondage to himself. (The poem's high, superb assonance seals the spell.)

Petrarch generated a swarm of imitators, and not just in Italy. Clément Marot, who called it a "plaisante invention Italienne," wrote the first French sonnet, in 1539. Also in France, Joachim du Bellay and Pierre de Ronsard (both mid-sixteenth century) were major influences on the sonnet's development. Their poems are sinuous, elegant in sound and sense. Their elevated interest in Platonic idealism influenced the Englishman Edmund Spenser, whose mellifluous sequence *Amoretti,* along with Philip Sidney's *Astrophel and Stella,* caps the development of the pre-Shakespearean English sonnet. Also in the 1530s, Juan Boscán and Garcilaso de la Vega introduced the sonnet to Spain. Between 1530 and 1650, Europe saw a vast outpouring of sonnets: about 200,000 of them, according to the scholar Hugues Vaganay. Most were not love poems, but poems of compliment or dedication appended to treatises in law, divinity, or other subjects.

Sir Thomas Wyatt and Henry Howard, the Earl of Surrey, brought the sonnet to England. George Puttenham writes in *The Arte of English Poesie* (1589) that Wyatt and Surrey "were the two chieftaines, who having travailed into Italie, and there tasted the sweet and stately measures and stile of the Italian poesie," mended the native English roughness ("our rude and homely maner of vulgar Poesie"). Wyatt developed the couplet ending, a device that gives his sonnets an epigrammatic sting. His focus is this-worldly, troubled; rougher than Petrarch, he yet looks back to Petrarchan tradition. A brusque courtier who served Henry VIII, Wyatt depicts complex social settings as well as scenes of solitary lament.

In the Renaissance, most poems circulated in manuscript; book publication occurred later, often after the author's death. Sonnets by Wyatt and Surrey appeared in *Tottel's Miscellany,* a landmark collection of lyric poems issued in 1557. It took another thirty years for the sonnet to hit its stride in England.

About 4,000 sonnets appeared in England between 1580 and 1600, the height of that country's sonnet vogue. Sixteenth-century England produced a generous handful of remarkable sonneteers, among them the gruff and steadfast George Gascoigne, the reflective Fulke Greville, and the sober, smooth Samuel Daniel (all included in this volume). Elizabethan sonnets inherited the familiar Petrarchan duo: longed-for, resistant beloved and adoring, suffering poet. The Elizabethan poet-lover, as the scholar Maurice Evans puts it, "will suffer the tempestuous and warring passions of love: he will lie awake all night, or if he sleeps, have erotic dreams of his mistress: he will hear her singing or watch her as she plies her needle or steal a kiss while she sleeps: he will itemize all her beauties and he will protest the power of his verse to keep that beauty alive in spite of the ravages of time." The poet's work took expression as a series of striking, governing images (called conceits). The poet was a soldier in love's wars, his passion a ship lost in a storm; an icy fire burned within him. His beloved's face was a garden or a set of assembled metaphors (known as a blason): her teeth like pearls, her lips like cherries, her eyes like bright suns.

Astrophel and Stella, published in 1591, sparked a sonnet craze among Elizabethan writers. Sidney was a catalytic influence: his Astrophel became the type of the frustrated, ardent lover. By the mid-1590s, the sonneteers were making prominent enemies among the literati. Sir John Davies, in his *Gulling Sonnets* (ca. 1595), mocked the "bastard sonnets of these rhymers base," the ornate and preening productions of conventional love poets. Sir John Florio, in his pamphlet *Second Fruites,* condemned the "active gallants" who, "devising how to win their Mistress' favours, . . . blaze and blanch their passions, with aeglogues, Songs, and Sonnets, in pitiful verse . . . and most for a fashion."

In his *Ortho-Epia Gallica,* Sir John Eliot spurned the authors of sonnets in even harsher terms. Formerly "cherry-cheeked" and "merry," the melancholy sonneteer (Eliot claimed) turns "lean, wan, pale, looking like one half dead": "You shall see him feign a sea of tears, a lake of miseries, wring his hands and weep, accuse the heaven, curse the earth, make an anatomy of his heart, to freeze, to burn, to adore, to play the idolator. . . . And by and by he exalteth in his verses that Diana whom he loveth best; her hair is nothing but gold wire, her brows arches and vaults of Ebenus: her eyes twinkling stars like Castor and Pollux, her looks lightnings: her mouth coral: her neck orient pearl: her breath balm, amber, and musk: her throat of snow: her neck milk-white: her dugs that she hath on her breast, mountains or apples of alabaster." In Eliot's comment, as in Shakespeare's Sonnet 130, "My mistress' eyes are nothing like the sun," convention is played off against crude reality. "If hairs be wires, black wires grow on her head," Shakespeare writes of his beloved, who, no goddess, walks on the ground.

The Elizabethan sonneteer aimed at the artful and reflective: he stood apart from, even as he inhabited, a passionate, love-struck self. The sonnet form offered welcome constraint as well as pleasure, "the certaine close of delight" (in Samuel Daniel's words). Expressing one's love was a genuine relief, but also a performance, and the performance often included erotic anecdote, moralizing, intimate confession, and satirical grace notes—a series of poetic poses.

One of Sidney's best modern readers, David Kalstone, emphasizes the "cutting, sardonic edge" that *Astrophel and Stella* maintains. The poet mocks moralizing doctrine, and garlands passion with wit. Conversational, tense, and playful, he contributes to the art of feigning (that is, fiction making) by fashioning a bold, dissatisfied persona, the lover Astrophel. The vivid, inventive Sidney plays off literary convention against experience, mere talk against action, and slyly marks his distance from what he calls "poor Petrarch's long-deceasèd woes." His Astrophel berates himself for abandoning his responsibilities to dote on love. He comforts himself with doses of idealism, the knowledge of Stella's high virtue and grace. "But ah" (Sidney writes), "desire still cries, 'give me some food.'" Astrophel's beloved Stella, "most fair, most cold," differs from the "soveraynebeauty" that Edmund Spenser praises in his *Amoretti*, another major achievement of the 1590s. Spenser's sonnet sequence creates a harmonious, even majestic, atmosphere. Erotic life, even in its frustrations, takes on the character of a stately ceremony. In its hallowed pace, the *Amoretti* pays tribute to Spenser's beloved, and to his own poetic ambition.

In the sixteenth century, women poets took up the sonnet avidly. In Italy, Gaspara Stampa and Vittoria Colonna wrote memorable sonnets, as did Louise Labé in France. We have chosen a poem from the sequence *Pamphilia to Amphilanthus* (1621), by the English Renaissance poet Mary Wroth, to illustrate how women adopted many of the Petrarchan themes. Often they added a twist based on the author's gender: Wroth, rather than picturing herself as a Narcissus figure like Petrarch, becomes the mirror for her male lover's self-admiration.

Samuel Daniel, in his *Defence of Ryme* (1602), considers the sonnet and asks, "Is it not most delightfull to see much excellently ordred in a small roome?" As the critic Michael Spiller remarks, the sonnet reins in the restless imagination, circumscribes it. But the sonnet was about to experience a radical expansion of its possibilities—a revolution, in the works of one man.

Modern readers agree (though earlier readers fought over it) that the most remarkable sonnets in the English language are those of William Shakespeare. His 154 sonnets experiment with ambiguities of tone in a daring, innovative way. Shakespeare exploits the dramatic potential of the sonnet form as no other writer does (as befits our greatest playwright). He refines the use of the concluding couplet so as to put his seal on the form. His sonnets surpass all others for sheer memorability and (often mysterious) power.

Published in 1609 (though begun, and perhaps even completed, in the 1590s), Shakespeare's sequence begins with more than a hundred poems voicing adoration of a young man; it ends with a much shorter series of cynical and wounded sonnets centering on the figure of a "dark lady." The pathos of Shakespeare's speaker, who is by turns proud, generous, self-deceiving, and self-hating—and through it all, helplessly, utterly in love—has proven irresistible to generations of readers. The singularity of the young man draws the poet's erotic attention: the poems credit themselves with establishing his worth, his enduring reality, in immortal verse. He is no mere idea, not a creature of the mind, as Dante's Beatrice, Petrarch's Laura, and their legion of descendents tend to be, but a troublesome, uncontrollable actor in a drama of betrayal.

Shakespeare's speaker (we are strongly tempted to identify him with Shakespeare himself) desperately wishes to know the young man, to find out "the substance whereof [he is] made"—yet he knows him all too well, as a corrupt soul who cannot be saved by praise. He is "too dear for [the poet's] possessing": too intensely loved, and worth too much, to be kept within a sonnet's confines. He outpaces every Shakespearean strategy, no matter how self-abnegating, shrewd, or resplendently assertive. Shakespeare's "I" talks to himself, his audience. and his beloved the way an actor on a stage does. Never before or since has a poet so richly, and painfully, depicted his own defeat; never has insecurity seemed so glorious.

Almost all Shakespeare's sonnets consist of three "open" quatrains *(abab cdcd efef)* and a couplet *(gg)*, the rhyme scheme now called either English or Shakespearean. In his poems, the octave-sestet division is overshadowed by three distinct and equal blocks, the quatrains—and by the couplet that looks back on the sonnet's action, often with acerbic, epigrammatic terseness or sweeping judgment. Much earlier, Wyatt and Surrey had relied on the couplet ending in their sonnets; but in Shakespeare's hands the couplet reflects on the poem it concludes in unprecedented, surprising ways.

Thanks to Sidney and Shakespeare, we may think of Renaissance sonnets as poems about secular love. Yet the sonnet in Renaissance England encompassed religious expression as well: the first sonnet sequence in English (obscure until recently, and without influence) seems to have been Anne Lock's *Meditation of a Penitent Sinner* (1560). The strongest sonnets of the early seventeenth century (after Shakespeare), those of John Donne and George Herbert, take up Christian themes. Donne's sonnets are contorted and passionate; they dominate the reader, and strike with exclamatory force. In the series usually called *Holy Sonnets* (most of them published posthumously in 1633), Donne gives tense, tormented expression to his spiritual struggle: he proves himself a great actor of his woes and his ecstasies. Donne's other contribution to the development of the form was *The Corona,* a series of sonnets linked by their first and last lines. Herbert's poems are compact, their conceits steady and intricate. In "Redemption," Herbert trades in surprise, and leads the reader to spiritual reassessment. In the more reassuring "Prayer (I)," the poet produces a beautifully rounded, satisfying tribute to the human act of devotion to God.

The profusion of sonnets in their era coincided with confusion about terminology. Though a posthumous collection of Donne's lyric poems was entitled *Songs and Sonets,* none of the poems in it counts as a sonnet by modern definitions: though "sonnet" had its modern meaning, and its fourteen-line norm, for some Renaissance writers, others applied the word to short songlike poems (in Italian, *sonetto* means a "little song"). Even sonnets properly so-called could vary in length: Greville's *Caelica* includes sonnets in which one, two, or five quatrains are followed by a concluding couplet. Despite the confusion of terms, practicing poets certainly regarded the fourteen-line, octave-and-sestet or quatrains-and-couplet form as a continuous tradition, as is evident in Wyatt's and Sidney's answers to the Italians, and in Shakespeare's to the sonnet writers of the 1580s and 1590s.

In the early seventeenth century, the Spanish writers Lope de Vega and Luis de Góngora perfected an ingenious, highly polished style, both lyrical and intellectual in nature. Lope is sometimes sober, sometimes light-hearted; Góngora, baroque and strenuous. The Spanish Golden Age had its influence on the major English sonnet writer of the mid-seventeenth century, John Milton. For decades, as Milton readied himself to write an epic (it turned out to be *Paradise Lost*), he wrote sonnets on his own youthful career ("How soon hath time," Sonnet 7) and, later, on his blindness (Sonnet 19), as well as sonnets on politics and friendship. We include Milton's Sonnet 23, on the loss and memory of a beloved wife ("Methought I saw my late espousèd saint"), as well as his fervent poem of protest against the massacre of Waldensian Protestants ("Avenge, O Lord, thy slaughtered saints," Sonnet 18). Milton also learned from the elevated voice of a great sixteenth-century Italian sonneteer, Torquato Tasso. But if Tasso's sonnets possess a kind of contoured eloquence, Milton's overflow with power. The momentum of his verse frequently overrides the distinction between octave and sestet, enjambments aid the drive toward culmination, and the whole becomes a statement of visionary strength.

Samuel Johnson's *Dictionary* (1755) declared that the sonnet form (defined as having fourteen lines) had "not been used by any man of eminence since Milton." Indeed, the English writers of the early 1700s had almost abandoned the form. Yet in Johnson's day, it was beginning a sort of revival. Thomas Gray's sonnet on the death of Richard West (written in 1742, published in 1775, and famously attacked by Wordsworth in 1800) combines the dignified rules of eighteenth-century poetic diction, and the eighteenth-century taste for balanced antitheses, with Petrarch's (and Sidney's) command to speak from the heart. "In vain to me the smiling Mornings shine," Gray's sonnet begins, "And reddening Phoebus lifts his golden fire; / The birds in vain their amorous descant join; / Or cheerful fields resume their green attire."

Gray's sonnet was an anomaly: he wrote no others. But Joseph and Thomas Warton, Gray's contemporaries, published sonnets in sets; William Bowles enjoyed popular success with sonnets during the 1780s; and by the 1790s the form was in bloom again, with contributions from Helen Maria Williams, Anna Seward, Charlotte Smith, the young Samuel Taylor Coleridge, his friends Charles Lamb and Robert Southey, and even Robert Burns, who wrote a comic sonnet about the sonnet: "What lucubrations can be more upon it?" Burns's poem ends, "Fourteen good measured verses make a sonnet." Mary Robinson's *Sappho and Phaon* (1796) presented itself as the first narrative sonnet sequence—and the first with Petrarchan rhyme schemes—since the seventeenth century. For all these writers, the sonnet becomes a way to reject the approaches we now call Augustan, the dominance of the couplet and blank verse (modes which allow a poem to take any length), and the preeminent discursive, descriptive, narrative, and satirical modes. The sonnet becomes a vehicle of nostalgia, even of mourning (as for Gray); of landscape, prospect, and the walking tour (as in Bowles and Smith); of lyric as a mode; and of an appeal to the ancients by which truth to feeling, not to reason or religion or society or duty, becomes what we ought to learn from ages past.

By 1800 the word "sonnet," in English, had come to mean, almost always, a fourteen-line poem in pentameter divided by rhyme into units of 8 and 6 (Italian or Petrarchan) or into 4, 4, 4, and 2 (Shakespearean or English).

The form had consistent connotations, too: Seward's *Original Sonnets on Various Subjects* (1799), which included attacks on Dr. Johnson's taste, also contained a sonnet to Henry Cary on the publication of his sonnets, celebrating the form's unique combination of strong emotion with "strict" restraint, and evoking its Petrarchan and (better yet) Miltonic heritage: "our greater Milton" had rendered the form respectable, and majestic, and English, too. (Though most readers already thought Shakespeare a great playwright, his sonnets remained a topic of controversy, not yet generally esteemed.) For the young Coleridge, as he said in his 1796 pamphlet, the sonnet was "a poem in which some lonely feeling is developed. . . . Poems, in which no lonely feeling is developed, are not Sonnets."

Coleridge, in 1796, was writing at nearly the last moment when it was plausible to define the sonnet in English, in general, by criteria of external form and at the same time by topic, theme, attitude. William Wordsworth was about to make it impossible. He had published a sonnet of sensibility in 1787 ("Sonnet on Seeing Miss Helen Maria Williams Weep at a Tale of Distress"); in 1802, he began to write sonnets copiously. By the end of his life, he had written more than five hundred, including sonnets devoted "To Liberty" (later, "To National Independence and Liberty"), modeled on Milton; sonnets in the tradition of Sensibility, about prospects, moments, or moods ("Composed upon Westminster Bridge," "Surprised by Joy," and many others); sonnets about "Steamboats, Viaducts, and Railways"; and a history in sonnets of the Anglican Church. Wordsworth also penned two of the most famous English sonnets about the sonnet form: one begins "Scorn not the sonnet," the other "Nuns fret not at their convent's narrow room." Both poems associate the form (as Anna Seward had done) with restriction, chosen limits, discipline, self-rule. John Keats's "On the Sonnet" (1819) instead urges poets to work well—and sensuously—within the inherited rules they did not choose: "So, if we may not let the Muse be free, / She will be bound with garlands of her own."

Anne Elliott, the heroine of Jane Austen's *Persuasion* (1815–1816), still defines sonnets in part by subject and mood: she muses, "The sweet scenes of autumn were for a while put by—unless some tender sonnet, fraught with the apt analogy of the declining year . . . and the images of youth and hope, and spring, all gone together, blessed her memory." Austen grew up reading, and sometimes mocking, the poetry of Sensibility (Anne, we learn, reads Walter Scott, and Byron). By the time of Austen's death—by the time of John Keats, and of Keats's epigones—the sonnet had almost become, thanks in part to

Wordsworth, what pentameter couplets were for the eighteenth century, a default form into which poets could pour almost anything. Leigh Hunt and his circle used the sonnet for impromptu competitions, one of which generated Keats's, and Hunt's, sonnets called "On the Grasshopper and Cricket." Sonnets became an appropriate choice when a poet required a fixed form, for any subject, fast.

A much older Hunt, introducing his anthology *The Book of the Sonnet* (compiled in 1857, published a decade later), declared that "with the exception of . . . the dithyrambic, which disdains all order and bounds . . . there is [no subject] unsuitable to [the sonnet]—whether light or serious, the humblest or the most exalted. . . . Every mood of mind can be indulged in a sonnet; every kind of reader appealed to." Charles Baudelaire, in France, agreed; he wrote in an 1860 letter that "the sonnet is suitable for everything: buffoonery, gallantry, passion, revery, philosophic meditation." Dante Gabriel Rossetti's "The Sonnet" (1880)—the most famous sonnet about sonnets, after those by Wordsworth and Keats—dubbed the form "a coin [whose] face reveals / The soul": a characterization that might fit, with equal facility, Romantic and post-Romantic lyric in general. (Louise Bogan's "Single Sonnet," included here, is another notable reflection on the sonnet form.)

"Those who wrote about the sonnet in the nineteenth century," says the scholar Jennifer Wagner, "permitted this small form to be a synecdoche for all lyric poetry." Victorian anthologies of sonnets (Hunt's, unfortunately, included) are full of predictably consolatory nature poems, pious resolutions, praise for friends and for public figures—precisely the goals that dominated other kinds of Victorian lyric verse. The best nineteenth-century sonnets, and the best sequences, show far more variety. Elizabeth Barrett Browning, in 1845–1850, used the sonnet sequence to depict a successful courtship, the first such use in English since Spenser. George Meredith, in 1862, published fifty sixteen-line sonnets about his failed marriage, the first set of short poems in English to pursue such a topic at length, and the first (in English) since the Renaissance to alter the fourteen-line form. Charles Tennyson Turner (Alfred's brother), Hartley Coleridge (Samuel's son), Gerard Manley Hopkins, Dante Gabriel Rossetti, his sister Christina, their brother William Michael, and, in America, Jones Very and Very's student Frederick Goddard Tuckerman wrote sonnets more readily and more frequently than they used any other form. Some of those names are remembered for nothing else.

Nineteenth-century sonnets found models in Milton and in the Italians, but also in Shakespeare. "With this key / Shakespeare unlocked his heart"—so

Wordsworth wrote in 1827. The American poet and playwright George Henry Boker (1828–1890), famous in his day, left for posthumous publication 313 skillfully Shakespearean sonnets about his extramarital affairs. (Boker's sonnets—along with thousands of others, by major and by minor poets, now in the public domain—appear in the remarkably capacious Internet anthology maintained by Eric Blomquist and his collaborators at www.sonnets.org.) Other writers turned sonnets to other purposes. Henry Wadsworth Longfellow translated Spanish devotional sonnets in the 1830s, at the very start of his career; his later sonnets encompass literary criticism ("Chaucer," "Milton") and reflective autobiography ("Mezzo Cammin," "The Cross of Snow"). Sonnets in sequence could suit marital love or illicit erotic love, but Victorians made them fit chaste familial love, too, as in George Eliot's *Brother and Sister* (composed before 1870) and in Augusta Webster's *Mother and Daughter* (published in 1895, a year after her death, with a preface by William Michael Rossetti). The sonnet could still respond to public affairs: Sydney Dobbell and Alexander Smith used them at length in 1855 to report on the Crimean War.

The Rossettis, whose father came from Italy, remained exceptionally conscious of the sonnet's Italian roots; so did Hunt, who could also read Italian, and who (like Robinson) considered the "legitimate" or Petrarchan sonnet (with just two rhymes in the octave) the only "perfect" kind. (Hunt points out that nineteenth-century editors did not classify Milton's "On the New Forcers of Conscience"—a caudate or tailed sonnet, with a six-line coda, a form familiar in Italian—as a sonnet at all.) While critics debated the limits of the form, poets extended its range. Meredith added lines; Gerard Manley Hopkins subtracted them, giving his three "curtal sonnets" (the most famous is "Pied Beauty") ten and a half lines apiece. Even Hopkins's fourteen-line sonnets (the vast majority, including both our choices here) seem, in their rhythms and timbres, startlingly new.

Dante Gabriel Rossetti's sequence *The House of Life* (1870–1881) helped to set off another sonnet boom. Almost every goal that a short nineteenth-century poem could adopt is served somewhere, between 1880 and 1910, in sonnets. There were erotic poems, of course, and divine meditations (such as Christina Rossetti's), and political commentaries ("Why I Am a Liberal" [1885], one of Robert Browning's few sonnets), but also much else—ekphrases, poems about works of visual art; compressed narratives, what today we might call short-short stories in verse; arguments about Nature and evolution; travel writing; and metaphysical tableaux (such as Meredith's famous 1883 "Lucifer in Starlight"). Anthologies of sonnets and books about sonnets flourished, among them *Sonnets on the Sonnet: An Anthology* (1898), edited by the Jesuit Matthew Russell, with multiple entries from Wordsworth and D. G. Rossetti, and single sonnets from (among many others) Edgar Allan Poe, Lope de Vega, and Théophile Gautier. Algernon Charles Swinburne, in 1882, wrote a sonnet about every Elizabethan and Jacobean dramatist, with a few left over for plays by authors unknown. Edward Cracroft Lefroy, in 1883, used the sonnet for deft, passionate adaptations of Theocritus. Eugene Lee-Hamilton's *Imaginary Sonnets* (1888) are dramatic monologues spoken by historical characters (Richard III, Cardinal Richelieu, Galileo). These writers of idiosyncratic sequences may stand for the trove of late-Victorian sonneteers who just missed inclusion here.

Even before the twentieth century begins, then, we might be tempted to say of the sonnet what Randall Jarrell once said about human beings: "Sonnets aren't like anything: there are too many of them." General claims about twentieth-century sonnets, claims about how poets use the form in general, ought not draw—as so many, alas, have drawn—on thumbnail sketches of the history of the form. It is simply not true that all modern sonneteers look back to Petrarch, to Petrarchism, and to anti-Petrarchism, or that they must choose between putatively English echoes of Shakespeare and putatively Italian, hence "foreign" forms. Nor is it true that the twentieth-century sonnet is, of its nature, more intensely personal than all other lyric forms.

Rather, modern and contemporary poets can choose among overlapping, competing, and often incompatible versions of what the sonnet as such, by virtue of its literary history, "means." W. B. Yeats seems to have seen it (we quote Helen Vendler) as "verse consciously aware of itself as written, not oral; verse from a European court tradition; verse knowing itself to be artifice, and often speaking about its own art; verse (although of Italian origin) associated with the essential English lyric tradition, from Wyatt . . . through Keats." Many other poets, though, especially those who write sequences, see the sonnet as a form for the impromptu: a *moment's* monument; a record of an instant, as if unrevised. Sonnets become important to the poetry of World War I, to national sentiment and national mourning, after Rupert Brooke's notorious 1914 quintet of patriotic sonnets ("If I should die, think only this of me"), which prompted appalled replies from poets in the trenches.

The sonnet became a domestic form, small-scale, fit for times of peace, for light verse, and for women, from Edna St. Vincent Millay (who attacked feminine propriety) to Phyllis McGinley (who often upheld it). The sonnet sequence mobilized the resources of journalism in W. H. Auden's *In Time of War* (1938, later retitled *Sonnets from China*), then rejected journalism for allegory in Auden's sequence *The Quest* (1941). The sonnet is secular, fit for records of day-to-day life, in sequences by contemporary poets ranging from Marilyn Hacker to Bernadette Mayer to Paul Muldoon; the sonnet is devotional, fit for the sublime, in Rainer Maria Rilke's *Sonnets to Orpheus* (1922), and more recently in the work of Donald Revell; while for e. e. cummings, John Berryman, and many others, it remained just right for erotic love. No poem, and few poets, can incorporate all those traditions at once. What until Wordsworth looked like a continuous story has become a dense portfolio from which individual poets and poems take their own stories about how to use the form.

Whatever line, whatever implications, about their own sonnets these poets embraced, though, one fact about the sonnet proved inescapable: the sonnet *had* a history—and to write a sonnet was to participate in a line of poets, stretching back for centuries, who had taken up the form. The sonnet by the early twentieth century, in English at least, stood less for particular historical lines than for history as such. And so the English-language modernist writers who wanted to distance themselves from literary history, or from a European past, refused to write sonnets, or used them only for parodies. William Carlos Williams wrote one sonnet per day in his undergraduate years, but in his modernist heyday, in 1938, he singled out the sonnet as a "fascistic form." He wrote one rhyming sonnet, in 1933, "Our (American) Ragcademicians" ("Oh what fools! what shattered fools we are, / What brainless, headless, bellywitted lumps"), as if to show that empty-headed scholars deserved no better than a creaky, obsolete sort of poem. Yet in 1939 he could praise Merrill Moore's copious modern sonnets, and by *Pictures from Brueghel* (1962) Williams himself could renew the form: "Sonnet in Search of an Author" is a tender fourteen-line scene of wild nature and sexual desire, with "Nude bodies like peeled logs." It even ends on something close to a rhyming couplet: "odor of a nude woman / sometimes, odor of a man."

As for other modernists, T. S. Eliot published no stand-alone sonnets, though there is one (beginning "Trams and dusty trees") embedded in Part Three of *The Waste Land,* and a quatorzain at the start of "The Dry Salvages" (from *Four Quartets*). Wallace Stevens wrote many conventional sonnets in his youth and some anomalous ones thereafter: "Nomad Exquisite," for example, and "Autumn Refrain," with its pentameter euphonies, its repetitions in place of a rhyme scheme, and its melancholy admission that the American Stevens "has never—shall never hear" Keats's nightingale. Ezra Pound wrote sonnets (among them "A Virginal," once an anthology staple) only in his archaizing youth; Marianne Moore and Hart Crane wrote sonnets (included here) that would have seemed, then, to occupy the very edge of the form.

Early twentieth-century poets who rejected overt modernism embraced the sonnet, among them Millay ("modern" in self-presentation but not in line and stanza), and Yvor Winters, an important antimodernist critic and an influential teacher of poets. Robert Frost, modernist and antimodernist at once, mastered the sonnet: he is the most recent of the eleven poets we represent more than once. As modernist demands for novelty, for breaks from the recent past, and for swerves away from popular expectations recede, the sonnet and the sonnet sequence return, first among British poets (Auden, Empson, Dylan Thomas) and then in postwar America, where poets (especially on the East Coast) look to Yeats and to Auden for models of formal control. Those Harlem Renaissance poets who embraced European and English forms in general (such as Countee Cullen and Claude McKay) produced well-turned sonnets; those who sought folk, vernacular, or modernist styles for African American experience (such as Langston Hughes) avoided the form, leaving Gwendolyn Brooks, a member of the next generation, to make the sonnet fit black American speech.

What is a sonnet now? How far can the form stretch? Brooks wrote fourteen-line, rhymed pentameter sonnets early in her career, but we represent her here by a jagged fifteen-line poem with no consistent meter. Elizabeth Bishop's "Sonnet," not in pentameters, has fourteen lines, a sharp turn, and rhyme; May Swenson's "Staring at the Sea on the Day of the Death of Another" has rhyme and an 8-plus-6 organization, but no regular meter. Five of the fifteen most recent sonnets in our book have no end rhyme: other features (length, structure, allusion) place them within the ambit of the sonnet form. To ask whether a given modern poem counts as a sonnet—to ask the question in modern terms—is to ask what we learn by calling it one. Titles matter—Lowell called his own poems sonnets—but they are not determinative either. Gerald Stern's *American Sonnets* (2002) consists of poems in free verse with no rhyme, no fixed length, and no particular allusion to prior sonnet sequences—they are simply shorter and less narrative than most of Stern's earlier poems. Albert Goldbarth's "The Sonnet for Planet 10" runs more than a page; it is not a sonnet by any definition (there is no tenth planet in our solar system, either). Goldbarth's poem ends by telling us that its unshapely, run-on form reflects the unshapeliness of Goldbarth's grief over his dying mother—he has not been able to find the concision, the resolution, the closure that his own definition of "sonnet" demands: "This poem was going to be a sonnet," he writes, "unfinished, diminished, / burial, funeral, etc. / But I'm weary, and I'm leaving it undone."

Inasmuch as we ask not "What are some durable sonnets?" or "Where are strong poems that just happen to be sonnets?" but "What is a sonnet? How do we know? What poems stretch, expand, or renew the sonnet form?"—inasmuch as we ask such questions, we seek limit-cases and self-consciously debatable examples. These are modernist questions, familiar also from arguments about painting, in which the most interesting, or most "advanced," examples of a form are those that press against the previously understood outer limits of prior practice. The strongest art (such arguments say) is the art that can ask and answer the deepest questions about itself. And so we should not be surprised that limit-cases, poems that might or might not count as sonnets (and as good ones) proliferate after about 1960, when modernism becomes a legacy. Moore notwithstanding, most of the limit-cases in our collection—the sonnets in free verse, in unrhymed two-line stanzas, in scrambled structures such as Brooks's—belong to the past fifty years. Once the quarrel between modernists who reject the sonnet as part of an obsolete literary history, and traditionalists who embraced that history whole, had itself become historical—once the innovations of modernism had been, so to speak, naturalized into "poetry" generally—poets could take up the sonnet on modernist terms. Talented poets continue to write "correct" sonnets too, and we have included them: Alison Brackenbury in Britain, Seamus Heaney in Ireland, Rafael Campo in the United States.

Among the important sonnet sequences of the twentieth century, Ted Berrigan's *The Sonnets* (1964) is the one least like anything the nineteenth century would have recognized. Unrhymed, never in regular meter, only sometimes anywhere near pentameter, and only sometimes fourteen lines long, Berrigan's sonnets make sense as sonnets—people who read them attentively and admire them must think of them as sonnets—because they have, along with their fourteen-line norm, such a strong sense of themselves as links in a lyrical sequence, a sequence with thematic echoes of Sidney and Petrarch, sharing their autobiographical vicissitudes and their disappointments in love. Berrigan's sequence, in turn, now has its own international avant-garde progeny, in work by Tony Lopez and Michele Leggott (included here) and by John Tranter in Australia, Bernadette Mayer in the United States, Robert Sheppard in the U.K.

Many of Berrigan's sonnets (we include an exception) are unsatisfying when read in isolation: you have to read the whole sequence to get the effect. And this is to say that we rely on Berrigan, as we rely on all poetry, to tell us how to read it, to tell us what kind of thing it is and how best to place it among works we already know. Poets, said Wordsworth, must create the taste by which they are to be admired; "you must rely on each particular poem," said William Empson, "to show you the way in which it is trying to be good." Sonnet sequences are well-positioned to do so, since a set of short poems in similar form—Meredith's sixteen-line units, Berrigan's scrambled sonnets, Lowell's blank-verse quatorzains—gives the poet extended opportunities to create our expectations: the first and the tenth sonnet change what we seek in the sixteenth. Each sequence, in turn, affects what we see in the next. Tony Harrison's sonnets, for example, count as sonnets not only because he called them sonnets, but because they echo George Meredith's sixteen-line form.

Contemporary poets—after Berrigan, after Williams—pursue limit-cases, expanding the range of the form, but they also understand (as Keats did) that the form is something inherited, that it brings with it the rules of the past; indeed, it sometimes signifies the past. Robert Lowell spent the years 1967–1973 writing unrhymed sonnets; one of the collections that resulted bore the title *History*. "History has to live with what was here," the eponymous poem begins, "clutching and close to fumbling all we had—/ it is so dull and gruesome how we die, / unlike writing, life never finishes." Lowell's clashes and gruesome dilemmas (he goes on to describe the murder of Abel and the death of cattle "against high-voltage wire") would not have looked much like a sonnet to Anna Seward, whose sonnet about "the rigorous sonnet" praised its "strict energic measures" as a "test of skill" for "duteous bards." Indeed it might not have looked like much of a poem. To us, though, it looks like another sonnet about sonnets: the poet, too, "has to live with what was here," has to contain the apparently uncontainable, incomprehensible carnage that marks human history within the electrified fence of pentameter form.

Sonnets mean limits, for Lowell as for Goldbarth, as they meant limits for Wordsworth and for Seward too; they also mean, for Lowell as for Berrigan, Hunt, and the Rossettis, some version (not always the same version) of literary history. Because we recognize the sonnet now—faster than we recognize any other form—as an inherited form, one with a history, the sonnet form works especially well when a poet wants to remind us that the present is surprisingly like the past, that we are like those far from us in history, that we do not differ so much from the people who love and fear and grieve in poems by

Sidney and Shakespeare, or for that matter in poems by Sappho and Virgil. Italian sonnets once seemed opposed to "Shakespearean" forms; sonnets in general, as vernacular, European-derived, urbane poems, once seemed antithetical both to "folk" culture and to a Latin or Greek inheritance. Now classical forms are simply "history," at one with the sonnet in the long perspectives the form itself should suggest. So D. A. Powell implies in the last sonnet we include here, which is also the last poem in his book *Chronic* (2009). It is a sonnet that works as hard as any contemporary poem to braid together defiantly contemporary experience both with the history of the sonnet, and with older—with ancient —poems. The sonnet remains for Powell what it was for Petrarch and for Sidney, for Mary Robinson and for Edwin Arlington Robinson, for Frost and for Yeats: a shape where strong emotion might make sense, where lyric invention might still take place.

"Whoso list to hunt"

THOMAS WYATT

1557

Whoso list to hunt: I know where is an hind,
But, as for me, helas, I may no more.
The vain travail hath wearied me so sore,
I am of them, that farthest cometh behind
Yet, may I by no means, my wearied mind
Draw from the deer; but as she fleeth afore
Fainting I follow. I leave off therefore,
Since in a net I seek to hold the wind.
Who list her hunt I put him out of doubt,
As well as I, may spend his time in vain.
And graven with diamonds in letters plain
There is written, her fair neck round about:
"Noli me tangere for Caesar's I am
And wild for to hold: though I seem tame."

WYATT HERE imitates Petrarch. This is no slavish copying: "imitation" is the Renaissance term for inventively adapting a text by a previous writer, and Wyatt performs this task with bold energy.

Petrarch's "Una candida cerva" (discussed in our Introduction) describes a spellbound fixity. The poet is entranced by the image of his own desire. Wyatt changes the scene to that of a hunt whose constant motion leaves the speaker-lover perplexed and jaded, yet still desperately afflicted by eros. In contrast to Petrarch, Wyatt expresses no cherishing of an occasion, no hypnotic attachment to the sight of the beloved. Instead, here all is swift, breathless pursuit. The poem's uncertain meter, which alternates strenuously between four and five beats per line, adds a rough, effortful impression (Wyatt wrote before the iambic line had become fully regular in English verse).

The scenario of "Whoso list to hunt" probably alludes to Wyatt's own career. Wyatt was a courtier and diplomatic ambassador employed by Henry VIII, a king whose glowering irascibility and domineering ways were legendary. Wyatt ran afoul of Henry at least twice. In 1536, he was arrested and imprisoned in the Tower of London, accused of being one of Anne Boleyn's lovers. Henry's court was full of romantic intrigue, backbiting, and slander; its inhabitants risked their lives whether or not they were dallying with the queen. With Anne safely beheaded, Wyatt returned to the king's favor. Then in 1541 he was imprisoned again, for reasons we still do not know. The terrified letters of self-defense that Wyatt wrote from the Tower make grim reading. Rather surprisingly, Wyatt escaped the executioner, and died of a fever in 1542.

There is a long tradition—beginning with the poet's son, George Wyatt—of reading "Whoso list to hunt" as veiled autobiography. George Wyatt reports that Anne Boleyn "had her usuall words, I am Ceasars all, let none els touche me." According to this interpretation, Henry VIII is the squinty-eyed, jealous Caesar; Anne, his protected hind, or deer. The rumor had spread that Anne was Wyatt's lover before Henry selected her for his queen.

The autobiographical reading seems plausible. Wyatt, in his poem, presents himself as one of a group of hunters (Anne's potential lovers), though he lags in the rear of the pack, frustrated, one of those "that farthest cometh behind." As a courtier, Wyatt would have participated in royal hunts—rugged, exhausting occasions, often lasting for many hours, during which the riders were anxious not to be seen outdoing the king in the manly art of the chase.

Is the speaker still hunting the hind, or has he given up? This is the crucial ambiguity that haunts the first two quatrains of Wyatt's sonnet. Putting on the voice of experience, the speaker begins by acknowledging that others will be tempted to take his place in the wearying search: there are always those who "list" (are inclined) to hunt. "But, as for me, helas, I may no more." Love's labors have made him a loser: it is time to quit. "Sore" conveys both mental and physical exhaustion: the man is ragged, bone-tired. "Vain travail," the speaker's phrase for his venture, means "futile work" ("vain" does not necessarily connote vanity; rather, it derives from Latin *vanum*, "empty" or "useless"). Travail, work or labor, also suggests traveling—here, a harsh journey that leads to no good result.

The second quatrain reveals that although the speaker has stopped in exhaustion, his mind remains bound to the deer, his quarry. "Yet, may I by no means, my wearied mind / Draw from the deer": Wyatt's caesuras (sharp pauses) in line 5 give force to his exclamation "by no means." He has tried and tried, but without success, to release himself from his psychic bondage. His mind is fixed to the deer (Anne) like an arrow stuck in the side of a hunted beast. The arrow of desire cannot be drawn out, though the frightened, elusive animal continues bounding on its way.

Still exhausted and "fainting" (failing, out of breath), but incapable of turning away, the speaker continues his pursuit. As "she fleeth afore / Fainting I follow," he acknowledges. In a virtuosic move, "I follow" leads to another caesura, and then a turn in the opposite direction: "I leave off therefore, / Since in a net I seek to hold the wind." Wyatt takes his apt image in line 8 from the Renaissance humanist Erasmus, who suggested that desire is by nature hopeless, an attempt to catch the wind in a net. The lover's object remains simply ungraspable. The deer now comes to represent something almost unearthly in the way she "fleeth afore." Teasingly close, she yet outspeeds her breathless pursuer.

The statement of philosophical resignation in line 8 marks the end of Wyatt's octave (rhymed *abbaabba,* as in Petrarch). The poet's concluding sestet *(cddcee)* begins in line 9: his tone now takes a canny, political turn. With "who list her hunt," he reiterates nearly exactly his opening words. The speaker decisively assures his reader, a potential fellow hunter, that such a quest is time spent in vain.

The deer now changes shape, from a wild animal to one of the protected creatures of the king's private lands, or deer park. With regal extravagance, diamonds (symbolic of chastity) spell out on the animal's neck the following saying, reported in the sonnet's final couplet: "Noli me tangere for Caesar's I am, / And wild for to hold: though I seem tame."

Though Wyatt says that these lines have been written "in letters plain," they cry out for interpretation. The risen Jesus says "Noli me tangere" to Mary Magdalene, who mistakes him for the gardener. In Petrarch's "Una candida cerva," this motto (in Italian) marks the beloved as an otherworldly phantom, the source of the poet's own bittersweet, self-directed toil. Petrarch's deer is not wild so much as evanescent, inhabiting her own realm (which shares its borders with the poet's mind). Wyatt's beloved, by contrast, remains "wild for to hold": dangerous, because of the cutthroat atmosphere of Henry's court. Her seeming tameness makes her all the more risky an object of desire. Rather than being free, as in Petrarch, she is clearly marked as Caesar's property. She belongs to her earthly lord, not to God.

No matter how prudent the advice the speaker gives himself, he remains drawn to a game that might be fatal. Desire cannot be separated from courtly power, the beloved's aura from the king's. With cool, intense nerve, Wyatt alludes to the all-mastering nature of kingly rule, and to the disappointment it has inflicted on him. This is an audacious, and unforgettable, gesture. The independent-minded poet comments on a monarch's authority as no sonneteer had done before. Wyatt, radically altering his precursor Petrarch, writes in "Whoso list to hunt" a daring, covert example of political poetry—and remakes sonnet tradition.

DM

"Norfolk sprang thee"

HENRY HOWARD, EARL OF SURREY

1557

Norfolk sprang thee, Lambeth holds thee dead,
Clere, of the County of Cleremont, though hight.
Within the womb of Ormond's race thou bred,
And saw'st thy cousin crownèd in thy sight.
Shelton for love, Surrey for Lord thou chase;—
Aye, me! whilst life did last that league was tender.
Tracing whose steps thou sawest Kelsall blaze,
Laundersey burnt, and batter'd Bullen render.
At Muttrel gates, hopeless of all recure,
Thine Earl, half dead, gave in thy hand his will;
Which cause did thee this pining death procure,
Ere summers four times seven thou couldst fulfill.
    Ah, Clere! if love had booted, care, or cost,
    Heaven had not won, nor earth so timely lost.

IN THIS moving poem Henry Howard, the Earl of Surrey, pays tribute to one of his soldiers, Thomas Clere. Like Surrey a proud Elizabethan nobleman, Clere cast his fortunes with his warlike lord. During the siege of Montreuil in September 1544, while caring for the injured Surrey, Clere received the wound that would lead to his death the following year. Surrey himself died two years later, at the age of thirty—executed for treason by the paranoid Henry VIII. The king was convinced that Surrey planned to usurp his throne.

The poet Surrey, a raw aristocratic free spirit, made a reputation for der-ring-do and crude roistering. In 1540, along with the evocatively named Sir John Wallop, he participated in a grand-scale, high-chivalric jousting match with six men on each side. In 1543, with a gang of friends, he went on a violent spree in London, breaking church windows and firing at people with stone-shooting crossbows. Commenting on a mysterious earlier offense that had landed him in jail, he had credited "the fury of reckless youth." This time, Surrey wrote a wild satire that turned his antics into a Jeremiah-like denunciation of wicked London.

Surrey soon channeled his rowdy impulses into Henry VIII's war with France. In battle, a fellow soldier noted, he spoke "vain, contemptuous words" to his own men. In "Norfolk sprang thee," Surrey assumes aristocratic privilege, as he did in life. But instead of excitement at bloody skirmishes, he demonstrates a collected, resolute admiration for his loyal kinsman, Clere.

In his poem's first word, Surrey points to the genealogical tie between himself and Clere. Surrey's father was Duke of Norfolk, and Norfolk was Clere's birthplace. The first line encompasses, with calm, moving epitaphic directness, Clere's birth and death: "Norfolk sprang thee, Lambeth holds thee dead." The caesura, or pause, between the two halves of the line adds a clipped solemnity. Clere is buried in St. Mary's Church, which adjoins Lambeth Palace; Surrey's poem is inscribed above his tomb. Lambeth, now a borough of London, was then part of the county of Surrey, where the poet's ancestors had lived for centuries. To be born is to be sprung from a place and an ancestry; to be dead is to be held, in the earth and in memory. Throughout this sonnet, place and name stay bound together. Birthplace and burial plot, as well as clan, tether Surrey and Clere to each other—and to their homeland and its wars.

Line 3 loftily alludes to Clere's maternal ancestry, the Ormond family, and his engagement to Mary Shelton, also a descendent of the Ormonds. Finally, line 4 rounds off the poem's first quatrain with a bold surprise: it invokes the doomed marriage of Henry VIII to Anne Boleyn (discussed earlier, in our commentary on Wyatt's "Whoso list to hunt"). Henry was, as Machiavelli remarked, "rich, ferocious, and greedy for glory," and especially eager for a male heir during his marriage to Catherine of Aragon. (Catherine gave birth to one daughter, Mary; but Henry, like every European monarch, wanted a son.) The raven-haired Anne, from the house of Ormond, was Clere's cousin, as Surrey's poem indicates. She was also Surrey's own cousin, and closely associated with him—another link in the dense thicket of kinship connections between Surrey and Clere.

After being Henry's mistress for some years, Anne became his wife, and was crowned queen in 1533 at a sumptuous, ornate ceremony. Anne marched forward in a flowing robe of purple velvet, whose folds concealed the fact that she was pregnant. (The child was Henry's—the future Elizabeth I.) A troop of ladies-in-waiting followed her, clothed in scarlet gowns. Three years later Henry charged Anne with adultery, and beheaded her.

Surely Surrey would have gone too far had he mentioned the name Anne Boleyn, or named her as his own relative. But even the evasive periphrasis "thy cousin" shocks us. Anne was reviled as a traitoress to the supreme monarch of England; the brazen Surrey reminds the reader that she was once queen.

Surrey's second quatrain begins with a presentation of Clere's double identity: he chose ("chase") Shelton for love (by becoming the fiancé of Alice Shelton), and Surrey for lord. In the power-obsessed, pragmatic world of Henry's England, love entwines itself with political might (as in the disastrous case of Anne Boleyn). Clere keeps his life clear, its two terms—desire and political service—properly separate, as Anne could not. But amorous passion is far less important in this sonnet than the male bonding that occurs during wartime. "Norfolk sprang thee" glides over Clere's love for Shelton. Instead, it progresses, firm and determined, toward its culminating scene: Clere's death. The hero's self-sacrificing love for his lord, the author of this very poem, far outstrips any heterosexual bond. As Surrey's biographer William Sessions notes, "love" leads to "Lord," and then to the "league" that holds the two men together.

In line 7 the faithful vassal Clere "trac[es the] steps" of his lord, Surrey. As in the first quatrain, he is an observer. There, he saw Anne crowned. Here, he witnesses a series of warlike triumphs in France and the Low Countries: the burning to the ground of Kelsall and Laundersey (Kelso and Landrecy), the surrender of "battered Bullen" (Boulogne) to relentless mining and bombshells. (Henry was excited by his army's conquest, but was too fat to march. Transported in a litter, he surveyed the town's ruins.)

The series of crude victories, pronounced in blunt fashion, yields to unexpected tenderness: the wounding of Surrey at the gates of Montreuil, in northern France (called "Muttrel" by Surrey, in English style). Surrey, "half dead" (as he curtly expresses it), "gave in thy hand his will." Surrey's will, his last written testament, stands for his very life, which Clere cared for so tenderly. And then Clere gave his own life, in exchange for Surrey's survival.

Is it Surrey or his loyal servant who is at death's door here, "hopeless of all recure"? The poem leaves it ambiguous. This uncertainty, melding the two soldiers into one, shows the heart of Clere's accomplishment. His death becomes necessary, and exemplary.

Surrey sums Clere's virtue in his final couplet: "If love had booted, care, or cost, / Heaven had not won, nor earth so timely lost." He replaces the earlier tender outcry "Aye, me!" with a subdued, carefully measured statement. Love, linked soberly here to "care, or cost"—the heavy burdens of such wartime friendship—might, the poet wishes, have "booted" (succeeded) in saving Clere from death. But the wish yields to a harder reality. "Timely" means both "soon" (that is, too soon) and "properly," "appropriately." The second sense ballasts the first. The premature sacrifice of Clere demonstrates his tenacity, his truth; and so his fate is fitting. By invoking his kinsman's end with lucid, measured pain, Surrey gives us a heartfelt testimony to the loss of Clere.

DM

"That self same tongue"

GEORGE GASCOIGNE

1573

That self same tongue which first did thee entreat
To link thy liking with my lucky love:
That trusty tongue must now these words repeat,
I love thee still, my fancy cannot move.
That dreadless heart which durst attempt the thought
To win thy will with mine for to consent,
Maintains that vow which love in me first wrought,
I love thee still and never shall repent.
That happy hand which hardly did touch
Thy tender body, to my deep delight:
Shall serve with sword to prove my passion such
As loves thee still, much more than it can write.
Thus love I still with tongue, hand, hart and all,
And when I chaunge, let vengeance on me fall.
    Ferenda Natura.

GEORGE GASCOIGNE was a scholar, a soldier, and by all accounts a well-known scoundrel. Born into wealth, he spent all his fortune, married a rich widow, and then, after a series of ruinous lawsuits, went to debtors' prison. One of his many enemies called him "a defamed person and noted for manslaughter," an atheist, and a "notorious ruffiann." Gascoigne wrote satire as well as love poetry; his work has a hard edge that befits his scurrilous life.

"That self same tongue," the sonnet by Gascoigne we have chosen, appeared in his charmingly titled collection *A Hundreth Sundrie Floures Bound Up in One Small Posie* (1573). The poem bore the title "The constancie of a lover hath thus sometymes ben briefly declared" (such explanatory titles were common in books of Renaissance lyric). A Latin motto caps "That self same tongue": *Ferenda Natura,* "Nature must be endured."

Constancy is the governing concept of Gascoigne's sonnet. So constant is he, in fact, that he appears paralyzed with steadfastness. Adherence to the law of desire, loyalty to one's implacable love: these aspects of Elizabethan sonnet writing can amount to an imprisonment of the self. So it appears in Gascoigne's disturbing poem.

"That self same tongue" starts on a deceptively light note. The poet recalls the first occasion when he invited his beloved to (as he tells her) "link thy liking with my lucky love." The series of *ell*-sounds trips off the tongue in quicksilver fashion: linking leads to liking, to luck, and then to love. The image of the link implies an agile, spontaneous connection—a far cry from the heavy bondage that the poet's love will turn out to be by his sonnet's end.

As the poem goes on, Gascoigne's alliterative phrases begin to convey a blunt, dogged force (see line 11, "Shall serve with sword to prove my passion such"). This stylistic habit connects "That self same tongue" with medieval English tradition, and marks Gascoigne as one of the so-called "drab" Elizabethan poets, whom C. S. Lewis opposed to the "golden" Spenser and Shakespeare. Yvor Winters reversed Lewis's judgment. Winters valued drabness: he favored poets like Gascoigne, who leaned toward the proverbial and the realistic. (The hardy, open-eyed resolve that confronts the reader in Winters's sonnet "The Castle of Thorns," given later in this book, owes something to the drab Elizabethans.)

By line 4 Gascoigne's speaker is already repeating himself, forever rehearsing his initial motto: "*I love thee still,* my fancy cannot move." "Trusty tongue" glints with irony. This tongue can indeed be trusted because, like the speaker's mind, it remains stuck in a groove. Infallibly rigid (and therefore reliable!): so the tongue speaks. Gascoigne finds himself condemned not only to unalterable desire, but to the changeless formula of the sad lover who says the same thing always: "I love thee still."

"Still" has here a double sense, both temporal and spatial (I love thee yet; I love thee without budging). The lover's "fancy"—a faculty somewhere between imagination and desire, and mediating between the two—"cannot move." To love is to be moved by someone. But Gascoigne rhymes "love" and "move" in order to deny motion to eros.

Gascoigne's second quatrain (*cdcd,* following the first quatrain's *abab* rhyme scheme) stakes its case on the speaker's "dreadless heart." The fearlessness, the lack of dread, that he attributes to himself is again ironic, because it consists not in warlike courage, but rather in a passive virtue—sticking to love. "To attempt the thought" that he will try to seduce his beloved is the main credit this speaker gives himself. His aim is stated in line 6: "To win thy will with mine for to consent." In Renaissance English, "will" can mean "desire"; and "consent," "attunement." But much as the poet wants them, the line refuses to yield these wished-for readings. For her desire to be in accord with his: such a result cannot be gained by this poet-seducer, whose strength is his straight, coercive loyalty to his one thought. The line must be read in more aggressive terms: will is volition (the poet's and the woman's, now at cross-purposes); and consent, the woman's surrender. The most he can hope for is victory, rather than the impulsive harmony suggested in line 2's lilting courtship. The showdown between male poet and female beloved will, it appears, never end. The "meet cute" charm that the speaker recalls in the sonnet's first two lines has devolved into a clenched battle.

Feminine resistance exactly matches masculine urgency. For the Elizabethans, a woman's chastity was her "honor," the equivalent of the martial valor that men were expected to demonstrate. The more chaste the maiden, the more she was worth; the more resistant, the more attractive. The likelihood of an impasse, rather than a joyous fling, was, accordingly, substantial.

Gascoigne's sonnet loosens up at the beginning of the sestet. He gives us an affecting, unguarded moment, a reminiscence of some early flirtation. The poet alludes to "that happy hand"—his own—"which hardly did touch / Thy tender body, to my deep delight." He brushed her fleetingly; the sensation was all the more powerful for its lightness, its transience. Gascoigne chooses his adjectives softly, decidedly: "Thy tender body," "my deep delight." And the small word "to" takes on, for a moment, a physical sense: her body grazes his delight itself. Perhaps, we think, the speaker should rest with such mementos, cherishing the near-miss: the thought of her, and of what might have been.

But he can't. Gascoigne reacts against the vulnerable, wistful lines I have just quoted. The hand that touched her "shall serve with sword" to prove his passion (by masculine aggression shown in military service, or by suicide?). The blade, he vows, will accomplish what the pen could not; action supersedes expression ("much more than it can write"). This poet might show the authentic character of his fervor by sticking his weapon in his own heart. (Or so he suggests.)

Gascoigne's concluding couplet wraps up "tongue, hand, hart and all": he lists the bold parts that have figured in his poem. The lover becomes a fighter in order to guard himself from change. If he is inconstant, he cries, "let vengeance on me fall." Deviating from his oath of love remains unthinkable; the oath, as much as the love, creates his identity. But we can detect a more fragile poem behind this determined one, built from the poet's memory of initial seduction and of the mild gesture he associates with it. Gascoigne joins (as sonnet writers often do) the fixity of self-reinforcing desire with the captivating slightness of erotic experience. He pictures a love brooded over, repeated endlessly by the poet to himself. Yet an intuition of fragility counters this grim monologue: the elusive, momentary encounter that gave birth to love.

DM

Astrophel and Stella 45

SIR PHILIP SIDNEY

Written 1582; published 1591

Stella oft sees the very face of woe
Painted in my beclouded stormy face,
But cannot skill to pity my disgrace,
Not though thereof the cause herself she know.
Yet hearing late a fable, which did show
Of lovers never known, a grievous case,
Pity thereof gate in her breast such place,
That from that sea deriv'd tears' spring did flow.
Alas, if Fancy, drawn by imag'd things
Though false, yet with free scope, more grace doth breed
Than servant's wrack, where new doubts honor brings,
Then think, my dear, that you in me do read
Of lover's ruin some sad tragedy:
I am not I; pity the tale of me.

WHEN IS a poem's speaker the poet, and when is he an imagined character? When can the speaker be anyone, even (or especially) its reader, you? When can we bring, to a particular poem, the information we have about its author, and when should we try to leave that information aside? How does a poet acknowledge that his sonnet will present—necessarily, since no one's whole inner life can be put into fourteen lines—a picture of him, and of his experience, that is in some ways abstracted, simplified, and altered for effect? Such questions may spring up when we talk about almost any lyric poem; they grow more complex when the poem has elements of narrative, and more complex still if parts of its story are true.

This sonnet from *Astrophel and Stella* is just such a poem. Unlike any earlier set of poems in English, Sidney's sequence arranges lyric forms (108 sonnets and eleven stanzaic "songs") into something like a narrative line; unlike his closest Continental precursors, Sidney presents characters with made-up names, in ways that blur fiction and historical truth. Astrophel ("star-lover," though "phel," pronounced "phil," echoes "Philip"), a gentleman poet much like Sidney himself, with the same equine and military skills, pursues Stella ("star"), identified with Lady Penelope Rich (other sonnets pun on her married name). The sonnets describe Astrophel's often fruitless pursuit, his momentary satisfaction (when she gives him virtuous friendship and a chaste kiss), and their later falling out. The sequence reflects on questions about truth and fiction, autobiography and falsification, persona and voice. They are questions that the sonnet form—with its unequal parts, so often divided into action and reflection, outer and inner, "then" and "now"—is well equipped to raise.

Sidney probably circulated *Astrophel and Stella* among friends at court. Its unauthorized printing in 1591, five years after his death, made Sidney the most imitated English poet of the Elizabethan age. Sidney's other important works include *The Countess of Pembroke's Arcadia,* a book of prose fiction whose shepherds and princes often declaim poems, and *The Defence of Poetry* (sometimes also called *An Apology for Poetry*), an argument in favor of what we now call imaginative literature, both prose and verse.

Following Aristotle, and imitating French defenses of French poetry (such as the one by Joachim du Bellay), Sidney's *Defence* argues that fictive works can affect us more strongly, and give us better models for our own conduct, than philosophy or history. Though "poetry . . . is an art of imitation," Sidney writes, "a feigned example hath as much force to teach as a true example, if not more." Yet the *Defence* is at best ambivalent about "passionate sonnets," love poems such as Petrarch's or Wyatt's: they often sound artificial and unconvincing, Sidney says, and even if skillfully fashioned they may entice us to "lustful love." *Astrophel and Stella* 45, like the *Defence,* makes claims for the superior power of fiction, but without the essay's moral frame. The poem does not ask whether love can lead us to virtue, or whether love poetry can do so. Instead, Sonnet 45—like other sonnets throughout the sequence—asks why artificial, fictive representations can move us, and when they might best convey an inner truth.

Astrophel wants, from Stella, at least her "pity," at best her love ("pity" may also mean sexual availability, as it does in the troubadour tradition). Stella does not pay much attention to his sad face, but weeps when she reads a story about doomed lovers. Astrophel therefore, in his sestet, wishes that he might offer her such a story: only thus will Stella, who cries only over fictions, "pity" him. But Stella heard a "fable" about "Lovers"; Astrophel will portray one unrequited "Lover" instead. Moved by his "ruin," Stella might even decide to spare Astrophel from a similar fate, though Astrophel will not allow himself so much hope, or think so far ahead. "Not though thereof the cause her self she know" means "though she knows that she herself is the cause" of his woe, with the added suggestion "though she knows very well (nobody has to tell her) its cause." Stella's honor brings new doubts to Astrophel, her amorous "servant," as he suspects that her notion of honor means that she will not grant him the favors he seeks; that suspicion "wracks" (tortures, as on a rack, but also "wrecks") him.

Having once read Sonnet 45, we may pity Astrophel the more ourselves. We are just as likely, however, to admire his invention: he is both lover and artificer, showing us how to represent self-consciousness, and why such representations may require fictions, even when what they represent is true pain. The critic Anne Ferry hears "Fancy" as if it were the name of a rival poet: Astrophel envies his skill. In her reading, "drawn by" means "attracted to," "moved to depict": Fancy, the rival, depicts "imag'd" (imaginary, envisioned) "things" with a free hand, thus winning more grace (from Stella) than does Astrophel, Stella's true servant, who has been constrained by his decision (until now) to stick to the facts. "Fancy" may instead mean the imaginative capacity within Stella, "drawn" (drawn out) by the fictional tales she reads, whose "imag'd things" affect her more than any facts can: fictions have "free scope," while Astrophel can only depict his genuine "wrack," along with mixed feelings about his, and her, "honor." Despite "new doubts" on his part or on hers, the poet continues to compete with Fancy for Stella's eyes, and heart, and hand.

No wonder the poem—with its keen interest in competition—shows so many technical flourishes. Like most of the *Astrophel* sonnets, this one begins with the demanding Petrarchan rhyme scheme abbaabba, and ends with the demanding requirement of a final couplet. Other technical challenges involve repeated words and internal rhyme: "spring," not a line-ending, introduces the rhyme words "things" and "brings." Sidney also displays his talent for elegant metaphor in a series of figures having to do with water. In the first lines, his face shows storm clouds, but no rain, because nobody cries. When Stella reads her fable, on the other hand, water comes forth: a sea, a spring. ("Gate" means "gat"—i.e., "begat," "produced"; Sidney's spelling may also imply that a sea-gate has opened.)

The octave also introduces competition between visual and verbal art. The painted woeful face cannot move Stella as the "fable" can: verbal art can create images (the word has the same root as "imagination") inside us, while visual art works only on the outside, not heart to heart but only face to face. To hold Stella's attention, Astrophel must become not a painting but a book, not something to see but something to "read." To repeat "face," once midline, once in rhyming position, is to give Astrophel two faces, both true ("very"), yet both obscured ("painted," "beclouded"). "To paint" in Sidney's era could mean "to depict," but also "to misrepresent," "to feign," or, for a woman, "to wear makeup" (paint one's face). Astrophel would not have imagined himself wearing makeup, but he does ask how to show—on his countenance and in his words—what storms are in his heart.

The answer he gives—the answer the sestet pursues—is that, to make his true feelings present to other people (especially to Stella), he must make things up. No wonder, then, that this sonnet about made-up stories, about when and how "I am not I," pursues a set of negations from first line to last: "cannot," "not," "never," "false," "new" (in place of "no"), and finally "not" once more. The *Defence* asserted that "the poet affirmeth nothing, and therefore never lieth": to suspend disbelief is not to take fiction for truth. This sonnet, however, invokes both the contrast between true and "false" images, lovers who exist and lovers who "never" were, and the contrast between truth and fiction. The turn in the last line makes the paradox clear: the "I" of a tale is not the "I" of the teller, even when they seem, to readers and listeners, to suffer the same events—yet the teller could not move us with the same force, might not even have become known to us at all, without the separate "I" of his fashioned tale. So the Astrophel who speaks the poem relates to the Astrophel he decides to present; so, we might think (so Sidney's readers have often believed), Sidney, the author, relates to "Astrophel."

It is one thing to suggest that a fiction might move Stella more than truth, that a tale might do more than a faithful, literal account in order to get across to somebody else the emotions that I already recognize within myself, as the mythical heroes named in Sidney's *Defence* inspired virtuous acts more effectively than did historical figures. But Sidney makes a stranger suggestion, too. What if we are, even to ourselves, imaginatively constructed characters? What if the process of making a "tale of me" is the only way we ourselves ever know who we are? Sidney's characteristic devices, Ferry says, "point to inner states as distinct from their outward show." Astrophel and Sidney, his implied creator, both struggle to catch up with an inner feeling that is always more complicated than any representation of it, in words or in pictures, can be.

So, they suggest, all poetry must struggle: so, perhaps, we make ourselves up all along. In Sidney's Renaissance world—so writes another critic, Stephen Greenblatt—"one can win pity for oneself only by becoming a tale of oneself, and hence by ceasing to be oneself." But Astrophel is himself and not himself, "not I" and "me," much as Sidney, Astrophel's creator, is Astrophel but is not Astrophel, and much as all poets are themselves, yet not themselves, whenever they speak through lyric poems. Though "I am not I" in the "I" of such representations, the reader or listener who understands rightly will hear not just a tale, but "the tale of me."

SB

Ruines of Rome 3

EDMUND SPENSER

1591

Thou stranger, which for Rome in Rome here seekest,
And nought of Rome in Rome percieu'st at all,
These same olde walls, olde arches, which thou seest,
Olde Palaces, is that which Rome men call.
    Behold what wreake, what ruine, and what wast,
And how that she, which with her mightie powre
Tam'd all the world, hath tam'd herselfe at last,
The pray of time, which all things doth deuowre.
    Rome now of Rome is th'onely funerall,
And onely Rome of Rome hath victorie;
Ne ought saue Tyber hastning to his fall
Remaines of all: O worlds inconstancie.
    That which is firme doth flit and fall away,
    And that is flitting, doth abide and stay.

THIS forceful sonnet of disappointment, with a moral lesson at its close, il-
lustrates the sixteenth-century uses of repetition and paradox. Every line con-
tains one or the other; most lines contain both. It also demonstrates the uses
of Renaissance translation, by which the sonnet form entered both English
and French. The third of the thirty-two sonnets in *Les Antiquitez du Rome*
(1558), by the French poet Joachim du Bellay (1522–1560), became the third of
thirty-three in Spenser's translation (published in 1591, perhaps written much
earlier; we give du Bellay's French below). In Spenser's English, as in du Bel-
lay's French, the sonnet pursues with concision and elegance three emotions
not normally juxtaposed: the disappointment of a "stranger," a tourist, at
reaching a famous destination and discovering that he cannot see what he

came to see; a tragic regard for the passing of great nations, for the long-term, one-way flow of history; and an ultimately religious view of a mutable, mortal earth, as compared to the fixed laws of heaven. Faithful in many respects to du Bellay's words, Spenser's sonnet adds technical feats of its own. It also adds, to the poetry of a Continental Catholic, Spenser's Protestant point of view.

From 1553 to 1557 du Bellay lived in Rome, where he worked as a diplomat under his cousin, a cardinal. As a member of the group of French poets called the Pléiade, du Bellay did as much as anyone to bring the models of the Italian Renaissance into French verse. He was the author of an important treatise, *La défense et illustration de la langue française* (The Defense and Illustration of the French Language; 1649), and also wrote the first sequence of love sonnets in French—his modern translator Richard Helgerson goes so far as to call him the French Petrarch. An ambitious, well-educated writer who composed verse in Latin too, du Bellay might well have yearned for some visible link between the Rome he saw and the Rome of Cicero, Virgil, or Ovid, especially since so many ancient Roman artifacts were unearthed and studied by Renaissance humanists.

Instead du Bellay saw, according to this sonnet, a dirty city nothing like the empire that its literature preserved. Rome is not Rome—a visitor to modern Rome has trouble even imagining the ancient empire—because the remaining ruins are not enough to let tourists imagine the Caesars' city, and because what ruins do subsist there remind us that Rome, like everything else, decays. Du Bellay turns a tourist's disappointment into classic, or rather medieval, themes: the mutability of the world, and the transience of earthly works and delights. That theme finds its evidence in the octave, with the descriptions of Rome; its symbol in the sestet, with the Tiber (the river that flows through Rome); and its proverbial summary in the last couplet, which (following Saint Augustine) sets the supposedly firm foundations of a worldly city against the insubstantial, yet immortal, human soul.

It makes sense that Spenser—who also translated Petrarch—would see himself in du Bellay: Spenser, like du Bellay, wanted to make a newly sophisticated national poetry that learned from, yet surpassed, older and foreign examples. It makes sense, too, that Spenser would alter, to fit his own version of English, du Bellay's Italianate form. Du Bellay's sonnets rhyme in Petrarchan fashion, *abba abba,* with variable sestets (this one rhymes *ccdede*); Spenser's translations of du Bellay normally rhyme in the "English" form introduced by the Earl of Surrey (and later taken up by Shakespeare), with three quatrains and a concluding couplet. Here, though, Spenser brings in one of his specialties, the interlaced rhyme that hooks one stanza on to the next. Rhyming *abab cdcd bcbc ff,* with the *a* and *c* rhymes differing by just one vowel, Spenser duplicates in the second quatrain the consonantal pattern from the first, and then brings back for the third quatrain the rhyme that launched the poem. Almost as in his later set of love sonnets, the *Amoretti,* the poem coheres around repeated rhymes, until the couplet cuts them loose.

It coheres, too, around densely repeated words. "Rome" occurs nine times, twice each in four lines, "old" three times in two lines, "what" three times, "fall" twice, "all" three times as a complete word and twice more as a syllable. We have, then, a sonnet in which sounds and words return again and again, most of all the word "Rome." These recurrences fit the question the "stranger" may ask: When is a name the same, but its meaning all changed? When does "Rome" cease to refer to what we have called Rome? Why is the meaning of words, like the meaning of places, subject to such drastic change?

They change, the sonnet implies, because everything does. All merely human projects, all attempts to take and hold earthly power, fail and fall; only in heaven can human beings find a lasting reward. (M. L. Stapleton notes that the recurring "all . . . fall" sums up the argument of the whole.) The absence, in Rome as it is, of Rome as it was, and the ironic persistence (in a city under foreign rule) of "olde walls, olde arches" as evidence of an empire's demise, remind us that all our claims to control our destinies will go the way of Augustus Caesar's empire.

Spenser's sense of antiquity, unlike du Bellay's, included the history of English words: Spenser's unusual spellings, here as in most of his poems, bring out homonyms and etymologies. Elizabethan English had no standard, single correct spellings, and Spenser puts the lack of a standard to poetic effect. In his Rome we behold "what wreake," that is, what a wreck (time has made of Rome), but also what time, history, and neglect have wreaked; we see "what wast," that is, what waste (of prior glory), but also what was (what no longer is). ("Pray" is the word now spelled "prey," from French "proie"; a pun on the religious "pray" seems unlikely.)

Spenser preserves, from du Bellay, the gap between the constructed Rome of the octave, characterized by decaying monuments, and the Tiber of the third quatrain, the river that still flows through Rome and "falls" (in du Bellay, "s'enfuit"—"flees," "drains out") to the sea. He also preserves, from du Bellay, the repeated formula "Rome . . . of Rome": Rome acts on itself (defeats itself, replaces itself), so that the new, visible "Rome" (whose sight is an emptiness) stands for the absence of the older "Rome" that claimed to rule the visible world.

For a French Catholic poet such as du Bellay, a sonnet (or a set of thirty-two sonnets) about the fall of Rome might well suggest the rise of the French language as a legitimate successor to Latin, and a rival to modern Italian. For an English Protestant poet such as Spenser, a set of sonnets on the same subject might also attack, by implication, the contemporary claims of the Roman Catholic Church. Du Bellay's ancient Rome put all the world under its laws ("lois") in order to rule it ("dompter," a cognate of English "dominate") before being tamed, or dominated, itself; Spenser, by replacing "lois" with "powre," removes any sense (if indeed there was any in French) that Rome ever deserved its dominion.

Spenser added, to du Bellay's Roman sonnets, a concluding sonnet, called "L'Envoy," all his own. That sonnet hails "Bellay, first garland of free Poësie / That France brought forth." "Free" here has religious implications, as if du Bellay had liberated French verse not just from the past, but from the pope. Du Bellay's sonnets deserve, Spenser continues, "prayse / Excelling all, that ever went before"—though not, perhaps, excelling what came afterward: "After thee, gins Bartas hie to rayse / His heauenly Muse, th' Almightie to adore." Guillaume du Bartas, the author of poems on religious topics including the seven days of Creation, was a Huguenot, a French Protestant persecuted by the Catholic state. By making du Bellay the precursor of du Bartas, Spenser (as Richard Danson Brown has implied) makes du Bellay almost Protestant. By replicating du Bellay's view of a ruined, and not remotely imperial Rome, Spenser suggests that not only temporal but spiritual power now rests far from the Tiber, and far from the pope.

Yet today we do not remember "Thou stranger" for its Protestant implications, present though they are; we reprint not Spenser's "Envoy," but his "Thou stranger." Nor did such Renaissance poets as Francisco de Quevedo, such moderns as Yvor Winters, C. H. Sisson, and Robert Lowell, retranslate du Bellay's "Nouveau venu" out of any sectarian fervor. Rather, we return to the sonnet—as they did—for the elegance of its repetitions, for the way it pivots from history in one city towards eternity and eternal "inconstancie." Spenser's version of du Bellay's "Nouveau venu" illustrates, as well as any single sonnet can, the passage of the sonnet form through Italian and French into English, the movement ("translation") of forms from one nation to others. It also crystallizes a disappointment at once international and metaphysical, a sense of loss that encompasses one visit, one city, one version of history, and a long view of the entire, frangible world.

SB

Les Antiquitez 3

JOACHIM DU BELLAY

Nouveau venu, qui cherches Rome en Rome
Et rien de Rome en Rome n'aperçois,
Ces vieux palais, ces vieux arcs que tu vois,
Et ces vieux murs, c'est ce que Rome on nomme.

Vois quel orgueil, quelle ruine: et comme
Celle qui mit le monde sous ses lois,
Pour dompter tout, se dompta quelquefois,
Et devint proie au temps, qui tout consomme.

Rome de Rome est le seul monument,
Et Rome Rome a vaincu seulement.
Le Tibre seul, qui vers la mer s'enfuit,

Reste de Rome. Ô mondaine inconstance!
Ce qui est ferme, est par le temps détruit,
Et ce qui fuit, au temps fait résistance.

Delia 38

SAMUEL DANIEL

1592

When men shall find thy flower, thy glory pass,
  And thou with careful brow sitting alone
  Receivèd hast this message from thy glass,
  That tells the truth, and says that all is gone;
Fresh shalt thou see in me the wounds thou madest,
  Though spent thy flame, in me the heat remaining:
  I that have lov'd thee thus before thou fadest,
  My faith shall waxe, when thou art in thy waning.
The world shall find this miracle in me,
  That fire can burn, when all the matter's spent:
  Then what my faith hath been thy self shalt see,
  And that thou wast unkind thou mayst repent.
Thou mayst repent that thou hast scorn'd my tears,
When winter snows upon thy golden hairs.

SAMUEL DANIEL was an Elizabethan poet influenced, like the better-known Spenser, Sidney, and Shakespeare, by the vogue for the Petrarchan sonnet. Daniel called his sonnet sequence *Delia,* after his beloved's fictive name (one of the appellations of Diana, the chaste goddess). It was first published in 1592, though several dozen of its sonnets had appeared the previous year, in an edition also containing Sidney's *Astrophel and Stella.* Delia (who may have been the real-life Countess of Pembroke, Sidney's sister) resists the poet-lover to the end, making his "joys abortive, perish'd at their birth" (Sonnet 55): he feels the pleasures of his desire and of his amorous chase, but no fulfillment. At times, Daniel seems to prefer thwarted desire over erotic happiness. "Each bird sings to herself, and so will I," Daniel exults near the end of his sequence

(Sonnet 54). Often, in *Delia,* the singer does not need the consummation that a shared life can offer. Never varying his smooth lament, he has, instead, the self-sustaining, birdsong-like consistency of his art.

At least, so it appears in some of *Delia*'s sonnets. In others, though, Daniel suggests an odd, persistent connection between himself and his beloved, even as she spurns him. Sonnet 36 is one of these poems: while the poet-lover punishes the beloved for his lack of success, he also lends her a pathos that ties him to her.

Daniel's central trope is Petrarchan: his love, he says, is a burning fire. But he offers a wry twist on the idealizing that goes along with Petrarch's influence. Instead of glorifying his beloved, and blessing her by means of his poetic talent, he uses his sonnet to pronounce sentence on her: she is rapidly becoming old, and will be sorry that she rejected the poet-lover's ardent advances. He begins with a cruel reference to what so many women dread, the disappearance of their beauty at the hands of age. Daniel's opening line combines two traditional images, the *carpe diem* or *carpe florem* motif (in which erotic action is compared to the taking of a flower: Latin *carpere,* "to pluck") and the glum motto *sic transit gloria mundi* ("thus passes the glory of the world"). Delia's faded glory is her unplucked flower; she is now withered without ever having experienced sexual enjoyment—or, more important, without having offered the male poet enjoyment.

The rest of Daniel's first quatrain rehearses an image more familiar from Shakespeare's Sonnet 2, which begins, "When forty winters shall besiege thy brow / And dig deep trenches in thy beauty's field." Like Daniel picturing his Delia with worried ("careful") brow before her glass (her mirror), Shakespeare threatens his beloved young man with the "trenches," or wrinkles, that age digs. (Shakespeare's Sonnet 62 applies the same idea to the speaker himself: "But when my glass shows me myself indeed / Beated and chopped [that is, chapped] with tanned antiquity.") The glass delivers an unmistakable message to Delia, as Daniel reports in the curt monosyllables of his line 4: "That tells the truth, and says that all is gone." The interlaced consonants of "that tells the truth," with its *th-t-t-th-t-th,* should lead a careful reader to slow down and give a measured, ominous tone to the performance. "All is gone," says the poet: your youth, your beauty, and, finally, the great romance you never allowed to take place. The last point is emphasized by the rhyme of "alone" and "gone": she is the abandoned one.

The second quatrain varies the picture. The poet imagines that the aged Delia now sees not just her own face, but also the "wounds" she made long ago in her poet-lover: injuries so deep they seem "fresh," now more than ever. Her flame may be "spent," exhausted (in Italian a burnt-out candle is *spento*, "extinguished"), but its heat remains in the poet.

"My faith" (the poet tells Delia) waxes even as you wane. He enforces his position as proud, solitary, and spurned. "What my faith hath been" is, it turns out, a refusal to give up his desire, matching her refusal to yield her honor. As in Gascoigne's "That self same tongue," the woman has refused to respond as the poet wished her to. But in contrast to Gascoigne's intransigence, Daniel displays a capable, pliant strength. He will show her his love, ever-fiercer over the years.

As he begins his sestet, Daniel finds in himself a "miracle." He replaces the message of Delia's glass with his own message, to her and to himself. Phoenix-like, he rises from the ashes of unconsummated passion. "All the matter's spent": the ceaseless reviewing of love's sorrows, the scrutiny of the beloved's gestures and her radiant appearance—all this was old (the reader suspects) long before Delia herself was. But this desire gets new life, even as age wears out the story's protagonists. The word "spent" is repeated from line 6: the poet has expended his energies just as she has wasted her beauty. (Spending is also a Renaissance euphemism for male orgasm, used wryly by Daniel, in a possible allusion to his future impotence. See Shakespeare's Sonnet 129, "The expense of spirit [that is, semen] in a waste of shame / Is lust in action.")

Significantly, "spent" rhymes with "repent." The conjuring aspect of the phrase "thou mayst repent," repeated at the beginning of line 13, gives a sense of the poet's powerful and anxious wish for a second chance—to have her turn toward him, finally. "Repent" means, in Renaissance English, to change one's mind, not just to feel remorse. This is no mere schoolboyish threat (you'll be sorry later on, when it's too late). Daniel has moved to a tenuous, affecting vision, still with a touch of resentment (he remembers her scorn, in the couplet), but with hope too. Perhaps, having missed her chance, she will turn back to him, in wonder at his love's potential to last—a potential embodied in his poem's own lasting statement.

The touching enigma of Daniel's sonnet appears in his conclusion. The reader may find it hard to decide whether the poet at the end turns against his disdainful beloved, or remains oddly attached to her. But attachment wins out, however subtly. The poet's love finds its place in the final couplet, in an almost magical picture of Delia. Winter snows fall on her "golden hairs." She has gone at least partly gray, but, the image implies, the youthful gold still lies beneath the wintry covering, shining as at first. Disappointingly, Daniel in a later edition changed "golden hairs" to "sable hairs," losing the point. Whether Delia was in fact blonde or brunette does not matter; but the brilliant, precious image does, suggesting Ovid's Age of Gold at the dawn of mankind, and gold as the standard of all worth.

Daniel decides to cherish the possibility of a future union between poet and beloved, both now aged. Daniel here attains some of the somber coloring of Yeats's marvelous, regretful "When You Are Old," based on his own missed love with Maud Gonne and indebted to another Renaissance poet, Pierre Ronsard. Ronsard's sonnet (published in French in 1578, and apparently known by Daniel) disarmingly depicts the poet, after death, taking his ease underground, while his beloved chants his verse and marvels, "Ronsard praised me when I was beautiful . . ." The Italian poet Torquato Tasso, another source for Daniel's poem, lacks Ronsard's compassion, as well as his eccentric imagination of a bond between poet and beloved. Tasso's sonnets on this theme are hard and triumphant, and exalt the poet's self-sufficient strength.

Daniel is closer to Ronsard than to Tasso. The tenderness of Daniel's concluding image surrenders the triumphal advantage proclaimed in his opening lines. He starts out writing at the expense of the beloved, excluding her in order to make a proud verse. But then the poet, now rueful and yearning rather than defiant, develops a muted, mature mood. Daniel stands by his love—and stands by himself. Thoughtful and ambivalent, he grants himself autonomy, yet remains affected by desire: he still wants Delia for his audience.

DM

Amoretti 78

EDMUND SPENSER

1595

Lackyng my love I go from place to place,
   lyke a young fawne that late hath lost the hynd:
   and seeke each where, where last I sawe her face,
   whose ymage yet I carry fresh in mynd.
I seeke the fields with her late footing synd,
   I seeke her bowre with her late presence deckt,
   yet nor in field nor bowre I her can fynd:
   yet field and bowre are full of her aspect,
But when myne eyes I thereunto direct,
   they ydly back returne to me agayne,
   and when I hope to see theyr trew obiect,
   I fynd my selfe but fed with fancies vayne.
Ceasse then myne eyes, to seeke her selfe to see,
   and let my thoughts behold her selfe in mee.

EDMUND SPENSER—Elizabethan gentleman, colonial official in Ireland, and author of the immense, gorgeously varied allegorical epic *The Faerie Queene*—stands out among English Renaissance poets for his lush and hieratic sensibility. Everything in his sonnet sequence, the *Amoretti* (1595), partakes of luxuriant ritual. By turns solemn and joyous, the *Amoretti* enjoys a regal pace. But its calm is disrupted, from time to time, by the furies of troubled love.

The amoretti (Spenser's invented term) are amorous sparks given embodied form, the little cupids that attend the poet's courtship. Ambient signs of erotic power, they represent the intimate gestures of love or resistance that pass between the speaker and his beloved. Spenser inherited the courtly love tradition

practiced by the troubadours of medieval Provence, in which the poet ad-
dressed his beloved as *midons,* "my lord," and waited for a sign from her—a
haughty, distant lady. Spenser gives his beloved a similarly noble, awe-inspiring
status.

Spenser's beloved, his bride-to-be Elizabeth Boyle, stands at the center of
the *Amoretti.* Goddess-like, she holds the law of desire in her hands. With
implacable assurance, her "stedfast might" (Sonnet 59) guides the poet. Spen-
ser shifts the focus away from Petrarch's rapt interest in the male lover's re-
sponses to his own desire. Instead, he studies the lady, her small indications of
favor and disfavor. In this respect he resembles Sidney, whose Astrophel pores
over Stella's responses to him. In Sonnet 78, though, Spenser has temporarily
lost his beloved. Deprived of her presence, he cherishes instead the image of
her he has internalized.

Spenser drops some autobiographical clues in the course of the *Amoretti:* he
is almost forty (Sonnet 60), and has loved Elizabeth for at least a year (Son-
net 63). After a long trial, she finally gives him her love (Sonnets 66 and 68).
This sonnet sequence stands out among its Elizabethan rivals because it ends
in marriage. Spenser caps the *Amoretti* with a long poem: the extravagant,
ceremonial *Epithalamion,* his "spousal verse" written for himself and Eliza-
beth. Four anacreontics—playful homages to Cupid's power, in imitation
of the ancient Greek lyricist Anacreon—provide an intermezzo between the
Amoretti and the stately, luscious *Epithalamion.*

At times in Spenser's sequence the beloved is a tiger or a ruthless storm,
virtually inhuman in her resistance to the speaker's pleas. He is vexed by her
combination of cruelty and beauty, envy and resistance. But the *Amoretti* ded-
icates itself to overcoming such frustration: in Sonnet 78, as the sequence
moves toward its conclusion, Spenser secures in his mind his image of the
ideal beloved. With the consummation of marriage, the ideal becomes fleshly
reality.

Spenser's Sonnet 78, from late in the *Amoretti*'s series of eighty-nine son-
nets, reflects on the Petrarchan scheme of stasis and restlessness: a combina-
tion that leads to narcissism, as we saw in Petrarch's "Una candida cerva" (dis-
cussed in the Introduction, and imitated by Wyatt in "Whoso list to hunt").
In Petrarch's poem the poet is frozen, unable to act, while the lady is chaste
and removed. Spenser turns this paralyzed situation to his advantage: the be-
loved becomes the fixed star of his affection, an inspiration that he carries
within him. The private devotion to the beloved's image is never desperate, as
in Shakespeare's sonnets. Spenser's adoration remains solid, reassuring.

As the sonnet opens, the speaker, mysteriously separated from his beloved (the plot of the *Amoretti* is at times unclear), wanders "from place to place." Previously united with him, she has now disappeared; this sonnet will allow him to secure her love within his own mind, before she returns. At the end of the *Amoretti,* the speaker is still wandering. We must wait for the *Epithalamion* to see Spenser's picture of mutual, fulfilled love.

Spenser's comparison of himself to a young fawn seeking its mother (the "hynd") provides a striking contrast to the numerous Renaissance sonnets, like Petrarch's and Wyatt's, in which love is pictured as a hunt, with the female supplying the role of the prey. In Spenser, the male poet-speaker is remarkably passive: drawn along in a trance-like manner from field to bower, haplessly following the absent beloved's footprints. The fields are "with her late footing synd"—that is, signed, bearing her imprint or seal. The speaker finds only her "aspect," rather than the woman herself. She has dissolved into a presiding deity or genius (the Renaissance term for the quasi-divine spirit of a place).

Spenser's rhyme scheme, tightly interlaced and containing only five rhymes, features open quatrains and a concluding couplet *(ababbcbccdcdee).* This arrangement enables Spenser to rhyme "hynd," "mynd, "synd," and "fynd." The lost hind becomes a creature of the mind only, sought for in her signs: the speaker's memory traces of their previous encounters. Like Wyatt in "Whoso list to hunt," Spenser gives us an implicit pun on "hind" and "(left) behind" (since he is outpaced by the woman). The speaker, caught up in memory and desire, remains behind, mournfully revisiting the places associated with his beloved. Meanwhile, she has fled, with a deft suddenness that resembles the agile vanishing of a deer.

The speaker tracks his lady, and hopes to feed his eyes on the remnants of her glorious, nourishing presence. He will be disappointed: and the volta (the poem's turn at the octave's end) brings home his loss. With line 9, Spenser turns from the fantasy of fulfilled presence ("Yet field and bowre are full of her aspect") to the bitter realization of her absence ("But when myne eyes I thereunto direct, / They ydly back returne to me agayne"). His gaze lolls "ydly" back to himself. The poet's endeavor proves both idle (useless or vain) and idolatrous. He sees not her, but rather himself, puffed up with empty "fancies": the delusions that lovers dote on. Like Petrarch, he floats irritably back and forth, addicted to images of satisfied love, and to his memory of the lady's beauty.

Spenser's closing couplet overcomes such distraction. "Ceasse . . . to seeke her selfe to see," he tells his eyes; instead, see "her selfe in mee." Rather than remaining driven by fancy (seeing himself in her, or in the faded remains of her), he firmly roots the beloved's image in himself. Secure in poetic imagination, she anchors his ardor and his high capacity. Like Mary Wroth in her *Pamphilia to Amphilanthus* (see below in this volume), Spenser hints at the Narcissus legend. In the *Amoretti,* the poet surmounts the baffled situation of Narcissus by making the beloved an aspect of himself. The lover succeeds, unlike the deluded Narcissus; turning his gaze inward, he knows that he sees at once both his own love and his beloved.

Spenser relocates the lady—from fields and bowers, the familiar pastoral haunts of love poetry, to the mind of the poet. He has triumphed over the tantalizing frustrations of Petrarch's *Rime sparse.* No longer distracted and vulnerable like Petrarch, Spenser is ready to build a palace for his bride, with its foundation in his poetic spirit. In *Epithalamion,* Spenser instructs his readers and himself to "open the temple gates unto my love, / Open them wide that she may enter in." The *Amoretti* are the necessary preparation for this glorious ceremony: the marriage of the poet and his bride, his imagination and his world.

DM

Caelica 7

FULKE GREVILLE, LORD BROOKE

Probably written in the 1590s; published 1633

The World, that all contains, is ever moving,
The Stars within their spheres for ever turned,
Nature (the Queen of Change) to change is loving,
And Form to matter new is still adjourned.

Fortune our fancy-God, to vary liketh,
Place is not bound to things within it placed,
The present time upon time passèd striketh,
With Phoebus' wandering course the earth is graced.

The Air still moves, and by its moving cleareth,
The Fire up ascends, and planets feedeth,
The Water passeth on, and all lets weareth,
The Earth stands still, yet change of changes breedeth;

Her plants, which Summer ripes, in Winter fade,
Each creature in unconstant mother lieth,
Man made of earth, and for whom earth is made,
Still dying lives, and living ever dieth;
    Only like fate sweet Myra never varies,
    Yet in her eyes the doom of all Change carries.

GREVILLE's finely tuned stanzas tell us that everything changes, that nothing in our experience of this world can sustain our hope or trust. Such claims gather up their pessimistic implications only slowly: the clockwork turning of the stars, the "grace" of sunset and sunrise, the circulation of fire and air, might delight our contemplation. But the reign of Fortune (another medieval commonplace), a fickle goddess set up by fancy (i.e., delusion), is nothing to celebrate, nor are erosion, winter, and the grave. All the changes in this poem about change collude to the same grim outcome, as seen in the eyes of Greville's lady, "Myra," who is less a beloved woman than a stark personification of our common end.

Greville was known in his own time as a figure at the court of Queen Elizabeth, a friend of Sir Philip Sidney (whose life he would later write) and a high official in the later administrations of King James I. He seems to have begun writing his only set of short poems, *Caelica,* sometime before Sidney's death in 1586; no one knows when he finished it. The sequence appeared in print only five years after Greville's death, in a collection containing almost all of his verse and prose. Most of the first seventy-six poems in *Caelica* concern, at least nominally, one or more cruel fair ladies, mistresses who without exception spurn or betray the poet. They bear the names Myra (suggesting the Greek *Moira,* fate), Cynthia, and Caelica ("sky-lady" or "heavenly lady," as in the Latin *caelum* and French *ciel*). The last thirty-three poems are explicitly religious, consonant with a Calvinist theology that emphasizes the fallen, corrupted nature of the material world and the pleasures therein.

Yet even the so-called love poems seem continuous with Greville's religious outlook. "On earth," writes the contemporary poet Thom Gunn, Greville "could be certain only of the weakness, mutability and uncertainty of all that surround[ed] him." Mutability, weakness, and uncertainty on earth certainly give Greville topics for this poem. So, however, do their opposites, the few certainties we can have about this changing world: those certainties tell us that nothing lasts, that all the variables we see, or do not see, come to equal the same constant, death.

Greville arranges his examples of mutability in order of decreasing size, from "the World" (meaning not the globe, but the universe) through the abstractions by which we make sense of it, down to the earth and then to the human beings on it. The cosmos holds everything, by definition, and yet everything in it moves with respect to something else, according to the Ptolemaic cosmology that set stars and planets in nested rotating "spheres." To adjourn is to defer a meeting (especially of a court or legislature) to another time and place: "Form" is always putting off the day when it will settle down and solidify, since "matter new" is always shaking things up. Greville adapts to his astringent temperament a medieval commonplace: "Fortune," who rules the material world, is its god, but unworthy of worship, since the one true God must be eternal, beyond change.

The passage of time, which brings change, seems to Greville a kind of violence: each new hour, as it "strikes," deals a fatal blow to the last. Air moves laterally, flame ascends, water flows downhill—all four classical elements seek constant motion; even the earth, which seems stable by comparison, makes possible the changing of the seasons, plants' growth and decay, and human life, which arises from earth ("dust to dust") and ends in earth again. Identified in Renaissance love poems with infidelity, "change" in theology can mean corruption and sin: earth is our "inconstant" (changing, unfaithful) mother because seasons change it (Greville may also allude to Eve, the sinful mother of us all).

Caelica includes fourteen-line sonnets, sonnets with "missing" quatrains (ten lines), sonnets with "extra" quatrains such as this one, "sonnets" with multiple six-line stanzas, and poems in unrelated forms (such as six- and seven-foot lines). All the sonnets and sonnet-like poems use the "English" construction invented by the Earl of Surrey, with quatrains and one or more six-line stanzas rhyming *ababcc.* These units fit the brief apothegmatic or philosophical units—the detachable abstract statements (what medieval writers called *sententiae*)—in which Greville tends to think. From most of those statements, in *Caelica* 7, Greville derives either paradoxes (earth "stands still" yet breeds change), or else the rhetorical figure of chiasmus, repetition with inversion ("Man made of earth, and for whom earth is made"). Each paradox, each chiasmus, represents the general contradiction that rules the whole poem. Everything changes, yet nothing does; nature's change follows the same cycles, ending in death. For all its symmetries, the poem (till its ending) seems almost ready to split up into its separable *sententiae,* into its component parts. It holds together because all the parts mean the same thing: everything in the world changes, and nothing stays still long enough to merit our trust.

Greville repeats himself not only in what he says, but in what his language does. No lines are enjambed; most are self-sufficient clauses. Almost all begin with a subject noun and end on a corresponding verb or verb phrase. Three in a row (lines 10–12) have the identical construction: subject noun—first verb—direct object—second verb. All the rhymes are verbs or verbal adjectives; eight (of eleven) present-tense verbs in rhyming position bear the -eth endings (liketh, striketh, etc.) already a bit archaic in Greville's own day. The poet thus makes stately, and considerably slower, lines, of eleven syllables rather than ten. He also makes lines that sound even more alike. (Because he rhymes past-tense verbs only with each other, we could read those rhymes as normal pen-

tameters, but we probably should hear more stately eleven-syllable lines—
"turnèd," "adjournèd," etc.)

Part of the poem's beauty, then, lies in Greville's ability to do and say the
same things over and over without monotony. Another part lies in how it
represents the ever-changing and intricate orders that it depicts. Like the
Ptolemaic cosmology of the first quatrain, the poem sets up a finely balanced
network of contrary motions and harmonies. Those motions seem, at some
moments, to suit us well ("for whom earth is made"); as much as it says other-
wise in some other key words (the pejorative "fancy," "striketh," "weareth"),
Greville's sonnet acknowledges the elegance in the metamorphoses that it de-
picts.

The very last phrases in Greville's cycle of quatrains, and the very last chias-
mus in this poem so full of them, remind us that bodies decay, but not im-
mortal souls: "Man . . . Still dying lives, and living ever dieth." But this poem,
like all of the poems in the first part of *Caelica,* will not admit explicit Chris-
tian doctrine. Despite its religious overtones, it takes place, as the scholar
Helen Vincent writes, in a "secular literary space," akin to that of earlier amo-
rous sonnets. The sonnet thus turns back to the world from which Greville
would flee, and finally to that world's epitome, the unsatisfactory, uncaring
beloved, whose position at the end of the poem—and whose eyes—suggest
no kind end.

"Sweet Myra never varies"—she is the unchanging star in Greville's sky, the
apex of devotion, the *ne plus ultra* of virtue or beauty: so we might expect if we
have read such sonnets as Sidney's, or Petrarch's. But Myra is less like a star,
less like Sidney's Stella (stars are, by contrast, "for ever turned") than she is
"like fate," not an especially erotic comparison. Rather, Myra personifies an
unalterable, and unfriendly, law. The word "doom" on its own, in Greville's
time, would have meant (like Myra's very name) fate, a cosmic decree, not
necessarily a catastrophe. But "the doom of all change" brings "doom" closer
to its more baleful modern meaning. It may also suggest the End of Days, the
Apocalypse, when change itself will cease. A centuries-old commonplace of
love poetry, the beloved's fatal gaze (Chaucer: "Your eyen two wol slee me
sodenly") becomes for Greville an anti-erotic condemnation. To devote one's
attention to a human beloved, or to any other earthly pleasure, is to give one-
self over to death.

Greville in life never married. One of his modern biographers, A. C. Reb-
holz, calls *Caelica* "a series of anti-love poems." Greville's prose "Letter to an

Honorable Lady" (like *Caelica,* almost impossible to date) advises the lady that "each degree of life in [flesh] is only a change, and variety of servitude." "The curse of our fall," Greville continues, appears to us "in the false changes of diseases, and cures; appetites and opinions. Neither can the confluence of worldly things yield any other rest, or stability, than such is in the kingdom of sleep; where the best is but a dream." The neo-Stoic distance that the "Letter" recommends, its detachment from anything in or of this world, shows already in this more delicate, and probably earlier, variation on the still-new English sonnet form.

Writing at a time of great change, and of increasing sophistication, in English poetry, Greville found some of his strengths in an older manner. His stanzas may seem to us, and may even have seemed in his own day, slightly old-fashioned, especially when set beside the more sensuously vivid, more psychologically complex poetry of his friend Sidney. And yet the austere geometries of Greville's lines, the forbidding warnings in his "anti-love" poems have inspired modern poets too: six lines in a row from *Caelica* 7 (from "The present time" to "change of changes breedeth"), quoted in full, make up the conclusion to one of the strongest poems by the living American poet (and former U.S. poet laureate) Robert Pinsky, his elegy for his difficult, reclusive mother, "Poem with Refrains."

SB

Sonnet 2

WILLIAM SHAKESPEARE

1609

When forty winters shall besiege thy brow
And dig deep trenches in thy beauty's field,
Thy youth's proud livery, so gazed on now,
Will be a tatter'd weed of small worth held:
Then being asked where all thy beauty lies,
Where all the treasure of thy lusty days,
To say within thine own deep sunken eyes,
Were an all-eating shame, and thriftless praise.
How much more praise deserv'd thy beauty's use
If thou could'st answer, "This fair child of mine
Shall sum my count, and make my old excuse,"
Proving his beauty by succession thine.
    This were to be new made when thou art old,
    And see thy blood warm when thou feel'st it cold.

SHAKESPEARE'S sonnets, published in 1609, present a story so perverse, so self-frustrating, and so varied in tone, that few readers have been able to resist trying to decode them. The sonnets range from elevated austerity, to a lush, measured grace, to near-lunatic emotional intensity. We have no idea whether Shakespeare himself decided on the poems' sequence: but, read in their familiar order, the 154 sonnets tell a disturbing, half-occluded story. The speaker, a poet like Shakespeare, obsessively admires a younger man. Ravished by his beloved's androgynous handsomeness, he urges the young man to marry and sire children, to give his beauty to succeeding generations. He also offers his own poetry for this mission: he can provide enduring fame for the one he praises. In the course of the sequence, the speaker makes the wrenching discovery that the young man, who does not reciprocate his love, has stolen the speaker's mistress. Unable to disavow his love, the speaker makes elaborate excuses for the young man's dreadful treatment of him: words intended to shame both of them. At times, he is coarsely unhinged and defiant; at others, self-punishing, when he adores his beloved at his own expense. Then, beginning with Sonnet 127, Shakespeare in the course of several dozen poems excoriates a demon-like female beloved (nicknamed the "dark lady" by later readers). He concludes with two weakly charming sonnets about Cupid.

All of this is strange enough, and clearly raises the possibility that our Top Bard (as W. H. Auden called him) was a bisexual. The young man, many have decided, is really Shakespeare's patron, the glamorous pretty boy Henry Wriothesley. Or perhaps, as Oscar Wilde decided, he was a young actor in Shakespeare's company, "Willie Hughes" (a Wildean invention). A strong candidate for the dark lady is the mysterious Lucy Negro, a celebrity courtesan in Elizabethan London. My commentary on three Shakespeare sonnets treads safer ground. I shy away from biographical inferences and confine myself to an analysis of Shakespeare's remarkable linguistic inventions.

Shakespeare revolutionized the sonnet in several ways. The Italian poets divided their sonnets into two uneven units, the eight-line octave followed by the six-line sestet. Shakespeare built his sonnets differently, as three block-like quatrains (four-line units) followed by a couplet. Shakespeare's quatrains are open (*abab,* rather than the closed *abba*), and each has its own rhymes: his sonnets rhyme *ababcdcdefefgg*. English poets before Shakespeare, including Surrey and Gascoigne, had used this rhyme scheme, and Wyatt first employed the couplet ending (in our collection, it appears in Wyatt's "Whoso list to hunt," Gascoigne's "That self same tongue," and Surrey's "Norfolk sprang thee"). But Shakespeare put his own stamp on the pattern, and it is now known by his name. Often Shakespeare's quatrains provide a series of scenes, a pageant followed by the final couplet's epigrammatic, summary gesture. But Shakespeare's strength may have made his signature pattern harder to imitate. The majority of English-language poets after Shakespeare have relied on the Italian sonnet form, though some have also written Shakespearean sonnets: the octave-sestet division, rather than quatrain breaks, provides the basic feature of most sonnets.

Shakespeare makes an intense and profound energy reside in certain words, which accumulate meaning as they are repeated from one poem to another, and within a single poem. For instance, "use," in the phrase "thy beauty's use," suggests the practice of usury (loaning money at interest). But as Shakespeare employs it—and he does so frequently in his sequence—it also has sexual overtones, as well as implications of manipulation (the young man's use of his beauty as a means of power; the poet's use of this same beauty in his sonnets).

Sonnet 2 begins aggressively, with a military image: the war against beauty. The youth's brow, like an enemy fortress, will be "besiege[d]" by the forty winters of middle age (age forty was rather advanced by Renaissance standards). In a few short decades, the poet predicts, the beloved's star-quality countenance will look like a battlefield carved by "deep trenches" (wrinkles). Shakespeare compares his beloved's "proud" (resplendent as well as self-satisfied) beauty to a gorgeous outfit turned to rags (a "tatter'd weed"). The poet predicts a grim, miserly future for the young man turned old: he will bury the treasure of his energetically sensuous, "lusty" youth within his own haunted, "deep sunken" eyes (a stark contrast to the "bright eyes" that Shakespeare imagines for the young man in the first sonnet of his sequence). There is only one remedy for this dire fate: the beloved must make a "fair child" to recreate himself, and incarnate his youth anew. Marred by age, he can then look back on his shining earlier self.

Shakespeare likes to make his sonnets converge on a paradox. Here, as often, it arrives in the couplet. The stunning final image of Sonnet 2 is that of the young man grown old, "feel[ing]" his blood cold and deathly, yet "see[ing]" it warm in the form of the son who represents his younger self. To be "new made" would seem to imply rejuvenation. Instead, it turns out to mean imprisonment in a paradox. The beloved, on his deathbed, will see before him the lively heir who bears a forceful, and painful, contrast. The son's vivid warmth tells the father of his impending death.

The experience invoked in Shakespeare's concluding couplet is utterly private—far removed from the sonnet's earlier emphasis on a public scene of avowal, in which making a child excuses one's old age in the eyes of all. The slow, decisive stress on two successive syllables, in the phrase "and sée thy blóod wárm," gives an almost uncanny, mesmerizing status to the appearance of the child. The line then skips forward to an iambic ending, a bone-dry resolution that cannot be evaded: "thou féel'st it cóld." Feeling should be trusted before seeing. At any rate, it has the last word: the cold blood that presages mortality. Shakespeare's conclusion, rather amazingly, offers a death threat directed at his beloved, the young man. But his verse, unlike its subject, lives.

DM

Sonnet 68

WILLIAM SHAKESPEARE

1609

Thus is his cheek the map of days out-worn,
When beauty lived and died as flowers do now,
Before these bastard signs of fair were borne,
Or durst inhabit on a living brow;
Before the golden tresses of the dead,
The right of sepulchres, were shorn away,
To live a second life on second head,
Ere beauty's dead fleece made another gay:
In him those holy ántique hours are seen,
Without all ornament, itself and true,
Making no summer of another's green,
Robbing no old to dress his beauty new;
    And him as for a map doth Nature store,
    To show false Art what beauty was of yore.

THIS POEM, with its exquisite pace and somber reflectiveness, forms—like our other two Shakespeare sonnets—part of the young man sequence. Shakespeare here meditates on beauty's preservation. Sonnet 68 displays the graceful perfection of a dance at a Renaissance court, with lords and ladies bowing and beckoning to each other, and the whole event infused with a sense of the fragile, memorable character of life's ceremonies.

Lauding the young man, Shakespeare turns away from the idea, expressed elsewhere in his sequence, that his face is a "field" that will be carved with age's damaging "deep trenches" (Sonnet 2). The wrinkles imposed by middle age, imagined in Sonnet 2, here take on a new light, as a nostalgic "map of days out-worn" (line 1). Instead of the earlier sonnet's shocking reminder of time's ravaging course, Shakespeare gives us a quiet, fond glance at a youth-fulness that he associates with a lost past. This beauty appreciates with age, rather than declining; the farther it recedes from the speaker, the more it is worth. The young man is still young, but superimposed on his face is an afterimage, as if he can become visible only through the lens of an older man's wan perspective. Looking ahead, the poet subtly suggests that his beloved's cheek is aging, becoming outworn: soon to be criss-crossed with lines, like a map.

The poet praises the young man as a true incarnation of the old notion of bare and honest beauty, before the artificial tricks of fashion ("these bastard signs of fair") came to be preferred. The older beauty was transient: it "lived and died as flowers do now." The somewhat furtive appearance of line 2's flower image, common in Shakespeare's sonnets, reminds us that all physical appearance, no matter how noble or graceful, is fleeting. A splendid face can be turned into a symbol (or "map," used to locate a bygone treasured ideal), but the face itself must wither, becoming rapidly unrecognizable.

Shakespeare's poetic lesson about time and the ideal of beauty necessarily detaches the beautiful countenance from its owner. In this poem, the young man is no longer an actor in a story, and therefore the poet has no call for am-bivalence toward him. Other sonnets present high drama, as the speaker works himself up over his beloved's misdeeds; Sonnet 68 gives us instead a cool allu-sion to the young man's beauty as symbol. The beloved's dangerous character has become irrelevant. Here, the stringent purity of the poet's presentation makes the point that lyric has the power to refine away all messy human inter-actions, leaving us with essential truth.

Shakespeare's second quatrain begins with a rather grisly image of "the golden tresses of the dead": human hair stolen from graves in order to be made into wigs. (The Elizabethan wig, very fashionable in Shakespeare's day, was akin to our hair extensions, pasted-on ringlets worn by both men and women.) Bas-sanio in Shakespeare's *Merchant of Venice,* about to make his correct choice of the lead casket over the glittering gold and silver ones, also describes such trea-sures of the tomb. Bassanio refers to the

> crispèd snaky golden locks
> Which make such wanton gambols with the wind
> Upon supposed fairness, often known
> To be the dowry of a second head,
> The skull that bred them in the sepulchre.

The wistful tone of Bassanio's speech moderates, without fully concealing, its hectic monstrosity: wantonness concealing death, golden curls that are really Medusa-like snakes. Of all the great writers, Shakespeare is by far the most adamantly opposed to cosmetics (though most poets seem to share his bias). His Hamlet rails at Ophelia, "God hath given you one face, / And you make yourselves another." Hamlet's harsh accusation of deceptiveness through makeup echoes in milder form in Sonnet 68, where artificial adornments like wigs become "bastard signs of fair": unnaturally bred loveliness. (Line 6's "sepulchres" are related via false etymology to the Latin *pulchrum,* beautiful.)

Like Robert Browning in "A Toccata of Galuppi's," sighing over the wondrous hair of Venice's "dear dead women," Shakespeare supplies a morbid twist to the idea of beauty's artifice. The lively frivolities of the *haut monde* and its "gay" highjinks contain a memento mori, a reminder of the tomb: all that gorgeous hair.

For Shakespeare, the young man represents a quite different kind of beauty, one infused with a still, sober perfection. You can see in him the "holy ántique hours," the loveliness of the past. By means of this haunting phrase, the poet endows a bygone era with a quasi-religious air. (In another sonnet, 73, Shakespeare refers in a similar vein to "bare ruined choirs, where late the sweet birds sang"—a nostalgic glance back toward the monasteries and churches wrecked by Reformation decree.)

Sonnet 68 proves Shakespeare a worshiper of beauty. In its service, he pursues a drastic refinement of phrase. "Without all ornament, itself and true" describes the poet's own words as much as the ideal he delineates. Truth consists in a stripped-down self-consistency that owes nothing to others, and has no need to steal their splendor. The second-hand labor of rival bards, who "rob" the treasury of hoary literary conventions, fades before this pure speech, which seems to derive from "Nature" itself.

The sonnet's final couplet returns to the image of the map identified with the beloved's cheek. A map, as suggested earlier, might be used to locate buried treasure (like the youthful "lusty days" of Shakespeare's Sonnet 2). It also means, in the Renaissance, an exemplary instance—someone might be the very map of virtue, or of vice. In Sonnet 68, Shakespeare shows us a map of his own values and methods in his strikingly unadorned final lines, which are spare and monosyllabic except for two dominating abstractions, "Nature" and "beauty." Here, the poet teaches "false Art" a lesson, showing it to be misdirected. But the beauty he invokes remains gone, a thing of the past: "what beauty *was* of yore." In earlier sonnets, the young man's beauty was said to be potentially eternal, as long as he had a loyal poet like Shakespeare to serve him (or as long as he produced a child so that his good looks could live on). Now, late in the young man sequence, beloved beauty has become a chaste separateness. Paired with his implacably "true" diction, Shakespeare's ideal defends itself perfectly.

DM

Sonnet 116

WILLIAM SHAKESPEARE

1609

Let me not to the marriage of true minds
Admit impediments. Love is not love
Which alters when it alteration finds,
Or bends with the remover to remove.
O no; it is an ever-fixèd mark,
That looks on tempests, and is never shaken;
It is the star to every wandering bark,
Whose worth's unknown, although his height be taken.
Love's not time's fool, though rosy lips and cheeks
Within his bending sickle's compass come;
Love alters not with his brief hours and weeks,
But bears it out even to the edge of doom.
    If this be error and upon me proved,
    I never writ, nor no man ever loved.

Shakespeare's Sonnet 116 is perhaps his most familiar, and cherished, poem. Often recited at weddings, its words have become so well known that they can be hard to read with fresh eyes. The sonnet is usually taken so ceremoniously that all drama is drained from it: we picture a happy couple at the altar, basking in Shakespeare's reassuring words. Yet Sonnet 116 is, in fact, quite suspenseful. No blandly encouraging praise of love, it is more akin to a high-wire act in which the embattled poet triumphantly rises above his beloved's treachery, the "impediments" that the young man's (and, later, the dark lady's) acts of desertion and betrayal have placed before him. Read along with the rest of Shakespeare's sequence, it is like an island of perfect security in a restless sea. Yet the poem is far from an act of deluded wish-fulfillment. Shakespeare brilliantly, and disconcertingly, admits skepticism about the actual course of love in order to build his high ideal of it. The more heartfelt he is, the more doubts he includes in his structure. And, amazingly, the mortar of doubt makes his poem more solid, rather than more precarious.

Shakespeare begins with a high-flown first sentence, based on the solemn language of the Book of Common Prayer. According to the wedding ritual in that text, used by the Church of England in Shakespeare's day (and for centuries afterward), anyone attending a wedding who sees any reason the couple should not be married must speak out. "If any man do allege and declare any impediment why they may not be coupled together in matrimony," then the ceremony must be deferred "until the truth be tried." (Such an impediment might be, for example, that one of the partners is already married.) The Book of Common Prayer pictures a trial that leads to the truth of the matter, and shows whether the couple's marriage is legitimate. In his sonnet, Shakespeare similarly testifies at love's trial.

With his opening three words, "Let me not," the poet pleads, in both senses of the word: he testifies and he asks for strength. We infer that he has been tempted to acknowledge impediments, to give them a place; now he vows to exclude them. Yet the rest of the sonnet goes on to "admit" these obstacles, alluding to them in order to overcome their significance.

Shakespeare now proclaims the value of steadfastness: "Love is not love / Which alters when it alteration finds, / Or bends with the remover to remove." When the beloved abandons him, the lover might be tempted to remove his affections—but this would be a mere parody of reciprocity, the poet suggests. Remaining inflexible is the way of truth: the lover must refuse to bend.

In his second quatrain, Shakespeare pursues the idea of inflexibility, which he attributes now to love itself, rather than the lover's loyal, unbending stance (as in the first quatrain). He establishes a fixed point that can monitor or oversee the lovers. "O no," the poet cries at the start of the second quatrain, before giving two images of love as a guiding, stable light. The first is that of the mark (probably a sea mark— a beacon or lighthouse), which saves mariners from running aground during "tempests." The second image is that of the pole star, which never changes position, and so guides ships ("wandering bark[s]") on their voyages. The star's "worth's unknown, although his [i.e., its] height be taken." The pole star's angle can be measured, but its power over our lives—its worth—remains unclear. Does the ideal's remoteness from the facts of a love affair lessen its definitive character, or (as the critic Stephen Booth suggests) is its influence simply too grand and ineffable to be comprehended? Within the single word "unknown," Shakespeare melds skepticism and belief. In the course of Sonnet 116, belief wins out: the higher the ideal, the more it compels our recognition.

Both the sea mark and the pole star define love as a faraway signal, beaming its influence down to lovers who might be at sea, lost or endangered. But this is not enough. In order to prove love's genuine worth, Shakespeare must go on, as he does in his third quatrain, to introduce the drastic pressure of death and time in place of the glimmering, indifferent guideposts of the second quatrain.

"Love's not time's fool," the beginning of the third quatrain, offers a much more vibrant image than that of the star and the sea mark. A "fool" is a dupe, but also (in Renaissance English) a darling: love, staunchly undeceived, knows that it cannot make time its affectionate ally. The two are bound together as predator and victim—and love becomes itself by cultivating an awareness of time's dangerous mastery.

"Rosy lips and cheeks" are a poignant emblem of youth, seen in anonymous terms (in contrast to the perspective of Sonnets 2 and 68, which celebrate the young man's unique face). The anonymity implies that we all come within the compass (that is, the reach) of death's "bending sickle." In a swooping phrase, Shakespeare conjures up the bend of the swing employed by the grim harvester to cut us down in death—a lethal echo of the bending mentioned in line 2. Shakespeare probably alludes to the draftsman's compass that, with its twin legs, charts the relation between a point and a line. Inevitable mortality has now become the fixed point, in place of the earlier pole star and sea mark. No matter how we take our course, we are still oriented and controlled by the hard reality of death, which has us within its scope. (John Donne would later use the compass image to depict the ineluctable connection between lovers in "A Valediction: Forbidding Mourning.")

True love requires unmoving stubbornness, strict loyalty to an idea: the beloved's faults are in fact just an aspect of time's capacity to erode human relations. Shakespeare has created a radically different world from that of so many other sonnets in his book, where he wrestles bitterly with the young man's and the dark lady's treacheries. Here, he moves past such real-life drama into a towering statement of faith.

Love "bears it out": endures, definitively shows its valor. Love finds itself ennobled by time, even as time beats it down. This contest is as majestic and conclusive as the Christian apocalypse. The "edge of doom" conjures up the terrifying scene of final judgment, when all souls will be put on trial. (In the formula used in the Book of Common Prayer, the priest tells the couple to swear that their union is legal "as you will answer at the dreadful day of judgment, when the secrets of all hearts shall be disclosed.") Finally, in his couplet-ending the poet puts himself under oath: "If this be error and upon me proved . . ." Again, he plays the witness at a trial, swearing that he has everything right. And, he implies, any lover would agree with him.

Sonnet 116 is not a poem about seduction (like our sonnets by Wyatt, Gascoigne, and Daniel), but a sublime, strict declaration by a poet-lover, proud because he has built an image that transcends the emotional chaos here below. Shakespeare depicts love as law, all the stronger because it is bound together with time and death: a mental anchor that makes the poet's aspiration the work of necessity.

DM

Pamphilia to Amphilanthus 46

LADY MARY WROTH

1621

Love thou hast all, for now thou hast me made
   So thine, as if for thee I were ordain'd,
   Then take thy conquest, nor let me be pain'd
   More in thy sun, when I do seek thy shade.
No place for help have I left to invade,
   That show'd a face where least ease might be gain'd;
   Yet found I pain increase, and but obtain'd,
   That this no way was to have love allayed
When hot, and thirsty, to a well I came,
   Trusting by that to quench part of my flame,
   But there I was by love afresh embrac'd.
Drink I could not, but in it I did see
   My self a living glass as well as she;
   For Love to see himself in, truly placed.

IN AN era that discouraged women from writing, Mary Wroth made a literary career. As a young girl, she gained the attention of Queen Elizabeth for her skills as a dancer, and later participated in lavish masques at the court of Elizabeth's successor, James. Niece to the great poet Philip Sidney, Wroth fell in love with a cousin, William Herbert. Herbert was married; and Wroth depicted her difficult situation in a sonnet sequence, *Pamphilia to Amphilanthus.* Pamphilia is the "all-loving," Wroth herself; Amphilanthus, her beloved cousin Herbert, the "lover of two." (The characters Pamphilia and Amphilanthus also appear in Wroth's lengthy prose romance, *Urania.*)

   This sonnet, which occurs near the conclusion of *Pamphilia to Amphilanthus,* begins by ceding the field to her victorious antagonist, love. From

Dante's *Vita nuova* on, amorous desire is often seen as a quasi-deity, tyrannical or presumptuous in his designs on the poet's heart. Love has "all" (the Greek word *pan,* altered to *pam,* in "Pamphilia"). So Wroth no longer resists desire as she has earlier in her sonnet sequence: I'm yours, she tells eros. She now belongs to love, as she wishes to belong to her beloved.

As in Dante, love remakes the protagonist, giving her a new vocation: the striving, and heroic stress, of the erotic life. To "ordain" someone (line 2) means, in Renaissance English, to determine her destiny; or to set her in a rank, as if for battle. Wroth has become part of love's army. Overtaken by love, she surrenders, but with one proviso. She wishes to settle in love's shade: to find a refuge there, rather than remaining painfully exposed, subject to the sun of fierce desire.

The rueful tone of this sonnet continues in its second quatrain. "No place for help have I left to invade": "invade" suggests an intrusion or violation, disturbingly yoked to the hope for "ease." (The wincing vowel repetition in "least ease" ekes out a slim possibility of respite; but "ease" is meant to chime with "increase," after all.) There is no relief in sight: the poet continues to be burned by love's energies. All that she has "obtained" (learned or acquired) is the knowledge that desire increases pain, rather than "allay[ing]" it. Yielding to love does not bring the wished-for solution; instead, it exacerbates her torment.

This is "no way . . . to have love allayed": so the sardonic, suffering poet attests at the conclusion of the octave. To allay is to overthrow, subdue, or quell. Here Wroth reflects on a familiar human dilemma. By surrendering to desire, we hope to allay it, to triumph over its pangs. Once the victim acknowledges that she is possessed by love, she should arrive at the harbor of fulfillment. But the one mastered by eros does not, in fact, become master in this way. As Freud notes, we find no satisfaction in satisfaction. We habitually seek out inaccessible objects of desire, teasing ourselves with love's difficulties. Such an object is Wroth's Amphilanthus, already committed to another woman. Hoping to win him from her rival, the poet thrusts herself eagerly into the amorous wars that she prefers to peace.

The poem's sestet allows it to move from the painfully resigned to the reserved and hopeful. Wroth rejects her captive, distressed stance in the octave: she now becomes strategic. Line 9 shows her on the move, as she arrives, "hot, and thirsty," at a well—a crucial location for magical psychic transformation in the medieval French *Roman de la rose* (Romance of the Rose) and in Spenser's *Faerie Queene,* two works that strongly influenced Wroth.

Love is treacherous, but Wroth, in her need, remains "trusting." She wishes to "quench part of [her] flame" in the well. Slaking her thirst, we at first suppose, might mean extinguishing desire, here depicted according to Petrarchan convention as a relentless fire. But she seeks to assuage only part of the flame, after all. Moreover, "quench[ing]" might actually mean consummation: fulfilling her desire and thereby, inevitably, strengthening it. The poet-lover remains a divided creature. She seeks to allay the restlessness of eros; but also, more earnestly, she wants to extend her anguish.

At this point, love "embrace[s]" the speaker "afresh," distracting her from her enterprise. "Drink I could not": the poet is stopped in her tracks, as she finds a radically new perspective imposed on her. She now draws on a central myth for the story of European love: the myth of Narcissus, originally narrated in Ovid's *Metamorphoses* and retold many times in the Renaissance. (Narcissus, enraptured by a reflection in a stream, fails to realize that it is his own image, and therefore ungraspable; the nymph Echo, equally frustrated, repeats his laments.)

In the Renaissance, Narcissus sometimes represents the resistant beloved, because he is punished for his cruelty by being trapped in an illusion; his hapless pursuer, Echo, stands for unrequited love. In addition to arrogant self-love, Narcissus can be the figure of a noble, hopeless desire for the unattainable: not a deluded failure, but a pattern of introspection. The Renaissance thinker Leon Battista Alberti conceived a theory of art in which Narcissus was the first painter; and in the Romantic era, A. W. Schlegel commented that a poet is always a Narcissus. The self-regarding nature of the Petrarchan poet, who so steadily scrutinizes his own desire, makes him resemble Narcissus. But the coy beloved, imprisoned by her attachment to self, makes an equally reasonable candidate for the role (so Petrarch himself charges in one of his poems).

In Wroth's sonnet, the Narcissus myth enables a reenvisioning of the protagonist's erotic dilemma. She becomes not a Narcissus, but the mirroring surface that enables him to communicate, unknowingly, with himself. She is a "living glass" (mirror), in the sense that she is herself responsive, wounded— bound to reflect the gestures and emotions of another. The figure of the glass also appears in the sonnets we have included by Daniel and Spenser. Often, the Renaissance poet aims to secure an ideal love by displaying its image (as a mirror does). The glass can tell the truth, or it can indulge the poet's fantasy.

In Wroth's corrected myth of Narcissus, the living mirror embodied by the suffering lover—the poet herself—offers accurate rather than distorted vision.

Two new players have entered: one of them is the "she" that the poet competes with, a presence only glancingly referred to here. ("She" is William Herbert's wife, figured as Amphilanthus' other love interest.) The other new presence is "love": now not an exterior, impersonal force, as at the poem's beginning, but a character in the story, Amphilanthus/Narcissus himself. From a rude, peremptory conqueror (as in line 1), love has been transformed into a careful observer who sees himself in the beloved, "truly placed."

These last two words of the sonnet are resounding. Love itself (that is, Amphilanthus himself) is placed by the poet, positioned just where she wants him to be. And she herself, in accord with this poetic adjustment, finds herself "truly placed," too. The Narcissus myth expresses the potential to mistake the self for the other. Wroth corrects the mistake: the poet becomes a faithful partner, conveying the beloved's value and reflecting it back to him.

"Yet love I will, till I but ashes prove": so Wroth writes in the final poem of her *Pamphilia to Amphilanthus* sequence. The poet states her all-consuming need. Both impulsive and committed, she frightens the reader with the absolutism of her passion. The self-abnegation so notable in Wroth's sequence, as she offers herself to an ambivalent beloved, sets her apart from the male sonneteers of her age. The male poets tend to place a far greater stake in poetic fame and in the assertion of their own skill. In this way they defend themselves against the damages inflicted by eros. (See, for example, Daniel's *Delia* 38.) Wroth remains undefended, and implacably devoted: determined to burn to the end.

DM

"At the round earth's imagined corners"

JOHN DONNE

Probably written 1615–1633; published 1633

At the round earth's imagined corners, blow
Your trumpets, angels, and arise, arise
From death, you numberless infinities
Of souls, and to your scatter'd bodies go;
All whom the flood did, and fire shall o'erthrow,
All whom war, dearth, age, agues, tyrannies,
Despair, law, chance hath slain, and you whose eyes
Shall behold God, and never taste death's woe.
But let them sleep, Lord, and me mourn a space,
For, if above all these my sins abound,
'Tis late to ask abundance of Thy grace,
When we are there; here on this lowly ground,
Teach me how to repent; for that's as good
As if Thou hadst seal'd my pardon, with Thy blood.

THIS famous sonnet typifies Donne's dramatic self-presentations, his stormy openings and his dramatic reversals. It also shows a poet accustomed to confidence, and to emotional extremes, striving for a humility that—as he acknowledges—he cannot quite find. The sonnet comes seventh in the set of sixteen on religious themes published in 1633–1635, soon after Donne's death. Three more turned up in manuscript in 1899, and all nineteen are usually printed together under the title (almost certainly not Donne's own) *Holy Sonnets*. All nineteen use the same uncommon hybridized rhyme scheme: *abba-abba* (Petrarchan) for the octave, *cdcdee* (Shakespearean) after line eight. The combination (when it works properly) makes the opening virtuosic (with only two rhymes for eight lines), and the conclusion emphatic, as here. This sonnet also breaks neatly, where Petrarchan sonnets usually break, in two: almost everything in the octave has a response—most often a reversal—in the sestet.

Donne begins by imagining the end of time—in fact, by imploring that end to begin: he not only describes (as in the Book of Revelation) what will happen at the end of days, but firmly tells the angels who will assist in these events that he wants them to take place now. (The assertive imperative nearly suggests—though it does not quite say—that Donne himself can bring these events about.) The first line ends with a monosyllable isolated by syntax from the rest of the line; with an imperative verb; and with an enjambment—all devices that keep it off-balance. Donne thus evokes insistent forward motion, following "blow" by repeating "arise, arise." If he imagines that he might command angels, he adds, to that power, another even more awesome, the power to resurrect the dead.

The third line speaks to the human bodies that will come back from the grave at the end of days. Those bodies, when "scattered," posed puzzles: if I lost my hand in a battle at Calais, and later died in Oxford, would my resurrected hand travel from France to England in order to join my body before the Last Judgment? Such questions prompted serious dispute in Donne's own day, and they reappear in his prose; the poet uses them here to introduce the pains and deaths that will be encountered at the end of time. The sentences themselves may seem dismembered: lines 5–7, their rhythms thrown off by a cascade of monosyllabic nouns, catalog ways to die, ways given in neither logical nor chronological order. The flood is Noah's, the first great man-slaying disaster in biblical history, as earth-cleansing fire will be the last. In between come secular causes of death, including disease ("agues") and suicide ("despair"). Donne had written a prose treatise, *Biathanatos,* defending suicide under certain circumstances (probably in the same years that he wrote this poem), and the inclusion of suicide here makes it simply another cause of death, like starvation ("dearth") and war.

Marshaling so many earthly powers (and imagining power for himself), the poet then moves to remind us who truly holds the power, who—according to Christian belief—is really in charge. "O'erthrow," the last verb that the octave places in rhyming position, redefines death as the replacement of one power or ruler by another. That power (see Donne's sonnet "Death, be not proud") turns out to be not mortality but divinity. Fire, flood, and the rest are God's instruments, by which God reasserts control over the bodies we borrow during our lives. No wonder, then, that the sonnet ends not with another cause of death, but with an invocation of God, sovereign over both angels and human beings, able to judge both the living and the dead.

We might expect Donne to follow up his account of the eschatological resurrection with an account of what will come next: the separation of the righteous from the unworthy during the Last Judgment (Revelation 20:12–15). Most, if not all, suicides would be damned. Those whom "law" put to death—executed criminals—might not be expected to fare well either. But Donne does not proceed to that next scene—he does not want to imagine that final judgment, and he does not have to do so, because he is not (despite his eventful opening) writing, or rewriting, biblical narrative. Rather, he is writing a lyric poem that incorporates dramatic (Donne's detractors might say melodramatic) elements. Those elements provide the sharp contrasts of mood, of scene, and of tone for which Donne's poems are known. The most important such contrast (in music, it would be a modulation) sets the large canvas and vaunting tone of the octave against the difficult humility which characterizes the whole of the sestet.

That sestet begins ("on time," as it were: at line 9) when Donne changes his mind. A man given to despair, a man of extremes, might well find himself temperamentally drawn to imagine apocalypse, even to hope it will come soon, as Donne has just done in lines 1–8. But the same man might well draw back, might retract his wish that time would come to an end, once he remembers that he himself might be a goat, not a sheep—that, should time end now, he might be damned. The proper relation for a Christian believer to have, the relation he wants to have, with respect to God is not one in which the believer stands eager for judgment, but one in which he humbly asks for grace, asks that his own sins be forgiven, and acknowledges God as "Lord."

Line 9 thus reverses exactly the imperatives that came before it: "let them sleep" reverses "arise, arise," and also places the agency of the Resurrection where it belongs—with God, rather than with human bodies. "Let . . . me mourn" reverses "blow," calling for quiet reflection rather than triumphant music. The repentant Donne now asks not for the end of time, but for more time. Rather than describe the Apocalypse with such vividness as to make it present to us, he asks quietly for abstractions ("abundance," "grace"). Rather than envision airborne angels on a scale that includes the whole earth, Donne sets his plea on "lowly ground."

The quatrain that concludes with "lowly ground" introduces the fulcrum of the poem, and the last verb: no command, this time, but a request, "Teach me how to repent." The emotional arc of the poem might have ended there, with the poet (his imagination still drawn to apocalypse) abasing himself, realizing that his "sins abound." Had Donne ended there, on that sentiment, he might almost have been addressing the Old Testament God, the omnipotent father figure who judges the world. He is not: he writes, instead, as a Christian believer, and the modulation of the final phrase is also a shift away from the Father, toward the Son. A sinner's repentance (Donne may have in mind the Prodigal Son of Luke 15) makes that sinner as welcome in heaven as any righteous man. That repentance comes through the blood of Christ, who has paid in advance, as it were, for the previous sins of all those who accept Him. Repentance is "as good / As if thou hadst sealed my pardon with thy blood": the counterfactual "as if" is a feint, since the Son has, in fact, "sealed" Donne's "pardon" on the Cross. That "as if" thus echoes, and balances out, the conditional in line 10. Since the second "as if" describes a condition already fulfilled, Donne may be saved, at the end of days, even if the first condition is also true.

Perhaps imitating Shakespeare, Donne has organized the sonnet around repeated key words. The key to the octave is "all": envisioning the whole world, and including (in lines 5–8) every person who has ever lived, the poet repeats "all" in two successive lines. The sestet instead modulates to the key of "abound": Donne certainly has in mind (and an early reader would have known) the uses of "abound" in the New Testament—for instance, Romans 5: "Being now justified by his blood, we shall be saved from wrath through him. . . . Moreover the law entered, that the offence might abound. But where sin abounded, grace did much more abound" (Romans 5:8 and 5:20).

This change of key, as it were, from "all" to "abound," is just one of many oppositions between octave and sestet, oppositions on which the sonnet turns. The octave remains dramatic, frequently visual, full of monosyllables, fast-paced, thunderous, confident, and relatively impersonal, with the poet speaking to an imaginary audience as if from a position of strength. There is no first-person pronoun, and all the second-person pronouns and pronominal adjectives are plural ("you" and "your"). The sestet is lyrical, almost without an image (the only concrete nouns are "ground" and "blood"), slower-paced, quieter, full of first-person pronouns, and humble, or as humble as Donne can be. A sympathetic reader must hear, at the least, an effort toward humility, for a poet whose temperament did not incline him in that direction. Others among the *Holy Sonnets* would see the poet humbler still.

SB

"Oh, to vex me, contraries meet in one"

JOHN DONNE

Probably written 1615–1633; published 1899

Oh, to vex me, contraries meet in one:
Inconstancy unnaturally hath begot
A constant habit; that, when I would not,
I change in vows and in devotion.
As humorous is my contrition
As my profane love, and as soon forgot:
As riddlingly distemper'd, cold and hot,
As praying, as mute; as infinite, as none.
I durst not view heaven yesterday; and today
In prayers and flattering speeches, I court God;
Tomorrow I quake with true fear of His rod.
So my devout fits come and go away
Like a fantastic ague, save that here
Those are my best days, when I shake with feare.

One of three sonnets discovered—and attributed to Donne—in a manuscript more than 250 years after he died, this poem is sometimes placed last among the *Holy Sonnets* because it may describe his later life: Donne became an Anglican priest in 1615, gave a sermon before the queen later that year, and from 1621 until his death commanded rapt audiences from his pulpit at St. Paul's Cathedral in central London. "Vows" may (or may not) refer to his ordination; "flattering speeches," to the sermons he gave. As with most of Donne's short poems, no one can be sure when he wrote it; critics offer speculations based in part on their sense of his mind.

    If the poem does consider the vocation of the poet's last decades, it also looks back to his earlier life. He alludes, almost certainly, to the Roman Catholic religion in which he was raised, a faith proscribed severely at the time—one of his uncles, a Jesuit, was executed for his secret missionary work in England. Looking back over his changing religious positions, Donne also looks back to the prevailing styles of lyric poetry (especially sonnets) familiar from his youth. The poem—especially its octave—sounds Elizabethan, as none of the other Holy Sonnets do. More specifically, it sounds Petrarchan. (Donne may have in mind, as the scholar Donald Guss believes, Petrarch's Canzone 264, "I' vo pensando," in which Petrarch reacts to the death of his beloved Laura. Another sonnet found in 1899, "Since she whom I loved hath paid her last debt," probably reacts to the death of Donne's wife.) Donne begins with the archetypal Petrarchan device: the poet deplores the nest of "contraries" that find their paradoxical home in his breast. Even the icy fire ("cold and hot") that seems, to modern taste, a Petrarchan cliché enters Donne's self-description; he tells us that he is constantly changing, but that he is paradoxically always inconstant, since his temper, his confidence, and even his beliefs change when he would far rather have them stay put.

These complaints—like a lover's complaint to himself or to a friend, but also like a churchgoer's confession—arrive in lines marked by Elizabethan technique. None contain elaborate descriptions; there is not even a concrete noun. Most are end-stopped, or else only lightly enjambed. The key words, and two of the rhyme words ("devotion" and "contrition," both pronounced with four syllables) are Francophone or Latinate abstractions, the "aureate" words that some Elizabethan poets (such as Sidney and Greville) emphasized. Donne appropriates for Christian purposes (like Greville before him, like George Herbert in the same years) the language most closely associated with Elizabethan sonnetry, and with secular, erotic ("profane") love.

Donne's spiritual and emotional troubles (like those of Petrarchan lovers) make him physically ill. "Distemper" suggests the reversal or bad outcome of the process by which steel is "tempered," which involves extreme heat and then cold; it also means illness, especially mental illness (as in our modern term "canine distemper," i.e. rabies). Another term brings in the medical theory, popular in Donne's time, that the human body contains four fluids, or humors, and that we fall ill when their proportions go awry: "humorous" therefore means not "funny," but "having to do with the humors," hence "liable to change." "Fits" means both intermittent bouts (of anything) and the shaking caused by illness (as we say "chills" or even "convulsions" today); a "fantastic ague" is an ague (a severe fever involving fits) so extreme it is hard to imagine unless you have experienced it, or a hypochondriacal ague, or an ague whose symptoms include delusions, or else an ague experienced in a dream.

Twentieth-century critics who admired Donne sometimes claimed that the best or strongest poetry (by any poet) always included paradoxes. To portray and reconcile contradictions, they claimed, was what good poetry always did. This sonnet might almost support that view: the contradiction that it deplores also prompts a theodicy, an attempt to explain why God's painful actions are just. The first line is not only a thesis statement (to introduce the examples of lines 2–8) but also a cry: Why should God make Donne so "inconstant" as he now seems? Is God's purpose, he asks, only "to vex me"? Why should Donne—a Christian believer, and part of God's creation—feel so "distempered," so "unnaturally" ill?

The answer is that Donne must fall before he can rise: he must become so ill, in body as in spirit, before he can become (if indeed he will ever become) spiritually well. Donne has written a poem about faith during illness, akin almost to the literature of deathbed repentance, and to the startling religious poetry and prose ("A Hymn to God My God in My Sickness," "Devotions upon Emergent Occasions") that Donne wrote when he believed he was mortally ill. In this sonnet, as in those works, Donne tells himself that in order to be "raised," to acquire the faith that the Christian God wants him to have, he must first be brought low. This often self-dramatizing, self-confident poet must come to know self-diminishment and humility before he can be saved.

The octave, though it describes worship, never names God; its only religious nouns describe human activities ("vows," "devotion," "contrition," "praying"). The sestet introduces "heaven" (line 9), "God" (line 10), "his rod": the poem begins to approach its solution (God vexes me to bring me low). Obtrusive Petrarchisms disappear. The sestet also changes diction drastically: the sestet includes no obtrusively Latinate words, and only a few that sound obviously French ("devout," "ague"). From the aureate terms of the sestet, Donne has come down to the most homely sectors of speech, the Anglo-Saxon monosyllables with which a child might say what he feels.

From a compact one-line statement of a vexing problem (line 1), Donne has come down to an equally compact sentence, the sort he might quote to himself as his troubles go on. He does not say that he now possesses a Christian humility, does not say that those troubles are over; he says only that he now knows whence and why they arise. Donne sounds humbled, though (typically) he also sounds newly confident, since he has solved the puzzle with

which he began: the paradoxical and Petrarchan affliction of inconstancy rep-
resents God's attempt to bring him low, to overthrow his "profane love" (in
the octave) and to replace the sinful arrogance ("flattering speeches") he might
have displayed from the pulpit. To achieve a proper religious self-abasement—a
monumental task for such a brilliant and self-dramatizing poet—Donne must
acknowledge his worst days as his best. To be ill, to have "fits," in this sense, is
the only way that Donne can ever get well.

SB

"Redemption"

GEORGE HERBERT

1633

Having been tenant long to a rich Lord,
    Not thriving, I resolvèd to be bold,
    And make a suit unto him to afford
A new small-rented lease, and cancel th' old.
In heaven at his manour I him sought:
    They told me there, that he was lately gone
    About some land, which he had dearly bought
Long since on earth, to take possession.
I straight return'd, and knowing his great birth,
    Sought him accordingly in great resorts,
    In cities, theatres, gardens, parks, and courts:
At length I heard a ragged noise and mirth
    Of theeves and murderers; there I him espied,
    Who straight, *Your suit is granted,* said, and died.

"REDEMPTION" tells a compact tale. The poem is a parable: a pointed, cryptic story like those narrated by Jesus in the Gospels (for example, the parable of the wise and foolish virgins in Matthew 25:1–13, or the parable of the sower, which appears in Matthew 13, as well as in Luke and Mark). As in the New Testament, Herbert's parable, provocative and efficient as it is, yet seems incomplete; it requires the thoughtful reader's response. In his first quatrain, Herbert sets the stage. The narrator is the tenant of a "rich Lord," who charges him exorbitant rents. Worried about his financial situation ("not thriving"), the narrator "resolve[s] to be bold," and prepares (somewhat nervously, one feels) for the upcoming interview with his landlord. He will "make a suit" (a request) for a "small-rented lease" (a cheaper monthly payment).

Herbert's story is, of course, an allegory. The "rich Lord" is God; the "old" deal he offers is the Old Testament covenant with the Israelites, who followed a great number of ritual laws (as orthodox Jews still do today). Seeking a new, less exacting contract with God, the narrator wishes to relieve himself of the burdensome yoke of such practices (which ones, the poem leaves unclear: dietary laws? obligatory charity?). This is the wrong quest, Herbert implies. Christ's new law is not less trouble than the old one; looking for an easier religion means missing a new truth that casts in doubt our usual distinctions between simple and difficult, the free and the bounded life. Christ does deliver ease, after all (so Herbert suggests)—but not in response to our ingenious striving.

There is something too knowing, too in control, about Herbert's narrator. He is secure in his boldness. He seems aware of his interests, determined to get himself a better deal. Yet, unbeknownst to him (as "Redemption" will show in its last line), he has already been released from his constraints. His labors are useless, mere symptoms of self-generated worry. The poet, arguing against his narrator, rests his case on simplicity and freedom, in contrast to the narrator's push to strenuously recast the terms of his existence.

The problem with this speaker, Herbert subtly lets us know, is that he remains oblivious to the enigmatic. He senses no mystery in events, though he is face to face with it. Failing to find his lord in heaven, he seeks him on earth. But this search reduces him to the merely earthly, the literal. He misses the point, unable to grasp the exalted-yet-humble fact of God's incarnation as man. To him, "dearly bought" means simply expensive (rather than purchased at the cost of the Messiah's own life); and "to take possession" has its customary legal meaning—as if God were a modern real estate developer. "Redemption" insists on the familiar Christian metaphor: Jesus redeems mankind as a buyer redeems (buys back) a piece of property. But the narrator takes the metaphor literally, and therefore fails to see its true power.

"I straight [that is, immediately] return'd, and knowing his great birth,/ Sought him accordingly in great resorts," the narrator says at the beginning of the third quatrain. Before reading the Gospels, one might expect God to be a king or a noble ruler, not a companion of "theeves and murderers" (nor of prostitutes like Mary Magdalene). But the Jesus story thwarts such expectations, based as they are on the idea that God in his earthly incarnation must be regal and powerful. (Herbert's own biography is relevant: born into a courtly family, he became a humble country parson.)

Jesus, in his shocking death by crucifixion, overturns the reasonable and

the decorous. Saint Paul, preaching the word of his Messiah, had to overcome
the prejudice that being crucified was shameful. The Romans used this form
of execution for criminals and lowlifes. The "ragged noise and mirth" that
heralds the God-man's brief appearance at the conclusion of "Redemption"
suggests something weird, even raucous, about this deity: he is disturbing not
only in the poverty of his milieu, but in the intensity of the joy he brings.

Herbert's Savior, like Paul's, shocks us into attention—but by informing us
that salvation is much subtler and swifter than we thought, not, as in Paul,
harder. (Herbert, though he alludes to the disreputable ecstasy his Messiah
brings, lacks Paul's frequently lurid emphasis on Christ crucified.) "Your suit
is granted" is God's message, radical and instantaneous. The "straight[ness]"
of this sentence—its immediacy, its directness—makes it a fitting capstone to
Herbert's efficient, graceful sonnet, his speech from the heart.

Jesus emerges only at the very end of "Redemption." I have already cited
the Messiah's words (as Herbert invents them). But his words do not conclude
the sonnet: the actual finale is "and died." This sudden ending unlocks Her-
bert's poem; the astonished narrator can do nothing but report Jesus' vanish-
ing. There is no indication that the Savior has cared about the narrator's life or
his particular troubles. He has delivered him, but in an offhand, and stun-
ningly provocative, way—and then he leaves. This new freedom may feel un-
comfortable: there is no consoling embrace, no reassuring presence offered.

The abruptness of Herbert's ending occurs by design. It is utterly different
from what the apprehensive narrator expected in the first stanza; but it raises
apprehensions of a new sort. Christ's self-sacrifice, his lifting of mankind's
burden of sin, makes no sense. The answer comes before the question: the di-
vine gesture is a gift. So Herbert offers his moving poem as a tribute to a sur-
prising God who foresees and calms man's worries. The redeemer comes to
free us from earthly care. But this release baffles us, more than it enlightens.
Herbert's poem expertly conveys the controversial mystery of such redemp-
tion.

DM

"Prayer (I)"

GEORGE HERBERT

1633

Prayer the Church's banquet, Angels' age,
   God's breath in man returning to his birth,
   The soul in paraphrase, heart in pilgrimage,
The Christian plummet sounding heav'n and earth;
Engine against th'Almightie, sinner's tower,
   Reversèd thunder, Christ-side-piercing spear,
   The six-days-world transposing in an hour,
A kind of tune which all things hear and fear;
Softness and peace and joy and love and bliss,
   Exalted Manna, gladness of the best,
   Heaven in ordinary, man well drest,
The milky way, the bird of Paradise,
   Church-bells beyond the stars heard, the soul's blood,
   The land of spices; something understood.

SURELY the most accomplished sonnet in English to lack a main verb, George Herbert's sonnet (one of fifteen in his book *The Temple*, all of them ending in couplets) consists of twenty-seven nouns or noun phrases, each an attempt to explain or describe Christian prayer. A Cambridge University graduate from an aristocratic family, Herbert briefly held a seat in Parliament, and could have pursued great secular distinction. Instead, he chose to devote himself to God, becoming the Anglican priest for a rural congregation, and turning the forms and devices of secular poetry to inventive sacred use. An earlier sonnet (not collected in *The Temple*) asks "My God . . . Why are not Sonnets made of thee?" Yet his most complex poems can end with sudden simplicity, as Herbert reminds himself that God seeks and rewards not intricate brainwork, but a humble and contrite heart.

Herbert was one of the first poets in English (Ben Jonson was another) who certainly gave his own titles to his lyric poems. The combination of title and list invites us to come up with rationales for the list's order: Has Herbert arranged these phrases, each a version of "Prayer," from least to most accurate? From least to most significant? From most collective, or "public," to most personal? In an order that tells a story? In an order that demonstrates (as Helen Vendler argues) self-correction, so that the poet says "Prayer is X; no, not X after all, but more like Y; not Y, or not Y alone, but also, and more important, Z"? Herbert's list fits all of those rationales. It also keeps up a set of oppositions: the exotic, the rich, and the faraway against the homely and the familiar; the violent against the peaceable; the novel, the paradoxical, and the "reversed" against the catechistic, the already-known. In each case the second set of terms "wins," and when (in the word "understood") it wins for good, the poem can end. Yet in each case the effect the whole poem exerts comes from the interplay of those opposites, from Herbert's sometimes back-and-forth movements among them.

Prayer is "the Church's banquet" because it feeds the soul, and (in church) feeds many souls at once; it is "Angels' age" because it links human time to eternity and because angels pray constantly (each angel is as old as his prayer is long). As God breathed life into Adam, so in prayer the children of Adam return that breath to its sender; as Christ descended from heaven to earth, so prayer, in its journey from earth to heaven, reverses the "plummet" (plumb line) that the Incarnation made. (Prospero, in Shakespeare's *Tempest,* drowns his magical, non-Christian book in the sea, "deeper than did ever plummet sound.")

The second quatrain represents prayer not as language ("paraphrase," "breath"), but as destructive, even military, force. An "engine" might be any "device," but here it is a weapon of war, a siege engine, like a catapult or battering ram. Moving from earth to heaven, making us closer to heaven (as if we were climbing a tower), prayer reverses thunder (which moves from the heavens to earth), and—since it is a way in which human beings get something out of God—it is like the "Christ-side-piercing spear" of John 19:34, where blood and water effuse from Jesus' wound. During the six-day achievement of Creation, God descended to arrange unformed matter; an "hour" of prayer is matter's upward response, disarranging time, as Joshua did when he made the sun stand still. Joshua's priests at Jericho played trumpets, then leveled the city on the seventh day. Prayer replays their "tune," which "all things" might indeed "fear," in answer to the classical poet-musicians, such as Orpheus and Amphion, whose songs were supposed to move stones.

These metaphors should provoke wonder, but they might also shock us; some of them could appall. Joshua and his trumpeters' "tune" served God, but the "sinners' tower" of Babel surely did not. And what believer would want to direct an engine of war "against" God, rather than on His behalf? Who would want most, in praying, to resemble the Roman soldier whose spear pierced Christ's side? There is something marvelous in these figures. How amazing to think that our thoughts and our words might reach God! But there is something aggressive, if not blasphemous, too: these figures imply that congregants' words may alter, or even attack, the holy presence. They are the wrong kind of praise for the power of prayer, emphasizing human ambition rather than divine condescension. Yet without these metaphors Herbert's account of how human believers actually do view prayer—in all our fallible, alterable, tempted capacities—would seem unsatisfying and incomplete.

Herbert cannot, however, end the poem there. Instead he modulates into gratitude, as expressed in prayers of thanksgiving, and in the "soft" third quatrain. God may provide relief, "peace," "joy," and the other desiderata of line 9; he has also provided us with "manna," sustenance from heaven, which we, by prayer, "exalt" (send back upward, to Him). The octave made prayer instrumental—a journey, a builder's tool, an "engine," valuable for what it would let us do. The sestet instead makes prayer something we value for its own sake, its own end. "Ordinary" is both an adjective meaning "everyday" (frequent, unexceptional) and a noun meaning "the daily, repeated part of the Mass." By praying, Christians encounter God every day (as an ordinary experience) in the prescribed (ordained) fashion, as part of a daily set schedule (an "ordinary," or rule).

Though ordinary in all these senses, prayer links us to extraordinary realms. The bird of Paradise (for Herbert a legend, though the name denotes a real species today) was supposed to lack legs, to "hover on the air, and feed on the dew of heaven," in the words of another clergyman, Jeremy Taylor, who used the bird as a figure for the soul: we are born "without legs, without strength to walk in the laws of God, or go to heaven; but by a power from above." That bird supposedly flourished in the Moluccas, in modern-day Indonesia, known then and now as the Spice Islands; "land of spices" suggests the Renaissance voyages there, but also perhaps the "spices" (1 Kings 10:1–5) that the Queen of Sheba brings to the wise King Solomon. Linking divinity to humanity, prayer links the everyday and the domestic to the exotic, the marvelous, the faraway.

Yet Herbert cannot end with exotica either: he must bring the poem, as it were, back home. "Something understood" is the best of all Herbert's figures for prayer, the most emotionally satisfying, the one that encompasses and replaces the rest. "Understanding," for Herbert (as for us), could mean either the mere reception of language, its decoding into sense, or the recognition of what is in a person's heart, of what he means by what he says. Here it means both: the couplet-rhyme with "soul's blood" emphasizes an "understanding" that includes not only the sense of words, but the content of hearts.

The last phrase becomes the greatest, the most extreme, in Herbert's series: the distance from us to God, the distance that a genuine prayer can cover, must infinitely exceed the distance from Britain to the Spice Islands, or from ground to sky. Yet "something understood" is also the quietest, and the most abstract, of all Herbert's phrases: it neither denotes, nor connotes, sensory experience. Herbert's last line recalls what musicians call a "Beethoven crescendo," a long series of louder and louder tones that resolves finally into a quiet chord. Herbert's finale seems less vivid, less powerful, than its more sensual precursors only until it is itself properly "understood."

Herbert ends other poems, too, with such effects. Sometimes those endings reject poetic invention as neither necessary nor sufficient for Christian life. Sometimes, however—and this sonnet shows one of those times—Herbert imagines his poetry, if and only if it helps him toward devout humility, as itself a way to approach his Savior, hence as something akin to prayer. "A verse is not a crown," Herbert writes in "The Quiddity," "Nor a good sword, nor yet a lute . . . But it is that which while I use / I am with thee" (that is, with God), "and Most take All" (that is, it is best of all). This sonnet is not itself, exactly, a prayer: it could not have been recited collectively, nor does it address God directly, with "My Lord," or "Thee," as Herbert does elsewhere. Rather, it demonstrates, in its series of figures, how it feels for this Protestant Christian to believe that when he prays, his God takes note.

"All Christians should pray twice a day, every day of the week, and four times on Sunday if they be well," Herbert wrote in "A Priest to the Temple" (sometimes called "The Country Parson"), his prose work of severe advice to himself. As a parish priest in a time of growing religious controversy, Herbert in his other writings could emphasize the collective, ritual aspects of prayer: it brings congregations together, and helps them to agree. "Though private prayer be a brave design," he writes in the long homiletic poem "The Church-Porch," "yet public has more promises, more love." Here, such contrasts are far under the surface, or else wholly absent. Herbert dwells in this sonnet not on exactly what believers say, nor on where they say it and how often, but on what it can mean, and on how much it can do. Herbert's first biographer, Izaak Walton, says that Herbert took care to explain to his congregants what each Bible passage meant, and why they should read it on that day, "so that they might pray with understanding." The sonnet's set of nouns, noun phrases, and symbols move cumulatively, not without reversals, until the poet has satisfied his own understanding too.

                                                                           SB

"On the Late Massacre in Piedmont"

JOHN MILTON

Probably written 1655; published 1673

> Avenge O Lord, thy slaughter'd saints, whose bones
>   Lie scatter'd on the Alpine mountains cold,
>   Ev'n them who kept thy truth so pure of old
> When all our fathers worship'd stocks and stones,
> Forget not: in thy book record their groans
>   Who were thy sheep and in their ancient fold
>   Slain by the bloody Piemontese that roll'd
> Mother with infant down the rocks. Their moans
> The vales redoubl'd to the hills, and they
>   To Heav'n. Their martyr'd blood and ashes sow
> O'er all th'Italian fields where still doth sway
>   The triple tyrant: that from these may grow
>   A hundred-fold, who having learnt thy way
>   Early may fly the Babylonian woe.

"ON THE Late Massacre in Piedmont" ("late" here means "recent") is a poem of historical trauma. Milton asks what poetry can do in the face of disaster, the destruction of a community through mass murder. Milton here takes on the realm of history, an unusual task for the English-language sonnet before his day. (After Milton, a number of sonnets address history, including, in our collection, Shelley's "England in 1819," Emma Lazarus' "The New Colossus," and Claude McKay's "America.") Milton's anguished response to mass death feels absolutely contemporary. It seems that every day we hear news of war and genocide: from Sudan, Congo, Afghanistan, and elsewhere. How can religious faith sustain itself, faced with such shocks?

Understanding Milton's sonnet requires some background. The Waldensians (also called the Vaudois) were Protestants who had lived for centuries in the Roman Catholic territory of Piedmont, in northern Italy. There they were massacred by Piedmontese soldiers in April 1655. Milton was Latin Secretary for Oliver Cromwell, the Lord Protector of England during the 1650s, after the execution of Charles I. In this capacity he protested to the Piedmontese rulers, on behalf of the arch-Protestant Cromwell. Horrified by the rumors of atrocities that he had heard from Cromwell's messenger, Samuel Morland, Milton expressed in his poem a desperate outcry against the killing of innocents.

Milton begins his sonnet by addressing God, and asking for vengeance: "Avenge, O Lord, thy slaughtered saints . . ." The Waldensians, followers of the twelfth-century reformer Peter Waldo, were true Protestants when the people of the British Isles, though nominally Christian, were still worshiping nature or crude idols, including Catholic relics ("stocks and stones"). The "bones" of the martyrs cry out; the "stones" of Britain are mere dumb matter. The heroic deaths of the Waldensians testify to their ability to keep God's truth pure (similarly, Moses and the prophets often enjoin the ancient Israelites to observe the law steadfastly, and avoid idolatry).

In Milton's eyes, the Waldensian victims of the Piedmontese have not merely been slaughtered—they have been "scattered." The poem witnesses the wholesale destruction of the human image. A new scattering will compensate for such heartless dispersion: the sowing of truth in the sonnet's final lines.

Milton begins his second quatrain with a new injunction addressed to God: not, this time, "avenge," but "forget not" (and then, later in line 5, "record"). Such memory might be seen as a substitute for vengeance, a sublimation of it into a higher realm. The God of the Hebrew Bible often warns the Israelites not to forget his covenant with them. Milton, turning the tables (and echoing Psalm 74, as well as the book of Lamentations), tells God not to forget his loyal subjects. After the Flood, God promises never to destroy mankind again; but faced with the devastation of the Waldensian massacre, Milton has some reason to doubt the promise. The Waldensians seem to stand for all of God's true followers; their loss threatens faith itself.

Milton's second quatrain presses forward with reckless power, first stopping short (after "Forget not") and then gathering strength from a series of enjambments. Lines 2 through 4 were not enjambed, but end-stopped, as if the poet were holding his fury in check. Now, though, Milton's sense rolls on from one line to another, just as the "bloody Piemontese . . . roll'd / Mother with infant down the rocks." The very name of the Piedmontese incarnates the scene of slaughter, the foot of the mountains *(pied-mont)* where the Waldensians lived. The murderers violate the closest, most protected human space, the connection between mother and infant; and Milton's closed quatrains envelop the tragedy.

Note that Milton, as he tells God to remember the martyrs, says that they "were thy sheep"—not "are." The Lord is no longer their shepherd; he has been unable to shield them. The poet drastically questions God's justice: What could possibly be the purpose of allowing such mass murder to happen? (A question often asked today, just a few years after the end of the most violent century in history.) The poet's disappointment hangs in the air like the moans of the Waldensian victims. At the end of line 8 the phrase "their moans," rhyming painfully with line 5's "groans," seems stranded in space, helpless.

This extreme cry, like the "rout that made the hideous roar" in Milton's "Lycidas" (as the Maenads tear Orpheus apart), is extended by the sonnet's next line, the beginning of the volta ("The vales redoubl'd to the hills, and they / To Heav'n"). Heaven is the destination for the beleaguered Waldensians' shouts of pain, but whether, and how, heaven will respond remains a question. The redoubling of the cries is intensely moving, more so in that it provokes no audible response from above. These martyred voices, seemingly abandoned, answer themselves.

Milton stops the echoing short and adds another imprecation, another statement directed to God. After "avenge," "forget not," and "record," the poet asks God to "sow" the victims' "martyr'd blood and ashes." (According to the early third-century Christian writer Tertullian, the blood of martyrs is the seed of the church.) From these seeds (an image from the parable of the sower in Matthew 13) "a hundred-fold" will grow. No longer the mere echoing of the traumatic groans, but rather a fruitful multiplication; no longer the single, imperiled sheepfold, but a dissemination, spawning faithful servants of truth.

Milton suggests, finally, that learning balances disaster: not merely the recording of the martyrs' deaths, nor the accurate memory of their tragedy, but the instruction of new Christians. He focuses on the *echt*-Catholic regions of Italy, where the "triple tyrant" holds sway (the pope, who according to Protestants claims a monstrous rule over heaven, earth, and hell). This new audience for truth will have "learnt thy [that is, the Lord's] way."

God's way is hard, even unsure. The sonnet's concluding mention of Babylon (where the Jews were exiled, longing for Jerusalem) emphasizes a common Protestant idea: Rome is Babylon, and the true church remains in hiding. Such exile is, needless to say, more tolerable than death. In place of the brutal downward trajectory of the martyrs, rolled down the rocks, Milton substitutes a horizontal "fly[ing]" from the face of oppression. But this escape is far from glorious, and the destiny of the true godly community, far-flung as it necessarily is, remains dangerously uncertain. The emphasis on "early," which begins Milton's final line with a new breath, a rapid push upward, speaks to the poet's agitated alertness. Milton refuses to picture God as a reassuring presence; instead, he makes his deity the spur to a future that can only seem perilous. Implicitly, he questions God, calls him to account. Through the inspiring pressure Milton places on his faith and his God, and the protest he makes against unjust destruction, he defines a task for religious poetry. Controversial and exalted, "On the Late Massacre in Piedmont" speaks with anguish to a permanent question: How can belief survive, and how does it change, in the face of violent persecution?

DM

"Methought I saw my late espousèd saint"

JOHN MILTON

1673

Methought I saw my late espousèd saint
   Brought to me, like Alcestis from the grave,
   Whom Jove's great Son to her glad husband gave,
Rescu'd from death by force though pale and faint.
Mine, as whom wash'd from spot of child-bed taint,
   Purification in the old Law did save,
   And such, as yet once more I trust to have
Full sight of her in Heaven without restraint,
Came vested all in white, pure as her mind:
   Her face was veil'd, yet to my fancied sight,
   Love, sweetness, goodness, in her person shin'd
So clear as in no face with more delight.
But O as to embrace me she enclin'd,
I wak'd, she fled, and day brought back my night.

MOST scholars think that Milton wrote this intensely moving sonnet (number 23 in the usual numbering) about his second wife, Katherine Woodcock, whom he married in November 1656. Katherine died less than two years later, three and a half months after bearing Milton a daughter. Milton's first wife, Mary Powell, also died after giving birth, in 1652. Milton's poem offers ardent testimony to the power of this female figure, who may be an amalgam of both lost wives. Yet rather than being reunited with her, the speaker is left poignantly in the dark at the poem's end. The sonnet is shadowed by the fact of Milton's blindness, which the poet calls "my night," and which descended on him in the 1650s.

"Methought I saw" asks fundamental questions about a poet's capacity to dream an object of desire into being, as Milton resurrects in imagination or memory the face of his lost beloved, and then, with terrible awareness, feels it slip away. The poem's first line begins with a word often used to introduce dream visions: "Methought." The remainder of the first quatrain is devoted to a mythological precedent: the story of Admetus and Alcestis, best known from Euripides' tragic play *Alcestis*. In Euripides' version, Heracles (the Roman Hercules), the son of Zeus (Jove), grants the mortal Admetus a favor: Admetus will be saved from death if someone agrees to die in his place. Alcestis, Admetus' wife, sacrifices herself for him, and Admetus mourns in agony. At the end of the play, Heracles, who is a roughneck, blustering comic presence in the tragedy, brings to Admetus a veiled female figure, and presents her to him as his next wife. The husband, still grief-stricken, refuses this new bride; but then, when Heracles unveils her, Admetus realizes that she is his own Alcestis. The play ends without an embrace—and, as in Shakespeare's *The Winter's Tale,* which tells a similar story, a disquieting gap remains between the reunited lovers.

In this first quatrain, the poet-speaker is the passive "glad husband," graced by Heracles' gift of his dead beloved. "By force" points to the prowess of Heracles the action hero: there is a noticeable contrast between his crude greatness and the wraithlike posture of the bride, still "pale and faint" from the realms of death.

In his second quatrain, Milton leaves classical mythology for the Hebrew Bible and Christian doctrine. His dead spouse was purified, "wash'd from spot of child-bed taint" according to the ritual for purifying women after childbirth, described in Chapter 13 of Leviticus. Not the paleness of death, as in the first quatrain, but the bloody evidence of new life distinguishes her. Though the taint has been removed, the very mention of it suggests the constraint of the Old Law, the Old Testament ritual that Christianity promises to overcome. According to Milton, the wife was "save[d]" according to law—but this validation seems merely technical. The heart of the second quatrain lies in its intense hope for a truer salvation, the apocalyptic sight of the regained wife: "yet once more I trust to have / Full sight of her in heaven without restraint." Saint Paul insists that, though we now see through a glass darkly, we shall "then"—when we are saved, whether in heaven or in messianic time—"see face to face" (I Corinthians 13:12). Milton shares Paul's hope for full sight, which for the poet means an unrestrained encounter between him and the beloved. The mutual acknowledgment he knows will come cannot take place in this poem, which remains fettered by the action of the dream. When dreams are abolished and wishes radically fulfilled, the thwarted yearning expressed in "Methought I saw" will pass away.

The beloved is "vested all in white," and "veil'd." The veil, a diaphanous barrier, suggests the hazy contours of dreaming; the white vestments are associated with angels, and with the apocalyptic purity depicted in the Book of Revelation. "Pure as her mind" is a strange, evocative phrase: the beloved's white robes extend the illumination that starts from her thoughts. The blind poet's imagination (his "fancied sight") eagerly receives this light, this blessed vision. Her presence is sheer idea, and yet tantalizingly whole; she exudes radiant virtues: "Love, sweetness, goodness, in her person shin'd." She beams delight, nourishing and clear, and seems ready to touch her dreaming spouse.

Milton's conclusion transmits the failure of wish-fulfillment, along with a dawning of truer insight. The sonnet's last two lines are linked by rhyme to the rest of the sestet, but they have the feel of a final couplet: "But O as to embrace me she inclin'd, / I wak'd, she fled, and day brought back my night." The dead beloved leans toward her husband: "inclin'd" describes a movement of gentle harmony, the intimacy that marks familiar love. But this beautiful inclination is suddenly broken: the speaker wakes, and the beloved takes flight. In an irrevocable instant, the speaker oversteps the bounds of the dream; he impulsively tries to turn the teasing of memory into the full-fledged presence he has lost. His waking, in response to her leaning toward him, disrupts the spell; and Milton's last line, monumental in its passionate resignation, speaks to continued desire as well as to the hard, ever-renewed reconciliation with loss.

Yet the speaker's migration from dream to reality opens him, unwillingly, to an inevitable fullness of knowledge. When Milton writes "my night," he means: the night that is mine alone even in daytime, the place of my poetic strength, lasting and necessary and therefore superior to the promises granted to imagination—even blessed imagination. This is the "ever-during dark" that Milton momentously evokes at the beginning of Book 3 of *Paradise Lost*, as he calls on a greater light than the merely visible one. Alive to the moment of loss, Milton refuses to flee into fantasy.

Readers of "Methought I saw" have often noted its resemblance to the moment in *Paradise Lost*'s Book 8 when the newly created Eve momentarily abandons her husband. Adam, under a divinely supplied anesthetic, has witnessed in dream her emergence from his side. "She disappeared and left me dark," Adam says: "I waked / To find her or for ever to deplore / Her loss." But then Eve returns "such as I beheld her in my dream": so Adam, rescued from desperation, poignantly remembers. Milton was probably writing *Paradise Lost* during the same period in which he produced this sonnet; in any case, the two scenes seem profoundly connected. Adam has a dream of Eve, and wakes to find it truth (as Keats summarized Milton's episode). But the truth includes painful separation—and in the fallen world, the final separation, death. One age-old fantasy of the poet's power imagines him able to master death, especially to resurrect an old love, as in the case of Orpheus and Eurydice (a myth much on Milton's mind throughout his career). Orpheus' failure to fully regain Eurydice suggests that the poet needs to accept the fact of a loved one's death, rather than hoping to undo it. So Milton, instead of enjoying the miraculous return of his love, wakes to find what is left to him: not what he can make, but what he is given. This dark discovery shines through the beloved's disappearance, and leaves Milton abandoned and steadfast, alone with his memory.

DM

Sappho and Phaon 24

MARY ROBINSON

1796

O thou! meek Orb! that stealing o'er the dale,
    Cheer'st with thy modest beams the noon of night!
    On the smooth lake diffusing silv'ry light,
Sublimely still, and beautifully pale!
What can thy cool and placid eye avail,
    Where fierce despair absorbs the mental sight,
    While inbred glooms the vagrant thoughts invite,
To tempt the gulph where howling fiends assail?
    O, Night! all nature owns thy temper'd pow'r;
Thy solemn pause, thy dews, thy pensive beam;
    Thy sweet breath whisp'ring in the moonlight bow'r,
While fainting flow'rets kiss the wand'ring stream!
    Yet, vain is ev'ry charm! and vain the hour,
That brings to madd'ning love, no soothing dream!

THIS sonnet represents an exquisite late stage of what we now called Sensibility: the verse and prose, lyrical, descriptive, and narrative, that flourished between about 1770 and 1800, just before the better-known and more broadly original writers now called the Romantics. Revolting against earlier emphases on reason, tradition, and self-control, the writers of Sensibility sought overpowering experiences, emotions too strong for reason to contain—grief at the death of a child, sympathy with the tears of a friend, self-destructive erotic devotion, even (as in the Gothic novel) morbid fear. Robinson's diction, in which no key noun lacks an adjective, marks her now as an eighteenth-century poet, but her rhetorical questions and exclamations marked her, for readers of the 1790s, as excitingly wild.

Or rather, they so mark the character who speaks in Robinson's poem. This sonnet, like forty-two of the other forty-four sonnets in Robinson's *Sappho and Phaon* (1796), is spoken by the ancient Greek poet Sappho, known in Robinson's day, as in our own, as one of the great poets of the ancient world, as a founder of European lyric tradition, and as a focus for centuries of debate about women and poetry. Sappho wrote verse about love for women and girls (our word "lesbian" denotes her home island, Lesbos). Eighteenth-century readers, including Robinson, had access to some of Sappho's verse, but they were more familiar with the "Sappho" depicted in Ovid's *Heroides* and in English poems inspired by Ovid: a woman poet of genius, and a former lover of girls, now tormented by her love for an unfaithful man. At the end of Robinson's sequence, as in Ovid, Sappho throws herself off a cliff.

The Sappho of Robinson's Sonnet 24 addresses the Moon, whose light is the light of reason. "Modest," "placid" and "temper'd," it imbues the earth with those characteristics as well. "Sublime" and "beautiful" were conventional opposites, the subject of a well-known treatise attributed to the ancient author Longinus and of a famous 1757 essay by Edmund Burke. For Burke, sublime objects were wild, forceful, illimitable, chaotic, and often dangerous, while beautiful objects were small, delicate, "clean and fair"—in other words, feminine. Robinson's Moon is "sublime" (extreme, impressive) in its stillness, but in Burke's sense it is not "sublime" at all: it is, and it makes the earth, "beautiful" instead.

To such a world Robinson's Sappho can never belong. This passionate female poet stands apart from a moonlit landscape given over at once to beauty and to reason, a landscape well-ordered, comprehensible, "sweet," and (in one more eighteenth-century term) picturesque. Impersonal (all water and air and light) in the first quatrain, that same landscape, with its flora, moonlit streams, and bowers, becomes, in the sestet, fit for people. "Temper'd" means both "tempered" (restrained, as by wise experience) and "temperate" (not given to excess). Here the beautiful, the feminine, the natural ("all nature owns thy temper'd power") and the reasonable or appropriate are almost one: they appear in harmony with one another, in a landscape that puts its best face forward, as clear in this moonlight as in the sunshine at noon.

That picturesque landscape might fit certain types of lovers well. (It might fit pairs of girls, or girls and women, mentioned clearly in Ovid, though only obliquely in Robinson: such loves would be neither animated nor troubled by destructively masculine force.) But the picture does not suit Robinson's Sappho: it neither represents, nor contains, nor brings any sort of calm to the passion she feels. That passion makes her, and her poetry, seek the sublime, the unnatural, or the more-than-natural. Indeed, she has been displaced from her own prior nature, separated from the visible world (as she feels) by her "madd'ning love."

In telling the Moon and the Night that she stands apart, that even the best of their charms cannot please her, Robinson may have in mind Milton's Satan, who addresses the Sun, as Sappho addresses the Moon, to mourn his exclusion from the beautifully ordered space that orb illuminates (*Paradise Lost* 4.35–37). Robinson also plays on the many religious and moralizing poems in which the "charm" of earthly beauty proves "vain," compared to the treasure of heaven. She is no religious moralist, though, and her Sappho remains pagan. Her other world, the one where she belongs, is more like Milton's Hell, a place of devils, darkness, and vertical motion, "where howling fiends assail." ("Gulph" could also mean a gap or gorge, anticipating the cliff from which she will leap.) "Mental sight" (imagination) has already presented to her such a gloomy chaos as fits her mood, a mood for which her first phrase is "fierce despair." This chaos, too, echoes *Paradise Lost,* where Satan flies through a vertiginous "darkness visible." She has seen, all along, that literally supernatural, frightening, or Gothic space, almost as if she were hallucinating, even while she looks at the moonlit lake.

What she wants to see instead, what she wishes that she could see, is the only dream that could soothe her—one in which her beloved Phaon returns. That final line also reminds us that Sappho observes all this moonlight (at midnight, "the noon of might") because she cannot sleep. Petrarchan sonnets often show lovers as sleepless, as hoping at best to see the beloved in dreams: Robinson's sleepless Sappho joins their number, as did Sidney's Astrophel.

Robinson's preface to *Sappho and Phaon* calls it the first set of "legitimate sonnets" since Milton. "Legitimate" means she has followed Italianate rules, consistently adopting the Petrarchan rhyme scheme (*abba abba cdcdcd,* with no concluding couplet), as against the Shakespearean or irregular forms that English poets of the day (such as Charlotte Smith and William Lisle Bowles) preferred. Octave and sestet work here as preeminent units: the first eight lines (addressed to the Moon) show Robinson's Sappho alone, defeated by a despair whose cause (within this sonnet) she has not named. The sestet, by contrast (addressed to Night), includes companions, lovers, implicitly present in natural "kisses" and "bowers," but absent, to her great regret, from Sappho's life now.

Eighteenth-century readers would have connected that life to Robinson's own. Robinson in her teens was a promising actress: at twenty-one, still new to the London stage, she caught the eye of the Prince of Wales. Their short liaison became the talk of London. When it ended in 1780, she was a "fallen woman," fodder for gossip, and unwelcome in polite society ever after. A famously talented woman undone by her unsanctioned love for an unreliable man—such is Sappho, in Robinson's depiction; so was Robinson, in the public eye. By the time of *Sappho and Phaon,* she had also become a well-known author, with three books of verse, four novels, a stage play, an operetta, and dozens of poems in periodicals, often under pseudonyms. "Through life the tempest has followed my footsteps," she wrote in her memoirs (completed and published after her death by her daughter, who also edited her poems); "I have in vain looked for a short interval of repose from the perseverance of sorrow."

That declaration reflects her almost lifelong difficulties—her unreliable husband and lovers, money troubles, one child to support, another who died quite young, and chronic pain (possibly from a botched delivery). Yet the same declaration reflects the tastes of the age in which Robinson wrote, an age that wanted, and got, depictions of emotional extremes. Sensibility cast attention on inward feelings, on depths of individual experience and on personal vulnerability, as against arguments, facts, or moral rules. The mood of the age thus encouraged its poets, Robinson among them, to revive the sonnet after a century of near-desuetude. These "legitimate sonnets," Robinson claimed, would restore the form from its low status as occasional verse to something worthy of Petrarch, and of Milton, and of the "precious fragments," "so exquisitely touching and beautiful," that survive of Sappho herself. If sonnets had existed in Sappho's day, Robinson nearly implies, then Sappho would have written them.

Sappho and Phaon presents its own accomplishment, along with that of its subject, as arguments for women's capacities generally—for "the talents of my illustrious countrywomen," Robinson says in her preface to the sequence, as well as for her own. Yet this Ovidian Sappho makes a puzzling feminist example. "Enlightened by the most exquisite talents," as Robinson's preface also says, "yet yielding to the destructive control of ungovernable passions," the Sappho of Ovid and of *Sappho and Phaon,* like Robinson herself, might seem to demonstrate that even the most self-possessed, most powerful woman could be undercut by the right man.

To this antifeminist argument the heritage of the Petrarchan sonnet gave

Robinson an ingenious implicit reply: any woman, even the genius of Lesbos, might be destroyed by the power of love, but so could any male poet—so could any man. No wonder this Sappho recalls Sidney, and Petrarch too. Robinson uses, for Sappho's passion, a form (not only the sonnet but the Petrarchan "legitimate" sonnet, and the Sidneyan amorous narrative sequence) usually allotted to men. In her sequence as a whole, and again in this sonnet, Robinson scrambles or complicates received ideas about which aesthetic qualities, which emotions, best fit women, and which fit men. The feminized, tender, picturesque landscape fits well with "solemn" reason, seen in the silver light of the mild Moon, while the woman poet harbors, by dint of her genius, a force stronger than any place on earth.

SB

"Huge vapours brood above the clifted shore"

CHARLOTTE SMITH

1798

Huge vapours brood above the clifted shore,
Night o'er the ocean settles, dark and mute,
Save where is heard the repercussive roar
Of drowsy billows, on the rugged foot
Of rocks remote; or still more distant tone
Of seamen, in the anchored bark, that tell
The watch reliev'd; or one deep voice alone,
Singing the hour, and bidding "strike the bell."
All is black shadow, but the lucid line
Mark'd by the light surf on the level sand,
Or where afar, the ship-lights faintly shine
Like wandering fairy fires, that oft on land
Mislead the pilgrim; such the dubious ray
That wavering reason lends, in life's long darkling way.

CHARLOTTE SMITH'S sonnet paints a murky, sublime picture, ominous and stirring. Her depiction of the "clifted shore" presages the seascapes of the great painter J. M. W. Turner: shimmering, obscure, and magnificent. Like Turner, Smith feels a mystic awe at the spellbinding, and delusive, effects of the shadowy sea, and the ships adrift on it. In "Huge vapours," the sonnet, so small and concentrated a form, becomes a vehicle for the immense powers of the shoreline, which seep into the soul of the spectator. Smith's talent for the atmospheric will have a significant influence on the Romantic poets, especially Coleridge.

By making the sonnet popular with a wide audience, Smith, along with other writers like Anna Seward and William Lisle Bowles, helped to bring it

back from the oblivion it suffered during the Restoration and eighteenth cen-
tury. Coerced into an unhappy marriage, Smith was imprisoned along with
her husband for debt in the 1780s. She became a novelist and poet in order to
make money, and was wildly successful. A sympathizer with the French Revo-
lution, Smith feared the revolutionary terror that had erupted in France by
1798, when she wrote "Huge vapours." (Napoleon's coup d'état occurred the
following year.) Her ambivalence about the events in France makes a subtle
appearance near the end of her sonnet, suggesting a larger political and his-
torical dimension for what might otherwise seem a private, meditative land-
scape poem.

In her first line, Smith harks back to John Milton, a major influence on her,
as on Mary Robinson and other writers of Sensibility. On the first page of
Paradise Lost, Milton evokes the Holy Spirit that "dove-like satst brooding o'er
the vast abyss, / And madst it pregnant." Milton is remembering the Creation
account in Genesis, when "the spirit of God moved upon the face of the wa-
ters." But he rewrites Genesis with his word "brooding," which suggests
at once childbirth and heavy contemplation. Smith, thinking of Milton, re-
moves his image from its religious context and transfers it to her own emo-
tions as she takes in her surroundings. She helps to create what we now call
the Romantic feeling for landscape; Romantic poems often evoke a melan-
choly, lonely place that echoes the feelings of the observer's own soul. The
brooding that leads in Milton to a world-changing (and world-creating) epic
plot remains, in Smith, an individual response, a pregnant mood. Like Co-
leridge in "Work without Hope" (discussed later in this collection), she adopts
a solitary and somber stance.

"Night o'er the ocean settles, dark and mute": Smith indulges in the myste-
rious, gloomy properties of the scene. Her affinity for a desolate, picturesque
setting is shared by Romantic poetry, and by the Gothic novel of her era.
"Huge vapours" first appeared, in fact, in Smith's own novel *The Young Phi-
losopher* (1798), where it bore the title "Written near a port on a dark evening."
Late in Smith's story, the penniless, passionate young suitor Delmont writes
the sonnet to his future mother-in-law, Mrs. Glenmorris, as he waits to cross
from Wales to Ireland. Shortly afterward, he visits the grave of a female sui-
cide: "beetling rocks, barren, cold, sullen, hung over a stony cove," Delmont
remarks, painting the Gothic scene.

The poet notices two sounds that spring from the otherwise silent shore.
The first is the "repercussive roar" of the surf. Repeated *r*-sounds, continued
in "rugged" and "rocks remote," conjure up the growling of the waves as they

pound the shore. These billowing tides are themselves "drowsy." An inter-change of emotion between the sea and the human observer leads Smith to attribute her own somnolence, slight yet heavy, to the ocean itself.

Smith begins her second quatrain by describing the second sound: distant calls of seamen, who announce the changing of the watch on an anchored ship. She notices in particular the solemn note sounded by "one deep voice alone, / Singing the hour, and bidding 'strike the bell '" The steadfast chanting of the sailor is analogous to the voice of a poet, who both sings and keeps regular time (in stanza and meter). The sailor in the dark of night is as lonely as the narrator of this poem: a wanderer at sea. Time's seemingly infinite ex-panse, like the vastness of the ocean, overshadows the human effort to shape and measure it. Yet we must remain loyal to the effort, anchoring ourselves to our task. The duties of the poet, then, are like those of the sailor: to strike a definite, safe course; to uphold the integrity of the vessel (sonnet or ship). But ambient sadness suffuses both of these characters.

The sestet begins with more atmospheric sweep: "All is black shadow." This generalizing flourish is modified in the next moment, as the poet takes note of the "lucid line" between surf and shore. Once again, as in the case of the ship's watch, a looming, all-encompassing panorama yields to a precise observation. Here, the observation has a nimble clarity: notice the dancing alliteration of the *l*'s in "the lucid line / Marked by the light surf on the level sand." Like the phenomenon they describe, these lines too are level, smooth, and light.

In her last four lines, Smith will veer away from such lucidity, toward the illusory and deceptive. Gazing at the ship's lights, she compares them to "wan-dering fairy lights" misleading the "pilgrim" (i.e., traveler). We now encounter Smith's second significant echo of Milton. In Book 9 of *Paradise Lost,* Milton compares Satan, creeping to tempt Adam and Eve, to "a wandering fire, / Com-pact of unctuous vapor," who "misleads the amazed night-wanderer." Milton refers here to the deluding, tricky illumination given off by a marsh light (also known as an *ignis fatuus,* or will-o'-the-wisp). Smith compares her wandering light to "the dubious ray / That wavering reason lends." The French Revolu-tion was fought under the banner of reason, and its English champions, like the philosopher William Godwin, exalted mankind's reasoning power as a more reliable guide than religion, custom, or national tradition. But reason proved to be ruthless in France, and Godwin, like Smith, was appalled. Rea-son seems to her "wavering" rather than firm; it is unclear where it might lead us—perhaps radically astray, as Satan leads Eve astray in *Paradise Lost.*

In *The Young Philosopher,* which is much occupied with political debate, one of Smith's sympathetic characters, Mr. Armitage, decries "the violence, cruelty, and perfidy, with which the French have polluted the cause of freedom." Yet he continues to hold, against the forces of political reaction, to "the boundless use of this power of thinking . . . the power of inquiry." The freethinker must save himself from a dangerous enthusiasm for Jacobin radicalism; he trusts unaided reason to do so. Yet Smith's sonnet hints that reason may not be a reliable guide.

In her final couplet, Smith rhymes "astray" with "way" (the distinctive poetic word "darkling" appears in Shakespeare's *King Lear,* as well as *Paradise Lost,* and will play a significant role in later lyrics). From her opening situation of a nighttime vista, she has shifted to the image of a journey (familiar in poetry, above all, from Dante, whose pilgrim begins the *Divine Comedy* lost in a dark wood). In 1798, the journey leads through the dark passageways of history, which tempt with glimmering lights: slogans proclaiming the rights of man, but also death to the enemies of the people. Though her poem never explicitly refers to war or revolution, these events lurk behind it, as surely as in our next poem, Wordsworth's "London, 1802." As the poet, now alert and isolated, continues to brood, she knows that the cliffs of England are not far from the chaos of France.

DM

"London, 1802"

WILLIAM WORDSWORTH

1802

Milton! thou shouldst be living at this hour:
   England hath need of thee: she is a fen
   Of stagnant waters: altar, sword, and pen,
Fireside, the heroic wealth of hall and bower,
Have forfeited their ancient English dower
   Of inward happiness. We are selfish men;
   Oh! raise us up, return to us again;
And give us manners, virtue, freedom, power.
Thy soul was like a Star, and dwelt apart:
   Thou hadst a voice whose sound was like the sea:
   Pure as the naked heavens, majestic, free,
So didst thou travel on life's common way,
In cheerful godliness; and yet thy heart
   The lowliest duties on herself did lay.

WORDSWORTH wrote "London, 1802" at a crucial moment in his own and his nation's history. In 1802 he was a former revolutionary appalled by the tyrant Napoleon's ascendancy, a patriotic Englishman frightened by France's threats of war against his homeland. The peace of Amiens between France and England had been signed in March 1802. It held for fourteen months; by the summer of 1803, the two great powers would be at war. In the midst of international crisis, Wordsworth calls upon an earlier poet: the staunch Protestant Milton, who had shown prophetic concern for England's integrity and its future. For Mary Robinson and Charlotte Smith, Milton is a source of the sublime; for Wordsworth in this poem, he is a source of moral strength.

   Like Shelley's "England in 1819," Wordsworth's sonnet addresses a turning-point in history. But the older poet's political attitude is different from that of the leftist firebrand Shelley. During the 1790s Wordsworth had collaborated with revolutionary circles in London and in Paris. His enthusiasm for revolution cooled as a result of the Terror in France, with its mass executions of priests, political opponents, and other "enemies of the people." Still, for twenty years after the Terror, Wordsworth ardently supported the republican cause. He spoke in 1809 of the "two wars waged against Liberty" by Britain, when his country battled the French and the American Revolution.

In his 1800 preface to *Lyrical Ballads,* the epochal book of poems he co-wrote with Samuel Taylor Coleridge, Wordsworth laments the "blunt[ing of] the discriminating powers of the mind." He ascribes such dullness, which blocks the sensitivity and moral intelligence that poetry relies on, to the pressure of "the great national events that are daily taking place" (this was an age of cataclysmic political disturbances), along with "a craving for extraordinary incident which the rapid communication of intelligence hourly gratifies." Urban life, he adds, feeds the hyped-up stimulations of journalism (the "rapid communication of intelligence"). Wordsworth chooses instead for his subject matter, in *Lyrical Ballads* and elsewhere, rural settings where social life is sparse, and where age-old habits guide human feeling. He stays attentive to the quiet power of custom—what "London, 1802" names "life's common way."

Wordsworth singles out Milton as his beacon in a time of trouble. Milton was a radical Protestant, a revolutionary who, like Wordsworth in the 1790s, advocated regicide. But he also supported what he called true authority in men. For Wordsworth, Milton provides an image of true citizenship; his hope that England will be a godly, virtuous nation coincides with Wordsworth's own. Like Milton, Wordsworth espoused the "unsuspicious dignity of Virtue" (as Wordsworth put it in 1809). He added a complaint—characteristic of his time—about the effects of industrialization: the "presumptuous Expediency" of the "Mechanic Arts, Manufactures, Agriculture, Commerce." Such brute commercialism, Wordsworth argued, damaged both the imagination and the conscience of the English people.

There is also a purely literary reason for Wordsworth to look back to Milton. In his sonnet writing, Wordsworth strove for what he named a "pervading sense of intense Unity." His image for the sonnet was that of "an orbicular body,—a sphere—or a dew-drop." Milton's sonnets are integrated in just this way: they blend octave and sestet, demonstrating the urgent strength that flows from the beginning to the end of each poem. (See, in this volume, Milton's "On the Late Massacre in Piedmont"—a political sonnet, like Wordsworth's.) In addition, the forthright plainness of Wordsworth's diction looks back to Milton, and contrasts with the often ornate and sentimental sonnet vogue of his day.

The first line of "London, 1802" makes an anguished cry. Milton's very name, the initial word of the poem, seems to sum up England's, and Wordsworth's, need. The mellifluous consonance of the vowels in "thou shouldst" and "hour" is amended by the clipped, urgent second line: "England hath need of thee." This is a blunt message, followed by a caesura that accents the emphatic quality of the poet's gesture. Then comes the dooming sentence: "she is a fen / Of stagnant waters." In "London, 1802," national tradition, the link back through the generations, is obscured by the swamp of preoccupation that sinks Wordsworth's nation.

The first quatrain ends with an expansive, resonant line: "Fireside, the heroic wealth of hall and bower." This is a leisurely, domestic, yet masculine image, conjuring up the strength of steadfast knights. Wordsworth pictures heroism as wealth—an investment, a place to reside in, centering the spirit of an individual and a culture.

Wordsworth's second quatrain begins by invoking the "Ancient English dower [i.e., dowry] / Of inward happiness." Then, in a stark, collective self-accusation, Wordsworth charges: "We are selfish men." The poet contrasts the happy state associated with native tradition to selfishness (the corrupt double of "inward[ness]"). Happiness is not complacency, but rather a true contentment based on self-sufficient, godly virtue. To attain such a state, Wordsworth's England requires the help of Milton. Just as Milton at the beginning of *Paradise Lost* pleaded to God, "what is low in me, raise and support," so Wordsworth asks Milton himself to "raise us up." Such elevation is a kind of reformation, undertaken in the individual soul.

At the conclusion of his octave, Wordsworth's closed quatrains *(abba)* produce a forceful rhyme: the "dower" of line 5 turns out to be "power"—the last noun in a dramatic, ascending series. "Manners, virtue, freedom, power": Wordsworth saves the best for last, the final term that caps the upward movement, Milton's "rais[ing] . . . up." Rooted in custom (manners), we reach for ultimate strength (power). In other Wordsworth poems ("Michael," "The Ruined Cottage"), the habits of rural life supply a firm foundation for his characters' virtues. They live starkly cut off from urban society; simple, solid manners sustain them. The pairing of freedom and power is Wordsworth's blow against the French Revolution, with its trampling of the free individual by an all-powerful state acting in the name of the people.

"Thy soul was like a Star, and dwelt apart": so Wordsworth begins his sestet. Milton was the "one just man" (as he calls Enoch in *Paradise Lost*): he stood against the evils that surrounded him, lonely in his far-shining, starlike virtue. In the *Prelude,* Wordsworth praised France as a nation "fresh as the morning star" (9.391). Stars, which guide us in our travels, are traditionally a locale for the heroic dead, especially dead poets; Shelley's elegy "Adonais" places the soul of Keats among the constellations. (Years later, after Wordsworth had become a political conservative, Shelley in his sonnet "To Wordsworth" used the star trope from "London, 1802" to rebuke the older poet. Once "thou wert as a lone star," Shelley tells Wordsworth, a beacon of "truth and liberty"—but no longer.)

Milton's voice, which Wordsworth first compares to the sea, then appears "pure as the naked heavens, majestic, free." The proud open quality of Miltonic speech seems bare and pure as the sky; he shows his majesty in the grandeur of *Paradise Lost, Samson Agonistes,* and his other works. But Milton's significance for Wordsworth finally resides in his humility. So "London, 1802" ends: "thy heart/The lowliest duties on herself did lay." Wordsworth has transformed Milton, his influential precursor, into one of his own stalwart, long-suffering protagonists, solitary yet obligated to common humanity. Yet he also gestures toward the elevated, prophetic inspiration that Milton might offer at a bleak moment in history. The intensity of Wordsworth's yearning is what makes his sonnet so moving: he reaches out toward the image of his great predecessor, and hopes to support himself and his country.

"London, 1802" is the cry of a man in need. Urgent and resourceful, it shows us Wordsworth's own poetic capacity, as well as his admiration for Milton's upright vigor.

DM

"Surprised by Joy"

WILLIAM WORDSWORTH

1815; revised 1820

Surprised by joy—impatient as the Wind
I turned to share the transport—Oh! with whom
But Thee, deep buried in the silent tomb,
That spot which no vicissitude can find?
Love, faithful love, recalled thee to my mind—
But how could I forget thee? Through what power,
Even for the least division of an hour,
Have I been so beguiled as to be blind
To my most grievous loss?—That thought's return
Was the worst pang that sorrow ever bore,
Save one, one only, when I stood forlorn,
Knowing my heart's best treasure was no more;
That neither present time, nor years unborn
Could to my sight that heavenly face restore.

THIS sonnet responds to the loss of William Wordsworth's daughter Catherine, who died suddenly at age four in July 1812. (The poet lost a son, Thomas, later that year, but he identified his daughter as the subject of this poem; his other three children survived him.) In the preface to the second edition of his *Lyrical Ballads* (1800), using phrases that critics have quoted almost ever since, Wordsworth had set out his belief that poetry requires "the spontaneous overflow of powerful feelings," adding that a poem "takes its origin from emotion recollected in tranquillity." The sonnet—his only poem about Catherine's death—pursues his powerful feelings, one after another, as they race through Wordsworth's self-analytical mind: tranquillity, for him, proves hard to imagine, much less to depict within fourteen lines.

The sonnet begins not with grief but with a joy that Wordsworth, at the moment of writing, does not even want to describe, since, in reacting to that joy, he discovered that he had—momentarily at least—forgotten his loss. "Surprised," Wordsworth turned (as a parent might turn to look for a child at his heels) to tell his daughter what he had just seen, and then remembered that she was no longer alive. (In the first version, published in 1815, Wordsworth "wished," rather than "turned"; we give the second, published in 1820, which also changed "long," in line 3, to "deep.") Wordsworth's memory sends him on a tumultuous chase through his own emotions, one that ends only when he remembers how he felt when he first learned that she was gone.

With swift dashes, sudden exclamations, and a recurring trio of rhymes in the octave *(abbaacca)*, Wordsworth pursues three kinds of awful sadness, each one following hard on the last: the grief of remembering that Catherine has died; the guilty shock of realizing that he has forgotten her death; and then, in the sestet, the memory of his first grief at the fact of that death. The fleeting events of the present, one following unpredictably upon another, stand in contrast to the permanence of the tomb; the flailing unease of enjambed phrases in the octave poses another contrast to the grim, stately, largely end-stopped sestet.

A vicissitude is "a change or alteration in condition or fortune; an instance of mutability" *(OED)*. The word recalls Thomas Gray's unfinished "Ode on the Pleasure Arising from Vicissitude" (first published 1775), which Wordsworth certainly knew, since he echoed it in other poems. Gray celebrates the end of winter, and the changeable spring, whose full pleasures only human beings can experience, since only human beings can mentally compare present, future and past: "'Tis man alone that joy descries / With forward and re-verted eyes," Gray wrote in that ode.

Such comparisons do not increase Wordsworth's sudden joy; instead, they straightaway demolish it. In the octave, a deeply unsettled Wordsworth rushes through dashes and very short phrases into a set of grammatically complete questions, asking, first, how he could ever share any joy with anyone other than Catherine, and then how he could have set aside her demise. Though he knows that she no longer feels "wind," or impatience—that she says nothing and hears nothing, silent, entombed—Wordsworth addresses his questions to her anyway: "with whom / But Thee," "how could I forget Thee?" Such grammatical choices recall his earlier feeling, in the first quatrain, that Catherine was still alive. The poet never did "forget" his daughter, though he momentarily forgot her death—a modern reader, informed by Sigmund Freud, might say (though Wordsworth himself could not have put it that way) that he unconsciously wants to believe she still lives.

That belief, or that wish, cannot survive Wordsworth's characteristically close attention to the workings of his own mind. In his third query, Wordsworth abandons the second-person pronouns, stops addressing Catherine, and instead addresses himself: "through what power . . . / Have I been so beguiled?" That such a "power" lies within himself, as within all of us—that the natural ebb of grief, like its flow, is part of the normal growth of the adult mind—shocks him even more. Is his ability to note present joy, to see the vicissitudes of a new day, a sign of impatience, a failure of "faithful love"? The still-bereaved father must wonder whether it is, and whether the failure reflects some fault all his own, or whether instead (as David Ferry puts it) "he was necessarily fickle, because he was still alive, and vicissitude is the ordinary human condition."

Wordsworth seems to wish that it were not. He can then think of nothing except her—or rather (since he has just reproached himself for thinking as if she were still alive), he will permit himself to think only of the fact that she is gone, and of how he felt on the day she died. That day—not today—was the worst day of this father's life (Wordsworth may be remembering *King Lear*: "The worst is not, / So long as we can say 'This is the worst'"). But today is the second-worst, today comes close: today is the day, important to students of mourning, when the mourner realizes—with whatever mixed feelings—that he has begun to give up his intense attachment to the deceased, that he has begun, however slightly, to turn back toward life. Astonished that he can forget Catherine's death for an instant, Wordsworth presents his disappointment that he has, in fact, moved onward, able to have and to share new experiences of joy (and of sorrow), but only with other people who are still on earth.

The work of making changing feelings vivid, performed in so many other poems through images, takes place here largely through pace (as the poem hurtles forward and then slows down), through syntax, and through grammar: sentence shapes and pronominal choices, punctuation, verb tense, and verb mood. The poem begins on a vivid verbal adjective, from which it might well have launched into the present tense ("Surprised . . . I see X"). Instead, the poet situates his occasion in the immediate past ("Surprised . . . I turned"). Rather than staying in that moment, telling us what he saw or found or heard, he then moves back farther in time.

That movement occupies most of the poem; it takes place in present-perfect ("have I been") and simple-past ("recalled," "Was," "stood") verbs. The last verb ("restore") belongs to a counterfactual clause: in it, the poet spurns both "present time" and any future ("years unborn"), since his daughter now belongs to the past alone. Wordsworth's conclusion holds the merest hint of the consolation expected in a Christian poem: Catherine's face looked "heavenly" while alive, but now it is heavenly in another sense, since she rests in heaven, unseen by mortal eyes, rather than in the terrestrial "tomb" of line 3. So much, and no more, of religion can the poem contain: anything greater than a hint would be more than the poet could bear.

People afflicted with grief—as Wordsworth has been—may well consider that grief, with all its pains, as a kind of connection to the deceased, fearing that when the pain diminishes, the connection will diminish too. Freud's most famous essay on grief, "Mourning and Melancholia," classified as "melancholy" people who did not want to get over their grief, who did not want to move on, because they did not want to admit that the dead (or otherwise lost) person was lost indeed. Wordsworth is not such a person, at least not within this sonnet—but he seems almost to wish that he were. His poem of sudden, uncontrollable feeling, in a quintessentially Wordsworthian transformation, turns into a poem of retrospective analysis: his poem of successive, spontaneous emotions (joy, and then astonishment, and then grief, and then the grief-suffused pathos of memory) becomes a poem of exemplary attention to the new frames we give our old experience, and about how he himself has changed over time.

SB

"On Seeing the Elgin Marbles"

JOHN KEATS

1817

My spirit is too weak—mortality
   Weighs heavily on me like unwilling sleep,
   And each imagin'd pinnacle and steep
Of godlike hardship, tells me I must die
Like a sick Eagle looking at the sky.
   Yet 'tis a gentle luxury to weep
   That I have not the cloudy winds to keep
Fresh for the opening of the morning's eye.
Such dim-conceivèd glories of the brain
   Bring round the heart an undescribable feud;
So do these wonders a most dizzy pain,
   That mingles Grecian grandeur with the rude
Wasting of old Time—with a billowy main—
   A sun—a shadow of a magnitude.

THE resplendent friezes from the Parthenon, known as the Elgin Marbles—because they were acquired from Greece's Ottoman overlords by Lord Elgin—arrived in England between 1803 and 1812, in separate shipments. They were housed in a private room, with permission to see them given to only a few. Today the marbles, still an object of international dispute between England and Greece, are located in the British Museum, where they continue to astonish the spectator.

The painter Benjamin Robert Haydon, a close friend of Keats, was one of the lucky Britons allowed to view the Elgin Marbles during their first years in London. The brilliance of the Parthenon reliefs obsessed Haydon; he drew them for as many as fifteen hours a day. He remarked on the "combination of nature and idea" embodied in them, and on their vast superiority to all other works of antique sculpture. (Haydon also defended the marbles against charges that they were not in fact Greek, but Roman copies.)

Haydon took Keats to see the marbles on the first or second of March 1817. Keats responded by writing two sonnets; the one we include is by far the more impressive of the two. In it, Keats confronts his own mortality, and experiences a solitary sense of the sublime: a vast loneliness, enforced by the sight of the Greek sculptures' unrivaled, enthralling power.

In Keats's hands the sonnet, a sharply delimited form, reaches toward the condition of the sublime ode. (Shelley will turn his sonnets in a similar direction: see his "England in 1819" and "Ozymandias," both in this collection.) The spellbinding grandeur of ancient Greek art revives in Keats's treatment of antiquity: the past transmits to him its pure, alien radiance.

This beauty does not comfort, but disturbs: the sight of the marbles reminds Keats of his mortal nature. He sees himself as a "sick Eagle looking at the sky." (Eagles were reputed to be able to stare at the sun; any eaglet that failed to manifest this ability was supposedly thrown out of the nest and condemned to die.) The consciousness of death initiates the movement of this sonnet, as it will provide the conclusion to "Four seasons fill the measure of the year," our other poem by Keats.

In another work of 1817, his lengthy romance *Endymion,* Keats refers to "things of beauty" as "an endless fountain of immortal drink." He wishes for a "bower quiet for us, and a sleep / Full of sweet dreams, and health, and quiet breathing." Such aspiration toward art as a replenishing source of lush comfort, and a refuge from human sorrow, is absent from "On Seeing the Elgin Marbles." Instead, the beauty of the sculptures overmasters the poet: his "spirit is too weak."

The poem's opening phrase is halted by a caesura (the dash), as if Keats were reluctant to speak the thought of death. But he does. "Mortality," that heavy word, completes the first line, and the poet soon identifies it with "unwilling sleep"—a restless lethargy unlike the sweet dreams imagined in *Endymion.* He scans the passionate heights of the Parthenon friezes: the grand hero Theseus, the furious battle of the Lapiths and Centaurs, the sublimely moving sacrificial procession (which features the unruly heifer that Keats likely alludes to in his "Ode on a Grecian Urn").

These artistic "pinnacle[s]" and "steep[s]" tell the poet one thing only, that he "must die." Keats himself is the sacrificial animal, helpless and doomed (he was to die at age twenty-five, of tuberculosis). But he is also a heroic figure, afflicted by "godlike hardship," like the suffering deity Apollo in his later poem "Hyperion." It remains unclear, at the end of the first quatrain, whether Keats is the victim of the ancient world's brilliance, a mere modern crushed by the Grecian grandeur, or (on the contrary) whether he will be inducted into that splendid antique world, so foreign to the poet and to us, and experience an apotheosis. The phrase "godlike hardship" suggests the latter possibility. (In "Hyperion," Apollo cries, "Knowledge enormous makes a god of me.")

The second quatrain opens a new motion: a wishful lapsing into soft indulgence. "Yet 'tis a gentle luxury to weep." The poet sheds tears, and yearns after an atmospheric protective power that he does not possess. If he had the "cloudy winds to keep / Fresh for the opening of the morning's eye," he would be equal to this experience—he could confront the brilliant relics of the Parthenon. Rather than the eagle who looks at the sun, he would be a friendly shield for that sun, for the "morning's eye," stimulating it to wakefulness (an antidote to the clinging sleep of line 2). The brisk pastoral flavor here recalls Milton's "Il Penseroso," with its figure of Morn "kerchief'd in a comely cloud, / While rocking winds are piping loud."

But the refreshing brio of pastoral, the innocence that attends the image of the morning's eye, will not suffice here. Newly vulnerable, the poet undergoes a kind of attack, a suffocating or stroke-like congestion. The "dim-conceivèd glories of the brain"—his own fantasies about his coming death, about the cloudy winds and the sun—"Bring round the heart an undescribable feud." There is a battle going on within this poet, but who the warring forces are, and why they fight, is as unclear to him as it is to us. The "wonders" (both the marbles themselves and his own thoughts in response to them) produce a "dizzy pain," a vertiginous disquiet. Keats here experiences the feeling of being overwhelmed that is associated with the sublime, but adds his own emphasis on the aching, internal confusion that, for him, burdens and defines the human.

Keats's sonnet is an ekphrasis, a poem created in response to a work of art (like Rossetti's "For a Venetian Pastoral," later in our book). But in contrast to Rossetti (and to his own "Ode on a Grecian Urn"), Keats describes nothing in the artwork itself. His feeling for the Parthenon reliefs is rare, acute, and as a result abstract; he is too dazzled to offer a verbal panorama, which would lessen the glory. The spare, removed images he gives us in his concluding lines evoke the vast might of nature, whose powers remain forever unknown to us. The "billowy main" (that is, ocean) is succeeded by "A sun—a shadow of a magnitude." This is an elusive last line. It flees the reader's understanding, and supplies at the same time an emblem of Keats's own cognitive obstruction.

"We hate poetry that has a palpable design upon us," Keats wrote in one of his letters. "On Seeing the Elgin Marbles" recoils from such design, from the brandishing of a motto or moralizing point. The poet sees no lesson in the marbles, unlike Shelley in "Ozymandias," and unlike Keats's friend Haydon, who was prompted by the friezes to "ponder on the change of empires." They are no friend to man: Keats refuses to give them a consoling function.

But the marbles do announce a theme: the alien splendor of art, its inhuman force. Keats gives us in his lines 12–14 an empty, though gleaming, atmosphere, utterly different from the elated picture of the fresh winds and sunshine in lines 7–8. We seem now to be on a distant planet, not our familiar earth. Like "keep / Fresh," "rude / Wasting" is a startling enjambment; it makes us wait for the initial word of line 13: wasting. "Old Time" both wastes and is wasted, its blunt rudeness visible in the marbles' broken surface. These sculptures seem both too close and too far away—utterly present, yet impossibly distant.

Keats ends with "a sun—a shadow of a magnitude." Magnitude is a technical term, the measurement of the brightness of a star (or a sun). By "shadow of a magnitude," Keats seems to mean the effect cast by the star's light, which diminishes us, the observers, as the Elgin Marbles dwarf the poet. This sun is aloof, remote; it outshines the human.

The Greek critic Longinus, in his treatise *On the Sublime* (first century CE), writes that true greatness is attained by the work of art that "is difficult or rather impossible to withstand, and the memory of which is strong and hard to efface." This description applies both to the Elgin Marbles and to Keats's poem about them. The content of the poet's vision overshadows the poet himself: he cannot grasp it. We tend to think of lyric poetry as emotional expression, what Keats imagines when he speaks of "gentle luxury": passionate or sensual, watered with tears and sighs. In "On Seeing the Elgin Marbles," the passionate impulse is curbed, turned back on itself. Keats transports himself, and his readers, to a new world (like the unknown planet swimming into view in another of his sonnets, "On First Looking into Chapman's Homer"). Strangely, this vista seems to exclude or even rebuke us.

The stark, blinding grandeur of this sonnet is Keats's fine tribute to the incommensurable splendor of the ancient world. His place in his own poem is obscure, threatened: crowded out by a greater illumination.

DM

"Four seasons fill the measure of the year"

JOHN KEATS

1818

Four seasons fill the measure of the year;
    Four seasons are there in the mind of man.
He hath his lusty spring, when fancy clear
    Takes in all beauty with an easy span;
He hath his summer, when luxuriously
    He chews the honeyed cud of fair spring thoughts,
Till in his soul dissolv'd, they come to be
    Part of himself. He hath his autumn ports
And havens of repose, when his tired wings
    Are folded up, and he content to look
On mists in idleness: to let fair things
    Pass by unheeded as a threshold brook.
He hath his winter too of pale misfeature
Or else he would forget his mortal nature.

MOST OF Keats's best sonnets (though not this one) are so famous that they are in almost every poetry anthology; they speak often to one another, or else, like this one, to Keats's other, longer poems. "Four seasons," composed in April 1818, had some popularity after his death (it appeared in the Victorians' favorite anthology, Francis Palgrave's *Golden Treasury*, under the title "The Human Seasons"), but it attracts modern interest first of all because it seems to predict the last of his great odes, "To Autumn" (1819). It explains what the later poem assumes—that to be alert to human life as Keats sees it is to understand, and to find symbols for, the inner conditions the four seasons can represent. To find such symbols is, in turn, to represent, and to realize, the fact that we will die.

Keats begins from an interest in analogy: What states of mind or attitudes are to "the mind of man" as the four seasons are to the land, to "the year"? "Mind," not "life"—he asks not about the growth and decay of the body, but about intellect, emotion, and memory, what Keats in a famous letter called "Soul-making." The first surviving version of the poem comes in an earlier letter of March 1818, from Keats to Benjamin Bailey. The letter investigates human perception, and praises the mental ardor that (Keats says) gives ephemera their value in a world where "nothing . . . is provable." There are, Keats speculates, "Things real—such as existences of Sun Moon & Stars and passages of Shakespeare—Things semireal such as Love, the Clouds &c which require a greeting of the Spirit to make them wholly exist—and Nothings which are made Great and dignified by an ardent pursuit." The sonnet itself Keats copies out as something "of a somewhat collateral nature"—that is, related to (though not exactly sprung from) the preceding thought.

This sonnet about the four seasons, seen in that light, describes cognizance and perception, the stages by which we take whatever attracts our notice—whether "real" or "semireal" or "nothing," a couplet from *Hamlet* or a stone in the street—into our consciousness so that it may affect us. Those stages, Keats suggests, correspond to the seasons in the calendar year. The first season of the mind is a "lusty spring," characterized not so much by sexual lust (the poem includes no begetting, and no generation) as by intake: the "fancy," one of the faculties of the mind, gathers impressions of beauty for later use. (Like the noun "fantasy" in more recent usage, "fancy" for Keats can also imply delusion, artificiality, or insufficiency: "Adieu! the fancy cannot cheat so well / As she is fam'd to do, deceiving elf," Keats wrote in "Ode to a Nightingale.")

The second approximate quatrain (lines 5–8, where the sentence ends midline) calls summer the season in which "man" makes, or remakes, "himself" from his stored "thoughts," in which impressions become reactions, and reactions become parts of ourselves. This remaking, in order to feel like summer, requires leisure, as the making of art requires some free time. If spring was youth, this summer is adulthood. While it takes place, we require no *further* impressions: we process, as it were, and recombine, the experiences and the forms of "beauty" we already know.

Keats represents that processing (lest it seem too exalted, too unfamiliar) by making his representative man a ruminant, chewing over again his earlier, springtime experience as a sheep or a cow rechews its cud. By the third quatrain (which begins "early," before the rhyme—"ports" / "thoughts," a full rhyme for Keats, as in parts of England today), man is no longer a beast of the field, but a bird, whose "tired wings / Are folded up": he neither takes in new experience (he lets it "pass") nor works to process the experience he has. Neither flying, nor acting, nor eating, the bird is a thing already complete, already made, unmoving and ready to stand outside time, as the birds elsewhere in Keats and in his successors (Keats's own nightingale, Yeats's "Sailing to Byzantium") stand outside time in order to represent art.

Another—less demanding—poet might end with the autumnal bird, perched, like an elderly man, at the end of life, his goals accomplished, his spirit prepared. Keats will do no such thing. The life of "man" (unless it ends far too early) includes a "winter" of physical decay, "pale misfeature," unattractive appearance (whereas the "tired bird" suggested not decrepitude but repose). The "mind of man" requires a concept of winter, in which we contemplate not the completion of any process (natural or manmade) but its ruin. The "mind of man" must have its winter too, if it is to represent adequately (and to make art that represents) human life. We ought, Keats suggests, to remember our "mortal nature," not out of fealty to any divinity (the sonnet conceives of none) but because not to do so would be to live with a false, or an incomplete, "soul." We notice decay and failure in other people—and by analogy from the effects of winter on plants, animals, soil, birds—years or decades (if we are lucky, as Keats was not) before we experience decay and physical failure ourselves. Four seasons thus take place within our minds long before they serve our their terms as analogies for our aging bodies. Keats does not say whether or how we might apprehend, in one mind, all four at once.

By incorporating winter, with its pale signs of mortality, into our minds, we may remind ourselves of our own difference from the calendrical cycle that gives Keats his initial subject. "Human life reaches, as seasons do not, an utmost verge," writes Helen Vendler in her book about Keats's odes; "human music ends." The four seasons alternate in a round, each winter giving place to spring (thus Percy Bysshe Shelley: "If winter comes, can spring be far behind?"). The annual revivification of everything save individual human lives is perhaps the most common motif in all Western poetry on the subject of the seasons. Keats, however, says nothing of it here: in his conception, winter (old age, disease) leads to no spring.

So the poem ends as a picture of human life. But what has happened to its account of perception? If spring corresponds to intake, summer to introspection, and autumn to contemplation, by which a "nothing," pursued, at last becomes stable and real, then winter must correspond to dissolution: in our mental winter, we forget what we discovered in spring. No wonder "forget" occurs in that final line. Conscious of our inevitable forgetting, which disfigures our mental composure, we know that neither bodies nor minds will last.

Keats's Shakespearean structure prescribes three quatrains and a couplet, but his syntax splits up the sonnet in other ways. He introduces the governing idea (four seasons occupy "the mind" as it grows) with a two-line sentence, gives two lines to spring, almost four to summer, just above four to autumn, and then a conclusive couplet to winter, for symmetry. The couplet for winter concludes with abstraction (none of the words in the last line describes any thing or person we can *see*). It also introduces teleology, as if the winter had entered our mind for a reason, as if somebody wanted it to be there. But the sonnet contains no hint of a divine designer (Keats, in an 1816 sonnet, called Christianity a "vulgar superstition"). The last line, with its emphatic disyllable rhyme, implies instead that something about our own minds remains incomplete, unsatisfied, until we have incorporated reminders of our fragility into our souls. That incorporation may well take place late in life (though for Keats it took place stunningly early), after "fancy" has filled our souls with "beauty." Without such incorporation, however, our comedy may seem shallow, our pleasures facile, our art mere fancy, and our consciousness off-balance, incomplete.

SB

"Ozymandias"

PERCY BYSSHE SHELLEY

1818

I met a traveller from an antique land
Who said: Two vast and trunkless legs of stone
Stand in the desert. Near them, on the sand,
Half sunk, a shatter'd visage lies, whose frown,
And wrinkled lip, and sneer of cold command,
Tell that its sculptor well those passions read
Which yet survive, stamp'd on these lifeless things,
The hand that mock'd them and the heart that fed:
And on the pedestal these words appear:
"My name is Ozymandias, king of kings:
Look on my works, ye Mighty, and despair!"
Nothing beside remains. Round the decay
Of that colossal wreck, boundless and bare
The lone and level sands stretch far away.

SHELLEY's friend the banker Horace Smith stayed with the poet and his wife Mary (author of *Frankenstein*) in the Christmas season of 1817. One evening, they began to discuss recent discoveries in the Near East. In the wake of Napoleon's conquest of Egypt in 1798, the archeological treasures found there stimulated the European imagination. The power of pharaonic Egypt had seemed eternal, but now this once-great empire was (and had long been) in ruins, a feeble shadow.

Shelley and Smith remembered the Roman-era historian Diodorus Siculus, who described a statue of Ozymandias, more commonly known as Rameses II (possibly the pharaoh referred to in the Book of Exodus). Diodorus reports the inscription on the statue, which he claims was the largest in Egypt, as follows: "King of Kings Ozymandias am I. If any want to know how great I am and where I lie, let him outdo me in my work." (The statue and its inscription do not survive, and were not seen by Shelley; his inspiration for "Ozymandias" was verbal rather than visual.)

Stimulated by their conversation, Smith and Shelley wrote sonnets based on the passage in Diodorus. Smith produced a now-forgotten poem with the unfortunate title "On a Stupendous Leg of Granite, Discovered Standing by Itself in the Deserts of Egypt, with the Inscription Inserted Below." Shelley's contribution was "Ozymandias," one of the best-known sonnets in European literature.

In addition to the Diodorus passage, Shelley must have recalled similar examples of boastfulness in the epitaphic tradition. In the Greek Anthology (8.177), for example, a gigantic tomb on a high cliff proudly insists that it is the eighth wonder of the world. Here, as in the case of "Ozymandias," the inert fact of the monument displaces the presence of the dead person it commemorates: the proud claim is made on behalf of art (the tomb and its creator), not the deceased. Though Ozymandias believes he speaks for himself, in Shelley's poem his monument testifies against him.

"Ozymandias" has an elusive, sidelong approach to its subject. The poem begins with the word "I"—but the first person here is a mere framing device. The "I" quickly fades away in favor of a mysterious "traveler from an antique land." This wayfarer presents the remaining thirteen lines of the poem.

The reader encounters Shelley's poem like an explorer coming upon a strange, desolate landscape. The first image that we see is the "two vast and trunkless legs of stone" in the middle of a desert. Column-like legs but no torso: the center of this great figure, whoever he may have been, remains missing. The sonnet comes to a halt in the middle of its first quatrain. Are these fragmentary legs all that is left?

After this pause, Shelley's poem describes a "shattered visage," the enormous face of Ozymandias. The visage is taken apart by the poet, who collaborates with time's ruinous force. Shelley says nothing about the rest of the face; he describes only the mouth, with its "frown, / And wrinkled lip, and sneer of cold command." Cold command is the emblem of the empire-building ruler, of the tyrannical kind that Shelley despised. Ozymandias resembles the monstrous George III of our other Shelley sonnet, "England in 1819." (Surprisingly, surviving statues of Rameses II, aka Ozymandias, show him with a mild, slightly mischievous expression, not a glowering, imperious one.)

The second quatrain shifts to another mediating figure, now not the trav-
eler but the sculptor who depicted the pharaoh. The sculptor "well those pas-
sions read," Shelley tells us: he intuited, beneath the cold, commanding exte-
rior, the tyrant's passionate rage to impose himself on the world. Ozymandias'
intense emotions "survive, stamp'd on these lifeless things." But as Shelley at-
tests, the sculptor survives as well, or parts of him do: "the hand that mocked"
the king's passions "and the heart that fed." (The artist, like the tyrant, lies in
fragments.) "Mocked" here has the neutral sense of "described" (common in
Shakespeare), as well as its more familiar meaning, to imitate in an insulting
way. The artist mocked Ozymandias by depicting him, and in a way that the
ruler could not himself perceive (presumably he was satisfied with his por-
trait). "The heart that fed" is an odd, slightly lurid phrase, apparently refer-
ring to the sculptor's own fervent way of nourishing himself on his massive
project. The sculptor's attitude might resemble—at any event, it certainly
suits—the pharaoh's own aggressive enjoyment of empire. Ruler and artist
seem strangely linked here; the latter's contempt for his subject does not free
him from Ozymandias' enormous shadow.

The challenge for Shelley will thus be to separate himself from the sculp-
tor's harsh satire, which is too intimately tied to the power it opposes. If the
artistic rebel merely plays Prometheus to Ozymandias' Zeus, the two will re-
main locked in futile struggle (the subject of Shelley's great verse drama *Pro-
metheus Unbound*). Shelley's final lines, with their picture of the surrounding
desert, are his attempt to remove himself from both the king and the sculp-
tor—to assert an uncanny, ironic perspective, superior to the battle between
ruler and ruled that contaminates both.

The sestet moves from the shattered statue of Ozymandias to the pedestal,
with its now-ironic inscription: "'My name is Ozymandias, king of
kings. / Look on my works, ye mighty, and despair!'" Of course, the pharaoh's
"works" are nowhere to be seen, in this desert wasteland. The kings that he
challenges with the evidence of his superiority are the rival rulers of the na-
tions he has enslaved, perhaps the Israelites and Canaanites known from the
biblical account. The son and successor of Ozymandias / Rameses II, known
as Merneptah, boasts in a thirteenth-century BCE inscription (on the "Mernep-
tah stele," discovered in 1896 and therefore unknown to Shelley) that "Israel is
destroyed; its seed is gone"—an evidently overoptimistic assessment.

The pedestal stands in the middle of a vast expanse. Shelley applies two al-
literative phrases to this desert, "boundless and bare" and "lone and level."

The seemingly infinite empty space provides an appropriate comment on Ozymandias' political will, which has no content except the blind desire to assert his name and kingly reputation.

"Ozymandias" is comparable to another signature poem by a great Romantic, Samuel Taylor Coleridge's "Kubla Khan." But whereas Coleridge aligns the ruler's "stately pleasure dome" with poetic vision, Shelley opposes the statue and its boast to his own powerful negative imagination. Time renders fame hollow: it counterposes to the ruler's proud sentence a devastated vista, the trackless sands of Egypt.

Ozymandias and his sculptor bear a fascinating relation to Shelley himself: they might be seen as warnings concerning the aggressive character of human action (whether the king's or the artist's). Shelley was a ceaselessly energetic, desirous creator of poetry, but he yearned for calm. This yearning dictated that he reach beyond his own willful, anarchic spirit, beyond the hubris of the revolutionary. In his essay "On Life," Shelley writes that man has "a spirit within him at enmity with dissolution and nothingness." In one way or another, we all rebel against the oblivion to which death finally condemns us. But we face, in that rebellion, a clear choice of pathways: the road of the ardent man of power who wrecks all before him, and is wrecked in turn; or the road of the poet, who makes his own soul the lyre or Aeolian harp for unseen forces. (One may well doubt the strict binary that Shelley implies, and point to other possibilities.) Shelley's limpid late lyric "With a Guitar, to Jane" evokes wafting harmonies and a supremely light touch. This music occupies the opposite end of the spectrum from Ozymandias' futile, resounding proclamation. Similarly, in the "Ode to the West Wind," Shelley's lyre opens up the source of a luminous vision: the poet identifies himself with the work of song, the wind that carries inspiration. The poet yields to a strong, invisible power as the politician cannot.

In a letter written during the poet's affair with Jane Williams, Shelley declares, "Jane brings her guitar, and if the past and the future could be obliterated, the present would content me so well that I could say with Faust to the passing moment, 'Remain, thou, thou art so beautiful.'" The endless sands of "Ozymandias" palpably represent the threatening expanse of past and future. Shelley's poem rises from the desert wastes: it entrances us every time we read it, and turns the reading into a "now."

The critic Leslie Brisman remarks on "the way the timelessness of metaphor escapes the limits of experience" in Shelley. Timelessness can be achieved only by the poet's words, not by the ruler's will to dominate. The fallen titan Ozymandias becomes an occasion for Shelley's exercise of this most tenuous yet persisting form, poetry. Shelley's sonnet, a brief epitome of poetic thinking, has outlasted empires: it has witnessed the deaths of boastful tyrants, and the decline of the British dominion he so heartily scorned.

DM

"England in 1819"

PERCY BYSSHE SHELLEY

Written 1819–1820

An old, mad, blind, despis'd, and dying king,—
Princes, the dregs of their dull race, who flow
Through public scorn—mud from a muddy spring,—
Rulers who neither see, nor feel, nor know,
But leech-like to their fainting country cling,
Till they drop, blind in blood, without a blow,—
A people starv'd and stabb'd in the untill'd field,—
An army, which liberticide and prey
Makes as a two-edg'd sword to all who wield,—
Golden and sanguine laws which tempt and slay;
Religion Christless, Godless—a book seal'd;
A Senate,—Time's worst statute, unrepeal'd,—
Are graves, from which a glorious Phantom may
Burst, to illumine our tempestuous day.

ONE OF the great poems of political anger in English, Shelley's sonnet about headline news (as we now say) commands attention for its tone (few poets have sustained such indignation for so long without monotony), for the way it condenses topical information (several radical pamphlets' worth), and for its odd structure: one sentence, mostly a stack of subject clauses, displaying an idiosyncratic rhyme scheme, with twelve lines giving reasons for despair, then two devoted to figures for violent hope. Shelley wrote the sonnet while living in Italy; anyone in England who tried to publish such sentiments would have risked prosecution for treason, and Shelley did not ask anyone to try. Instead, he enclosed it a letter to a friend, the poet and publisher Leigh Hunt, who shared Shelley's radical, antimonarchical politics, and who had been imprisoned for sedition. It first appeared in print in 1839, when Mary Shelley collected her late husband's poetry (Hunt was still alive and writing, and must have given the letter to her). Mary also gave the sonnet (untitled in the poet's letter) the title that has stuck to it ever since.

"England in 1819" contains just one sentence, its main verb, "Are," delayed till line 13. All the lines before "Are" form a list, a set of things, conditions, people, and legislation to be found in the England whose condition the radical Shelley assailed. That list becomes the compound subject for Shelley's verb, a stack of despised entities piled one on another and then at long last overthrown.

As in George Herbert's "Prayer (I)," we expect lists in poems to imply reasons behind their order. A list of good things should shift from better to best; a list of bad things should descend from bad to worse. Yet Shelley's first example of England's parlous state seems hard to top: it is the head of state, George III, known in the United States today as the king against whom America staged a revolution, known to Britons in 1819–1820 as the eighty-one-year-old monarch whose unbalanced mind required the Regency, a legal arrangement by which the king's son, the prince regent, ruled in his stead. Though without direct political power, the old king retained his title, and gave the radical poet a fine first symbol for the elements he hated in his native country: deference to hereditary order, conservatism (a temperament, not just a political movement), willed ignorance of what seemed to Shelley (and to anyone else who sympathized with the goals of the French Revolution) the inalienable rights of man.

The Hanoverian line of descent flows downward, from mad king to prince regent, growing more polluted as it goes on, like a "muddy spring." Hanoverian rulers and governors (George III, the prince regent, and the ministers under them) are not only blind, but without sympathy, as if they also lacked the sense of touch. (Shelley may have in mind the scene from *King Lear,* another harsh masterpiece about a divided kingdom, in which the mad Lear tells the blinded Gloucester, "You know which way the world goes"; Gloucester responds, "I see it feelingly.") Muddy springs may hold real leeches, which have medical use; the Hanoverian line, so close to the dirt already, disgorges only the useless leeches of ministers and kings who "cling" to England, gorging themselves on its blood, spending the riches they did not work to produce, until they collapse from some toxic combination of satiety, old age, and turpitude.

The first six lines form the sestet of a Petrarchan sonnet, rhymed *ababab*—

Shelley appears to put the conclusion first (England, too, is morally upside-down). When the rhyme changes, England looks worse still. A nation whose vilest enemies were the aristocratic "leeches" of lines 4–6 might be saved by time alone, but this England requires (in Shelley's view) disruptive action—a revolution easy for Shelley to imagine, but hard to carry out. The sonnet reacts to the Peterloo Massacre of August 1819, in which British troops on horseback charged and fired their weapons into a crowd assembled in St. Peter's Square, in the industrial city of Manchester ("loo" alludes sarcastically to the Battle of Waterloo). Sixty thousand people attended the meeting, where radical orators spoke for universal suffrage (one man, one vote). Hundreds of civilians were wounded, and at least a dozen died. Britons who shared the orators' goals, and many who did not, were horrified; peaceable social change seemed far away—Shelley wrote to Leigh Hunt in December 1819, "I suppose we shall soon have to fight." "Two-edg'd sword" implies that (as in many countries today) a nation that puts down domestic dissent with its army risks encouraging a military coup. It also alludes to Psalm 149, in which the righteous, with "a two-edged sword in their hand," will "execute vengeance upon the heathen . . . to bind their kings with chains."

Shelley was (or, at least, often writes like) what philosophers call an Idealist—someone who believes that abstractions such as Liberty or Justice are at least as real as tables and lemons. It makes sense, then, that his list of bad things in his England should begin with a bad person, continue through bad or badly treated groups of people (the victims at Peterloo, the standing army), and conclude with abused or traduced ideas. English laws do not represent justice: "golden" is sarcastic in one sense (the laws violate ordinary morality), straightforward in another (the laws serve the rich), and allusive in a third (laws protecting private property make it into an idol like the Golden Calf).

"Sanguine" is also double-edged, meaning "bloody, blood-colored," or else "confident": the laws shed innocent blood with unearned confidence. Expelled from Oxford University for writing a pamphlet called "The Necessity of Atheism," Shelley was no friend of the Christian God, but this sonnet does not exactly attack Christianity; rather, the insincere worship of a God set up as Christian, a state church that in practice worshiped the state, seemed to Shelley even worse than sincere belief. Worst of all, in the poem's first couplet, is one particular bad law. Which one? Most critics identify one or another statute denying political rights to Catholics, though some (among them the formidable scholar James Chandler) propose the very existence of the "senate"—that is, Parliament—itself.

The concluding couplet alters the mood entirely, away from anger, toward a vertiginously qualified hope. "Are graves" stands out not only for what it means, not only for its long-delayed main verb, but also for the early caesura it makes—early enough to feel odd. By contrast, lines 1–7 and 10–12 constitute grammatically complete noun clauses, and line 8–9 break between a subject and its verb. The caesura (internal pause) within line 14 comes even sooner than the pause in line 13. It comes after just one syllable, "burst," suggesting the shock that a revolution might bring: few people will expect it, until it arrives.

Will it ever arrive? The "glorious phantom," the triumphantly revenant spirit of liberty, may (or may not) "burst" up from this succession of graves; if it does, it will resemble a sun reappearing from behind dense clouds. (For centuries, English radical thinkers—John Milton among them—invoked an "ancient liberty" identified with England before the Norman Conquest, so that any future revolution would also be a reappearance, a rebirth: Shelley's language of resurrection and reappearance suggests this tradition, though faintly.) "Tempestuous day" summarizes the violence of the list that precedes it, but makes clear, too, that the darkness over England is like a stormy day, not a night. It will clear up (if it does clear up) suddenly and unpredictably, rather than as part of any gradual, regular order that nature can bring.

The last couplet feels conclusive, emphatic, as final couplets often do in Shakespearean sonnets. Shelley's form, though, is certainly not Shakespearean: inverted and odd at the outset, it concludes with a couplet and then another couplet, as if the poem—like its England—had lost its balance. To these doubled couplets, Shelley adds doubled metaphors (a phantom from graves, the sun from behind storm clouds). England requires sudden change so urgently that no one image will do.

SB

"Work without Hope"

SAMUEL TAYLOR COLERIDGE

1825

All Nature seems at work. Slugs leave their lair—
The bees are stirring—birds are on the wing—
And Winter slumbering in the open air,
Wears on his smiling face a dream of Spring!
And I the while, the sole unbusy thing,
Nor honey make, nor pair, nor build, nor sing.

Yet well I ken the banks where amaranths blow,
Have traced the fount where streams of nectar flow.
Bloom, o ye amaranths! bloom for whom ye may,
For me ye bloom not! Glide, rich streams, away!
With lips unbrightened, wreathless brow, I stroll:
And would you learn the spells that drowse my soul?
Work without Hope draws nectar in a sieve,
And Hope without an object cannot live.

BY contrast to more songlike forms, the sonnet can seem—did seem, to many poets, for centuries—retrospective, self-conscious, fit for second thoughts. Stanzaic lyric, in this view, suits song and spontaneity; sonnets, instead, suit men and women looking back at their pasts, left out on their own. So it seemed to Henry Howard, Earl of Surrey: one of his sonnets bears the title "Description of Spring, Wherein Each Thing Renews, Save Only the Lover." So it seemed to John Milton, who asked himself (in only the second sonnet he wrote in English) why his twenty-three years seemed unproductive, why "my late spring no bud or blossom shew'th." So it seemed, as well, to the sonnet-writers of the 1780s and 1790s, such as William Bowles, Mary Robinson, and Charlotte Smith. Smith's sonnet "Composed during a Walk on the Downs, in November 1787" concludes that, soon enough,

> propitious spring
> Crowned with fresh flowers shall wake the woodland strain;
> But no gay change revolving seasons bring
> To call forth pleasure from the soul of pain,
> Bid Siren Hope resume her long lost part,
> And chase the vulture Care—that feeds upon the heart.

Coleridge in his own youth admired these sonneteers—especially Bowles—without restraint. In 1796, he printed and sent to his friends a pamphlet of then-recent sonnets (by authors including Seward, Smith, Bowles, and Coleridge himself), designed to show what could be done with the form. This is the pamphlet quoted in our introduction, defining the sonnet as a fourteen-line "poem, in which some lonely feeling is developed." Coleridge wrote few sonnets in his maturity, but he kept on thinking about the form: a note of 1811–1812 pleads "the enormous difficulty" of duplicating Petrarchan rhyme in English. For Coleridge, true sonnets, like all true poems, had to exhibit not strict conformity to preset rules but an organic, lifelike unity, whose felt wholeness provided the reason behind all its parts.

Written in 1825, "Work without Hope" follows that prescription. It follows, as well, the dictates of Coleridge's youth, finding amid the harmonies of spring an irresolvable "lonely feeling," and a poet who cannot quite sing. The fourteen pentameter lines place a sestet first, then follow it with four couplets, as if to shift not from a question to its answer, nor from a problem to its solution, but from an apparent reason for joy to an irresolvable problem, one that leaves the poet lonely still.

The sonnet begins in a garden, with birds, bees, temperate air, even "slugs." Coleridge was probably looking at the garden that adjoined the house where he lived, in Highgate, in suburban London, apart from his long-estranged wife and his adult children, as a permanent guest of the doctor James Gillman and his wife, Ann. Coleridge quarried the sonnet from a longer set of lines preserved in a notebook, apparently addressed to Ann, his "greatest confidante" (so says Coleridge's biographer Richard Holmes), and "the last really close emotional attachment of his life." The notebook lines end, "I lost my

Object and my inmost All / Faith in the Faith of The Alone Most Dear." The sonnet is less biographical, and perhaps less self-involved: it submerges any romantic disappointment into a more general desolation, and a sense of artistic collapse, amid the productivity of early spring.

Coleridge's opening lines, on a first reading, may sound celebratory; reread, they introduce a poem of solitude, or else of sterile age. "All Nature" implies that Coleridge, "sole unbusy thing," does not belong to Nature. He stands apart, unnatural, nearly immobile, while "birds are on the wing." Coleridge then drives the contrast home, concluding his sestet with a volley of verbs that negate every major aspect of human life: he can neither sweeten the lives of others through kindness and friendship ("honey"), nor find erotic fulfillment ("pair"), nor provide security for himself and his family ("build"), nor make successful art ("sing").

Coleridge has not always felt so lost; he says he has known, has "traced," the sources of powers he cannot now wield—though he does not say that those powers were ever his own. Perhaps he has "known" them only as a critic, friend, first reader, and midwife to some other, more confident creator: if we read the lines that way, they allude to William Wordsworth, who collaborated with Coleridge throughout the 1790s on his way to a more productive, and far more self-sufficient, poetic career. Coleridge's verb tenses, in any case, duplicate the contrast, made famous by Wordsworth, between the poet as he is now and the poet in his more spontaneous, confident youth. In typical Coleridgean fashion, the lines promise no recompense—the poet has lost his promise, his own "dream of Spring," and gets, from Nature, nothing in return.

Coleridge turns away from the garden at Highgate (which, in February in London, might well be blooming), toward classical and Miltonic symbolism. Amaranths were the flower of immortality ("fadeless, or never-fading," says Coleridge's own note, "from the Greek *a*, not, and *maraino*, to wither"). These flowers accompany the laurel wreath, given to poets, and "nectar," the drink of the gods. Coleridge, with "lips unbrightened, wreathless brow," once knew such immortal literary beauties —he has seen the Muses' fountain—but he cannot go there now; nor can he raise beauties of his own.

Saying that amaranths would not bloom for him, that he cannot experience spring, Coleridge echoes *Paradise Lost* (3.41–44): "Seasons return, but not to me return / Day, or the sweet approach of ev'n or morn, / Or sight of vernal bloom, or summer rose." Thus Milton described his blindness. Coleridge compares his own passive impotence to Milton's lack of sight—the blind poet could not see, but he could sing. Coleridge may have had in mind, too, the words of his former friend William Hazlitt, who in 1824 wrote that Coleridge would have been "the finest writer of his age," producing "immortal fruits and amaranthine flowers," had he not spent his energies on conversation and on political prose.

The last lines proceed as syllogisms reversed: A (fruitful work) requires B (hope) and B (hope) requires C (an object). If no C, then no B; if no B, then no A. Coleridge is "unbusy," his life and work fruitless, because he has no "object"—neither a task that his art, once made, could accomplish, nor anyone who can fully return his love. "Object" can mean "goal, purpose to be accomplished," and by extension "terminus, place to end"; also "beloved, object of love," as in Coleridge's own poem "Constancy to an Ideal Object." Coleridge lacks an object in every sense. No wonder, then, that the poet and critic, alone in the garden, lacks hope: he kept on working—that is, writing—but without any sense that his labors could come to an end.

With his brief, exclamatory imperatives—"Bloom . . . bloom . . . Glide!"—the poet laments, and flaunts, his apparent impotence, telling Nature to do just what it would do in any case: flowers bloom, and streams flow to the sea, whether or not they have anyone to watch them, and whether or not they benefit us. They will not benefit Coleridge. Why not? By trying (however abstractly) to answer that question, Coleridge ends the poem—or brings it to a point where he cannot bear to go on. His question ("Would you learn . . . ?") casts his readers as surrogate doctors, diagnosing the illness behind the symptoms ("spells") of lassitude and hopelessness ("spells" and "drowse" also suggest his addiction to opium). Having begun in the present tense of description, Coleridge concludes in the timeless present of proverbs, as if to suggest that his hopeless, fruitless situation will not change as long as he lives.

Coleridge's history as a poet is full of self-proclaimed failure, outlined most famously in his "Dejection: An Ode" (1802): failure to achieve the public success of Wordsworth, failure to finish the great works of philosophy, theology, and poetry that for decades he wanted to write. Yet Coleridge's most powerful, most personal poems (as Holmes also remarks) turn the feeling of failure into an aesthetic success. This sonnet stands among them, representing sharply how it felt for Coleridge—and not only for Coleridge—to believe that spring would come, but not for him.

SB

"Swordy Well"

JOHN CLARE

Probably written 1820s; published 1908

I've loved thee Swordy Well, and love thee still.
Long was I with thee tending sheep and cow
In boyhood, ramping up each steepy hill
To play at roly poly down—and now
A man, I trifle on thee, cares to kill,
Haunting thy mossy steeps to botanise
And hunt the orchis tribes: where nature's skill
Doth like my thoughts run into fantasies,
Spider and bee all mimicking at will:
Displaying powers that fools the proudly wise,
Showing the wonders of great nature's plan
In trifles insignificant and small:
Puzzling the power of that great trifle man
Who finds no reason to be proud at all.

CLARE, a self-taught rural laborer, here shows his feeling for home: he affectionately devotes his sonnet to a quarry near his village in Northamptonshire. ("Well" here means pit or excavation: a place of stone rather than water, but still a source of life; "swordy" derives from "sward," a grassy expanse.) He begins with a blunt, heartfelt exclamation: "I've loved thee Swordy Well, and love thee still." In this first line the poet effortlessly joins past and present. But Clare's sonnet will go on to contrast youthful play with grown-up care. He considers the nature of poetry: Does it revive childhood energy, or reflect on the mature status of man in the world? Both young and old in spirit, the unfortunate Clare (who ended his days in a lunatic asylum) praises innocent vigor as well as the contemplation that experience brings. Experience wins out in Clare's poem: by the time he reaches his last line, he has traveled far from childlike joy.

Clare's great precursor in this arena is Wordsworth (born twenty years earlier, and tremendously influential on Clare's work). "I cannot paint/What then I was," Wordsworth writes in "Tintern Abbey"—but he depicts himself as a boy, bounding like a deer among the woods and fields of his old home. After so many years, Wordsworth's childhood can still be recovered in memory. Clare's transition from boyhood to maturity is more abrupt: reflection distracts him, rather than connecting past and present as in Wordsworth. Clare's disconcerting shifts mark his difference from his great precursor, who valued continuity above all. Giving up Wordsworth's desire for mastery, Clare has a greater openness to life, a capacity to be puzzled or even stunned by its twists and turns. This appealing looseness appears in his poem's rhyme scheme, too. The first rhyme pair becomes an unusual chain that spills over into the sestet in giddy fashion, weaving from "still" and "hill" to "kill," "skill," and "will."

"Swordy Well" opens in a pastoral mood, underlined by the poet's boyhood vocation of "tending sheep and cow." (In another poem, "The Lament of Swordy Well," Clare shows his solidarity with nature by speaking for Swordy Well in the first person. There the stone pit denounces the "greedy pack" that "rend and delve and tear/The very grass from off my back," and replace the meadow with ploughed field and barren land.) The young shepherd's care for nature involves not merely work, but high and intense play. Romping joyously, the boy Clare sprints up hills in order to roll down them ("To play at roly poly down"). The silly exuberance of this activity marks its distance from the works of "that great trifle man," considered in Clare's conclusion. The exhilarating childhood game was innocent, played for itself only, undirected to any ulterior end. The older, experienced poet, by contrast, uses nature as therapy, or as a means of escape. "Now/A man, I trifle on thee, cares to kill," he writes. The carefree playing of youth has become a care-killing adult "trifl[ing]." Trifling implies the trivial but self-satisfying character of the mature poet's enterprise. The word shows Clare's winning, somewhat reckless exuberance: "I think to please all & offend all," he wrote to a friend on the publication of his first book. But this trifling, so lighthearted in the octave of "Swordy Well," will take on gravity when it reappears near the end of the poem.

Clare now shifts to the description of an adult form of play, and one that much occupied him: botany. (He discovered hundreds of species of plants in his wanderings through Northamptonshire.) A slight uncanniness, derived

from Wordsworth, surrounds the second quatrain, with its image of the poet
"haunting" Swordy Well's "mossy steeps." The scientist-hunter tracks the "or-
chis tribes," the flowers of his native place. This is no merely sober, analytic
endeavor. Instead, nature's extravagance mirrors and supports the poet's own
imagination. "Skill" naturally inclines toward fantastic imagination, an imagi-
nation shared by the landscape and the rural poet who studies it: "nature's
skill / Doth like my thoughts run into fantasies," Clare writes. The rollicking
zest of the poem's beginning modulates into a quiet admiration directed both
to nature and his own mind, a brown study attentive to marvels.

Clare's sestet delves further into these fantasies, the "mimicking" of "spider
and bee": two creatures with symbolic powers. The spider is the archetypal
intellectual web-weaver, associated with the modern spirit of inquiry (by Fran-
cis Bacon, Jonathan Swift, and others). The bee, by contrast, is a solid archi-
tect, devoted (like the ancients) to constructing his sweet, firmly made cells.
The spider, a solitary, spins its web out of itself; the sociable, productive bee
works in common. The protean Clare here announces his ability to take on
the styles of both spider and bee, "at will." But he is more a spider than a bee.
He inclines toward an oddly dissatisfied, curious stance—one influenced by
the Augustan poets, and above all Alexander Pope, who scrutinized human
presumption. He exults in his ability to demonstrate "powers that fools the
proudly wise / Showing the wonders of great nature's plan." Clare champions
his own talent as a naturalist, and (by implication) as a marginal, rural charac-
ter who gets the better of the "proudly wise," the ones installed at the centers
of power and intellect.

"Great nature's plan" outwits and astonishes the learned, who remain caught
in their vain preoccupations. The plan is the design that permeates and con-
trols all, unveiled by Clare himself, and operative even—especially—in "trifles
insignificant and small." With this phrase, Clare joins in one of the classic ar-
guments for poetry, its ability to portray much in little *(multum in parvo)*.
This small art contains worlds. And in doing so, it matches nature's own pow-
erful miniatures. (In an essay, Clare criticized the "fashionable popularity
[that] changes like the summer clouds, while the simplest trifle, and the mean-
est thing in nature, is the same now as it shall continue to be till the world's
end.") Elsewhere in his poetry, Clare sometimes implies that nature is a self-
sustaining power independent of human perspective; often, he is purely de-
scriptive. In "Swordy Well," however, nature and the poet's consciousness run
parallel to each other. Both are skillful fantasists; and both deal in marvels.

But there is a downward turn at the end. The simple "wonders" of line 11 make up one half of Clare's aim: he relishes nature profoundly, right down to its "trifles." The other half of "Swordy Well," though, is suggested by line 13's "puzzling" (i.e., baffling) —a word that introduces a different sense of "trifle," which now suggests frustrated preoccupation. There is something cryptic and even ominous about the poem's concluding object of study, "that great trifle man." A vague, persistent shadow hovers over Clare's conclusion.

Man remains a riddle. The poet, who early named himself a trifler, must be included here in the object of study. Like Socrates he inquires into his nature, obeying the Delphic dictum "Know thyself"—and "finds no reason to be proud at all." Clare rejects the self-congratulatory ambitions of his fellow men and women, their sin of pride. He shows his own colors: he is a modest, thoughtful, poetic soul, who retains his innocence before nature, and muses on our place in the cosmos. But the diminished note of this sonnet's last line may sound slightly frantic, too. Striking out at all human accomplishment, it reminds us of poor Clare's perplexity, and perhaps even his final fate: he was a man of exultant, appreciative spirit distracted into madness.

DM

"Mysterious Night"

JOSEPH BLANCO WHITE

Written 1827

Mysterious Night! when our first Parent knew
    Thee, from report divine, and heard thy name,
    Did he not tremble for this lovely Frame,
    This glorious canopy of Light and Blue?
Yet 'neath a curtain of translucent dew,
    Bathed in the rays of the great setting Flame,
    Hesperus with the Host of Heaven came,
    And lo! Creation widened in man's view.
Who could have thought such Darkness lay concealed
    Within thy beams, O Sun! or who could find,
    Whilst fly, and leaf, and insect stood revealed,
    That to such countless Orbs thou mad'st us blind!
Why do we then shun Death with anxious strife?
    If Light can thus deceive, wherefore not Life?

BUILT around an analogy to Adam's first night in Eden, White's sonnet ends not in Eden but with us, his imagined listeners, bringing a carefully qualified consolation in matters of faith—and of half-concealed doubt. "Mysterious" means not "spooky," not (or not only) "puzzling," but "hidden from human knowledge or understanding; difficult or impossible to explain" *(OED)*. Night seems mysterious now (it was more so, and for other reasons, to Adam) because it stands for something beyond our rational ken, in the province of religion—in this case, for what happens after we die. White seems to argue by analogy that, just as Adam was mistaken if he feared sunset, we should not "shun," nor even fear, our deaths. The poet speaks at first to personified Night, and then, in the third quatrain, to the Sun. He finally turns to us, to mortal human beings (a category that includes the poet, but not the Sun, Night, or the stars), to ask questions with no clear answers: our very inability to give such answers might lead to a less "anxious" contemplation of our less-than-eternal lives on earth.

The sonnet has the structure of a homily: it begins with a character (though not a scene) from the Bible, and ends with a lesson for us. It proceeds, too, through three scenes, three times of day, corresponding neatly to the three quatrains of White's Shakespearean structure: first, Adam's first day, with "Light and Blue" overhead. Second, evening, when Hesperus (the evening star) accompanies the sunset, shining through "translucent dew," whose droplets, neither transparent nor opaque, appropriately distinguish day from night. Third comes Night itself, when "fly, and leaf, and insect" grow indistinct, and when we see, in more than just compensation, the "countless Orbs" of the separate stars. Astonishing enough when we expect them, the stars must have been a wonder for Adam in Eden, who could not have known, on that first night, what he would see. As spectacular stars succeed the sunset in Eden, one beautiful scene giving place to another, so might the splendor of the afterlife (which we cannot apprehend while we are alive) compensate for the loss, to us, of this world.

The analogy works in other ways too. God (for a believer) created the night, just as (and just when) He created the day (Genesis 1:4–5): the maker of the heavens, with their starry host, is the maker of heaven too. The glories of this earth, however transitory, may "blind" us to the rewards of another life, as the Sun (in this reading almost a Satanic figure) blinds us to the beauty of constellations. For White as for many other poets (Dante Alighieri among them) the "countless" stars become symbols of the unknowable divine order that governs the universe. Read that way, White's sonnet becomes compatible with most varieties of Christian doctrine; so it must have struck the many readers who, throughout the nineteenth century, found beauty and solace there.

And yet, for any form of religious orthodoxy, this sonnet is a sort of trap. If it reminds us that there may be, beyond our earthly lives, greater beauty in heaven, it also concludes by telling us we cannot know. If we give up our anxieties about death, we must do so not upon doctrine or proof, but out of trust in a benevolent creator whose intentions remain mysterious.

How do we know that the sonnet admits such a position—that we are not being anachronistic by finding, in White's poem, both faith and doubt? We cannot know for sure—but we can test the hypothesis against the poet's other writings, and against his remarkable life. Born in Spain in 1775 to a mercantile family of Irish Catholic descent, José María Blanco y Crespo, the future Blanco White ("White White"), grew up bilingual in Spanish and English, and became a Roman Catholic priest—his only alternative to the family business—despite his early doubts about church doctrine. After Napoleon's armies invaded Spain, he wrote on behalf of the insurrectionary, anti-Napoleonic government until it fell; he then, in 1810, fled Spain for England. There, taking permanently the name Blanco White, he became a prolific political and religious journalist, writing about Spain in Spanish and in English, and often attacking the Catholic Church. In 1814 he became an Anglican priest, though his skeptical, searching temperament, and his voluminous reading in theological controversies, led him eventually out of that church as well; in 1835 he became a professed Unitarian. "There is not in my composition a particle of that which can produce . . . unhesitating zeal," he wrote in his autobiography. "This characteristic breaks out in everything I have written: I must 'come and see.'" Blanco White's autobiography describes the evolution of his religious views; it also describes the painful chronic illness that colored his thinking about life and death.

White's accomplishment shows how the sonnet, in the early nineteenth century, remained the occasional form par excellence, the form that suited talented amateurs. White (who also composed verse in Spanish) never published a book of his English poems; instead, he sent his compositions to friends, among them the poets Robert Southey, Felicia Hemans, and Samuel Taylor Coleridge. White sent this sonnet to Coleridge in 1827; in his reply, Coleridge called "Mysterious Night" "the finest and most grandly conceived Sonnet in our language,—(At least, it is only in Milton's and in Wordsworth's Sonnets that I recollect any rival)." Coleridge also sent the sonnet (without asking White) to a magazine, *The Bijou,* which published it in 1828. It would reappear, under several titles ("To Night," "Night and Death"), in many nineteenth-century anthologies, sometimes accompanied by a dedication to Coleridge, or else by editors' effusive praise.

White's earlier sonnet about turning fifty, "On Hearing Myself for the First Time Called an Old Man," had used the equation between death and night in a more predictable, and an unconvincingly consoling, way: "Oh Death, thy gloom / . . . Is to the Christian but a Summer's night." "Mysterious Night" reflects a more unsettling outlook. To see the sonnet in the frame of White's life is to see how well it reflects both belief and doubt; its language and central analogy serve at once reason (which knows where its powers end) and religion—the latter meaning, for White, not a set of articles, but an attitude toward the divine. Shortly before he copied out his final version of "Mysterious night" (the one we print here) in his journals for 1838, White returned in a prose meditation to the subject of that sonnet: "God cannot have formed his intellectual creatures," he wrote, "to break like bubbles, and be no more. To die with implicit trust in Him, but without drawing absurd Pictures of a future life, is the only rational conduct of which the subject admits." So he had already implied in the images, and in the unanswered questions, that make up this long-admired poem.

SB

"To-morrow"

HENRY WADSWORTH LONGFELLOW

1833

Lord, what am I, that, with unceasing care,
    Thou didst seek after me,—that thou didst wait,
    Wet with unhealthy dews, before my gate,
    And pass the gloomy nights of winter there?
O strange delusion!—that I did not greet
    Thy blest approach, and O, to Heaven how lost,
    If my ingratitude's unkindly frost
    Has chilled the bleeding wounds upon thy feet.
How oft my guardian angel gently cried,
    "Soul, from thy casement look, and thou shalt see
    How he persists to knock and wait for thee!"
And, O! how often to that voice of sorrow,
    "To-morrow we will open," I replied,
    And when the morrow came I answered still, "To-morrow."

THE MOST famous American poet of his day, Longfellow remains in American memories a sign of what nineteenth-century readers sought: clarity, uplifting sentiment, consoling versions of traditional forms. Yet although he sometimes provided these desiderata, his adult life had another mission too. By lecturing and teaching (at Bowdoin College and then at Harvard), by writing critical essays and prefaces, and most of all by his adaptations and translations, Longfellow tried to bring "the poets and poetry of Europe" (a phrase that formed the title of an enormous anthology he compiled, in 1845) to American eyes and ears. He translated verse into English from Anglo-Saxon, Icelandic, German, French, Italian, Swedish, and Danish, but he retained particular affection for the poets and poems of Spain, which he visited as a young man—one of few Americans to do so, since, at the time, it was dangerous and impoverished, compared to Germany, northern Italy, or France.

We give here one of the most melodious and most sensitive of Longfellow's many translations, a sonnet from the Spanish of Lope de Vega Carpio (1562–1635; the Spanish original is below). It comes from the first book that Longfellow published, an 1833 collection of verse translated from Spanish, intended partly for classroom use. Longfellow's note in *The Poets and Poetry of Europe* calls Lope "perhaps the most prolific author who ever lived," and one of the most celebrated too: in Golden Age Spain, "his name became a proverbial expression for whatever was most excellent." Lope penned at least five hundred plays, along with improbable quantities of nondramatic verse: epic, mock-epic, literary pastoral, and hundreds of sonnets, sacred and profane, including the 1614 sequence entitled *Rimas sacras* (Sacred Rhymes), from which this sonnet (sometimes given the title "Mañana") comes. The sonnet is one of few by Lope widely known to readers of English verse; Geoffrey Hill made his own harsher, but beautiful, version in *Tenebrae* (1979).

The poem, in Longfellow's English and in the original Spanish, pursues a startling, self-abasing, almost self-canceling piety, scrutinizing—without even attempting to remedy—the poet's deep-seated guilt. George Herbert's "Redemption" (which Lope could not have read, though Longfellow knew it) imagined the poet as a petitioner seeking Christ, and finding him amid the beggars at a Jerusalem gate. Here it is Christ who seeks, incessantly, undiscouraged by human indifference, ignorance, "ingratitude," as a determined traveler might press on through snow. The Son appears as both supplicant and tramp, seeking the unworthy poet, the human sinner, and remaining, in "unhealthy" weather, "before my gate": Christ as the Man of Sorrows, but also Christ as infinitely patient Savior, able to wait for us for as long as it takes.

Lope has "Qué tengo yo"—literally, "What do I have?"—where Longfellow has "Lord, what am I . . . ?" adding an echo of Psalm 8, "What is man that thou art mindful of him?" Longfellow's version of Lope, like Lope's original, implies another question, one familiar to all writers on ethics, ancient and Christian and otherwise: How can we know what is good, what is right, and not do it? How can we see a stranger at our door, "wet with unhealthy dews" and bleeding from his feet, and decide not to take him in? How (as Euripides' Medea says) can I know the better course, but follow the worse? How can we believe that salvation lies in Christ without dedicating our lives, irrevocably and wholly, to His Word? (Lope, though he entered the priesthood, did not lead an especially pious life.) Yet Longfellow's Lope does not ask that question directly; rather, he seems to take for granted that he will never find an adequate answer, never turn toward the good. Why should Christ try to save me, if I will not be saved? What "delusion" explains my ingratitude?

In another sort of text—a sermon—the questions and exclamations of the octave would lead to an exhortation. The speaker might say to himself, or to his audience, that now, at last, we may make ourselves turn toward Christ. The Son waits at our door still; it is not too late to embrace his message, to bind his wounds. (Those "bleeding wounds" come from the nails in the Cross: this wandering Jesus is at once the traveler on his rounds in ancient Palestine, ready to cure ills and exorcise demons, and the lifeless body of the Pietà.)

Yet such exhortation never arrives: the sonnet becomes neither hortatory nor even pious so much as resignedly diagnostic, with no consolation at all. Not only has Jesus, ready to save any sinner, waited through "gloomy nights" outside Lope's gate; Lope has heard an angel (in Longfellow's English, a "guardian angel"), a voice of conscience, telling him daily that Jesus is waiting for him, and yet Lope (that is, the "I" of the sonnet) will not even open his door. "Casement" (for Lope's "ventana," meaning "window") is a Keatsian term (prominent in Keats's "The Eve of St. Agnes," "Ode to Psyche," and "Ode to a Nightingale"), and in Keats it suggests the pleasures of the senses: "A bright torch, and a casement ope at night / To let the warm love in!" ("Ode to Psyche"). For Longfellow, though, this "casement"—if the soul would only let itself look out and down—should instead reveal an ascetic salvation: the beggar, Jesus, who is always at the door.

"Mañana le abriremos," the Spanish says: "To-morrow we will open," a kind of quiet hypocrisy (the tribute that vice pays to virtue) paid again and again each day, as the word "morrow" recurs three times in the last two lines. "Sorrow . . . tomorrow" also stands out as the only polysyllabic rhyme. Longfellow's last line, as it were, procrastinates further by means of its meter: the poem, like many nineteenth-century sonnets (but unlike the original), ends in hexameter. The condition of knowing the better but doing the worse, of postponing indefinitely, over and over, what action religion or ethics absolutely require—this is, for Longfellow's Lope, the human condition. It is what "we" all do, without knowing why.

"To-morrow and to-morrow and to-morrow"—the triple "morrow" on which Longfellow concludes—has a Shakespearean resonance as well: it recalls Macbeth's despairing speech, in which "all our yesterdays have lighted fools / The way to dusty death." Lope's repeated "tomorrow" ("mañana") has its own ancient source: as the Spanish critic José Manuel Blecua has pointed out, Saint

Augustine in the *Confessions* asks why he once said to himself, "Tomorrow, tomorrow? Why not today? Why do I not end my turpitude this very hour?" Lope also wrote a poem (not a sonnet) in the voice of Saint Augustine speaking to God. We may read the sonnet as Lope's own self-condemnation: he asks why *he* in particular keeps putting off, and putting off, the moment of reckoning, in which he may accept Christ. We may also, though, read it as condemning us all. Indeed, the first-person plural in the sestet, after the first-person singular of the octave, almost requires that "we" condemn ourselves—we sinners, we who dwell uneasily along with our guardian angels and our own souls. ("We" also means, here, "my soul and I.") Lope's memorable sonnet diagnoses as spiritually flawed, perhaps even (we do not know yet) beyond repair, all of us who procrastinate first and last things, all who postpone matters of spirit or obligation, never knowing—as none of us knows—when it will be too late.

SB

Rimas Sacras 18

LOPE DE VEGA

¿Qué tengo yo que mi amistad procuras?
¿Qué interés se te sigue, Jesús mío,
que a mi puerta, cubierto de rocío,
pasas las noches del invierno escuras?

¡Oh, cuánto fueron mis entrañas duras,
pues no te abrí! ¡Qué estraño desvarío
si de mi ingratitud el yelo frío
secó las llagas de tus plantas puras!

¡Cuántas veces el ángel me decía:
"Alma, asómate agora a la ventana,
verás con cuánto amor llamar porfía!"

¡Y cuántas, hermosura soberana:
"Mañana le abriremos"—respondía—,
para lo mismo responder mañana!

"The Fish, the Man, and the Spirit"

LEIGH HUNT

1836

To a Fish

You strange, astonish'd-looking, angle-faced,
    Dreary-mouth'd, gaping wretches of the sea,
    Gulping salt-water everlastingly,
Cold-blooded, though with red your blood be graced,
And mute, though dwellers in the roaring waste;
    And you, all shapes beside, that fishy be,—
    Some round, some flat, some long, all devilry,
Legless, unloving, infamously chaste:—

O scaly, slippery, wet, swift, staring wights,
    What is't ye do? what life lead? eh, dull goggles?
How do ye vary your vile days and nights?
    How pass your Sundays? Are ye still but joggles
In ceaseless wash? Still nought but gapes, and bites,
    And drinks, and stares, diversified with boggles?

A Fish Answers

Amazing monster! that, for aught I know,
    With the first sight of thee didst make our race
    Forever stare! Oh flat and shocking face,
Grimly divided from the breast below!
Thou that on dry land horribly dost go
    With a split body and most ridiculous pace,
    Prong after prong, disgracer of all grace,
Long-useless-finn'd, hair'd, upright, unwet, slow!

O breather of unbreathable, sword-sharp air,
   How canst exist? How bear thyself, thou dry
And dreary sloth? What particle canst share
   Of the only blessed life, the watery?
I sometimes see of ye an actual *pair*
   Go by! linked fin by fin! most odiously.

The Fish Turns into a Man and into a Spirit and Again Speaks

Indulge thy smiling scorn, if smiling still,
   O man! and loathe, but with a sort of love:
   For difference must its use by difference prove,
And, in sweet clang, the spheres with music fill.
One of the spirits am I, that at his will
   Live in whate'er has life—fish, eagle, dove—
   No hate, no pride, beneath nought, nor above,
A visitor of the rounds of God's sweet skill.

Man's life is warm, glad, sad, 'twixt loves and graves,
   Boundless in hope, honor'd with pangs austere,
Heaven-gazing; and his angel-wings he craves:—
   The fish is swift, small-needing, vague yet clear,
A cold, sweet, silver life, wrapped in round waves,
   Quickened with touches of transporting fear.

THE nineteenth century in England (especially its middle decades) was a fine time for light verse: some poets wrote, or wrote well, almost nothing else. Yet the great trove of Regency and Victorian light verse holds surprisingly few examples of the sonnet, which remained an implicitly serious form. Fortunately that rule permitted exceptions. Here we present a trio of linked sonnets by Leigh Hunt, the prolific belletrist, political writer, newspaper editor, and critic, remembered now as a mentor to John Keats. We give three sonnets by just one other poet, Shakespeare. Nobody thinks Hunt as good a poet as Shakespeare or Keats, but almost everyone who reads Hunt at all admires his congenial wit, his affable temper, and his jokes—which, like most jokes, need time to set up. Those jokes—and the lightness of tone they permit—let Hunt close his triptych with both a serious judgment in favor of "difference," forbearance, and tolerance, and a gently mocking glance at large theological and scientific debates.

The first, and most purely comic, sonnet comprises apparently unmotivated insults delivered, by a man, "To a Fish." Fish may look "strange," to a man, compared to men, but not as strange as a man who lets loose with fourteen lines of invective against perch and trout. The improbable tide of insults throughout the octave—none resolved into a completed sentence or question—rushes along into a sestet that simply repeats the tone and the goals of that octave, though with a new syntax. Hunt's Man now asks grammatically complete questions, at a fast and ridiculously angry clip, the comedy heightened by polysyllabic rhymes. "Wash" means water. "Boggles" are botches, messes, bad situations; "joggles," slight movements from side to side; and "goggles," wide-eyed stares, as from a fish's eyes. All three words would have sounded as odd in a poem in 1836 as they sound now. The comedy throughout the sonnet comes from a flagrant disproportion between tone and topic (no one really gets that angry at fish), but also from a glimmer of recognition. We know that it would be frustrating (not to mention impossible) for us to lead a piscine existence—deprived of sex, "cold-blooded," helpless, monotonous, lonely in crowds (or schools), dependent on frequent drinking, never at rest—and yet, described that way, the lives of fish may sound uncomfortably like our own.

Having permitted a man to insult a fish, Hunt now lets a fish sass back at a man. "The laughter occasioned by wit," Hunt wrote in 1844, arises from "a sudden and agreeable perception of the incongruous"; we may see incongruity in a talking fish, but the fish himself sees it in people, who—amazingly, distressingly—walk upright, holding hands. This second sonnet includes, as the first did not, a bevy of evaluative adjectives ("amazing," "horrible," "ridiculous," "blessed") and adverbs ("horribly," "odiously"), as if to underline the implication that what we approve, or disapprove, depends on what we know and on how we live: the fish's perspective seems no more absurd than the man's. If a fish seems to stare at us ("goggles"), the fault lies with us: human beings (the fish says) are so ugly and so strange that when fish see us, they cannot look away.

Hunt has had it both ways, so to speak, allowing the fish to speak in language no different from our own in order to show how completely fish differ

from us. This oxymoronic effect, fit for broad comedy, finds a serious expla-
nation in metempsychosis: the same "spirits" can inhabit us all, can "Live in
whate'er has life"—people, eagles, perch, trout. The particular spirit who
speaks the third sonnet has been the fish of the second, and speaks master-
fully, almost philosophically, to correct the attitude of the man who spoke the
first. Had the man once been a fish—so the spirit implies—he would under-
stand why trout enjoy being trout. (The same might be true, Hunt implies,
for Scots and Englishmen, rural folk and city dwellers, women and men.) To
see life widely (not only human life) is to give up "hate," "pride," and "scorn":
to see man and fish together is to see the fitness, the appropriateness, in the
life proper to each.

It is to see the benefits of humor as well. "Indulge thy *smiling* scorn, if *smil-
ing* still," says spirit to man, repeating a key word: anger and scorn and resent-
ment, the negative emotions we saw at length in man and in fish, become
tolerable, worth indulging, if and only if allied to humor, which discourages
open conflict and improves our mood. "Quickened" means "given life" (fe-
tuses "quicken" when they move in the womb), but also "made to speed up,"
as are fish that escape predators (including human anglers). Fish, Hunt's spirit
implies, have feelings too, and may be more like us than we think, even as we
learn not to despise their "difference" from us. As the contemporary poet Al-
bert Goldbarth (himself a master of comic verse) has pointed out, Hunt seems
to anticipate modern environmental thinking, in which fish, however "small-
needing," have moral claims on us. Hunt makes that sort of thinking appeal-
ing by making it funny, too.

Hunt also recalls debates, alive in his own time, about how and whether
"man" might be just one more animal. Charles Darwin's *On the Origin of Spe-
cies* would not appear until 1859, but Charles's grandfather Erasmus had writ-
ten verse on the origin of animal species as early as 1803: "Allied to fish, the
lizard cleaves the flood / With one-celled heart, and dark frigescent blood."
Writing in his own newspaper, the *London Journal,* in May 1834, Hunt re-
viewed Georges Cuvier's controversial *Théorie de la terre* (Theory of the Earth;
1821), newly translated from the French. Cuvier's work, an important anteced-
ent to Darwin's, explained the stark differences between fossils and living spe-
cies through a series of catastrophic extinctions, or floods; Hunt's review sum-
marized earlier accounts of the origins of life on earth. According to one such
account, by William Whiston, "the heat which remained from [the earth's]
first origin . . . excited the whole antediluvian population, men and animals,
to sin, for which they were all drowned in the deluge, excepting the fish,

whose passions were apparently less violent." Hunt also said that in another early account, by Benoît Demaillet (or de Maillet), "man himself began his career as a fish; and he asserts that it is not uncommon, even now, to meet with fishes in the ocean, which are still only half men, but whose descendents will in time become perfect human beings."

English Christian thinkers in Hunt's time sought evidence of providence through creation, as in the weighty Bridgewater Treatises of the 1830s; most denied that one species could change into others, since each retained its own, God-given place. Both proponents and opponents of "evolution" asked, about fossils and people, about types of fishes and doves and rocks, "How canst exist?" Though Hunt was allied with atheists (such as Percy Bysshe Shelley) in his youth, he here acknowledges God's disposition, and mankind's hopes of heaven, as determinants of human action—even as he gives equal attention to fish. People and fish, in Hunt's poem, have the same kind of "spirit"—both are animals (like the eagle and dove) whose opposite habits and tastes belie their common origin in divine creation, every part of which adduces "God's sweet skill." The deduction of divine order from earthly evidence—the "research" into divinity by what we now call geology and biology—had in Hunt's day the name "natural theology." It was a topic on all educated tongues, and Hunt's three sonnets parody that enterprise, even as they also endorse its aims.

The evolutionary controversies of the nineteenth century do not ride on the surfaces of Hunt's polished sonnets, but instead lie behind them. Those controversies might have made the sonnets look, to contemporary readers, like lighthearted reactions to the weightiest, most troubling, theological and scientific debates of the era. Whether or not we set Hunt's sonnet amid those debates, we might see how his wit encourages us to take the claims of animals seriously, to remember that tastes grow from circumstances, and to notice how much even human tastes differ. Before and after that lesson in tolerance, Hunt supplies rare delights: goggles and boggles and joggles, the unlikely adjuration "loathe, but with a sort of love," the fish's revulsion at human beings, who dare to stand still (why would they?), who go about linked (how *could* they?) "fin by fin."

SB

"The Columbine"

JONES VERY

1839

Still, still my eye will gaze long fixed on thee,
Till I forget that I am called a man,
And at thy side fast-rooted seem to be,
And the breeze comes my cheek with thine to fan.
Upon this craggy hill our life shall pass,—
A life of summer days and summer joys,—
Nodding our honey-bells mid pliant grass
In which the bee half hid his time employs;
And here we'll drink with thirsty pores the rain,
And turn dew-sprinkled to the rising sun,
And look when in the flaming west again
His orb across the heaven its path has run;
Here left in darkness on the rocky steep,
My weary eyes shall close like folding flowers in sleep.

JONES VERY, born in Salem, Massachusetts, in 1813, was the son of a sea cap-
tain. During his senior year at Harvard, he began to hear the voice of God. In
response to this stark inspiration, he produced a flood of poetry, mostly son-
nets, beginning in 1838 (when he was briefly confined in McLean's asylum,
near Boston). Before his breakdown, he wrote hearty drinking chants; after it,
songs of innocence. The born-again Very was a religious enthusiast whose in-
tensity sometimes frightened his friends; but they also noted his gentle, mod-
est character. His poems, full of an assured contemplative mood, demonstrate
this gentleness.

"The Columbine" is a meditative, quietly ecstatic lyric, in the tradition of
the seventeenth-century poet Henry Vaughan. Very's subject, the columbine,

is a small flower. Its petals make a bell shape, with long nectar spurs in the center. In European folklore the columbine was sacred to Venus; its name derives from the Latin *columba,* "dove" (the bird of peace). Symbolizing peace and love, the flower provides a shelter, a calm enfolding influence: here the poet can reside.

Very's sonnet begins with the hypnotic repetition "Still, still": the poet creates a soothing spell. He looks with fixed, receptive eye at the columbine, and addresses it in the second person. Entranced by his encounter, he moves, without resistance, toward union with nature.

In his first quatrain, Very aims for loss of the distinctions that language imposes between the human and nonhuman parts of God's creation ("till I forget that I am called a man"). Obliviousness and illumination prove near allied. Note the disoriented, deliberately strange phrase "I am called a man": all such definitions, the customary ways of social speech, will fade under the spell of Very's wholehearted gaze. Like Wordsworth, whose heart "dances with the daffodils" (in his famous lyric "I Wandered Lonely as a Cloud"), Very wants an accomplished innocence. Here he goes beyond Wordsworth, picturing himself metamorphosed into flowerlike stasis (as in Ovid's *Metamorphoses,* which features a series of humans transformed into plants and animals). Guided by grace, he becomes part of what he calls, in another sonnet ("The Garden"), a "glorious whole." Finally, it seems that the only way for Very to achieve the serene harmony he desires is to cease to be a man, and become a flower.

The poet's simple approach embodies a delicate ambiguity: in lines 3 and 4, the flower is both "fast-rooted" and fanned by the breeze. The columbine participates both in nature's firmly planted aspect and in its gently wavering, "pliant" character. Very's "summer days" provide a carefree life, relaxed and dependent on "summer joys." His landscape is a realm of inspired loafing, free from the pressures of worldly occupation.

Line 7 depicts the "nodding" of the "honey-bells" (that is, blossoms), an action performed by poet and flower, side by side (even cheek to cheek—see line 4). The nodding is both a quiet assent and a mark of sweet somnolence. As in the first quatrain, forgetfulness harmonizes with concentration. The friendly, open character of the flower and of its blossoming friend, the poet, stands in contrast to the legendarily busy bee, who "half hid his time employs." In Andrew Marvell's "The Garden," a source for Very's poem, "th'industrious bee / Computes its time as well as we." In Very's garden, unlike Marvell's, life is timeless and cheerfully passive, with the bee's industry hidden away. The word "employs" looms as a mild threat, deflected by the protective enclosure of the honey-bell (the columbine's concentric petals).

The poet begins his sestet with a calm litany of *and*'s at the beginning of each line. He offers a plan of action, but action in the form of observation and enjoyment rather than physical activity (such activity is happily impossible for the flower, of course). "Thirsty" and eager, Very and his companion the columbine imbibe the rain; anointed with the dew (a sign of God's grace) they face the sun at dawn. Then, with the course of the day itself elided in dream-like fashion, they will watch it set in "the flaming west": a resplendent image, and the only time this sonnet comes close to fierceness. The interwoven rhyme words of this third quatrain, with the two rhymes so close to each other in sound ("rain"/"again"; "sun"/"run"), bind Very's image of the day together. The sun, running its race, scarcely seems to work at all. The day is over before one knows it.

The poet's concluding couplet suggests the thought of death: the end of life, as sunset and darkness are the end of day. Strangely, comfort and abandonment here seem to be blended into one. The poet is "left in darkness on the rocky steep"—an image that appears, for a moment, threatening. But the threat dissipates. The vowel sound of "steep" is echoed in "weary" and then, finally, in "sleep": an envelope structure that supports the speaker, guiding him toward a soft, sufficient end. The repeated, cooing *oh*-sounds of the last line's "close like folding flowers" reassure poet and reader, lulling us toward sleep. But there is nothing siren-like or drowsily magical about this conclusion: it speaks sober and wholehearted. In "The Columbine" Very takes his nourishment from a clarified, blessed universe, and invites us to share his faith.

                                                                        DM

"Written in Emerson's Essays"

MATTHEW ARNOLD

Written 1844; published 1849

"O monstrous, dead, unprofitable world,
That thou canst hear, and hearing hold thy way!
A voice oracular hath pealed today,
To-day a hero's banner is unfurled;

"Hast thou no lip for welcome?"—So I said.
Man after man, the world smiled and passed by;
A smile of wistful incredulity
As though one spake of life unto the dead—

Scornful and strange, and sorrowful, and full
Of bitter knowledge. Yet the will is free;
Strong is the soul, and wise, and beautiful;

The seeds of godlike power are in us still;
Gods are we, bards, saints, heroes, if we will!—
Dumb judges, answer, truth or mockery?

DESCRIBING the young Arnold's first encounter with the writings of Ralph Waldo Emerson, this sonnet portrays at once the powers that Arnold found in those writings, and his frustration at realizing how little his contemporaries cared about the literary efforts he loved. Those powers would remain an object of admiration for Arnold throughout his long, successful career as a literary and cultural critic; that frustration would help to make him the critic he became. Arnold's best short poems ("Shakespeare," "To Homer," "To a Friend") show his unsurpassed capacity for emotional response, not to people he met or to scenes he viewed, but to the books and authors he had read. This lesser-known sonnet makes a superb example. With its self-reproach, its "bitter" turn, and its unanswerable conclusion, these lines also point up the difference between a writer like Emerson (as Arnold saw him) and a poet and critic like Arnold: the first an indefatigable and self-reliant creator (the author of the essay "Self-Reliance"), the second a writer attentive, despite his own wishes, to what his contemporaries believed.

Lecturing in America in 1884, Arnold remembered how eagerly he and his friends read Emerson "forty years ago, when I was an undergraduate at Oxford." Emerson remains for the mature Arnold what he had been to the student: "a friend and aider of those who would live in the spirit," a bringer of "inexhaustible . . . hope." "By his conviction that in the life of the spirit is happiness," Arnold continues, "and by his hope that this life of the spirit will come more and more to be sanely understood, and to prevail . . . by this conviction and hope Emerson was great." But will that hope bear fruit? Can we truly live "the life of the spirit" (as Emerson encourages us to do) when our contemporaries seem not to care, when they discount whatever we come to love? Can we find hope—as artists, as readers, as citizens—in our own times? These questions—an undercurrent in Arnold's lecture—animate his earlier, more painful, poem.

Arnold's title lets us imagine the poem as an impromptu, started and finished on the same book's flyleaf. In fact, the poem went through multiple drafts, as Arnold tried to do justice to the effects that Emerson's writings provoked in him, if not (alas) in other, older Britons. The strongest effect was cheer: the second-strongest, for the self-skeptical Arnold, was disbelief. He begins with an ardent echo of Hamlet, who calls the world (in his first soliloquy) "weary, stale, flat and unprofitable." That world—by which Arnold means human society (the social world, not the world of nature)—must be "monstrous" indeed, must have lost track of its own best nature, if it remains unaffected by such a strong writer as Emerson. Arnold envisions him as a prophet, even a conqueror: Emerson deserves (but does not get) his own public, triumphal parade.

Like many young readers, Arnold has trouble believing, or even understanding, that most people (even most serious readers of literature) might not feel as he does about his favorite books. The second quatrain pans out from the agitated Arnold to that indifferent crowd. "Man after man, the world" has ignored Emerson, as if that "world" were a larger, duller parade, moving obliviously in the wrong direction. To speak of Emerson's individualism and his inward fire to a business-minded, disillusioned society is as fruitless as making a speech to a corpse.

Frustration with Britain's lack of aesthetic attention, its lack of interest in things of the spirit, would characterize Arnold's entire career. He would decry that lack, later, as "Philistinism," a word he made popular (though not a word he coined). Here the crowd may be Philistines, or (more darkly) people who know better than this young man, who have outlived the excitements of their own youth: they, not he, stand "full / Of bitter knowledge." Grammatically, the smilers in the crowd (the people who might as well be dead) must be the people expressing sorrow and scorn, but the string of adjectives gravitates, too, toward the speaker (a device that students of classical poetry call a transferred epithet). It is as if the poet has projected his own sorrow onto them, or does not want to admit that he feels sad himself. (Echoes of Emerson's own poem "Days" are a felicitous coincidence: Emerson had not yet written it.)

We then see Arnold trying to look away, to follow the advice he found in Emerson, who recommended in "Experience" (part of the book that the young Arnold probably read), "Trust thyself! Every heart vibrates to that iron string. Accept the place the Divine Providence has found for you. . . . Great men have always done so." (Arnold would quote just those sentences in 1884.) Concentrating on Emerson's individualistic prescriptions, the sonnet overlooks—as Arnold's later lecture also overlooks—the tragic sense also present in "Experience"; Arnold celebrated in the American writer only what Arnold had not found in the literature of the European past.

They are prescriptions the young Arnold could not quite take. Seven of Arnold's fourteen lines are independent clauses; four within the sestet (from "Yet the will is free" to "if we will!") are hortatory admonitions that conclude cleanly at the end of a line. These phrases seem meant to lift spirits, and to make themselves (by lifting our spirits) more nearly true. In Emerson's prose, such sentences come thick and fast. In Arnold—and here is this sonnet's emotional force—they instead sound like the young poet's not-quite-successful attempts to cheer himself up. The future critic, the devoted reader, cannot bring himself to stand so wholly apart from other readers, from other books, and from his own society, as his Emerson would have him do.

"The will is free," Arnold says, to escape its own or other people's "bitter knowledge"; he then renames it—not the "will" but the "soul." When the word "will" reappears, it has become a verb: we have only to "will" it, to make an emphatic decision, and we will become "gods," or at least "bards, saints, heroes." But the anticlimactic order of nouns is a giveaway, undermining the claim that Arnold has tried to make. The line begins with the most powerful, and the farthest from human society, of its categories ("Gods"), then moves through literature and religion to worldly (political or military) success. Perhaps we cannot become gods. Bards, then? At least heroes? But perhaps not even that.

Arnold ends on a question whose answer we might not want to know. Are these exhortations—"The seeds of godlike power are in us still," for example—"truth or mockery?" An entirely Emersonian reader might say that I am the best and only judge: only I can determine what seeds lie in my soul. But Arnold cannot make himself believe it. He turns therefore, characteristically, to an undefined authority, to "judges" outside himself, without telling us who those judges are. An earlier draft of the sonnet concluded, bathetically, "O barren boast, o joyless Mockery." Arnold's final version instead locates judgment in other people, beyond the poet's own "soul." At worst, these judges are the contemporary readers who "smiled and passed by," dead to the hope the American thinker offers. At best, they are imaginary gods (who stand outside time) or future readers (an idealized posterity) who might give the human spirit, and the writing that embodies it, the esteem that they deserve. Either way, though, these judges are now "dumb" (meaning not "dimwitted," but "mute"): they will not endorse, or echo, and may not hear, the trumpet blast Arnold gave on behalf of Emerson thirteen long lines ago.

Such nonresponse is—maddeningly, for a born critic such as Arnold—what really new literature almost always receives, a silence sometimes indistinguishable from "mockery." A poet whose soul is, as W. B. Yeats would later put it, "self-delighting, / Self-appeasing, self-affrighting"—who is, or feels, entirely self-reliant—can go on working in spite of that lack of response, can simply ignore whatever "the world" believes. But a literary and cultural critic, practicing an applied art, attempting almost by definition to change other people's minds, must live with the dual vision that Arnold, in this poem of his youth, already displays: he cannot ignore, on the one hand, what he discovers for himself, in books, nor, on the other hand, can he cease to care what other people already think. That dual vision comes out in the unanswerable question—it might be better to call it a protest, a cry—with which Arnold concludes his poignant early poem.

SB

Sonnets from the Portuguese 28

ELIZABETH BARRETT BROWNING

1850

My letters! all dead paper, mute and white!
And yet they seem alive and quivering
Against my tremulous hands which loose the string
And let them drop down on my knee to-night.
This said,—he wished to have me in his sight
Once, as a friend: this fixed a day in spring
To come and touch my hand . . . a simple thing,
Yet I wept for it!—this, . . . the paper's light . . .
Said, *Dear, I love thee:* and I sank and quailed
As if God's future thundered on my past.
This said, *I am thine*—and so its ink has paled
With lying at my heart that beat too fast.
And this . . . O Love, thy words have ill availed
If, what this said, I dared repeat at last!

ELIZABETH BARRETT BROWNING's exciting and excited sonnet takes part in the centuries-old tradition of amorous sonnets and sonnet sequences (as old as the sonnet form, as Dante and Petrarch), but also draws on the new Victorian kind of poem called the dramatic monologue, which her husband Robert Browning helped to invent. In dramatic monologue a single character's speech, depicted in real time, reveals by irony or indirection that character's inmost thoughts, and makes him or her seem present, as if on stage. In dramatic monologue, however, the speaker is never the poet herself. Here, we must identify the vivid, distractable lover who speaks as Elizabeth Barrett Browning—indeed, we can set the poem beside what we know of her life.

That life involves one of the great love stories in literary history. Well-known as a poet by the early 1840s, Elizabeth Barrett lived as an invalid in the London house of her strict father, who supported her writing but did not want her, nor her siblings, ever to marry. Robert Browning, five years younger and much less successful, admired her poetry, as she admired his. They exchanged letters, he paid her weekly visits, and their literary friendship soon became something stronger: "I love your verse with all my heart, dear Miss Barrett," he wrote in January 1845, "and I love you too." Despite her illness, the pair made plans to elope and live in Italy: in September 1846 those plans were fulfilled. (The Brownings would live there together until her death in 1861; they had one son.)

Over the twenty months of their clandestine courtship, Elizabeth and Robert wrote each other almost six hundred letters, most of which were published after her death. In those same months, Elizabeth also began a series of sonnets about their courtship, shown to Robert only after their elopement, and published in 1850 under the title *Sonnets from the Portuguese*. The Portuguese poet Luís de Camoëns was famous for his love sonnets; Barrett Browning's title referred, as well, to her earlier poem "Caterina to Camoens," one of Robert's favorites. The title also allowed the pretense—albeit a flimsy one—that the sonnets were merely translations, with no basis in the poets' lives. Parts of the sequence, if not the whole, remain popular today, especially the penultimate sonnet, which begins, "How do I love thee? Let me count the ways."

We chose Sonnet 28 in part for its distance from that one. "How do I love thee?" seems to take place outside space and time; it takes the Brownings' love as already mutual, already confirmed, and perhaps already eternal, concluding, "if God choose, / I shall but love thee better after death." Sonnet 28, by contrast, takes place on earth, at a particular time in the midst of their courtship, and in a particular space. Elizabeth presents herself alone and indoors, overcome with joy at the written evidence (still new, or as good as new) that her beloved hopes for their union too. Having bound Robert's letters together with string (to hide them, or to keep them in chronological order) she unbinds and rereads them as if to stave off disbelief: his love still seems too good to be true.

Like other Victorian poets—and as skillfully as any—Barrett Browning puts to lyric, expressive purpose the devices of the realist novel and of the theater, with "stage directions" (she picks up the letters, she drops them) and "props." On those devices the dramatic monologue depends. We seem not only to hear, but to see, the character who speaks these lines, almost as that character (i.e., Elizabeth) comes to envision Robert before her: the lines end in outbursts, impassioned and impromptu. Midline interruptions, repeated demonstratives ("This . . . This . . . And this"), and asides ("the paper's light") help to create the sense that we are there in her room.

Barrett Browning also musters bodily senses—sight, touch, hearing, temperature, kinesthesia, even pulse rate—to make the scene as vivid as she can. The sonnet begins with touch—her hands keep trembling, adjusting themselves to the papers' slight weight. We then find the word "sight," the memory of the first time she saw him in person, and then again "touch" and "hand." The turn after line 8, introducing a new set of rhymes, introduces the sense of sound as well: Barrett Browning remembers a heartbeat that felt like "thunder," then a "heart that beat too fast." She introduces, finally, her entire body (not just the octave's "hand" and "knee"): Robert's epistolary declarations have affected her whole frame ("I sank and quailed").

Sonnets from the Portuguese seems to have been the first English sonnet sequence since Edmund Spenser's *Amoretti* (1595) whose courtship concluded in marital union. As the scholar Natasha Distiller writes, Barrett Browning depicts herself "coming to terms with having love, not . . . with wanting love." She finds those terms, but not without inner turmoil, not without self-doubt, not without surprise. The paper letters Barrett Browning rereads in this sonnet become evidence, shocking evidence, of love returned—not only words to that effect but also physical evidence, objects, tokens: the words, and the physical letters, grow more and more "alive" in the course of the sonnet, as the poet remembers how it felt to read them. The letter that said "I am thine" has grown almost faint because she has been clutching it to her chest, or secretly wearing it, as lovers wear tokens and lockets: she has kept it as close to her heart as she could.

Barrett Browning's sonnet takes pains to distinguish itself, and love poetry generally, from the love letters, the personal letters, described and reread by the character within the poem. We do not read, in Elizabeth's sonnet, the words that came to her in the letters that Robert wrote. Instead, for most of the sonnet, we read their paraphrase, and we see how his words worked on her. Then, in her last exclamation, as she turns to him—just when the love letters seem most animated, most committed to their future union—even paraphrase disappears. Barrett Browning shows just how intimate, and how important, the correspondence between the two poets felt by telling us that she cannot reveal what it said.

By withholding whatever that last letter meant—and by addressing Robert as she does so ("O Love")—Barrett Browning makes a brilliant joke, a partly flirtatious ending to a nonetheless serious sonnet: she declares herself unable to finish the poem while making that declaration itself an emphatic conclusion. This sonnet so attentive to the body's various senses, and to sound (the sounds of speech, the "thunder" of a quickened pulse), falls suddenly silent. This love poem about love letters thus speaks to the gulf between the two forms—the latter private, literal, meant for one reader alone; the former, because it is poetry, "departicularized" (to use the poet Allen Grossman's term), drawing on knowable conventions, able to move people the author will never meet. Anything meant for a lover's eyes alone may remain in a love letter, but has to be subtracted from love poems, as Barrett Browning subtracts the last memory here.

Sonnet sequences from Petrarch forward have portrayed the progress, or regress, or romantic love; they have also depicted human interiority, finding and displaying the language of the inmost self. In sequences that describe unrequited love—such as Petrarch's, or Sir Philip Sidney's—there need be no contradiction between these two goals. The poet sets down on paper, for himself and later for others, the record of what he feels, how he feels, alone.

In a successful courtship, on the other hand, the two goals sooner or later collide: if my heart belongs to you and you alone, it cannot wholly belong on the printed or circulated page. William Empson thus decided that "the better the marriage, the less you can write about it": the already-married couple are "presumed to be combined against the world." Barrett Browning describes not a marriage, but a successful courtship, and she does so here by showing, first, its moments of excitement, and then its disappearance from view. As they find, embrace, and fulfill promises to each other, the paired lovers finally move away from the conventions and from the literary traditions that make romantic love, and the poems that describe it, intelligible to an audience beyond the lovers themselves. In doing so, she brings together Victorian and Renaissance conventions, the sonnet sequence with its hearts revealed and the dramatic monologue with its sets, its props, its demonstratives, its aural immediacy. She shows how these lovers came to know each other through the written word, and how their words became at last too intimate for further exposure—even in paraphrase, and even in poems.

SB

Sonnets, Third Series 6

FREDERICK GODDARD TUCKERMAN

Written before 1873; published 1931

I look'd across the rollers of the deep,
Long land-swells, ropes of weed, & riding foam,
With bitter angry heart: did I not roam
Ever like these? and what availeth sleep?
Or wakefulness? or pain? and still the sea
Rustled and sang, "Alike! and one to me!"
Ay! once I trod these shores too happily,
Murmuring my gladness to the rocks and ground;
And while the wave broke loud on ledge and reef,
Whisper'd it in the pause: like one who tells
His heart's dream & delight! and still the sea
Went back & forth upon its bar of shells,
Wash'd & withdrew, with a soft shaling sound,
As though the wet were dry, and joy were grief.

THIS POEM of dramatic, persistent, wracked grief pays close attention to the shore it describes. It is a nature poem, in the sense that Tuckerman records the beach, the waves, the minutiae of nonhuman nature, and yet it sets the poet against nature, against the great forces that cannot change how he must feel.

Tuckerman was one of few gifted poets of the American nineteenth century neglected both in his lifetime and in our own day. He studied at Harvard with Jones Very (author of "The Columbine," in our collection), joined the literary society of Boston, traveled to Britain in 1855 to spend several happy days with his literary model Alfred, Lord Tennyson, and spent the rest of his years in relative seclusion in western Massachusetts. There, in 1857, his wife, Hannah, died of complications during the birth of their third child. Tuckerman's

five sets, or "series," of sonnets, most of them addressing his grief for her, con-
stitute his major literary achievement. Tuckerman collected the first two series
in his only book, printed in 1860 and sent to friends; series 3, 4 and 5 saw print
only decades after he died. (We give this sonnet as it appeared in manuscript.)

Like an explorer who brings his best, imported, instruments, Tuckerman
used his transatlantic formal repertoire to describe the fauna, flora, and physi-
cal geography of New England and New York, and the blasted landscapes of
his own interior life. Few of Tuckerman's sonnets use the same rhyme scheme,
yet most sound fluent, and very few sound forced; none of his sonnet-writing
American coevals—and there were many—managed anything like his bra-
vura technique. He usually portrays himself alone, wandering over beaches or
woodlands; he is, in his wanderings, resolutely nostalgic, driven to sonnets
and to solitude by the loss of the woman he loved. Divided in his relation
to society, a solitary who wishes he were otherwise, Tuckerman also shows a
divided relation to nature. On the one hand, he cannot help depicting the
emotions that his mountains, seasides, and stormy skies suggest. On the other
hand, he knows that nonhuman nature does not feel as we do, that any emo-
tions we discover in landscapes and seascapes are the emotions we put there.

The poet begins and ends with onomatopoeia—direct imitation, in lan-
guage, of nonlinguistic actions and sounds. Liquids, rhotics, and sibilants
("soft" consonants: five *l*s, four *r*'s, five *s* sounds) pursue the rolling waters of
the first two lines. Onomatopoeia returns when the ocean's sounds do: break-
ers echo in the consonance of "loud . . . ledge," and again in the final passage,
with six *w* sounds in two lines. "Rollers" are rolling waves; "land-swells" are
likely the moving shapes on the sea surface that the shape of the coastline, af-
fecting the waves, creates. Tuckerman almost certainly describes the Atlantic
Ocean as seen from Long Island, where Walt Whitman's great seashore poems
also take place.

Like Whitman, like Tennyson ("Break, Break, Break"), the Tuckerman of
this sonnet sees the ocean from the shore, and sees his emotions in its unrest-
ing force. Yet when he imagines that the sea speaks to him, that sea says noth-
ing of anger or pain: rather, the sea "says" that it cannot care how he feels, and
has no feelings of its own. This imagined response makes a neat paradox: the
sea seems to speak, but only to say that it bears no sentiments, that all its
speech is fiction, that it never shares our grief. The English Victorian critic
John Ruskin called the attribution of feelings to nonhuman nature the "pa-
thetic fallacy" (from "pathos," meaning emotion in general). Poets, as Ruskin
recognized, may either rely on that "fallacy" or turn against it.

That turn gives Tuckerman the turning points here. Like Coleridge in "Work without Hope," Tuckerman has inverted normal sonnet structure, writing a sestet with a concluding couplet (rhymed *abbacc*), and then placing that sestet first. Tuckerman's ventriloquized "conclusion" (in which the sea says, "Alike! and one to me!") finishes that sestet. It also concludes what we might call Scene One, a time in the recent past when the poet walked along Long Island's coast in a "bitter angry" mood. The octave (rhymed *cdefcfde*) begins with Scene Two, in the same place but in the more distant past, when Tuckerman "trod these shores too happily" during Hannah's lifetime. The adverbial phrase suggests that he tempted fate: perhaps, as he walked along the beach, he was composing poetry about his marriage, reciting his new lines between the crashes of waves. "Nature never did betray / The heart that loved her," William Wordsworth wrote, but the nature-loving, yet bereft poet here knows that for him Wordsworth's promise was false. Nature has already betrayed Tuckerman: it has taken his wife away.

Yet nature intended nothing of the sort. Nonhuman nature intends nothing at all—it simply occurs, as the sea occurs to the land, indifferent whether it drowns or saves. The sea's indifference to outcomes along its shore, the fact that nobody can direct it (and that it cannot "direct" itself), informs the syntactic shifts of the last few lines: where the sestet had a clear direction—"across," from land to sea—Tuckerman's final sentence instead moves "back and forth," going nowhere. Scene Two differs from Scene One in Tuckerman's mood, and in the particular sound that he heard—"soft" then, loud enough to wake a sleeper now—but it does not differ in the indifference that its sea gives to human need. Despite the restless mood of the first few lines, the sea cannot be, could not ever have become, a partner in Tuckerman's sadness, since years ago, when Tuckerman felt happy, the ocean sounded exactly the same. So the last line says again—so it says outright. It also suggests (though it does not state) that in retrospect, on Tuckerman's return to this site, these counterfactuals felt like new facts. His joy, remembered after Hannah's demise (as in Wordsworth's "Surprised by Joy"), now causes fresh grief, and nothing can wash it away.

This poem about boundaries, binaries, and false equations—land and sea, poet and nature, past and present—incorporates a flurry of conjunctions, *and*'s. Most of these *and*'s connect words that serve as near-synonyms: the sea "rustled and sang," the poet murmured "to the rocks and ground," "the wave broke loud on ledge and reef," the murmurs contained (or betrayed) "his heart's dream and delight," "the sea / Went back and forth," "washed and withdrew." (Such pleonastic pairs occur often in Shakespeare, especially in his later plays.) But Tuckerman does not end with such redundant conjunctions: the sea as he remembers it, the sea that can neither remedy nor ratify his melancholy heart, behaved "*as though* the wet were dry and joy were grief." Wet and dry are not synonyms but antonyms. Joy and grief are (or at least should be) antonyms too, and only the forever-uncaring, unlistening, undying sea can purport to equate them.

Horror at nature's indifference—followed, sometimes, by reluctant, secularizing acceptance—is hardly Tuckerman's discovery: it became standard in Victorian poems, especially after Charles Darwin's *On the Origin of Species* (1859). Thomas Hardy's sonnet "Hap" (1866) complains that Hardy (or his ill-fated speaker) suffers at the hands of supposed "gods," weak stand-ins for a godless universe, who do not care whether he feels bliss or pain. Tuckerman (other sonnets make clear) was no atheist, but he comes close to Hardy's outlook here. Tuckerman's sonnet stands out not because it contemplates the so-called pathetic fallacy, not because it portrays an indifferent nature, but because of the resources with which it does so. It brings, to a frequent late nineteenth-century theme, at once the reinvented aspects of sonnet form, the line-by-line aural mimesis of tide-wracked seaside, and the sadly trustworthy self-knowledge of a man who spent years seeking, and often finding, fit language for his loss.

SB

"Retreat"

CHARLES BAUDELAIRE

(Translated by Rachel Hadas)

1861

Come in, sweet Sadness, take your ease, sit back.
You asked for twilight—see! And here it is,
Enveloping the city in its mist,
Soothing to some, to others an attack.

Leave millions squirming under Pleasure's sway.
Flicking his whip, that cruel bully drives
Them to fresh orgies. Oh, what sordid lives!
Come here, dear Sadness, take my hand—away,

Goodbye to all that. Look, the years gone by
Are leaning down from Heaven's balcony.
Out of the sea Regret arises, smiles;

The sun curls up to die. For miles and miles
A shroud unfurls along the eastern sky.
Listen, my darling, Night is walking by.

CHARLES BAUDELAIRE's "Retreat" ("Recueillement") has the tranquillity of a dream: halcyon and profound, with a touch of mystery—yet touched by nightmare, too. The sonnet imagines a dignified, even sedate relation between the poet and his muse, whom he names Sadness (Douleur). The poet seeks solitude and grace, tinged by a funereal tone.

First published in a magazine in 1861, "Retreat" was included after Baudelaire's death in the third edition of his masterwork, *Les Fleurs du mal* (The Flowers of Evil). (We give the French original below.) There, it accompanies visions of miserable, anguished sensuality, and efforts to find a perverse beauty in gruesome subjects (including a famous poem about a dog's corpse). The poet is often darkly obsessive, contemptuous of himself or others, afflicted by intense, skin-crawling boredom. Yet he retains a fierce pride in his pleasures. A grimace often accompanies Baudelaire's murky celebrations. Suggestive and magical, "Retreat" provides an escape from the immobilizing anxiety and degradation depicted so often in *The Flowers of Evil*. It opens a door to another world, where the poet transforms the perturbing ache of desire into restfulness.

The sonnet opens in a quiet mood: the first quatrain provides the peaceful entrance to the tumult of the second quatrain, which pictures a frenetic multitude. In his first line, the poet tames his temperamental mistress, his Sadness ("ma Douleur"). He calms her as one would a child, and tells her to settle down ("tiens-toi plus tranquille"). Like a sorcerer, he produces an enveloping mist, and gives her the twilight atmosphere she wants. Twilight, a major presence in Baudelaire's poetry, here brings peace to some and gnawing worry to others ("aux uns portant la paix, aux autres le souci").

In the second quatrain, Baudelaire projects his dismal, compulsive tendencies onto the unhappy masses, who live "sordid lives" under the whip of the "cruel bully" Pleasure. Slaves of appetite, they squirm and ready themselves for "fresh orgies." The crowd's frenzied actions resemble the torments of the damned: a neurotic *Inferno*. After this disturbing tableau (a passage of the poem scorned by one of Baudelaire's successors, the great poet Paul Valéry), the sonnet achieves composure in the sestet.

Now the poet effortlessly commands his muse; the dim, dusky scene soothes both of them. He spirits her off to a new land: the change of scene commences with the poem's volta. In the French, the phrase "par ici, / Loin d'eux" ("over here, / Far from them") glides effortlessly across the stanza break between octave and sestet. Sadness gives her hand to Baudelaire. Freed from the dirty crowd and their passions (left on the other side of the volta), he prepares to take flight. Yet no delight in escape, but rather an elegiac, bittersweet tone tempers the sestet. The lost years are "leaning down from Heaven's balcony," in their old-fashioned dresses ("robes surannées," not translated in this version). Another personification, matching Sadness, arises: Regret, who smiles, born from the sea like Aphrodite. Baudelaire's sestet might remind the reader of his "Invitation au Voyage" (Invitation to the Voyage), with its refrain, beautifully translated by Richard Wilbur: "There, there is nothing else but grace and measure, / Richness, quietness, and pleasure." As in that poem, in "Retreat" Baudelaire fantasizes into existence a realm of pure grace and perfect repose.

But the sonnet's charm has bite. Translator Rachel Hadas aptly conveys the small shock of mortality that initiates line 12: "The sun curls up to die." The darkening clouds are like a shroud unfurled in the East ("l'Orient," in Baudelaire a rich, evocative place of dreams), over the mansard roofs and chimneytops of Paris. In its last line, "Retreat" invokes the evening with a grand, calm theatrical flourish. Intent and devoted, the poet again addresses his muse, calling her "ma chère" ("my darling"). He begs her to attend to a subtle, ghostly arrival: "Night is walking by." (The repeated "entends"—"listen"—suggests that he still needs to coax her into serenity.) Night is the last of the series of personifications that preside over this poem: Sadness in the first quatrain, Pleasure in the second, Regret in the first tercet of the sestet. (We might wish to add three other capitalized entities that appear in Baudelaire's original: the evening, "le Soir"; the years, "les Années," who lean over the balcony of the sky; and the East, "l'Orient." And the translator capitalizes Heaven, in Baudelaire's French simply "ciel," or "sky.")

The odd man out among the personifications is Pleasure, the cruel master. In the light of Baudelaire's other poems in *The Flowers of Evil,* his presence implies ennui, disgust, horror—all the emotions that attend sensual craving. Night does away with these agonies, and with the coolly teasing presence of Regret. Joined to Sadness, who hearkens to her presence, Night becomes a somber, smooth guide, and seals the poem. All turbulence is cast out.

The title "Recueillement" could also be translated as "meditation": a deep, almost reverential state. A *recueillement* is a gathering of oneself, a salutary retirement or withdrawal. The word glances forward to a key verb in the second quatrain, "cueillir," "to catch": in this case, to catch, or be struck by, remorse—what the crowd does under the cruel sway of pleasure, when they reap enjoyment and are themselves harvested (another meaning of *recueillir*).

With this play on related words, Baudelaire reflects on modernity. The crowd's frantic experience differs from that of the man of *recueillement,* who communes with himself and collects his thoughts. For Baudelaire, modern life proffers an endless stream of impressions: it absorbs, fascinates, and at times even convulses the spectator. Sanity demands insulation from this wild pageant. So one of Baudelaire's heroes is the *flâneur,* who strolls through the city, enjoying its variety without letting it overwhelm him. The *flâneur,* a leisurely urban wanderer, maintains a distance from the strange goings-on that fill the streets of Paris. His privilege, Baudelaire writes in his essay "Le Peintre de la vie moderne" (The Painter of Modern Life)' is to remain hidden. Faced with the contemporary world's dynamic surface, he is, Baudelaire exults, "a *prince* who everywhere rejoices in his incognito."

In "Retreat," Baudelaire seeks a refuge from intoxication. He distills excitement into a lucid calm. The refuge proves ambiguous. Baudelaire in "The Painter of Modern Life" calls twilight "that strange, equivocal hour when the curtains of heaven are drawn and cities light up." The coming-on of night suggests a chill of uncertainty, despite its tenderness: a subtle disturbance within repose. Baudelaire's genius makes us feel this frisson.

The critic Christopher Miller notes that Baudelaire's meditation on evening has a significant echo in later poetry. T. S. Eliot in "Preludes" and "The Love Song of J. Alfred Prufrock," Miller writes, learns from Baudelaire to juxtapose "the beauty and serenity of twilight with tawdry, menacing images of the city." But Baudelaire, in "Retreat," also reflects on the sonnet tradition. The form is in its origins meditative, the turning of the self toward a contemplation both erotic and ideal. With his second quatrain, Baudelaire splits off the erotic from the thoughtful: he poses the distractions of the passionate, unsatisfied crowd against the majestic, somewhat morbid clarity that comes with the twilight. In his conclusion, he will change the formula, and instill a refined excitement, a purified version of passion, into the final picture of evening. Baudelaire's last line presents a scene both aloof and quietly thrilling. The poet enthrones the contemplative aspect of the sonnet, and links it to newly calm desire. At the veiled heart of thought he feels the charms of Night, his serene eros: that dear, sad goddess.

DM

"Recueillement"

CHARLES BAUDELAIRE

Sois sage, ô ma Douleur, et tiens-toi plus tranquille.
Tu réclamais le Soir; il descend; le voici:
Une atmosphère obscure enveloppe la ville,
Aux uns portant la paix, aux autres le souci.

Pendant que des mortels la multitude vile,
Sous le fouet du Plaisir, ce bourreau sans merci,
Va cueillir des remords dans la fête servile,
Ma Douleur, donne-moi la main; viens par ici,

Loin d'eux. Vois se pencher les défuntes Années,
Sur les balcons du ciel, en robes surannées;
Surgir du fond des eaux le Regret souriant;

Le soleil moribond s'endormir sous une arche,
Et, comme un long linceul traînant à l'Orient,
Entends, ma chère, entends la douce Nuit qui marche.

Modern Love 50

GEORGE MEREDITH

1862

Thus piteously Love closed what he begat:
The union of this ever-diverse pair!
These two were rapid falcons in a snare,
Condemned to do the flitting of the bat.
Lovers beneath the singing sky of May,
They wandered once; clear as the dew on flowers:
But they fed not on the advancing hours:
Their hearts held cravings for the buried day.
Then each applied to each that fatal knife,
Deep questioning, which probes to endless dole.
Ah, what a dusty answer gets the soul
When hot for certainties in this our life!—
In tragic hints here see what evermore
Moves dark as yonder midnight ocean's force,
Thundering like ramping hosts of warrior horse,
To throw that faint thin line upon the shore!

THIS IS the final poem in George Meredith's harrowing sequence *Modern Love,* written shortly after the death of his estranged wife and published in 1862. Like the previous forty-nine poems, this one is sixteen lines long, based on the sonnet form but with an additional two lines. The rhyme scheme is *abba cddc effe ghhg:* four closed quatrains. Meredith clearly derives the *Modern Love* stanza from the Shakespearean sonnet, though his quatrains are closed rather than open, and though he substitutes a final quatrain for the traditional concluding couplet.

Meredith's sequence remains unrivaled in English-language poetry for its picture of a conflicted, dissolving marriage. (Mary Nicolls, whom Meredith married in 1849, left him for a pre-Raphaelite painter eight years later: there was evidently an autobiographical foundation for *Modern Love*.) In his first poem the couple lies on their bed like "sculptured effigies," the knight and lady on a medieval tomb. There is an uncrossable line between them, the rigorous division their quarreling has drawn. So they remain, "each wishing for the sword that severs all." By the end of the sequence, the path is clear: these two, spared the death they have wished, have been separated forever. In the early poems of the sequence Meredith's narrator is close to the husband, maddened by jealousy and grief; at the end of it, he has achieved a cold, distant attitude. Meredith's dire summing up of the case looks down from a height on the "ever-diverse pair," surveying the scene of their mutually accomplished destruction. ("Diverse" in Meredith's phrase has its older meaning of "split" or "divided.")

Meredith's opening words, "Thus piteously," bring forward a savage irony, with their wicked allusion to the Renaissance sonneteer's frequent request for pity from his beloved (Sidney's Astrophel, for example, asks it from his Stella, as in the Sidney sonnet included here). To take pity on the chivalric lover was to yield to him amorously. Here, by contrast, love itself takes pity on the ravaged couple, and releases them from his bonds. Love "begat" this marriage; now he "close[s]" it ("close" is also a musical term, for a harmonious chord: again used ironically).

In the first quatrain, Meredith first compares the lovers to "rapid falcons in a snare," then to nervous, nocturnal bats. The falcon, a bird of prey (and associated with love in Chaucer's *Troilus and Criseyde*), here becomes a victim, caught in a trap. The gruesome bat, which haunts caves and old ruins, is an antiromantic symbol, suggesting the bad magic that afflicts this unsympathetic pair. The chivalric falcons "condemned" to behave like bats are animals driven—like the couple in *Modern Love*—to act against their better natures.

Meredith's second quatrain gives us a snapshot of the lovers as they appeared at the beginning of their union: "beneath the singing sky of May, / They wandered once . . ." He regards them in a state of easy pastoral cheerfulness, spurred by hope (of which the dew is a symbol). But this relationship is past-, not future-oriented. Not guided by the "advancing hours," they look backward: they want to recover their innocent beginning, the "buried day" that died long ago, and will never return. (Meredith may have been thinking of Matthew Arnold's image of the "buried life" in his poem of that name: Arnold's speaker, in "nameless sadness," dwells on the authentic self hidden away within and inaccessible to him.) Meredith's word "cravings" powerfully implies the gnawing, unsatisfiable appetite that afflicts his couple.

The third quatrain begins lethally: "Then each applied to each that fatal knife, / Deep questioning, which probes to endless dole." These relentless inquiries erode happiness by asking too much of it—they prod and poke, laying open to scrutiny the man and the woman. There is no turning back from such skepticism once it has begun. "Hot for certainties," we want, like Shakespeare's Othello, to prove the worst. The result is a "dusty answer," a sign of our nature as beings that are but dust and ashes (as the Bible puts it): desiccated, bound to return to the deathly state that denies all love, all joy. The single word "dusty" portends our inevitable end. Meredith takes it as definitive, the sentence of nature on the soul (here rhymed significantly with "dole," sorrowful pain).

Meredith's final quatrain, his couplet-like conclusion, pictures the drastic submission of love to law. The "ramping hosts of warrior horse" are Meredith's image for the thundering of the surf. Such martial upheaval ends quietly, though: all the ocean's force acts to "throw that faint thin line upon the shore." The poet has moved from the quest for "hot certainties" to "tragic hints," imaged in the evanescent border between sea and land. The monosyllabic final line, sober and steadily paced, recapitulates in its "faint thin line" (with its tenuous, wavering *i*-sounds) the fatal division between the couple.

All that remains is the feeble, yet persistent, presence of two unlucky people, pictured in that faint thin line. *Modern Love* 50 is the story of their love's desolate end, told with Meredith's exceptional harshness and sophistication.

DM

"A Dream"

CHARLES TENNYSON TURNER

1864

I dream'd a morning dream—a torrent brought
From fruitless hills, was rushing deep and wide:
It ran in rapids, like impatient thought;
It wheel'd in eddies, like bewilder'd pride:
Bleak-faced Neology, in cap and gown,
Peer'd up the channel of the spreading tide,
As, with a starved expectancy, he cried,
"When will the Body of the Christ come down?"
He came—not It, but He! no rolling waif
Tossed by the waves—no drown'd and helpless form—
But with unlapsing step, serene and safe,
As once He trod the waters in the storm;
The gownsman trembled as his God went by—
I look'd again, the torrent-bed was dry.

CHARLES TENNYSON TURNER, the elder brother of Alfred, Lord Tennyson, spent his life as a country clergyman—and ardent sonnet writer. He published his first volume of sonnets in 1830, when he was still an undergraduate at Cambridge. "A Dream" dates from 1864, when Turner was firmly ensconced in his parish in rural Lincolnshire, and brooding over Victorian developments in religion and science. The poem expresses Turner's baffled, yet thoughtful response to a new age.

The 1830s marked the beginning of the Oxford Movement, a fervent championing of mystical Christian feeling on the part of students and clergymen. Gripped by sacred enthusiasm, they criticized what seemed to them to be the lazy secularism of the Anglican Church. The biographer Lytton Strachey later

wrote that the leaders of the Oxford Movement "saw a transcendent manifes-
tation of Divine power, flowing down elaborate and immense through the
ages; a consecrated priesthood, stretching back, through the mystic symbol of
the laying on of hands, to the very Godhead." Turner was deeply influenced
by the Oxford Movement, which wished for what the doubtful Strachey called
a "manifestation" of God's power.

On the other side of the debate, advances in science and religious scholar-
ship questioned an older faith. The most influential of these developments
was the publication of Charles Darwin's *On the Origin of Species* (1859). His
theory of evolution posed a direct challenge to a literal-minded reading of the
biblical creation story. The Higher Criticism of the Bible was almost as trou-
bling: the discovery that the Christian scripture was built from strands of
writing composed at different times, and compiled by unknown editors to
form a whole. Finally, Ernest Renan, in his immensely influential *Vie de Jésus*
(Life of Jesus; 1863), treated the Messiah as a historical figure, rather than a
God-man, and depicted him in the real landscape of first-century Palestine.

In the midst of this tumult, the pious Charles Tennyson Turner slept fit-
fully. He responded with voluble energy to the new attacks on religion. In
his 1864 book of sonnets (which also includes "A Dream"), he heaped scorn
on Renan and blasted the newfangled approach, charging, in his poem "The
'Higher Criticism,'" that it "substitute[s], for our sound faith in Christ, /
A dreamy, hollow, unsubstantial creed." Elsewhere in his volume, though,
Turner expresses sympathy for the doubting priest, and hopes that the "Neol-
ogist," whose knowledge erodes faith, will be cured by the "simple creed" of
primitive Christianity. (The German Neologians were the original Higher
Critics of the Bible, in the late eighteenth century; they hoped to reconcile
scholarship and belief.)

"A Dream" is Turner's potent, compressed response to the intellectual revo-
lution of his time. His "morning dream" presages a powerful awakening. (The
dream vision is an important poetic genre, in which dream brings forth truth.
Turner, we should also note, was briefly addicted to opium.) The sonnet's cen-
tral presence is a "torrent," "rushing deep and wide." The image of the sub-
lime, bounding river was an important one for Turner. In scripture, it usually
gives life: its grandest appearance is in Amos 5:24, "Let judgment run down as
waters, and righteousness as a mighty stream." In Revelation 22:1, an apoca-
lyptic river gives life to the dead. But the river image can be frightening as
well. Isaiah issues a terrible prophecy that the land of Judah will be drowned
by overflowing waters sent by an enraged God: the waters represent the Assyr-

ians, who are about to invade Judah (Isaiah 8:7). Turner, who feels uncertain and abandoned, in need of God's presence, stands somewhere between the dreadful promise of Isaiah and the saving one of Revelation.

Turner's torrent comes from "fruitless hills" (unlike the hills that offer God's help, toward which Psalm 121 beautifully tells us to lift up our eyes). The poet's stream is frantic and disoriented, rushing from place to place. It has "rapids," where helpless vessels are dashed to pieces. Here, in the river of the restless, skeptical mind, pride and impatience join hands. The "bewilder'd" scholarly investigator, determined to undermine Scripture, undermines himself in the process.

The sonnet's second quatrain begins with a doddering, donnish figure: "Bleak-faced Neology, in cap and gown." Neology is disillusioned, "starved" of hope: he "peer[s]" cautiously at the stream, and then—with bursting emotion, restrained until now—he "crie[s], / 'When will the Body of the Christ come down?'" Neology's anguished question sounds both skeptical and intensely desirous. He wishes for proof, for a definitive sign that will assure him of the faith he now seems to be losing. He wants his Messiah now: a genuine mark of the enthusiastic Christian, but also the desperate move of someone striving to save himself from doubt. So things stand at the end of the poem's octave.

The sestet brings the hoped-for apparition of Christ. With astonishment, the poet announces, "He came—not It, but He!" The Savior is here in all his glory (in Turner's dream, that is: as Freud noted, dreams fulfill wishes). This is not a "drown'd and helpless form," but a living Messiah. Turner alludes to Matthew 14:24–31, when Jesus comforts his storm-tossed disciple Peter, as well as to Milton's pastoral elegy "Lycidas," which praises "the dear might of him that walked the waves."

Turner's agitated sonnet testifies to a divided mind and a sincere heart. The poet cannot shrug off the vast difference between his age and an earlier one that had been spared questions about the validity and worth of religion. The poet's struggle with doubt surfaces in the concluding couplet of "A Dream." A few lines earlier, the dream-vision Christ appeared "unlapsing" in his progress, "serene and safe." It seemed for a moment that the serenity and safety were to be transferred from God to the humans who beheld him. Now, however, the skeptic Neology reacts with a shudder, not joyful relief, to the holy apparition: "The gownsman trembled as his God went by." This trembling witnesses a divine power, but not one that promises safety. The gownsman may be punished by God, or may be disregarded by him. The return of divine force does not deliver what the poet hoped for; it threatens, instead of consoling.

With the final line of the poem, we arrive at a troubled prospect: the end of the dream suggests an arid, perplexed world. "I look'd again, the torrent-bed was dry." Turner's second look at the scene, from a sober, "fruitless" perspective, suggests that the powerful, superhuman stream may have been a passing phenomenon after all—not a sign of enduring faith, but a momentary epiphany.

Here Turner parts from his scriptural source. In the Matthew passage that stands behind Turner's sonnet, Jesus appears, walking on water, to the disciples whose ship is roiled by the storm. They cry out in fear, thinking him a demonic spirit (compare Turner's trembling gownsman). But the Savior instantly calms the storm, and comforts the disciples; he makes Peter walk on water toward him. Embracing Peter, "Jesus stretched forth his hand, and caught him, and said unto him, O thou of little faith, wherefore didst thou doubt?" (Matthew 24:31).

Turner the Victorian poet, buffeted by the winds of secular inquiry, cannot achieve the safe harbor promised by the Gospels passage, in which a reassuring God transfers miraculous power to his follower Peter. The world has changed. In this sonnet's confrontation of disillusioned knowledge and yearned-for faith, poetry stands between, gazing in both directions at once.

DM

"I know not why, but all this weary day"

HENRY TIMROD

1867

I know not why, but all this weary day,
Suggested by no definite grief or pain,
Sad fancies have been flitting through my brain;
Now it has been a vessel losing way,
Rounding a stormy headland; now a gray
Dull waste of clouds above a wintry main;
And then, a banner, drooping in the rain,
And meadows beaten into bloody clay.
Strolling at random with this shadowy woe
At heart, I chanced to wander hither! Lo!
A league of desolate marsh-land, with its lush,
Hot grasses in a noisome, tide-left bed,
And faint, warm airs, that rustle in the hush,
Like whispers round the body of the dead!

HENRY TIMROD was born in 1828 in Charleston, South Carolina. He worked in a law office and then taught school, but his true vocation was poetry. Timrod won the favor of the New England literary scene: he was praised by Longfellow and Tennyson for his first volume of poems, published in 1860, and John Greenleaf Whittier judged that he had "the true fire within." When the Civil War broke out, Timrod enlisted in the 30th South Carolina Regiment, but his poor health barred him from active duty. Instead, he worked as a war correspondent for the *Charleston Mercury.*

For the *Mercury,* Timrod reported on the Confederate retreat from Shiloh, in the spring of 1862. Shiloh was the bloodiest battle in American history. In the dismal wasteland between the two armies, dying soldiers screamed in agony through the night. Timrod's bitter experience of the war proved too much for him. The tubercular and frail poet died just two years after the Confederate defeat, an impoverished, broken man. "I know not why," published in 1867, the year of the poet's death, recalls Timrod's desolate, shattering time on the battlefield.

Timrod remains the closest Southern rival to the great Northern poets of the Civil War, Herman Melville and Walt Whitman. He wrote in a variety of genres, but he is best known for his evocations of the Confederate nation in poems like "Ethnogenesis." In "I know not why," Timrod casts aside the righteous Southern pride of "Ethnogenesis." Instead, he reflects somberly on the losses imposed by America's bloodiest conflict (the Civil War killed about 160,000 soldiers and civilians, nearly as many as have died in all of America's other wars put together).

"I know not why" begins with a picture of the wandering, distraught mind of the poet. The "weary day" confirms his ennui. Languid and wrapped in futility, he cannot identify the source of his discontent. His black melancholy is comparable to Baudelaire's or Coleridge's. In his Dejection Ode, Coleridge describes "a grief without a pang": amorphous and dull, lacking the sharpness of definition that would enable the poet to confront and understand it. Similarly, in Timrod, the dismal mood envelops all, and seems to have no objective correlative ("suggested by no definite grief or pain").

In Timrod's sonnet, the poet's "brain" becomes a field for "sad fancies," "flitting" around like bats, peripheral and distracting. The swarm of fancies, subtly eluding conscious control, vexes the poet's brain, which he compares to "a vessel losing way, / Rounding a stormy headland." Timrod might be thinking of the Union ship that attempted to resupply Charleston's Fort Sumter in 1861, and was fired on by the newly seceded state of South Carolina—the first shots of the war. The poet also invokes a great precursor in the sonnet tradition, Thomas Wyatt's "My galley chargèd with forgetfulness." In Wyatt's sonnet, based on a Petrarchan original, the poet pictures his love as a battered ship driven off course. Timrod's vessel images not erotic drive, as in Wyatt, but the mind itself, perplexed and anguished.

After depicting the ship battered by winds, Timrod moves on to the "dull waste of clouds above a wintry main" (ocean): this bleak, scoured seascape is his second picture of his sensibility. The third, culminating image of the second quatrain is the most significant for the poem's trajectory: "a banner, drooping in the rain, / And meadows beaten into bloody clay." Timrod here comes upon the scene of war, with an army's banner sagging dolefully above

the slaughter. The meadows, emblem of a vivid life in nature, have been ru-
ined, turned into "bloody clay." With these words, Timrod reverses the mo-
ment in Genesis 1 when God, like a potter, makes the first man from the clay
of the ground. In "I know not why," destruction overmasters creation: the hu-
man clay returns to its source, and the soldiers' blood, like Abel's, cries out
from the ground (Genesis 4:10).

The near-assonance of "drooping" and "bloody," and of "meadows" and
"beaten," conveys the severe quality of this nightmarish battlefield setting.
This landscape is stark and empty. We see no corpses, only an earth soaked
with blood. Timrod here recalls the two days of rain that soaked the Shiloh
battlefields (one of them nicknamed Bloody Pond), along with Shiloh's neigh-
boring swamp, the dismal Owl Creek. The end of Timrod's octave reveals the
root cause of his pain, which earlier appeared so obscure. "I know not why"
expresses the reverberation of history, not just the ambient melancholy of an
individual soul.

The sestet describes a desolate marsh that matches Timrod's Civil War
memory. "Strolling at random," the poet now wanders physically, just as he
wandered mentally in the octave. By chance, he comes upon a place that an-
swers his psyche's troubled recollection. A marsh is the most fertile of natural
environments, embodying the interchange of land and water that gives rise to
life. Here, though, the "lush, / Hot grasses" are fetid, not wholesome ("noi-
some" means noxious and foul-smelling). This mephitic place, symbolic of
the warm American South, is overgrown with subtle suggestions of mortality.
Like the flitting fancies of the first quatrain, the "rustle" of the marsh grasses
provides a quiet, morbid buzz. The marsh sounds resemble the overheard
voices of mourners: "Like whispers round the bodies of the dead."

The eerie, eldritch tone here is poles apart from Whitman's death whisper,
which, in his poem "Out of the Cradle Endlessly Rocking," guides us steadily
toward life. And Timrod's final tableau, with its insidious winds and overripe
vegetation, contrasts sharply with the rejuvenating sprig of lilac offered in
Whitman's elegy for Lincoln, "When Lilacs Last in the Dooryard Bloomed."
Unlike his Northern counterpart, Timrod finds no heartening sacrificial sym-
bolism in the Civil War's deaths. The poet remains immersed in melancholy,
so profoundly identifying himself with those lost in battle that he does not—
cannot—introduce them into his poem. He is unable to pass on to the phase
of mourning, which involves (as Freud argues) an acknowledgment of loss
and a separation of oneself from the dead.

The very striking reversal of the couplet and the third quatrain in Timrod's poem is a sign of this resistance to closure, the poet's refusal to pass on from melancholy to mourning. The couplet (here, lines 9 and 10) normally stands at the end of a Shakespearean sonnet: it summarizes, revises, and sometimes undermines the first twelve lines of the poem. But "I know not why" deprives itself of this encapsulating finish. The poem, like the poet, remains stranded. The ominous concluding rhyme of "bed" and "dead" implies that the lush marsh grasses blur, in the poet's mind, with the rotting corpses of the war dead. This is where Timrod remains, in his art as in his life: fixed in the permanent aftermath of battle.

The poet and critic J. D. McClatchy notes that novelists and painters mostly avoided depicting the battlefields of the Civil War. Instead, they offered an oblique or impressionistic response to historical crisis. This response may seem to have more to do with private traumas and obscure memories than with monumental public occasions. But in Timrod's case, such indistinction serves the poem's purpose: the evocation of a war that occupied not just the cities and the countryside, but the souls of Americans.

DM

"Renouncement"

ALICE MEYNELL

Written 1869; published 1875

I must not think of thee; and, tired yet strong,
 I shun the thought that lurks in all delight—
 The thought of thee—and in the blue Heaven's height,
And in the sweetest passage of a song.

Oh, just beyond the fairest thoughts that throng
 This breast, the thought of thee waits hidden yet bright;
 But it must never, never come in sight;
I must stop short of thee the whole day long.

But when sleep comes to close each difficult day,
 When night gives pause to the long watch I keep,
 And all my bonds I needs must loose apart,

Must doff my will as raiment laid away,—
 With the first dream that comes with the first sleep
 I run, I run, I am gathered to thy heart.

THIS ONCE very popular sonnet begins with a familiar paradox: to say "I must not think of" something or someone is perforce to think of it, or of him. The poet who tells herself over and over, in increasingly lofty terms, to "shun . . . / The thought of thee" comes to realize that she cannot do it. Indeed she seems to think of little else; the sonnet itself thus "stops short" again and again. If she cannot stop herself from thinking of him, at least—so the octave concludes—she can promise to do no more than think: she will never touch him, nor even see him again.

That octave, with its distraught repetitions, portrays a tumultuous, self-imposed frustration. "Think" and "thought" occur in the octave five times (but not at all in the sestet); "must" and "never" appear twice, close together, as she tries in vain to discipline her mind. The absent, unattainable beloved has also become, by the end of the octave, intangible, identified with the empyrean ("the blue Heaven's height"), with a song that seems to have no words, and with a light that suggests divine inspiration, the aniconic blessing whose true source can never be seen. Avoiding clear visual images, relying instead on sound, pace, and tone, Meynell creates both an expression of unrelieved yearning and a promise never to cross a line, never to act on even so fierce a passion.

Unsatisfied on earth in waking hours, that passion is fulfilled, instead, in a kind of heaven, at night and in dreams. In a song, the shift from one mood to another might be signaled by a change of key; in this sonnet, the change, the volta, is signaled instead by the changed meaning of one word. "Day" in line 8 means a twenty-four hour-period; so we at first must think that to do something day after day, each and every day, is to do it unceasingly, if not without complaint. "Day" in line 9 means, instead, the daylight hours: the sestet corresponds to the night, and brings relief. (It also reverses the usual meaning of "watch," a vigil—as on a ship or in a military camp—kept throughout the night.)

With relief comes the absence of repetition: no important word (no noun, no verb) occurs more than once in lines 9–12, whose conditional clauses flow smoothly, without midline stops. Night replaces day, as confident freedom replaces arduous self-restraint. But to what end? To the end that "must never, never" occur, except in dreams: reunion with the beloved. Doffing her "will" with her clothes at the end of the day, the poet allows us to imagine her as momentarily naked, even as sexually available (to an appropriate, welcome man) in her sleep. (John Keats used the same device in "The Eve of St. Agnes," a poem that Meynell would have known.) Yet the same lines evoke passages from Saint Paul, who imagines the Christian soul, at the end of time, leaving behind the "corruptible" garment of flesh in order to "put on" immortality (I Corinthians 15:53–54). Meynell's diction reinforces this echo, turning antiquated and even biblical ("raiment" occurs fifty-six times in the Authorized Version of the Bible). To go to sleep, and then to dream erotically of the beloved, is like being redeemed at the End of Time.

Meynell thus sets in motion a peculiarly Victorian combination of chaste and feminine piety with sexual suggestion. That combination takes over at the very end of the poem, when the separated lovers reunite. At this climactic moment (it works like a couplet, though it does not rhyme as one) Meynell offers climactic repetitions: "first dream . . . first sleep," "I run, I run, I am." Repeated words here imply not struggle but joy: not only in dreams, but with "the first dream," "the first sleep," "I run, I run." (She goes to bed early, in order to dream as soon as she can.) Where the octave kept stopping (and flaunting its internal stops), the final clause accelerates instead. Meynell pivots from the promissory ("I must not . . . it must . . . I must") to the indicative ("But when sleep comes . . . I run"). The poet can tell herself what to do while awake, but she cannot help or control her dreams, and therefore bears no guilt for what goes on there: she ends up pathetically grateful for the blameless release they afford.

Drawing on the many earlier sonnets in which lover meets beloved in a dream, Meynell also draws on earlier sonnets of commemoration: on, for example, John Milton's "Methought I saw my late espousèd saint." Sleep, Meynell implies, is as close as she comes to the afterlife—to the "blue Heaven" that is, in waking life, no farther from her than her beloved's hand. Yet Meynell does not say that her beloved has died. Indeed she implies, with "must," that a moral rule, not a natural fact, keeps these would-be (or former) lovers apart—and so it was in her life when she wrote the poem.

Born Alice Thompson, to literary English parents—Charles Dickens considered her father a friend—the poet grew up in Italy; her family moved back to England when Alice was nineteen. By that time she was already taking her poetry seriously. The year before their move, she had written in a diary, "I must try to cultivate that rhyming faculty which I used to have, if it is not quite gone from me. But whatever I write will be melancholy and self-conscious, as are all women's poems."

In her early twenties Alice became a Roman Catholic, following her mother's conversion a few years before. The English priest who brought Alice into the church became a close friend, one of the first people other than blood relations to read and respond to her verse. When their attachment risked becoming sexual, they broke off all communication rather than jeopardize his vows. Another sonnet, "Thoughts in Separation," gives the reasons behind their break. That sonnet ends in what sounds now like a moment of bathos: "Thou to thy crucifix, I to my mother."

"Renouncement," probably written in the same months, stands above and apart from the biographical circumstances that seem to have prompted it: with its combination of youthful passion and arduous chastity ("I must stop short of thee"), it might fit any lover trying to force himself, or herself, to give up a desire. (Meynell thus joins the many nineteenth-century women who took up—as Joseph Phelan put it—the sonnet's "association with an interior and often secret life of longing.") Yet if its distance from the facts of her life can help explain its continued power, the facts of that life can help us read it, too. The sestet itself renounces, or rejects, the moralizing octave, whose rules she escapes in her dreams: the poem places religious language at the service of personal passion, rather than the other way round. Meynell begins by telling herself what she will do, what she believes that she must do (and in fact did), yet ends by showing what she cannot but feel.

SB

Brother and Sister 7 and 8

GEORGE ELIOT

Written before 1870; published 1874

7

Those long days measured by my little feet
Had chronicles which yield me many a text;
Where irony still finds an image meet
Of full-grown judgments in this world perplext.

One day my brother left me in high charge,
To mind the rod, while he went seeking bait,
And bade me, when I saw a nearing barge,
Snatch out the line lest he should come too late.

Proud of the task, I watched with all my might
For one whole minute, till my eyes grew wide,
Till sky and earth took on a strange new light
And seemed a dream-world floating on some tide—

    A fair pavilioned boat for me alone
    Bearing me onward through the vast unknown.

8

But sudden came the barge's pitch-black prow,
Nearer and angrier came my brother's cry,
And all my soul was quivering fear, when lo!
Upon the imperilled line, suspended high,

A silver perch! My guilt that won the prey,
Now turned to merit, had a guerdon rich

Of songs and praises, and made merry play,
Until my triumph reached its highest pitch

When all at home were told the wondrous feat,
And how the little sister had fished well.
In secret, though my fortune tasted sweet,
I wondered why this happiness befell.

   "The little lass had luck," the gardener said:
   And so I learned, luck was with glory wed.

MARY ANN EVANS—"George Eliot" was her pen name—gained and de-
served transatlantic fame as a novelist, but those who have read her novels
(especially *Middlemarch*) will remember the many short pieces of verse she
uses as epigraphs for her chapters; when she gives no source, Eliot usually
wrote them herself. She also wrote book-length verse dramas, and claimed
(plausibly) that her shortest, least realistic novel, *Silas Marner,* could easily
have been a tale in Wordsworthian narrative verse. Ideas appropriate to narra-
tive—of why and how one event gives rise to another, of how characters find
outcomes (skill, virtue, fate, luck?)—propel this wry, nostalgic diptych, the
best (and funniest) part of Eliot's sequence of poems.

Brother and Sister records the shared Warwickshire childhood of Mary Ann
and Isaac Evans, the older brother she adored. Beginning in 1857, the adult
Mary Ann (already known as George Eliot) lived with the writer and editor
G. H. Lewes, though Lewes could obtain no divorce from his first wife. When
Mary Anne, in 1857, told Isaac about her new status ("You will be surprised, I
dare say, but I hope not sorry to learn that I . . . have someone to take care of
me in the world"), Isaac, who had remained in Warwickshire, responded to
her only through his lawyer, and refused further contact for the remainder of
their lives. The sonnets thus record not just a paradisal childhood, but a para-
dise wholly lost. The judgmental older brother, and the passionate, intellectu-
ally gifted, ill-fated little sister (who admires her brother more than most read-
ers can) also gave Eliot the basis for her 1860 novel *The Mill on the Floss.*

Most of the sonnets in *Brother and Sister* are lyric or meditative, or else
paint scenes. This pair, by contrast, uses Eliot's gift for narrative, and for the
changing perspectives of past and present, engagement and irony, that turn
narrative (a series of events) into character (a person shaped by, though not

wholly by, those events). The irony of this childhood incident becomes an "image meet" (an appropriate symbol, and an example) of the sorts of "judgments" we make without sufficient evidence, judgments that may guide, or deform, adult life.

Sonnet 7 begins as if it were part of a sermon, a homely religious parable, or a moral lesson found in daily life; it ends by invoking, with its dreamy boat, the comparatively unmoralized, gorgeous legacy of verse romance. The practical, perhaps dictatorial brother (much like Tom in *The Mill on the Floss*) has tasked the dreamy, distractable little sister to mind the line with which they are fishing in their "brown canal," on whose "banks" (says the prior sonnet, 6) she liked to sit and dream. She must take the line from the water when a barge comes near, lest the passing boat sever the line. Like Tom's sister Maggie in *Mill,* Mary Ann cannot keep her attention on practical matters: she imagines the barge, before it arrives, as a boat that might take her who knows where, drifting into archaic diction ("fair-pavilioned") as she does so. She does not withdraw the imperiled line, despite the advancing barge, until her brother returns and tells her to do so. When she does pull the line up, "lo!" (the word becomes comic in rhyming position, a pun opposite "high"), through her inattention, she has caught a fish.

Once Mary Ann lands her perch, everything changes: not only her older brother, but the adults in the family ("all at home") praise her conduct, and she gives their praise an archaic term ("guerdon," reward) fit more for a fair pavilion than for a brown canal. The adults' praise not only implies that Evans has shown talent or diligence ("aptitude," as we say now) in fishing; it also suggests that worldly success is sufficient evidence, if not of moral goodness, then of talent that merits praise. For Eliot, there is always something suspect about skill without wisdom (see the fate of Tertius Lydgate in *Middlemarch*), hence about praise for demonstrations of skill. The cozy family, though their praise is "sweet," seems doubly fallacious in retrospect: praising talent that may not exist, on wildly insufficient evidence, they mistake talent for goodness, and both for luck.

Sonnet 7 paraphrased the brother; Sonnet 8 quotes, of all the people "at home," only the gardener, a low-status adult outsider, who understands that "the little lass had luck," but maintains, like a committed gambler, that luck merits praise. The adult author now disagrees. "Luck was with glory wed" meant (back then, to the girl) something neutral and descriptive—"when you get lucky, then people will praise you." But once the full lesson sank in, the phrase meant something more. It implies that praise, even from adults, even from the adults you love and trust, does not necessarily mean that you have done something good, nor even that you have mastered a skill: it may simply mean that you got lucky, whether or not you know (as Eliot came to know) that that is all it means.

All the sonnets in *Brother and Sister* use Shakespearean form, three quatrains and then a couplet. That form fit Eliot's temperament, because it almost requires a conclusion, a generalization, something that sounds like (whether or not it is) a "moral" to the "story" the quatrains relate. Sonnet 8 here provides a meta- or anti-moral, telling us that the conclusions we draw (in poems and in life), and the conclusions adults draw for us (especially if we are children), may have nothing to do with the truth. The marriage of event and moral, outcome and explanation, may just be the marriage of glory and luck. Eliot's temperament led her to draw morals, but that same temperament, aided by her broad learning, led her to warn against narrow or hasty moralizing: over and over, her novels tell her readers not to pass judgment until they have learned all the facts. You can see this self-consciousness about morals and moralizing, about glorification and dispraise, in the final couplets of both these sonnets, since the "pavilioned boat" that might have borne the young Mary Ann through "sky and earth" is at least as illusory, hollowed, and unmerited as the "guerdon" she gets when she brings home a fish.

We may not find in *Brother and Sister* the play of overtones and implications, word by word and line by line, that we find in the sonnets of Shakespeare or Keats. Eliot offers, instead, moral reflection, and a verbal nuance meant to illuminate character. That nuance can turn up only on rereading, in her novels as in her best poems. Here, for example, a key phrase from Sonnet 7 changes its sense once we have read Sonnet 8: "full-grown judgments"—those made by full-grown adults, whose faculty of judgment has had time to ripen—seem as unreliable as the hasty judgments of children, and the judgments themselves (not only the world, or the people in the world) are often perplexed (crossed, contradicted) by subsequent events. The race is not to the swift, nor the fish to the strong—as Ecclesiastes did not quite put it—but time and chance affect all things.

SB

"For a Venetian Pastoral"

DANTE GABRIEL ROSSETTI

1870

Water, for anguish of the solstice:—nay,
    But dip the vessel slowly,—nay, but lean
    And hark how at its verge the wave sighs in
Reluctant. Hush! Beyond all depth away
The heat lies silent at the brink of day:
    Now the hand trails upon the viol-string
    That sobs, and the brown faces cease to sing,
Sad with the whole of pleasure. Whither stray
Her eyes now, from whose mouth the slim pipes creep
    And leave it pouting, while the shadowed grass
    Is cool against her naked side? Let be:—
Say nothing now unto her lest she weep,
    Nor name this ever. Be it as it was,—
    Life touching lips with Immortality.

DANTE GABRIEL ROSSETTI's "For a Venetian Pastoral" is an ekphrastic poem (a poem that responds to a work of visual art). Perhaps the most famous example of ekphrasis in poetry is Keats's "Ode on a Grecian Urn"; Shelley's "Ozymandias" (in this volume) is another well-known instance. Whereas Keats and Shelley describe imagined works of art (the urn, Ozymandias' statue), Rossetti pictures a real one: the *Fête champêtre* (Pastoral Concert), probably by the sixteenth-century Venetian painter Titian.

Both a poet and a painter, Rossetti (the son of an Italian expatriate who had settled in London) was a member of the circle known as the pre-Raphaelites, who were profoundly influenced by medieval art. In "For a Venetian Pastoral," the poet turns to a later tradition: the masters of the Venetian Renaissance. Rossetti saw the Titian painting—then attributed to another Venetian artist, Giorgione—in the Louvre, on a visit to Paris in 1849. He wrote a first version of the poem, which was published the following year. Twenty years later, he radically revised it for the 1870 edition of his poems; we give the later version.

Titian's painting features a pastoral landscape with two clothed, seated men in deep conversation, one playing a large lute (or "viol," in Rossetti's poem). The men are flanked by two nude women. The woman on the left has just dipped her water pitcher in a well, which she leans on. Her torso is gracefully turned, her face somber and abstracted. The woman on the viewer's right is seated, turned away from us so that her face is hidden; she plays a flute-like instrument (Rossetti's "pipes"), which she holds a few inches from her lips. The center of the painting is the lute-player's shadowed face, and his hand arrested in the act of strumming his instrument. The entire painting gives a sense of beautiful equilibrium, of human forms that respond to one another even as they remain absorbed in their individual activities. It is fluent, poised, muted in sensibility.

Rossetti's sonnet, like Titian's painting, mingles soft beauty with a reverent, reflective sadness. The poem's opening gesture is exquisite. "Water, for anguish of the solstice": it is the height of summer, and the heat brings on a spontaneous cry in the poet, as if from sympathy with his mute protagonists. Rossetti is surely thinking of the etymology of "anguish": it comes from the Latin *angustus,* meaning narrow, close, but also concise or subtle. The anguish he sees in Titian's painting is less desperate than finely desirous: the feeling epitomizes the scene.

In the rest of his first quatrain, Rossetti moderates the pace. He issues a direction to the woman in the *Fête champêtre:* "nay, / But dip the vessel slowly"— and then, in an intent, focused tone, he urges on her a subtle attentiveness similar to his own: "nay, but lean / And hark how at its verge the wave sighs in / Reluctant." Rossetti is now addressing the reader (and viewer of the Titian) and himself, more than the female figure in the painting. She is leaning on the well. We "hark" along with her, and listen for the barely audible rush of water. We seem to be there, in the painting. With quiet virtuosity, Rossetti enjambs lines 3 and 4: the wave "sighs in / Reluctant." (In Titian's painting, the water in the glass pitcher held by the woman shines through it, luminous and faintly restless against the stone wall of the well.) Again an etymological hint: "reluctant" comes from a Latin term meaning to struggle or resist (wonderfully, Eve in *Paradise Lost* shows toward Adam a "sweet reluctant amorous delay"). Resistance, desire, and poised hesitation are all blended in the nude woman's fine gesture, which hypnotically suspends the action.

The sigh in line 3 seems an expression of appreciative regret. It surveys experience and forecasts the culminating phrase of the octave, "Sad with the whole of pleasure." The characters' cherishing of the necessarily tenuous moment, pressed by heat, fatigue, and the passing day, puts them in accord with the way the viol-string "sobs." (A few years after Rossetti, the French poet Verlaine speaks similarly of "les sanglots longs des violons de l'automne," "the long sobs of autumnal violins.")

A new exclamation adorns line 4: "hush!" The spectator is enjoined to respond lightly lest he disturb the balance of the scene, which is poised at the "brink of day" (it is twilight). Like "verge" in line 3, "brink" gives a gingerly transitional aura to the moment in the painting, making it equally spatial and temporal (this is why Rossetti uses the word "verge," rather than "edge," for the lip of the glass pitcher). The female figure's eyes "stray," yet remain hauntingly anchored to the grassy place.

The sestet begins with a gentle surmise. We cannot see the face of the woman playing the flute, but Rossetti imagines a secret life for her. Her lips are "pouting": the embouchure she uses to make music also expresses discontent, contrasting with the cool grass that soothes her nakedness. She is on the verge of weeping, the poet reveals, as he advises that we curb our impulse to console her ("Let be:—/ Say nothing now unto her lest she weep").

With sacerdotal solemnity, the poet then issues a monosyllabic instruction: "Nor name this ever. Be it as it was . . . " Rossetti wants to "let be" the scene and its characters: to refrain from intruding, from naming the significance of this drama. We may want to know who these people are, the motives for their sadness and their pleasure. But the spell cast by the *Fête champêtre* requires that we not know. Painting, even when it represents a realistic human setting, bars us from the kind of curiosity that we exercise in everyday life concerning the people we meet. Art captures experience by not violating that experience, by holding its hand suspended over the world it depicts. This is as true of Rossetti's sonnet as of Titian's painting. Both venerate a mystery. If we speculate, or inquire too closely, we infringe on a hallowed place.

Rossetti's final line firmly contains his sense of the pastoral tableau he has evoked: "Life touching lips with Immortality." The phrase recalls statements from the Hebrew Bible, most prominently the assurance in Psalms 85:10 that "righteousness and peace have kissed each other." The kiss is traditionally the sign of a compact, a firm agreement; in the Psalms passage, it signals the reconciliation of two contrasting virtues. Rossetti diverges from his biblical sub-text by presenting not a full-fleshed kiss, but a touching of lips, slight and barely felt. The gesture captures the quality of "For a Venetian Pastoral": it moves us in its delicate approach, touching on life without claiming possession.

For Rossetti, the sonnet was "a moment's monument." So he announced in the prefatory poem to his 1881 collection, *The House of Life*. In Rossetti, the sonnet becomes consummately about the moment: not a moment of decision or a critical turning-point, but a fragile refuge, a shelter against time's depredations. "For a Venetian Pastoral" provides a memorable example of Rossetti's characteristic effort to find a harbor in the instant, to hold to the present the way one holds a pose. In this sonnet, Rossetti paints a picture of arrested motion, an intuitional respite from the forces of the outside world. He knows that the refuge cannot last—that, as a slender lyric form, the sonnet cannot win the argument against time. But its frail perfection stands forth for sympathetic reading: we know our own vulnerability in Rossetti's characters. In keeping with the traditions of pastoral poetry, Rossetti's scene lives lightly but well, and shadowed by melancholy.

DM

"A Superscription"

DANTE GABRIEL ROSSETTI

1870

Look in my face; my name is Might-have-been;
  I am also called No-more, Too-late, Farewell;
  Unto thine ear I hold the dead-sea shell
Cast up thy Life's foam-fretted feet between;
Unto thine eyes the glass where that is seen
    Which had Life's form and Love's, but by my spell
    Is now a shaken shadow intolerable,
Of ultimate things unuttered the frail screen.

Mark me, how still I am! But should there dart
    One moment through thy soul the soft surprise
    Of that winged Peace which lulls the breath of sighs,—
Then shalt thou see me smile, and turn apart
Thy visage to mine ambush at thy heart
    Sleepless with cold commemorative eyes.

DANTE GABRIEL ROSSETTI'S "A Superscription" presents a brilliantly enigmatic, summarizing moment in his influential sonnet sequence *The House of Life* (1870). (A superscription is a caption for a painting or drawing, summoning its meaning into words.) Rossetti wrote the sonnet in 1869, seven years after the suicide of his wife, Elizabeth Siddal. For many readers it testifies to the anguish the poet must have felt over the loss of his wife—or over his subsequent tragic, frustrated love affair with Jane Morris, the wife of the poet and artist William Morris.

The House of Life consists of two sections, "Youth and Change" and "Change and Fate." It traces, with labyrinthine intensity, the poet's devotion to (at least) two muse-like beloveds; many of the poems are colored by allusions to the cruel destiny of loss and separation that overshadows erotic happiness. What is the mysterious power that presides over "A Superscription"— and that says "I," addressing poet and reader with grim finality? The strange, powerful "I" and the addressee or "thou" seem knit together in trancelike manner; the "thou" (we surmise) tacitly complies with the words of the "I," as if in a dream. The "I" figure is clearly related to the tyrannical eros of Dante's *Vita nuova* (which was elegantly translated by Rossetti). She also resembles Moneta, the cold, admonishing muse of Keats's "Fall of Hyperion: A Dream." Rossetti's "I" also defiantly tells the poet, or "you," who he is; her spell is threatening and reductive. But unlike Keats's muse, this one incites no fight for creative life from the poet. Instead, she mirrors Rossetti—just as his beloved reflected his profound self back to him earlier in the *House of Life* sequence. But whereas the beloved enraptured him, this figure renders him nearly extinct, a mere "shaken shadow intolerable" (as he appears in the mirror).

She translates his existence by giving her own four-fold motto: "my name is Might-have-been; / I am also called No-more, Too-late, Farewell." These four names are the muse's explanations of herself, which also encompass the poet in their relentless grip. She is one of a series of potent female personifications in *The House of Life,* goddess-like apparitions who form a crucial part of his personal mythology. (John Hollander identifies Persephone, Pandora, Lilith, and Dante's Beatrice as major models for Rossetti's life-giving and life-threatening women.)

There is another prominent source for Rossetti's opening line: Shakespeare's Sonnet 2, which begins with the speaker commanding the young man, "Look in thy glass, and tell the face thou viewest / Now is the time for face to form another." Shakespeare urges his young man to create a lasting version of his beauty by fathering a child. So in Shakespeare the image in the glass (mirror) is masterful, intended to reinforce the young man's power to envision a proud, tenacious self. Rossetti turns his mirror-image in the opposite direction: he implies the futility of the identity claimed by the "thou." This implement of the eye, the glass, is matched by one of the ear, a shell. Rossetti shies away from the visual in this poem, in contrast to his method in "For a Venetian Pastoral." T. S. Eliot accused Rossetti of indulging in the merely decorative; but his true métier is difficult, thwarted words, not ornate picture making. He gives no visual description of the form in the glass, only an allusion to its ghostly frailty.

The muse holds up to the poet's ear the "dead-sea shell" that the sea has cast up between his "foam-fretted feet." (Rossetti probably derives the image of the shell from the Dream of the Arab in Wordsworth's *Prelude*.) The shell transmits only echoes, not active voice; the sounds it makes are dead, a mere trace of the past, as is the vision that emerges in the glass in the second quatrain. Like Coleridge in "Work without Hope" or Stickney in "Mt. Lykaion" (later in this book), Rossetti in this sonnet is a man without prospects, abandoned by life.

Rossetti's second quatrain (rhymed *abba* like the first, in the Italian style) produces an elaborate periphrasis: what appears in the glass held up to the "thou" is "that . . . / Which had Life's form and Love's." This shadowy entity seems to be a beloved who has vanished; along with her, an aspect of the poet himself has disappeared. The "I" or muse figure throws doubt even on the past: in the rhapsodic heights of erotic love, represented earlier in *The House of Life,* we saw (we are now told) only the "form" of life and love, not their capable reality. Old passion, instead of being dwelt on nostalgically, is bitter, even "intolerable," because it has been revealed as shadowy and insubstantial, a "frail screen." The screen is a thin, inadequate defense against necessity—a force too frightful to invoke by name, and therefore designated here only as "ultimate things unuttered." Many of Rossetti's sonnets gravitate toward the unuttered. Their plots are elaborate and cryptic, their diction hard to untangle.

Rossetti's obliqueness is no mere stylistic flourish: an insomniac terror resides behind his evasions. The sonnet's sestet unveils the torment that continues to lurk as a possibility for the speaker, though his life and his love are gone. Even in the stillness of emotional death, a ghostly, momentary frisson darts through his soul—"the soft surprise / Of that winged Peace which lulls the breath of sighs." Eerily, hopeless resignation may for a brief time take on the look of peace. But this gift of reconciliation with his fate conceals a stinging arrow: the insidious smile of the muse who has bewitched him, and who is now ready to entrap him in renewed agony. She will, she tells the speaker, "turn apart / Thy visage to mine ambush at thy heart / Sleepless with cold commemorative eyes." "Turn apart" sounds like "tear apart": she has taken him by surprise, whether to his utter destruction or for a less dramatic, but equally fatal, vigil of lost desire.

The sonnet's last word is "eyes": the eyes of the poet (perhaps reflected by those of the muse). They will never be healed by the oblivion of sleep, but continue to brood endlessly. "Commemorative" suggests an emblem of something past and definitively gone (like a commemorative coin); and the prefix "co-" (meaning "with") implies the lasting bondage of the poet to his muse, who ambushes his heart as Dante's eros feasts on Beatrice's heart in the *Vita nuova*. Rossetti's grammar makes it possible that both "thou" and "I" are sleepless, that both have cold eyes; they share a spectral communion.

In "For a Venetian Pastoral," Rossetti sees the moment as a refuge; the sonnet is a protected space for acute, bittersweet thought. "A Superscription" offers no such possibility: in this sonnet, experience is alienation, unshaded by any pastoral shelter. The poem's conclusion depicts a turning apart into hopeless solitude, a fixation or imaginative limbo from which the "thou" will never escape. "A Superscription" disturbingly announces Rossetti's final descent into drug addiction and obsessive, brooding melancholy, which began about the time of this poem's composition. It remains one of the most personal and essential works of this poet, whom the critic Walter Pater esteemed for his "mystic isolation" and for his odd flights from paradise to nightmare. Pater described *The House of Life* as a haunted house, in which Rossetti was "but the 'Interpreter.'" The "thou" in "A Superscription" is indeed the displaced, despairing poet, who, subject to an obscure ritual sentence, wanders through a condemned realm. Rossetti is sustained only by the severe intricacy of his art, which both baffles and mesmerizes the reader.

DM

"The Cross of Snow"

HENRY WADSWORTH LONGFELLOW

Written 1879; published 1886

In the long, sleepless watches of the night,
    A gentle face—the face of one long dead—
    Looks at me from the wall, where round its head
    The night-lamp casts a halo of pale light.
Here in this room she died; and soul more white
    Never through martyrdom of fire was led
    To its repose; nor can in books be read
    The legend of a life more benedight.
There is a mountain in the distant West
    That, sun-defying, in its deep ravines
    Displays a cross of snow upon its side.
Such is the cross I wear upon my breast
    These eighteen years, through all the changing scenes
    And seasons, changeless since the day she died.

IN 1861 the poet's wife, Fanny, the mother of their six children, died in a fire in the library of their Cambridge home (Craigie House, now a National Historic Site). Henry was badly burned as he tried to save her; he wore a full beard for the rest of his life to hide the facial scars. He would not write about her death directly until 1879, when he composed, but chose not to publish, "The Cross of Snow," considering it too personal, or too painful, to share. The sonnet (one of dozens he composed in the last decade of his life) describes his continuing grief over Fanny, and, in doing so, violates standards of Victorian and postbellum American taste, by which (as Matthew Arnold put it) suffering should find "some vent in action," grief (especially grown men's grief) some end. Discovered among his papers and first published in a biography written by the poet's brother, the sonnet now stands among Longfellow's most famous poems: its entire lack of religious consolation (despite its focus on the image of the cross), and its depiction of wholly unrelieved pain—precisely the aspects that might have repelled, or disturbed, his contemporaries—suit it better to our taste now.

Longfellow has organized the sonnet around two scenes that offer stark contrasts: a darkened bedroom, dominated by a portrait only the widower sees, and a "mountain in the distant West" whose sight makes a public spectacle. Both scenes, we learn, give him signs for his unchanging grief. The octave sets Longfellow's loss of his wife, represented by her portrait, beside the recorded achievements of his career, represented by the books on their shelves, almost valueless when compared to her. One such achievement involved the sonnet itself, a form that Longfellow, through his poems and translations (among them "To-morrow," included in this volume), did as much as anyone to bring to America. Longfellow also adapted and translated European narrative poetry, some of which described the lives and martyrdoms ("legends") of Catholic saints. Those martyrs presumably ascended to heaven, where their holy deeds found eternal reward: Fanny Longfellow, by contrast, stays on earth, not in person (alas) but in the form of an image, gazing down at Longfellow in the bedroom that Henry and Fanny once shared. Visitors to Craigie House today see that image, a chalk drawing of Fanny in three-quarter profile, done by Samuel Rowse in 1859; her likeness (youthful, serious, beautiful) hung on the wall across from the bed, so that Henry would have seen it upon retiring, and on awakening, each day.

Fanny died the day after the fire, most likely in bed. Her portrait looks down at the poet, eighteen years later, as if from heaven, under the "night-lamp," a secular and domesticated halo: by its light the sleepless Longfellow can brood, or read, or, *in extremis,* write (there are chairs in the bedroom, but no desk). Longfellow would have known John Milton's final sonnet ("Methought I saw my late espousèd saint," also included in this book), in which Milton's late wife comes to him in a dream. Later sonnets of mourning (including some of Frederick Goddard Tuckerman's) also used the device of the dream-visit, in which the beloved flees as the poet wakes up.

Here, by contrast, there is no dream-visitation, because there is no dream: Longfellow cannot sleep. "Watches" are units, a few hours each, for nocturnal sentries, as in a military camp; Longfellow puns on the term. What can he watch, what does he care to see, except her? Why bother to read any books, when the best moral lesson, the most blessed life, can be discovered not in them, but in her face? Longfellow may look to her as if she could speak, but of course she can say nothing to him, being dead. Her portrait neither blames nor absolves him for his failure to save her in 1861. Except for "watches," the octave hews to ordinary diction, and to ordinary rhymes, until the few medievalizing terms bring the comparison to a saint's story into relief: "legend" for "story" or "narrative," and the archaic "benedight," meaning "blessed."

With the sestet, the scene changes—from private to public, indoor to outdoor, night to day, and Europe (the source of saints' legends) to western America—and the language snaps back into modern American English. Only Longfellow's grief remains unchanged. We have moved from saints' lives to the Passion of Christ; we have also moved from a bedroom in Cambridge to "the distant West," to the Mountain of the Holy Cross, in Colorado. There, as the art historian Linda Hults writes, "in late summer, when filled with the winter's remaining snow, two perpendicular ravines form a Latin cross about 1,100 feet tall." First described in 1869, the mountain became famous through Thomas Moran's 1875 painting; Longfellow likely saw Moran's image in one of its many color reproductions, though he may also have owned William Henry Jackson's 1873 photograph (the photograph is in the Craigie House collection now).

Preserved in the midst of change, a bright cross seen on high, the mountain might indeed resemble a miracle, some evidence of God's presence in this world, and of a Christian blessing bestowed on America through its sublime landscape. On view at the Centennial Exposition in Philadelphia in 1876, the painting and the photograph were seen just that way, as patriotic icons of Manifest Destiny—the doctrine that America had to expand, and was morally justified in doing so. Longfellow rejects that interpretation, of course, because he is writing a memorial poem; but he rejects other, properly religious interpretations too. In another sort of memorial poem—a poem with the hope of Christian resurrection—the cross in the mountains would stand for the promise that Christ conveyed in the sign of the Cross: the believers, the meritorious, shall not die. The sleepless Longfellow remembers Saint Paul's words, "Behold, I show you a mystery: we shall not sleep, but we shall all be changed" (I Corinthians 15:51), a text often read at funerals. (By "changed," Saint Paul meant "resurrected, and taken to Heaven": for the believer, Christ will conquer death.)

Here, though, the "sun-defying cross" is ironic, found in an American nature that holds no sign and no promise that the dead shall live. The cross is preserved thanks to merely natural means: all year, the mountain shadows prevent the snow from melting, since they block the sunlight. This American cross stands not for any resurrection (much less for any public destiny), but for the durability of grief. Longfellow carries *this* kind of cross "upon his breast" (like the hairshirt of a penitent, or like a scar), because he, too, knows "changeless," perdurable sadness. His heart never melts (the poet did not marry again): his cross resembles the cross on the western mountains because it, too, is a product of unbroken shade.

The sestet in this Italian sonnet breaks neatly in two parts, their rhymes matching *(abcabc)*. The sharpest enjambment in the poem, and the only one in the midst of a clause, takes place in the penultimate line. "And seasons" becomes an intensifier, succeeding the blandness of "changing scenes," as if Longfellow were replacing, rather than following up on, the earlier plural noun. Longfellow may again have had Milton in mind, since "Methought I saw my late espousèd saint" ends, "I wak'd, she fled, and day brought back my night: "day" becomes the final noun in Longfellow's last line, as "night" was the most important noun in the first. Where Longfellow began by measuring time, dividing the night into "watches," by the end of the poem the measures of time have lost meaning. Winter and summer, day and night, each of the eighteen years since 1861 all prove equally pointless, meaningless, since none of them can efface, reverse, or alter Fanny's death.

Longfellow inclined temperamentally to give comfort: those of his poems most famous in his own time may sound, in ours, full of false cheer. (One sonnet finds him "confident, that what the future yields / Shall be the right, unless myself be wrong.") The octave to "The Cross of Snow," reread, takes some small comfort in the memory of Fanny's virtuous life, a lesson that survives for the poet and others, a lesson more virtuous than any book. By the end of the sestet, however, that lesson is not canceled, exactly, but almost without consequence. The sonnet thus looks forward to the modern poems about mourning, studied at length by Peter Sacks and by Jahan Ramazani, in which a reluctantly secular poet finds no sufficient consolation, no good end for durable grief. The memory of Fanny's life holds lessons, but the scarlike, unpromising "cross" on Longfellow's breast has nothing more to teach him, and no way to change us. It is, simply, unchanging and unrelieved memory.

SB

Later Life 17

CHRISTINA ROSSETTI

1881

Something this foggy day, a something which
  Is neither of this fog nor of to-day,
  Has set me dreaming of the winds that play
Past certain cliffs, along one certain beach,
  And turn the topmost edge of·waves to spray:
  Ah pleasant pebbly strand so far away,
So out of reach while quite within my reach,
  As out of reach as India or Cathay!
I am sick of where I am and where I am not,
  I am sick of foresight and of memory,
  I am sick of all I have and all I see,
  I am sick of self, and there is nothing new;
Oh weary impatient patience of my lot!—
  Thus with myself: how fares it, Friends, with you?

THE bilingual daughter of an Italian émigré, Christina acquired at least as much poetic reputation in her time as her brothers Dante Gabriel and William Michael, and many of her poems are remembered now: among them, the *sui generis* narrative "Goblin Market," with its uncanny sexual symbolism; the Christmas carol "In the bleak midwinter"; and such quiet, sad lyric work as "Up-hill." She had a reputation for piety, too: a devout Anglican, she turned down at least one suitor for reasons of religious incompatibility, and devoted her mature years to literature and to charitable works. Christina Rossetti's oeuvre includes verse in English and in Italian, narrative poems for adults, songs for children, and sonnets in almost every mode available to her day. "This my tome / Has many sonnets," says Rossetti in the prefatory poem to her volume *A Pageant* (1881), as indeed it has: that book collects her two most important sequences.

The first, *Monna Innominata* (My Lady Unnamed), portrays a chaste lady's successive answers to a courtly lover. Each of its fourteen sonnets bears two epigraphs, one from Dante and one from Petrarch. A conscious response to the Italian amorous tradition, the sequence concludes—typically, for Rossetti—with Christian renunciation: "I will not seek for blossoms anywhere," the lady promises, "Except such common flowers as blow with corn."

The second sequence, *Later Life* (its title refers to Rossetti's fiftieth birthday), is less concerned with Petrarchan questions of courtship, and more fully Victorian: wider in range, tones, and models, with sonnets on seasons, moods, and travels, imitations of Shakespeare (see the twenty-fifth in the series, "When we consider what this life we lead"), and sonnets that might do double duty as prayers. The sonnet discussed here in certain ways summarizes Christina Rossetti's powers, since it is at once a poem of travel, of landscape, of memory, of mood, of melancholy, of spare diction, of elegant self-analysis, and of dismay with the ways of this world. Yet it is also atypical of her verse: however deep its melancholy, it substitutes, for any more pious conclusion, an unexpected, almost cheerful humor. It also considers the completed circuit, the link between author and reader, that any finished poem implies.

Rossetti's antitheses and contradictions evoke frustration and a baffling vagueness, a mental fog laid over a meteorological one. The sonnet begins as a landscape poem, and opens as if to project a Petrarchan rhyme scheme *(abba)*. Yet it veers away from the conventions it evokes, both in its imagery and in its organization (the octave turns out to rhyme not *abba abba,* but *abba bbab*). Otherwise-unexplained mental associations normally connect like with like, and spray-wracked beaches are, like London fogs, full of mist. We might expect an impression of "this foggy day," akin to the beach scenes and nocturnes of James McNeill Whistler, whom Christina had met and Dante Gabriel knew well. Instead, the "foggy day" brings "Something" that does not belong in the impressionistic poem (a poem about weather and scenery) that Rossetti might prefer to write, but cannot write today. (She did write such poems on other days: see the beautiful, refreshing *Later Life* 21).

Rather than sensory similarities, Rossetti's octave offers contrast and inner confusion. "Today" and the prior day at the beach ("strand") turn out to be opposites: the latter "pleasant," the former anything but. Beaches and cliffs mark off the sea from the land, and English shores distinguish home from abroad. Yet for Rossetti these bounds might as well not exist, since the beach and its cliffs are as "far away" for the poet as nations overseas. Perhaps she cannot, whatever her wish, leave London: Christina and her elderly mother spent the summer of 1880 at the seaside town of Eastbourne, but returned to the city together that fall. Yet travel might not help, even were it an option: anywhere now seems to her as good, or as dismal, as anywhere else. All scenes of relief, or of renewed interest in life, seem equally impossible to the poet adrift in her own psychological mist.

After such involutions and such vagueness, the sestet comes as a mild shock: following a lengthy, multiply subordinated sentence whose subject is "something," Rossetti gives independent clause after independent clause, each the length of one line, each with the subject "I," each with a predicate clear, general, crisp and grim. The beach scene, we realize, came into the poem as Rossetti's finally unsuccessful attempt to distract herself from her internal state, from the grim unease, the "something" in her soul, that generates the poem, and that she spells out in her sestet. Yet octave and sestet both confound paired opposites: in both, things that should be the same are really antithetical (beach mist and London fog), and things that should be antitheses seem synonymous (English and foreign shores). So it falls out in her "I" statements too: "where I am" might as well be "where I am not," the future might as well be the same as the past, "all I have" (what already belongs to the poet) seems as worthless as "all I see" (what she might learn or acquire at some future date), since all provoke in her the same ennui.

With these insistent equations come hammered repetitions: "I am sick of" (five times in four lines), "out of reach" (twice, plus "within my reach," in the same two lines), "where I am" (twice). The same lines also deliver oxymorons ("impatient patience"), a familiar feature of the Petrarchan sonnet, with its icy fires. Rossetti's unerotic oxymorons, though, signal not lovesickness (fixation on one erotic object) but a causeless, objectless enervation, an inability to fix on any object at all. All objects seem equal because they are equally uninspiring. Such equations arise not from external circumstances ("neither of this fog nor of today") but from her own character, her "lot."

Few readers consider Rossetti, in general, funny, though her poems for children show lightness of touch. We have to hear sadness ("I am sick . . . I am sick . . . I am sick") in the parallels of her emphatic line. Yet her closing question sounds jaunty, if not indeed comic: "How fares it, Friends, with you?" The question suddenly places all the preceding lines, with their fogs and their fears, in the past; not coincidentally, it uses six words that appear nowhere else in the poem. Alone for thirteen lines, Rossetti suddenly notices that she might have an audience, an awareness that must console her no matter what answer her question gets. If we feel unlike her (sunnier, less foggy), perhaps tomorrow she will feel more like us; if we feel like her—if we share her restlessness—at least she can know that her pain is shared.

Rossetti's other sonnets also explore extremes of ennui, acedia, or despair. They come close to what we now call clinical depression (as "this foggy day" comes close to Sylvia Plath's "Sheep in Fog"). One early poem imagined a world made of "Cobwebs," "with neither night nor day," "no pulse of life through all the loveless land." Bleak for thirteen lines, that country becomes at the last attractive, since it promises no "fear forevermore." Christina Rossetti never published that sonnet (William Michael saw it into print after her death): its featureless classical underworld could not fit her Christian belief, which provided some uplifting endings to other sad poems. *Later Life* 7, for example, turns away from this "insipid" life toward Christ, who "Can satisfy all hearts—yea, thine and mine."

There is no Christian consolation, though, in *Later Life* 17. Instead, Rossetti asks how a poem itself, simply by representing its author's moods, might solace its author, and its readers as well. Tired of herself, she turns to us: tired of "me," "I," "my," and "myself" (the only pronouns in her first thirteen lines), she turns toward a plural "you." John Stuart Mill argued that true poetry, or at least lyric poetry, is overheard—that in it the soul speaks only to itself. Gerard Manley Hopkins suggested instead that a lyric poem was akin to a musical score, not so much the voice of the poet alone as a composition for performance by an attentive and sympathetic reader. Both accounts make sense; neither alone explains the power of a lyric poem to fix itself in readers' memories, to describe "something" (Rossetti's word) within the poet even as it describes "something" within readers too. So Rossetti implies. And so she turns, not to a friend, nor to a lover, nor even to God, but to us, asking if we have ever felt this way ourselves. Simply to ask, to realize that "Friends" might be able to answer, is, for this wry moment, enough.

SB

"The New Colossus"

EMMA LAZARUS

1883

Not like the brazen giant of Greek fame,
With conquering limbs astride from land to land;
Here at our sea-washed, sunset gates shall stand
A mighty woman with a torch, whose flame
Is the imprisoned lightning, and her name
Mother of Exiles. From her beacon-hand
Glows world-wide welcome; her mild eyes command
The air-bridged harbor that twin cities frame.
"Keep, ancient lands, your storied pomp!" cries she
With silent lips. "Give me your tired, your poor,
Your huddled masses yearning to breathe free,
The wretched refuse of your teeming shore.
Send these, the homeless, tempest-tossed to me,
I lift my lamp beside the golden door!"

THE COLOSSUS of Rhodes was a gigantic statue of Helios, the Greek sun god. One of the Seven Wonders of the World, it stood more than a hundred feet high—an ancient skyscraper. The dedicatory poem for the statue, thought to have been inscribed on its pedestal, read, "To you, Sun, the people of Dorian Rhodes erected this statue that reaches Olympus, having laid to rest the brazen wave of war and crowned their city with the foe's spoils." (The men of Rhodes built the statue partly from melted weapons, captured in a battle against Demetrius, an invading general.) The poem concluded: "Not only on sea but on land, they set the lovely light of freedom and independence. To the descendents of Herakles belongs dominion on sea and land."

These lines on the Colossus of Rhodes, available in the Greek Anthology

(6.177), provided clear inspiration for Emma Lazarus' famous sonnet about the "new colossus," the Statue of Liberty destined for New York harbor. Lazarus was the daughter of a prominent New York Sephardic Jewish family, a friend of Emerson, Longfellow, and Henry James, and a talented woman of letters: she translated into English the verse of the German Jewish writer Heinrich Heine, as well as medieval Hebrew poetry.

Lazarus wrote "The New Colossus" in 1883, spurred by the campaign to raise money for a pedestal for Frédéric-Auguste Bartholdi's statue *Liberty Enlightening the World,* which the French government had promised to give to the United States. At the time, the monument, not yet known as the Statue of Liberty, was still in pieces. (Bizarrely, the gargantuan hand with its torch was on exhibit in Manhattan's Madison Square Park; much of the rest of the statue remained in France.) Joseph Pulitzer's *New York World* promoted the cause of Lady Liberty. Pennies poured in from schoolchildren and working people. Three years later, the statue was finally assembled and dedicated.

Freedom was as important to Lazarus as it was to Bartholdi and Edouard de Laboulaye, the French law professor who conceived the project of the liberty statue. She saw an intimate connection between liberty and social justice. Throughout her brief life (she died at the age of thirty-eight), Lazarus worked on behalf of the poor, particularly the Jewish immigrants from eastern Europe and Russia then flooding into America. Encouraging her to join in the fundraising for the liberty statue, her friend Constance Harrison told her, "Think of that Goddess standing on her pedestal down yonder in the bay, and holding her torch out to those Russian refugees of yours you are so fond of visiting at Ward's Island." Except for the hand, Lazarus had only seen photographs of the statue. But she set to work. "The New Colossus" became her most popular poem, and was inscribed on the statue's pedestal in 1903. And long after Lazarus' death, a passage from "The New Colossus" greeted international arrivals at Idlewild Airport, later JFK.

Lazarus begins her sonnet by contrasting Lady Liberty with "the brazen giant of Greek fame," the Helios that towered over Rhodes. "Brazen" here (an echo of the Greek Anthology epigram) has a double sense: made of bronze, and showing a warlike boastfulness. The "conquering limbs" of Helios announce the dominion of Rhodes over sea and land, as the poem on the ancient colossus emphasizes. Yet the Greek poem also sees in the sun god a torch of freedom: Lazarus will rely on this image in her response to the Liberty statue.

The "twin cities" that Lazarus mentions are Brooklyn and Manhattan, not yet incorporated as one. New York harbor is "air-bridged" because joined by the Brooklyn Bridge, which was first opened in 1883, the same year that Lazarus wrote "The New Colossus." The cities "frame" the harbor, supporting and surrounding it. But the harbor, an emblem of security and welcome, remains at the center of the picture. (An earthquake destroyed the Colossus of Rhodes only fifty years after it was built, in the third century BCE. But pictures from the Renaissance and later periods imagine Helios standing astride the harbor of Rhodes. Ships pass to and fro between his monumental legs.)

New York harbor presents "our sunset gates." The West is, as the Germans called it, the *Abendland* ("evening-land")—the latest, and youngest, outpost of the civilization stemming from Europe. The "mighty woman with a torch" replaces Helios with a maternal, yet powerful and ardent, image. "Mother of Exiles" Lazarus names her, after a breathless enjambment. Like a lighthouse beacon, she guides ships to land—the ships of immigrants, who were in Lazarus' era flocking in increasing numbers to America. In 1882, immigration reached a new peak of nearly 790,000 for the year; more than 23 million immigrants arrived between 1880 and 1920. Henry James, repelled and fascinated by the influx, noticed that only a few scraps of English could be heard among the speakers of Yiddish and Italian who thronged the Lower East Side streets. Lazarus' Liberty is more sympathetic than James. With her "mild eyes," she shelters the refugees. (Their status as "refuse" has nothing to do with trash, but rather means that they were rejected by their native countries.)

"Whose flame / Is the imprisoned lightning," Lazarus writes of the statue's torch. Lazarus' biographer, Esther Schor, points out that these lines hark back to a foreboding image in one of her earlier sonnets, "Progress and Poverty." In that poem, Lazarus writes, "Science lights her lamp / At the brief lightning's momentary flame." But the voyages of discovery and the scientific advances of the Enlightenment also require suffering. Workers live in a "deep, reeking hell," below the decks of the explorer's ship. "What slaves be they, / Who feed the ravenous monster," Lazarus asks in "Progress and Poverty." With "The New Colossus," Lazarus transforms the "huddled masses" from the forgotten slaves who power the brilliant, yet dreadful, machine of progress into a group "yearning" for freedom. But Lazarus' image of imprisoned lightning continues the theme of "Progress and Poverty." It implies a captive power, straining against the forces that keep it contained. (Who will free the lightning, and make it a true beam of enlightenment?)

In the sestet, Lazarus, who called Emerson "Master and Father," reiterates an Emersonian theme: self-reliance (see Arnold's response in "Written in Emerson's Essays," earlier in this book). America does not require the Old World's renowned culture—its "storied pomp," as Liberty puts it in her speech. In stirring lines, Liberty announces that America reaches out for and welcomes, in fact needs, the immigrants of the "ancient lands" across the sea. "Give me your tired, your poor, / Your huddled masses yearning to breathe free": these lines are so familiar that it may be impossible to see them with fresh eyes. Many American schoolchildren still learn them by heart. The implication of the lines—that America offers a refuge, and a new chance—remains fundamental.

As a contrast to her own poem, Lazarus may have been thinking of English poetry's most familiar example of a monumental but hollow boast, that of Shelley's "Ozymandias." Lazarus sets her figure of Liberty, with her mild "command," against the tyrannical speech of rulers like Shelley's pharaoh. Instead of presiding over a desert, and trumpeting her fame with a "sneer of cold command," as Ozymandias does, Liberty devotes herself to the "homeless" and "tempest-tossed," the migrants buffeted by fate.

For Jews escaping pogroms in eastern Europe, for southern Italians fleeing dire rural poverty, and for the Irish looking for an end to their suffering under British rule, America in the 1880s was a *goldene medina* ("golden land," in Yiddish). The New World had its own miseries: the filthy, crowded tenements of the Lower East Side, the barbarous factories. But America still opened a door to the future. When we turn back to "Progress and Poverty," or reflect on Lazarus' own efforts to assist the poor, we can see that she was troubled, as well as made hopeful, by the America that the immigrants were entering. Lazarus, like other reform-minded citizens of her day, wanted to ensure a decent life for the "huddled masses." In her eyes the monumental colossus, France's recent gift, goaded America not to self-congratulation, but to further striving toward justice. The statue raises us up to welcome the stranger at the door, the immigrant about to become one of us. By making it clear that Liberty means a challenge, not merely a reward, Lazarus made a permanent contribution to America's sense of itself.

DM

"As kingfishers catch fire, dragonflies dráw fláme"

GERARD MANLEY HOPKINS

Written by 1883; published 1918

.

As kingfishers catch fire, dragonflies dráw fláme;
As tumbled over rim in roundy wells
Stones ring; like each tucked string tells, each hung bell's
Bow swung finds tongue to fling out broad its name;
Each mortal thing does one thing and the same:
Deals out that being indoors each one dwells;
Selves—goes itself; *myself* it speaks and spells,
Crying *Whát I do is me: for that I came.*

I say móre: the just man justices;
Kéeps gráce: thát keeps all his goings graces;
Acts in God's eye what in God's eye he is—
Chríst—for Christ plays in ten thousand places,
Lovely in limbs, and lovely in eyes not his
To the Father through the features of men's faces.

HOPKINS, an English Roman Catholic and a Jesuit priest for almost all of his brief adult life, here explains with a brace of examples how his vividly patterned poetry, and his eye for the details of the created world, drew on his Catholic beliefs. That argument begins from notions Hopkins found in his favorite theologian, the medieval English thinker John Duns Scotus. According to Scotus, every thing—animal, vegetable, or mineral—in God's creation has its own essence, its *haecceitas* or "thisness," put there by the Creator. We can come closer to God, and know more of Him, as we know more about— and as we admire—the visual, auditory, tactile, and kinesthetic properties of the animals, plants, and objects in God's creation. Hopkins called the unique spark, the God-given energy, in each created thing its *instress;* he called the impression it makes on our senses (once we look at it closely enough) its *inscape.* To watch a bird, or a flower, or a stone, attentively and generously enough is to discover its inscape, and then to contemplate the inner energy, the unique spirit, that made that inscape possible—a spirit put there, of course, by God.

To study the Creation closely enough, to attend to inscape and instress, is thus to pay homage to its Creator, and that is what Hopkins's descriptive language does; in this sonnet he also explains why he does so, how this mode of homage operates. The sonnet thus instructs us in right perception, starting with compact and highly colored examples. Kingfishers "catch fire" and dragonflies "draw flame" because both iridesce when they fly or perch in the sun (the kingfisher is also an emblem of Christ). Because they move so beautifully, with such brightly visible energies, bird and insect make especially good demonstrations of inscape, of divine powers coming to our notice through the creatures in the visible world. Bird and insect reveal their inner uniqueness visually; stones dropped in wells (out of sight) reveal theirs via sound. Each creature, each object, reveals its note, "goes itself," when perceived in action, as a violin string is most truly itself when played (when bowed or plucked). And the divine Creation (unlike a violin) is forever perceived (by God), forever in action, forever harmonious and in tune.

In many of Hopkins's sonnets, as Joseph Phelan says, "the octave sets out the beauty and glory of this world, and the sestet reorients the reader toward . . . God": so it is here. Since the octave describes the nonhuman parts of Creation, it omits both morality and theonymy: God and Christ are never named. Created things without consciousness have no choice about how they display their inscape; they can neither reject, nor choose to pursue, the unique qualities that God gave them. Human beings, however, can act in harmony or out of harmony with their essences. To act out of harmony with one's own essence is to sin, for Hopkins always unlovely. To act in harmony with one's own best essence is to imitate the human being who acted most in harmony with himself: Christ, both fully human and fully divine. To act so—to "justice" (Hopkins makes the noun into a verb, as we might say that the dragonfly of line 1 "dragonflies") is to "keep grace," to show piety and mercy, to be Christ-like. When we do so, as the Son did, the Father is pleased.

The sonnet amounts to an argument, with a general claim (reduced to a proposition, it would be something like "God admires expressions of unique natures, since He put them there") and then two clusters of evidence for that claim, drawn from nonhuman and then from human life. It also revels in details, and in local aural effects. The first four lines include no agents capable of human speech, and what satisfies there consists mostly in imitative and intricate sound: flares of alliteration and chiasmatic (A-B-B-A) patterns of consonance ("fire," "dragonflies," "draw," "flame") introduce further alliteration ("rim," "roundy") and then a riot of internal rhyme ("ring," "string," "tells," "bell's," "swung," "tongue," "fling," "thing," "thing," "dwell," the "sell" in "self" and "selves").

These intense, infolded aural patterns abate as the octave draws to its close, throwing emphasis less on sound and more upon semantic nuance. "Each mortal thing" speaks for itself, explaining that by acting according to its unique nature, it acts out God's purpose on earth (Hopkins here adapts Scotian theology). Dragonflies fly and iridesce—at least, they do when they are most fully dragonfly-like; just men (human beings) act justly—at least, they do when they are most true to their best natures, most Christ-like. The sestet thus depends not only on aural effects, but also on the changing meanings of its repeated words: "just," "grace," "lovely," "eyes." "Goings" means actions (what we do as we move through the world), but also motions (how we stride or stroll from place to place). Had the poem ended at line ten, the conjunction of these two meanings would imply that people who act mercifully have better carriage or posture, that beautiful people are morally better than physically unattractive ones, and that to be gracious is to be graceful too. Though Plato implied as much, such an equation of mercy with elegance, graciousness with gracefulness, for modern human beings might seem improbable—as improbable, perhaps, as Hopkins's analogy between "justicing" and the sparkling glide of a dragonfly.

We know that beautiful people can be cruel, that ugly and disfigured people can be kind: if we ask only about our own notions of beauty, Hopkins's sestet may seem false to experience. If we ask instead what looks beautiful, graceful, to God, "in God's eye," Hopkins's equations make much more sense. God watches us even more attentively than the best human observer can watch a dragonfly. Watching us, God the Father looks for Christ's nature, the Nature of his Son, which is beautiful to Him, just as we look for dragonfly essence in dragonflies, which are beautiful to us. When God sees people who love and imitate Christ, who partake of Christ's nature, God therefore finds them "lovely," whether or not we find them attractive. Since the poem has to do with notions of beauty, with what seems "lovely" to whom and why, Hopkins does not address sin (which required grace in the first place): he shows, as it were, the Creation on a good day, when the relation of the divine to the human works as it should. The introduction of Christ (twice) at line 12 also replaces justice with mercy, the old dispensation with the new. As if to celebrate that new dispensation, Hopkins can end with virtuosic, almost nonstop alliteration: "plays"-"places," "ten"-"thousand," "lovely"-"limbs"-"lovely," "father"-"features"-"faces." The last line also climbs out of what, by Hopkins's standards, has been a nearly regular meter: triple feet (anapests) and a triplet of prepositional clauses ("to the . . . through the . . . of . . .") drive the emphatic twelve-syllable close.

Hopkins made almost no effort to publish his poems, whose idiosyncratic language and at times unorthodox theology might have displeased his Jesuit superiors; they survived because he sent them in letters to literary friends, such as the Anglican clergyman R. W. Dixon and the future poet laureate Robert Bridges. Hopkins wrote to Bridges during the late 1870s, the same years in which he likely wrote this poem: "No doubt my poetry errs on the side of oddness. . . . But as air, melody, is what strikes me most of all in music and design in painting, so design, pattern, or what I am in the habit of calling 'inscape' is what I above all aim at in poetry. Now it is the virtue of design, pattern or inscape to be distinctive and it is the vice of distinctiveness to become queer." Not only does Hopkins's sonnet explain instress and inscape, finding in each creature's being (including our own human natures) evidence of God's presence; the poem also defends Hopkins's search for goodness and beauty, not only in doctrinal universals, but in the particular physical and moral quality, the timbre or luster or style, unique to each part of the created world.

SB

"Thou art indeed just, Lord, if I contend"

GERARD MANLEY HOPKINS

Written 1889; published 1918

*Justus quidem tu es, Domine, si disputem tecum; verumtamen justa
    loquar ad te: quare via impiorum prosperatur? &c. (Jerem. xii 1).*

Thou art indeed just, Lord, if I contend
With thee; but, sir, so what I plead is just.
Why do sinners' ways prosper? and why must
Disappointment all I endeavor end?
    Wert thou my enemy, O thou my friend,
How wouldst thou worse, I wonder, than thou dost
Defeat, thwart me? Oh, the sots and thralls of lust
Do in spare hours more thrive than I that spend,
Sir, life upon thy cause. See, banks and brakes
Now leavèd how thick! lacèd they are again
With fretty chervil, look, and fresh wind shakes
Them; birds build—but not I build; no, but strain,
Time's eunuch, and not breed one work that wakes.
Mine, O thou lord of life, send my roots rain.

HOPKINS'S apparently bleak—but in some ways triumphant—sonnet be-
gins as a translation from the prophet Jeremiah, who wondered, as Hopkins
did, how his misery might comport with the ways of a just God. Hopkins's
sonnet does not, however, end there: if its first glories involve the verve with
which Hopkins can make the prophet's words fit his own case, its last include
the ways in which Hopkins and Jeremiah diverge.

    Near the end of his life almost every poem that Hopkins finished was a sonnet, and most of those sonnets were wrenchingly sad; later critics called them, collectively, his "terrible sonnets" ("terrible" as in "terrifying") for the depth of their bleak moods. "Thou art indeed just" is probably one of his last, sent in March 1889 (when Hopkins was living in Ireland) to Robert Bridges: "it must be read adagio molto and with great stress," Hopkins advised. In what seems to have been his very last, the sonnet "To R.B.," Hopkins apologizes to Bridges for his lack of "inspiration," his inability to sustain the rich praise for God's work—"the roll, the rise, the carol, the creation"—that his earlier poems (such as "As kingfishers catch fire") had shown.

Instead, Hopkins in his last months wrote of impatience, of loneliness, and even—despite his faith and his vocation as a Jesuit priest—of despair. "Thou art indeed just" is a poem about despair, and also a poem about infertility in spring, when everything blooms and flourishes save only the poet himself. Such lonely spring poems comprise a tradition of their own, from Surrey to Coleridge (see "Work without Hope," in this collection) and beyond. Hopkins adds his own, paradoxically vigorous, complaint, and his own vivid description of the lush green nature amid which he cannot find any symbol for himself.

Hopkins's sonnet begins as if the author planned to offer a theodicy, an argument that explains why God is (despite appearances) fair and just. Hopkins tried a full-scale theodicy in his own sublime long poem "The Wreck of the *Deutschland*" (1876); here he does not so much construct a theodicy as yearn for one. Hopkins's sonnet also begins as a translation: most of the octave renders into Hopkins's strenuously rhymed English the passage he quotes in Latin from the Book of Jeremiah, Chapter 12 (he may or may not have considered the Latin a title). The classically educated Hopkins, like most Jesuits, would have preferred to read the Bible in the Latin of Saint Jerome; the King James Version has, for Jeremiah 12:1: "Righteous art thou, O Lord, when I plead with thee: yet let me talk with thee of thy judgments: Wherefore doth the way of the wicked prosper? Wherefore are all they happy that deal very treacherously?"

Hopkins's version of the same passage highlights its sense of argument, of impassioned but almost legalistic dispute. We see not only "just" but "contend" and "plead"; we hear "why," twice, and then the counterfactual question, "Wert thou my enemy . . . / How wouldst thou worse . . . thwart me?" Repeated words and sounds emphasize Hopkins's frustration: "endeavor" and "enemy" reinforce four rhymes on "end." Jeremiah—who seeks to reform his

community, to turn an erring Israel back toward the ways of the Lord—
emphasizes the threat that a just God may pose to sinners, however much
those sinners prosper now. Hopkins emphasizes instead his own misfortune:
"all *I* endeavor," "thou dost / Defeat, thwart *me*" (phrases not in the biblical
source). Those first-person pronouns are also singular pronouns: Hopkins
evokes groups of sinners, and then, as against them, himself.

The translation, and its Latin title or headnote, might make the poem—for
a present-day reader—look and feel like a sermon, with Jeremiah 12 as its text,
such a sermon as Hopkins (who had been a parish priest in Liverpool) might
give. But the inward and personal sentiments in the poem, and its turn to ad-
dress God (not a congregation), bring the poem closer to a kind of religious
prose less familiar today: the record of a spiritual meditation, as practiced in
particular by Jesuits, and as invented by Ignatius Loyola, the Jesuits' founder.
Hopkins takes from Ignatian meditation the practice of starting from a par-
ticular text, the use of the senses to imagine a place, and the concluding direct
address to God, though he does not follow its full set of rules.

A meditation, a sermon, or a theological argument might pose a problem
and then propose a solution. A translation, on the other hand, would stay
with the text: if the first part of the sonnet adapted Jeremiah 12:1, the second
might adapt what the prophet says next. Yet Hopkins, at the sonnet's turn,
does neither: he abandons the structure and the terms proper to argument,
and he swerves away from the tone and the sense of the prophet's words. Jere-
miah continues (12:2–4, in the King James Version again): "Thou hast planted
them, yea, they have taken root: they grow, yea, they bring forth fruit: thou
art near in their mouth, and far from their reins. But thou, O Lord, knowest
me: thou hast seen me, and tried mine heart toward thee: pull them out like
sheep for the slaughter, and prepare them for the day of slaughter." The plants
in Jeremiah are figures for people who flout divine law (he then compares the
same people to horses and sheep). Those people face "slaughter," he warns, if
they do not change.

Hopkins, by contrast, compares himself to the birds and the plants that he
sees, which God will not punish, and which can have done nothing wrong.
The flora and fauna here represent God's bounty, in "banks" and "brakes"
(hedges and groupings of plants) "thick" enough to provide relief from the
wind: Hopkins admires and emulates their vital interpenetration in his syn-
tax. ("Chervil" is cow parsley, whose flowerets remind Hopkins of a "fret," a
net of jewels for the hair.) Hopkins has shunted Jeremiah's malediction into

an earlier sentence (lines 7–9) about "sots and thralls of lust"—people who seek fertility of a sort, but do not otherwise resemble vegetation—as if to clear space for the flourishing and blameless foliage of the sestet. Alliteration heightens the emulation of fertile nature: "fretty chervil . . . fresh," "birds build." Alliteration also reinforces the contrast between the poet, who "builds" and "breeds" nothing, and birds who breed in their built nests.

Hopkins brings out, in Jeremiah, the sense of complaint, of the faithful man's misfortune as a problem for the believer. The lyric poet leaves behind, however, the prophet's mission, his demands that his nation reform. Indeed he addresses no nation, wishing only that he himself be well planted, bear fruit. Hopkins registers a temperamental distance from the biblical prophet too, deemphasizing the punishment of sinners and emphasizing the benevolence of God. In a sermon of 1880, Hopkins preached on John 16: "Justice in the Scripture means goodness. . . . Cheering men on against sin is not the same as cheering men on to justice, though now the two things go together." That sermon continues, adapting John 12:47: "*God did not send his son into the world,* Christ said, *to judge (or condemn) the world but that by him the world might be saved.*"

Hopkins's sestet alludes to his priestly vocation: celibate, he will not "breed," and may feel like a "eunuch." But the fertility for which he yearns has little to do with begetting children; rather (as in other late sonnets), he wants to "build," to create "one work," one poem, that pays homage to his God—a work that need not do something *to* someone else (for example, make sinners mend their ways) in order to take on the vivid energy "that wakes," the energy Hopkins wishes his poems would have. Hopkins's turn to immediate nature in the sestet is also a turn away from his poem's opening, with its hint of theodicy, its legal-argumentative language, its anger against "sots and thralls," or even a turn against notions of *judgment* as such.

Having made that turn, Hopkins ends with a one-line prayer: "Mine, O thou lord of life, send my roots rain." This sentence has no equivalent in Jeremiah 12 (though it does echo Jeremiah 14:21–22), and it is the only complete one-line clause in the poem. Here, too, Hopkins flaunts playful alliteration—"lord . . . life," "roots rain"—wrapped up (as nowhere else in the poem) with echoes that link the start of the line to its end: "Mine . . . rain." Hopkins here sounds calmer, less desperate, if still unsatisfied. He no longer wants to know something, or to prove something, or to answer a "why" question, nor does he attend (like Jeremiah) to the fate of a community of believers, to whether and how they might change. Instead, he prays that a merciful God might reward his struggle, or alleviate his pain, with the same benevolence that the Creator shows, every March, to chervil and to nesting birds.

To notice Hopkins's prayer for refreshment, his turn away from his own resentment and anger, is not to deny this sonnet its sad mood, its place amid the "course of loathing and hopelessness" that afflicted the last years of Hopkins's "wretched life" (the phrases are his own, from a journal of 1888). Yet the sonnet also stands as a monument to Hopkins's observation, to the details he found—and found afresh, even when he himself felt exhausted and grim—in visible nature, in the created world.

SB

"Mt. Lykaion"

TRUMBULL STICKNEY

1905

Alone on Lykaion since man hath been
Stand on the height two columns, where at rest
Two eagles hewn of gold sit looking East
Forever; and the sun goes up between.
Far down around the mountain's oval green
An order keeps the falling stones abreast.
Below within the chaos last and least
A river like a curl of light is seen.
Beyond the river lies the even sea,
Beyond the sea another ghost of sky,—
O God, support the sickness of my eye
Lest the far space and long antiquity
Suck out my heart, and on this awful ground
The great wind kill my little shell with sound.

MOUNT LYKAION, in the southern Peloponnese, is the legendary birthplace
of Zeus, king of the Greek gods. In antiquity, the mountain's summit con-
tained Zeus's altar and, in front of it, two columns topped with golden eagles.
No shadow is cast by any creature, human or animal, that passes within
Mount Lykaion's central area, the shrine of Zeus: so reports the ancient Greek
historian Pausanias. Trumbull Stickney's "Mt. Lykaion" conjures the trance-
like, dreadful atmosphere that Pausanias attributes to the mountaintop. The
poet, like the historian, depicts Mount Lykaion as eerie and hallowed.

"Mt. Lykaion" may respond to Keats's "On Seeing the Elgin Marbles." Both
poems convey a resonant encounter with antiquity. Like Keats, Stickney is
confronted by a sensation of, as he puts it, "sickness." He feels overmastered

by the ancient world, weak in its presence. He has met the canonical grandeur of Greece, and finds himself dizzied by it. But unlike Keats, who actually viewed the Elgin Marbles, Stickney did not see the columns with Zeus's eagles. They have been gone for many centuries, recorded only in ancient writers. Stickney describes a hallucinatory landscape.

The hallucination answers Stickney's own fragile psychic state. Born in Geneva, taught Latin and Greek by his father, Stickney attended Harvard and the Sorbonne, and traveled extensively through Europe. In 1903, he became an instructor of Greek at Harvard. That summer, on a trip to Greece, he began writing his *Sonnets from Greece,* from which "Mt. Lykaion" is taken. Stickney was probably already suffering from a brain tumor, which caused faintness and partial blindness; he would be dead the next year, at the age of thirty. (His death uncannily seems to confirm Pausanias' claim that those who trespass on the mountain's summit will live no longer than a year.) Stickney's illness figures in the concluding lines of "Mt. Lykaion": it represents his sense of diminishment in the face of the ancient world he loved.

Stickney's affection for the past remains, in the bleak world of his sonnet, unreciprocated. Amid this hard, bright landscape, the numinous presences of antiquity are absent (there had been a shrine to Pan, as well as the one to Zeus, on Mount Lykaion). The poet stands "alone"—so the first word suggests. Grammatically, "alone" refers to the two columns, but the word also implies Stickney's own isolation and illness: an unsteady wanderer, he has no companion in his travels.

With the signal enjambment that joins lines 3 and 4, Stickney draws our attention to the word "forever," ironically set like a banner at the beginning of its line. The eternal presence of divine power promised by the cult of Zeus could not, in fact, sustain itself; the old gods are dead. Stickney's imaginary eagles look east in mute, hopeless expectation, as if waiting for new divinities from Asia (the source of many aspects of Greek religion). Instead, modern history moved westward, toward France, England, and then America. Stickney can call forth only the static emptiness of a lost world, however beautiful. The repetitive, meaningless action of the sun, whose rising fails to rouse either the poet or the scene it shines on, seals the first quatrain.

After looking up at the sun, Stickney casts his gaze down, toward "the mountain's oval green," where "an order keeps the falling stones abreast." The "order" he evokes is mysterious yet dull, unadorned with mythic resonance. The poet's sight has been reduced to mere notation, conveying no higher sense. With the movement from line 6 to line 7, order has turned to "chaos":

the abyss that one sees when one looks down from a steep mountain like Lykaion. But Stickney, we may assume, is also suffering from the onset of his blindness. The river he finally detects, deep within the void, is "like a curl of light"—a mere trace, off in the distance, and too remote to matter. The Greeks attributed divinity to rivers, too; river gods are important in pastoral poetry. Here, however, the river makes a visual disturbance, and a slight one. It supplies no animating pastoral presence.

Stickney never uses the pronoun "I" in "Mt. Lykaion." He never attributes to himself an act of seeing, nor an act of any kind. The river "is seen"; his eye does not grasp it, can make nothing of it. And this tenuous sight yields, as Stickney begins his sestet, to a dismal, uninviting vista: "Beyond the river lies the even sea, / Beyond the sea another ghost of sky." The phrase "ghost of sky" is the most marked instance of figurative language in the poem. It suggests that even the primal facts of the world, sky and sea, seem ghostly, insubstantial. Stickney calls the sea "even": flat, and incapable of the disturbing energy of Frederick Tuckerman's rolling breakers (in "I looked across the rollers of the deep"). Whitman's sea whispers death (in "Out of the Cradle Endlessly Rocking"); Stickney's sea whispers nothing.

The last four lines of "Mt. Lykaion" shift the tone. They are a desperate prayer, addressed to a God who—we fear—may not be listening. (Is it Zeus or Christ?) With poignance, Stickney begs God to "support the sickness of my eye"—to sustain him in his misery and disorientation, to save him from the worst. He asks not for healing or rejuvenation, but only for a shielding from absolute doom. The ensuing monosyllabic image of the poet's fear is violent: "Lest the far space and long antiquity / Suck out my heart." Those last four words give a profound shock: they plunge us into blankness, and rob the poet of his very life.

"Antiquity" rhymes with "even sea," and it seems similarly level or blank: it is a "long" expanse, uncharacterized except for this one adjective. "Long" here means "long ago"—inconceivably distant in time, and therefore allied to the "far space" extending from the summit of the mountain to its foot. This is "awful ground," a dread, fearful site. The very vacancy of the place, imbued somehow with vestiges of Zeus's power and our awe, threatens to make an empty shell of Stickney, in his vulnerable, physically weakened state.

The "great wind" is the torrent of inspiration, but here it merely blows aggressively against the poet, rather than filling him with rapture. The body without a heart (in the sonnet's penultimate line) is succeeded by a similar image, the "little shell" that has been "kill[ed] . . . with sound" (in the final line;

the assonance of "kill" and "little" quietly devastates). The sound of the wind, coming from nowhere and directed nowhere, contrasts with the mellifluous song that the poet should be making. Stickney here evokes the tortoise shell used to build the first lyre (as recounted in the "Homeric Hymn to Hermes"). The shell, so small against the vast wastes of space and time, is the poet's humble instrument (we may have been expecting the word "soul" instead of "shell," but Stickney returns us to the question of poetic art). Stickney's illness blends now with his sense of his lesser poetic stature. He treads the dark ground that reduces him to a man without a shadow (as in the legend Pausanias relates).

In "Near Helikon," another poem in his *Sonnets from Greece*, Stickney records his unhappy sense of abandonment. As in "Mt. Lykaion," he here recounts a disoriented lapse into the barely perceptible, the onset of a blindness. As in "Mt. Lykaion," too, the poet sees in his fate an exclusion from song:

> To me my troubled life doth now appear
> Like scarce distinguishable summits hung
> Around the blue horizon: places where
> Not even a traveler purposeth to steer,—
> Whereof a migrant bird in passing sung,
> And the girl closed her window not to hear.

As in "Mt. Lykaion," the frail, deeply painful beauty of these lines haunts the reader, who aches for the dying Stickney. Where he traveled, none returns.

DM

"Nests in Elms"

MICHAEL FIELD

1908

The rooks are cawing up and down the trees!
Among their nests they caw. O sound I treasure,
Ripe as old music is, the summer's measure,
Sleep at her gossip, sylvan mysteries,
With prate and clamour to give zest of these—
In rune I trace the ancient law of pleasure,
Of love, of all the busy-ness of leisure,
With dream on dream of never-thwarted ease.
O homely birds, whose cry is harbinger
Of nothing sad, who know not anything
Of sea-birds' loneliness, of Procne's strife,
Rock round me when I die! So sweet it were
To die by open doors, with you on wing
Humming the deep security of life.

To SEE how this sonnet works, and why it might have shocked its initial readers, you must first envision the birds who nest in these elms. They are rooks—big, loud, black, European birds closely akin to crows; in some parts of England, "rook" and "crow" are interchangeable. The most famous rooks in English literature show up in *Macbeth,* where they announce the coming of murder and night: "Light thickens; and the crow / Makes wing to the rooky wood: / Good things of day begin to droop and drowse; / Whiles night's black agents to their preys do rouse." In W. B. Yeats's poem "The Cold Heaven" (1916), "the cold and rook-delighting heaven" holds no delight, but rather terror, for the poet, who envisions the bleak "injustice of the skies." Any reader who knows what a rook is, or how a rook sounds, would associate rooks in poetry (especially rooks seen or heard en masse) with fear or gloom.

Field's opening sentences are therefore a surprise: first in their casual, un-afraid exclamation (Field speaks of the rooks as a more conventional poet might speak of robins or wrens), and then in stating outright that the rooks' unmusical "caw" is something "I treasure." Their sound implies high sum-mer, probably a summer night ("Sleep at her gossip" is Sleep portrayed as an old woman, at her round of social tasks). It implies, for Field, attractive "mysteries"—secrets of a forest (dark forests brought doom for Macbeth) and perhaps the pagan rites or "mysteries" of Celtic Britain or ancient Greece. The caws are like "runes," pagan letterforms (which might record such mysteries). They help Field imagine a pre-Christian hedonism, a preindustrial and Arca-dian life of "ease," as if such a life still existed (could we but envision it) among English birds, in treetops, at night, out of view.

The octave flaunts euphonies and soft, "leisurely" rhymes: *abbaabba,* with all the consonants in the rhyming syllables either sibilant ("ess" sounds) or nearly silent (final *r,* suppressed in most British English). With no mention of death, and only suggestions of night, it makes a positive case for the rooks and their sound: they permit a vicarious fantasy of "never-thwarted" treetop life. The sestet, admitting that the birds are "homely" (both "familiar" and "not beautiful") and that their cry is unmusical too, makes a negative case for them instead: their "cry is harbinger / Of nothing sad." Uttered by a whole flock, among nests, the cry never connotes solitude or homelessness; uttered by a bird that figures in no famous myth of dispossession, the cry compares favor-ably to the nightingale's song, a reminder in Ovid and many later writers (see his *Metamorphoses,* Book 6) of cannibalism and rape. (Procne, in Ovid, dis-covers that her husband, King Tereus, has raped her sister Philomel and then cut out Philomel's tongue. The sisters take bloody revenge, and the gods then change them into birds, a swallow and a nightingale.) Never alone, Field's rooks are also never historical: they exist in a natural, life-giving order which yet contains no human disappointments, because it finds food and strength even in death. (Rooks are not, strictly speaking, carrion crows, but Field may be thinking of the carrion crow's ability to feed on offal.)

Field uses the rooks, their crowds and their forests, to find (as Field's poems often try to find) an almost ecstatic joy in the present moment, a celebration of this-worldly life. And yet that celebration, in a poem of intellectual hon-esty, cannot long remain without the idea of time passing, the thought of the threat of death. A death surrounded by the cry of rooks, and by their wings' loud motion (rather than by any human mourners) would be a death sur-rounded by reminders that the life of nature goes on, reminders that reassure ("rock") almost like lullabies. Robert Frost wrote, in "The Need of Being

Versed in Country Things" (1920), about birds who made their nests in a burnt-out farmhouse: "for them there was really nothing sad." Speaking of these loud rooks, Field seems to make the same point; and Field (unlike the Frost of that later poem) can express open gratitude at the flights and the changes of nonhuman nature, finding "pleasure" in their dissonant sound. That sound, those changes, give Field a sense of "security" (the longest word in the poem, and a rare one in lyric) against the disappointments and the isolation endemic to merely human "life."

Field concludes with serious praise, not for a lushly imagined, unseen Arcadia, but for the homely sounds of northern woods. "Now more than ever seems it rich to die," John Keats wrote in his "Ode to a Nightingale," "To cease upon the midnight with no pain." (Field would have known Keats's verse quite well.) Repudiating the nightingale, Field's close becomes anti-Keatsian in tone and in sentiment. The last sentence implies not a continued dwelling on death, nor a self-conscious embrace of beauty, but an almost bracing return to health, a vision of wild birds as a cure for ennui, and a sense that these rooks, with their nocturnal industry, set an example for our diurnal lives.

"Michael Field" was not one poet but two who wrote as one. Katherine Bradley and her niece Edith Cooper published ten books of poems, and thirty-one plays, under that pseudonym between 1884 and 1914, including elaborate adaptations of Sappho. Their work won early praise from Robert Browning, and attention from Yeats, before falling into near-total neglect for much of the twentieth century. Bradley and Cooper were also lovers, and said as much in their openly amorous poems, connecting their own shared life to what they saw as its pagan (especially ancient Greek) precedents. *Wild Honey from Various Thyme,* their first book of lyric verse in fifteen years, followed their joint conversion to Roman Catholicism in 1907, but contained many poems ("Nests in Elms" likely among them) written earlier, from non-Christian points of view. Though the sonnet eschews the archaizing, pseudo-Greek language that Bradley and Cooper, as Field, affected in their verse of the 1880s and 1890s, "Nests in Elms" is a pagan poem, with no sense of Christian humility, no afterlife, and a setting that evokes both druidic rituals (runes in forests) and Greek myth. It finds sufficient consolation, with the rooks, where other poets might not find "zest" at all: these "homely" birds and sounds give Field (Bradley and Cooper) all the "security" they need.

SB

"Archaic Torso of Apollo"

RAINER MARIA RILKE

(Translated by Edward Snow)

1908

We never knew his head and all the light
that ripened in his fabled eyes. But
his torso still glows like a gas lamp dimmed
in which his gaze, lit long ago,

holds fast and shines. Otherwise the surge
of the breast could not blind you, nor a smile
run through the slight twist of the loins
toward that center where procreation thrived.

Otherwise this stone would stand deformed and curt
under the shoulders' transparent plunge
and not glisten just like wild beasts' fur

and not burst forth from all its contours
like a star: for there is no place
that does not see you. You must change your life.

RAINER MARIA RILKE arrived in Paris in 1902 as a young man of twenty-six and, within his first two days in the new city, sought out the sculptor Auguste Rodin. Three years later, he had become Rodin's secretary, and a devoted student of the great artist's work. His observation of Rodin's methods led Rilke to write what he called *Ding-Gedichte:* "thing-poems," hard and definitive. Everyday selfhood would be transformed into the fiercely conclusive world of things. In the fall of 1907 Rilke also discovered the paintings of Paul Cézanne. "Making real," in the manner of Cézanne and Rodin, became for him the task of art.

Rilke published the first book of his *Neue Gedichte* (New Poems) in 1907. He wrote the second volume, which contains "Archaïscher Torso Apollos" (Archaic Torso of Apollo), in about a year, beginning at the end of July 1907; the book appeared in November 1908. (We give the sonnet in German at the end of this essay.) Both books of *New Poems* draw on objects, people, and creatures that Rilke saw on his walks through Paris: a panther at the zoo, the cathedral of Notre Dame, a blind man in the street. The poet fixes his imagination, with great concentration, to the physical world. In "Archaic Torso," Rilke directs his gaze toward a powerful but fragmentary artwork, the Torso of Miletus in the Louvre. The statue looks back at the poet, and at us, with tremendous intent: the artwork itself guides the poet's awareness. Rilke's earlier work depended on his sensibility; his shifting, exploratory moods gave rise to memorable poems. Here, by contrast, the poet claims to inherit insight from the object he describes. In "Archaic Torso," Rilke's insistence on the objective is, as his translator Edward Snow comments, "disconcerting" and "almost ruthless." A near-compulsive force drives the sonnet to its urgent, surprising conclusion.

Rilke's poems provide a kind of mirror for his readers, one that confirms their inwardness. The poet addresses us directly, with pure, primordial integrity, or so we feel. Instantly drawn in, we consent to the poem's authority over us, the authority of (as the critic Sven Birkerts puts it) "a world comprehended." Rilke's poems, both soothing and rigorous, answer our need. Rilke's continuing popularity is proof that our appetite for transcendence, a legacy of Romanticism and high modernism, remains with us. His words suggest a saving possibility: a reconsecrating of one's life.

We see this possibility in "Archaic Torso." Attention leads to urgency; the pressure of occasion rises and breaks loose into a command. Beauty, the lightning bolt of transcendence, somehow sees into us. In "Archaic Torso," Rilke produces a paradoxical conjunction of what is most deeply inward and "what feels furthest away and most inhospitable" (as Michael André Bernstein comments). Transcendent beauty shocks us: we are forced out of our usual defensive, possessive stance. We suddenly have a task: the world waits for us to realize it, and wants this realization. This world stands forth, a presence both intimate and alien.

Rilke begins with a lack of knowledge: we never knew the torso's head. The German phrase is "unerhörtes Haupt," "unheard-of head"—the adjective "unerhörtes" is often used for something unbelievable, astonishing, or absurd. The missing head remains beyond our ken. This is another realm, invisible to us. But the fragmentary sculpture itself, what remains of it, glows like a lamp that has been turned low. "Kandalaber," Rilke's word for the lamp, probably means a chandelier with gas flames that can be turned up or down. The word Edward Snow translates as "dimmed" is, in German, "screwed back" ("zurück-geschraubt"), a term that images the statue's dense, curved core of meaning. The light of the statue's torso, Rilke continues, "holds fast and shines." Its power stays contained, a tight source.

The octave of "Archaic Torso" spirals downward. Rilke descends from the mechanical (the gaslight chandelier, associated with the figure's unknown head) to the sexual center, depicted in harshly biological terms. The German "Zeugung" ("procreation") is a recondite scientific term. Rilke's choice of words implies that creation is purely instrumental, technical. But Rilke, at the same time, refuses the bristling scientific vocabulary he invokes. He reminds us that the statue's genitals are actually broken off. Whatever was there is now an absence—so the glow of imagination steps in and supplies the missing center. The artist's subtle, slow ripening of his work appears in the work itself. And so the reference to procreation is mitigated by the soft turning, the "slight twist of the loins" ("leisen Drehen"). (The perfect economy of Rilke's German is notable in the octave, and is brilliantly reproduced, so far as is possible, by Snow.)

The sestet returns to the effect of the stone fragment itself, godlike and gleaming ("blenden" means not just "to blind," but "to dazzle"). It begins with the precipitous, repeated u-sounds that make a sonic plunge ("stünde," "und kurz," "unter," "Schultern," "durchsichtigem Sturz"). Then it levels out, and traces borders for experience. "Rändern," meaning "edges" or "contours," rhymes drastically with the sonnet's final word, "ändern" ("change"). With the removal of just one letter, r, composure yields to radical demand. In the final line's phrase, "die dich nicht sieht" ("that does not see you"), two short i's are contained by two long ee-sounds: a verbal image for the utter self-containment of the statue, and the seamless unity of the command that exposes the reader in the middle of life. (The directive "du mußt," "you must," is all the more forceful since it follows a series of negative and conditional phrases.)

The statue itself makes the oracular statement at the end of "Archaic Torso": the force outside us breaks in. The statement sounds oracular, as in Keats's "Ode on a Grecian Urn" ("Beauty is truth, truth beauty . . . "), another poem about an artwork. But in contrast to Keats's line, Rilke's does not promise an integral world. Rather, it sounds like a reproach. Art reaches across the gap that separates it from life and finds that life falls short. Like the statue it describes, Rilke's poem has a jagged edge; it jolts our minds. The statue's command transports us away from our ordinary habits and into an unexplored realm—perhaps a frightening one.

Rilke's "Archaic Torso" has had a lasting impact on American poets, from Randall Jarrell to Robert Lowell to Louise Glück. But the *New Poems* (which contain several other remarkable sonnets) were not his last contribution to the sonnet form. In February 1922 Rilke wrote, in a few weeks, his *Sonette an Orpheus* (Sonnets to Orpheus). Unlike the *New Poems,* these sonnets locate themselves not in an object or an experience of contemplation, but in a far-reaching transitive power: the might and precision of poetry itself. Their intricate dance of words is unique to the original German; it cannot be reproduced in translation. Implacable, taut, and wild, these poems have been freed from the things of this world. The *Sonnets to Orpheus* lack the scenic grounding that the *New Poems* supply. They remain, almost a hundred years later, at the furthest frontiers of poetic art, testimony to the virtuosic energy that the sonnet form inspires.

DM

"Archaïscher Torso Apollos"

RAINER MARIA RILKE

Wir kannten nicht sein unerhörtes Haupt,
darin die Augenäpfel reiften. Aber
sein Torso glüht noch wie ein Kandelaber,
in dem sein Schauen, nur zurückgeschraubt,

sich hält und glänzt. Sonst könnte nicht der Bug
der Brust dich blenden, und im leisen Drehen
der Lenden könnte nicht ein Lächeln gehen
zu jener Mitte, die die Zeugung trug.

Sonst stünde dieser Stein entstellt und kurz
unter der Schultern durchsichtigem Sturz
und flimmerte nicht so wie Raubtierfelle;

und bräche nicht aus allen seinen Rändern
aus wie ein Stern: denn da ist keine Stelle,
die dich nicht sieht. Du mußt dein Leben ändern.

"A Church Romance"
(Mellstock: circa 1835)

THOMAS HARDY

1909

She turned in the high pew, until her sight
Swept the west gallery, and caught its row
Of music-men with viol, book, and bow
Against the sinking sad tower-window light.

She turned again; and in her pride's despite
One strenuous viol's inspirer seemed to throw
A message from his string to her below,
Which said: "I claim thee as my own forthright!"

Thus their hearts' bond began, in due time signed.
And long years thence, when Age had scared Romance,
At some old attitude of his or glance
That gallery-scene would break upon her mind,
With him as minstrel, ardent, young, and trim,
Bowing "New Sabbath" or "Mount Ephraim."

THOMAS HARDY is a brilliant, and a peculiar, poet. Nostalgic, sometimes bitter, he looks at the world with ironic yet empathetic eyes. In his best poems, like "A Church Romance," Hardy refuses to tamper with our sense of the plot. Left to ourselves, we share the author's gravity and his intuitive power. Hardy's ironies, the poet and critic James Richardson remarks, "verge on meaninglessness"—yet they move us deeply. In the wake of the Romantics and the heroic Victorians Tennyson and Browning, Hardy espouses a poetry of limitation. Instead of fiery, relentless personalities, he offers a gallery of ordinary men and women; no spellbinding incantations, but plain-spoken verses. His subtle, weary, and rich sense of the everyday has been profoundly influential on later British poets. (In "A Church Romance," Hardy writes deftly; the poem ranks with compact masterpieces like "During Wind and Rain" and "In Time of 'The Breaking of Nations.'" Elsewhere, he is occasionally uncouth, awkward by design or by fault.)

Hardy locates "A Church Romance" in Mellstock, one of the fictional towns featured in his novels. (Hardy's invented region, Wessex, closely resembles the author's native Dorset.) The scene is the Anglican Sunday service, with the crowd assembled for worship and for music ("New Sabbath" and "Mount Ephraim" are favorite hymns). The songs spur the courtship of Hardy's characters, and prove less godly than erotic: not heavenly but earthbound. The event could well come from one of Hardy's novels, where slight encounters, worked by chance, often determine his characters' lifelong fates. Though better known for his novels, Hardy for the last thirty years of his life devoted himself exclusively to poetry.

The first quatrain of "A Church Romance" depends on three muscular verbs: "turned," "swept," and "caught." Hardy's proud woman takes in the scene from her "high pew" and grasps it instantly. (A high pew has a high back and sides; she is below the gallery, in the middle or near the rear of the church.) She masters with her gaze the setting of the first quatrain, and we expect her to direct the rest of the action as well. In fact, she yields to the occasion, though hers is still the poem's controlling consciousness.

The somber background of line 4 frames the first quatrain with ominous suggestion. The late afternoon submits to darkness; youthful spirits will fade too. Here Hardy produces a gesture of metrical virtuosity, not uncommon in his poetry. He inserts an anapest in the middle of his line 4 in order to graphically convey a heartsick, disoriented swoop: "the sink/*ing sad tów*/er-wind/ow light." (An anapest is a foot consisting of two unstressed syllables followed by one stressed syllable.) We expect "sad" to be stressed, but it is not. This small downward leap responds to the declining sun of twilight, glimpsed through the church window. The ebbing day will become, in the sonnet's sestet, the aging of the protagonists.

The second quatrain shows a reversal: the male musician "claim[s]" the woman—he has turned the tables on her. Like a medieval troubadour, he attracts her through the power of song. Instead of the troubadour's words, however, he uses his violin. In this way he conquers her: she responds "in her pride's despite." She resists, haughty like a medieval lady, then yields to the passionate lover. But she retains an independence of mind that reappears in the sonnet's sestet.

Hardy's father and grandfather played bass viol in Stinsford Church, in Dorset. In Hardy's biography—credited to his wife, Florence, but mainly written by himself—the poet reveals that "A Church Romance" describes the courtship of his parents. The elder Mrs. Hardy told her son that his father appeared in Stinsford's west gallery wearing a "blue swallow-tailed coat with gilt embossed buttons, . . . a red and black flowered waistcoat, Wellington boots, and French-blue trousers." He was, the young lady judged, "rather amusingly old-fashioned, in spite of being decidedly good-looking." Hardy implies the sympathy and the pathos of the (now grown-up) child who imagines his own parents' early love, and the fading of their desire with age. In a poignant fight against time, he becomes both of them.

Hardy, himself a skilled violinist, clearly identifies with his father in this sonnet. The passionate young musician (the "strenuous viol's inspirer") "throw[s]" his "message" to the woman. The violinist's rather stiff, formal declaration—"I claim thee as my own forthright!"—moves us away from youthful fervor and toward the formality of marriage. Hardy's octave culminates in "forthright." The word sounds frank and blunt; its final syllable, "right," carries a legal overtone. The rhyme with "despite" enforces an ironclad factuality.

The man's claim, commanding and binding, provides a transition to the sestet. We sense the stolid, predictable path toward marriage. Instead of describing a joyous wedding ceremony, Hardy dryly mentions "their hearts' bond . . . in due time signed." When this couple consents to wed, they make a mere contract, with all danger, all possibility gone: the word "due" connotes obligation rather than happiness. So far, the sestet, though neutral, feels grim. The tone becomes even more complex in line 10. Now Hardy, along with the wife, looks back from the perspective of years. He paints bleakly, with a curt phrase: "when Age had scared Romance." Romance has been frightened, but how seriously? Has it been frightened away?

Has this been a happy marriage? The poet makes it hard to tell. This couple's life remains closed off from us, available only in a few quick glimpses. What the woman notices, we also see; but a richness of experience, denied to us, informs her perceptions. The middle-aged husband's spontaneous, unmeant gesture revives the wife's loving past self. "Some old attitude of his or glance" brings back a hint of the long-ago church scene, which shines against the dull present. Now the "gallery-scene" of the poem's opening, the seed of her whole future life, "break[s] upon her mind." Does this remembrance of youthful enthusiasm, the image of the "ardent" and "trim" young man eagerly courting her, depress her with its incongruity? Or does it convince her that the glow of love persists, though usually invisible? Hardy does not say; the pang of this ambiguity now presides over his sonnet.

It is not the legal, social truth of marriage that matters here—not the husband's right of possession, nor any chronicler's description of the couple's travails together. The woman's one fleeting thought contains all; we need no further detail. Hardy's reticence demonstrates one way that poetry defines us: his sonnet centers on a nuance of memory whose meaning is immense, yet inconsequential. The poet presents life as common and extraordinary, near-hopeless and vivid, all at once.

In "A Church Romance," Hardy combines humane concern and detachment. Neither cynical nor sentimental, he pursues a gentle irony. The antithesis of young love and withering age remains unresolved (such lack of resolution is typical in Hardy's poetry, as the critic Samuel Hynes suggests). Hardy refuses to unmask love as an illusion. Time wears down his protagonists. Yet age is not more genuine or more persuasive than the memory of youth.

DM

"Mowing"

ROBERT FROST

1913

There was never a sound beside the wood but one,
And that was my long scythe whispering to the ground.
What was it it whispered? I knew not well myself;
Perhaps it was something about the heat of the sun,
Something, perhaps, about the lack of sound—
And that was why it whispered and did not speak.
It was no dream of the gift of idle hours,
Or easy gold at the hand of fay or elf:
Anything more than the truth would have seemed too weak
To the earnest love that laid the swale in rows,
Not without feeble-pointed spikes of flowers
(Pale orchises), and scared a bright green snake.
The fact is the sweetest dream that labor knows.
My long scythe whispered and left the hay to make.

"MOWING" appears in Frost's first book of poems, *A Boy's Will*, published in 1913, when the man who would become America's iconic poet-sage was almost forty years old. Speaking about *A Boy's Will* in a letter to Gorham Munson, an early champion of his work, Frost reflected on the genesis of the volume in the years 1900–1906. He spent this period with his wife and children in remote New Hampshire, trying to make a go of it as a farmer. "That's where I got my sense that I have forever for accomplishment," Frost wrote to Munson. "If I feel timeless and immortal it is from having lost track of time for five or six years there. . . . My infant industries needed the protection of a dead space around them. Everybody was too strong for me, but at least I was strong enough not to stay where they were. I'm still much the same. What's room for if it isn't to get away from minds that stop your works?"

"Mowing" offers the vision of self-protection that Frost invoked in his letter to Munson: the poet working alone and timelessly, saved from the stress of human society. Here, Frost characteristically treasures "any small man-made figure of order and concentration" (as he put it in a 1935 letter to the *Amherst Student*). The poet as rural laborer, depicted in "Mowing," produces such figures. He stands out against the background of a nature that seems indifferent, yet ready for the imposition of human work, both physical and poetic.

At the beginning of "Mowing," nature is soundless and imperturbable. Frost mentions "the heat of the sun," but at first gives no real description of landscape. The fact of the setting suffices. Against its background, we see a solitary harvester, not singing (as in Andrew Marvell's "Damon the Mower" or Wordsworth's "Solitary Reaper") but merely working. By refusing the precedent of these earlier poems, which participate in the pastoral tradition of sweetening labor with poetic expressions of love (Marvell) or exotic strains of music (Wordsworth), Frost stakes his place as a later, harder writer. He also turns against a mood of lush indolence, perhaps associated for him with late Victorian and Georgian verse. "It was no dream of the gift of idle hours, / Or easy gold at the hand of fay or elf": with these lines Frost kills off the luxuriant tones of romance. He refuses to be the master of a sensual fairyland where daydreaming and rich, golden harvests sway the reader's imagination.

In his essay "Prudence," Frost's intellectual ancestor Emerson writes with appreciation of the "whetting of the scythe in the mornings of June." (June is the usual beginning of the hay harvest in New England.) Emerson goes on to criticize "scatter-brained and 'afternoon men,'" those who do not, as he does, "love facts." He warns, "Do not clutch at sensual sweetness before it is ripe on the slow tree of cause and effect." Frost, who clearly knew Emerson's essay, echoes the Concord sage's rejection of a too-facile "sensual sweetness," opting with Emerson for a steady, committed observation of fact. In "Mowing," Frost oversees the growth of cause into effect.

During this boiling summer day, the poet hears no full-throated song, but rather a whisper, the hissing of his scythe cutting dry grass stalks. (The critic John Elder, reflecting on Frost's poem, describes his own experience of mowing hay: "As we learned to keep the blades of our scythes down we advanced from the percussiveness of swinging and chopping to a continuous, beautiful rustling. That subtle sound was in fact the surest guide to effective technique.") This subtle, dry undertone is pitched too low to be made much of by the listening protagonist of "Mowing." "Perhaps it was something about the heat of the sun, / Something, perhaps, about the lack of sound." The repetition, with variation, of "something" and "perhaps" in lines 4 and 5 bears witness to the incremental manner of "Mowing," the way Frost stubbornly and slowly mulls over significance. With the addition of just two letters, "sun" gradually yields to the firmer syllable "sound."

Marvell's lovesick Damon, who seems ready to dissolve into the landscape, gives us a characteristic pun on "scythe" and "sigheth." Frost wants instead to hear a more integral, stronger message, one nothing more than true. Frost's volta, his turn from the phantom of "fay or elf" that ends the octave, begins with these lines: "Anything more than the truth would have seemed too weak / For the earnest love that laid the swale in rows." (A swale is an isolated strip of low-lying meadow that requires mowing by hand. In Frost's day, as now, mowing was usually done by machine.) Frost enacts a movement away from Romantic projection and toward his own investment in activity, in the work that he identifies with poetry itself. The rows of hay bales form an age-old image for lines of poetry, backed up by the etymology of "verse": in Latin, *versus* is a furrow.

His is a work of "earnest love," Frost tells us, opposed to the imaginative tricks played by "fay or elf." A laconic steadfastness is required here, betokened by the rhyme of "speak" and "weak" that frames Frost's transition from octave to sestet. To say too much would be to give way to easy enchantment: a false kind of poetry, more interested in self-comfort than truth. For Frost, love is not indulgent and sympathetic, as we are inclined to think. Rather, it keeps its counsel, showing a New Englander's independence. The spiky flowers and "bright green snake" that adorn the landscape are the signs of this poet's hardy and strange spiritual state. (Frost refers to the round-leaved orchis, whose pallid flowers are arranged around a loose, fragile-looking stem.) The snake shares in this Eden—not a sly tempter, but a suggestion that nature (rather than man) has been exposed or surprised.

Frost's final two lines are the equivalent of a couplet, though they are not rhymed; they provide an epigrammatic finish. (The poem's strange, interwoven rhyme scheme is odder than that of any other sonnet in this book; it suits Frost's proud design on his readers.) The penultimate line is choice: "The fact is the sweetest dream that labor knows." (Here Frost gives the answer to "I knew not well myself" in line 2.) The action of mowing becomes, ineluctably, result. Frost the expert classicist knew that "fact" derives from the Latin *facere*, "to make" or "to do." This is a wide-awake conclusion, clear-eyed and factual. Yet Frost calls it a dream—and a sweet one at that. Often when we dream, we imagine a clarified world, more lucid than the one we are used to, almost hallucinatory. Such a phenomenon has the cold sweetness of an apple picked from the tree. It is a form of knowing, not a soft, unsteady wish-fulfillment.

"My long scythe whispered and left the hay to make," Frost ends. The process of harvesting goes on, it seems, without him; he has done his part. The scythe's whispering, from line 2, is recapitulated in this final line. Frost here plays with a familiar idiom, "to make hay while the sun shines" (that is, to profit when conditions are right). As he often does, Frost twists the sense of common speech, turning it in a direction all his own. Here, he moves away from the convenience of too-familiar everyday talk and toward an innovative awkwardness. "Left the hay to make" sounds faintly ungrammatical, even confusing. It derives from the rare intransitive use of "make" (in Frost's New England, ice can be said "to make"—that is, to form; and a flood tide "makes"). The poet was traditionally called a "maker"; but Frost's world makes without his action. (The heat of the sun, not the mower, produces hay.)

Frost tells us, when he concludes "Mowing" with the word "make," that his sonnet has not so much accomplished a job as pointed to the work of the world. Frost's counsel is: leave the hay to make. Instead of hauling it into bales, he listens again in memory to the rhythm of the scythe, and to his own meditation. The poet stops labor, entranced by what has been done. "Mowing," like much other Frost, gives us a combination of hard-mouthed Yankee proverb and visionary fulfillment.

DM

"Bluebeard"

EDNA ST. VINCENT MILLAY

1917

This door you might not open, and you did;
   So enter now, and see for what slight thing
You are betrayed. . . . Here is no treasure hid,
   No cauldron, no clear crystal mirroring
The sought-for truth, no heads of women slain
   For greed like yours, no writhings of distress,
But only what you see. . . . Look yet again—
   An empty room, cobwebbed and comfortless.
Yet this alone out of my life I kept
   Unto myself, lest any know me quite;
And you did so profane me when you crept
   Unto the threshold of this room to-night
That I must never more behold your face.
   This now is yours. I seek another place.

MILLAY became a celebrity during her twenties for poems—including a series of sonnets—about her scandalously Bohemian life. The readers of the late 1910s and 1920s saw her as a modern young woman whose sexual verve and sometimes cynical wit energized her verse line, and whose contemporary lingo replaced the Victorian attitudes and antiquated diction of earlier verse without otherwise altering its forms. Some saw her as a poetic ingenue; others as a sort of poetic flapper. Her most famous sonnets (the ones found in most other anthologies now) portray in what look like autobiographical terms her complicated, even rakish, sexual life, with its instant trysts and its resonant regrets. "Bluebeard," by contrast, has nothing of current events, and makes no effort to describe a new demographic cohort. It is a fable, even an allegory—and before it can be read for its psychology, it has to be read as a work of art.

Millay updates a famous, and grisly, story. In the most famous version (recorded in French by Charles Perrault, and put into English later by Andrew Lang), the wealthy Bluebeard tells his young bride that she may see and use any part of his well-equipped house, save only one locked closet or chamber. When the bride, overcome by curiosity, unlocks the chamber anyway, she discovers the corpses of previous wives, whom he has murdered one by one. Bluebeard returns from a journey, and finds her out. He is about to kill her, too, when her brothers arrive and kill him instead, leaving her the mistress of his great house.

Not the violence in the fable, but the centrality of its domestic secret, propels this poem. Millay's Bluebeard begins with the same compact warning as in Perrault's version of the tale. Will we see a closetful of corpses, and a hair's-breadth escape? We will not: most of the octave rehearses, and cancels, the expectations the fairy-tale title should bring. Millay's other sonnets performed a similar evacuation of fabular (and of European) content, replacing courtly lovers, declarations of loyalty, and flowery symbolism with urbane, apparently autobiographical fact. This sonnet replaces its time-worn symbols with . . . nothing. (The ellipsis in line 7 drives home that point.) The secret that this Bluebeard must keep from a partner, the secret space that, opened up, proves fatal—if not to the partner, then to the life they share—is a space with no content, or nothing but cobwebs. Why should it matter? Why should anyone care?

Without a sign of "distress," the secret chamber lacks any sign of "comfort," any visible consolation, any reason to go there. Nor do we know that this household, more than other households, requires consolation. We see nothing here of the domestic labor, the endless demands on energy and affection, that made a poetic subgenre, by Millay's time, of the wife's and mother's complaint. Instead, we see a complaint about scrutiny: this Bluebeard had to keep an empty closet, a secret chamber with no secret save its own existence, "lest any know me quite." ("Never shall one room contain me quite," says another sonnet Millay published in the same book.) For Millay's Bluebeard, psychic stability, continued social life, depends on the sense that something has been left out of that social life—that there is an "inner" life, as we say now, distinct from the outer: to be me, to live among others, I must believe that nobody can know all about me, that there is some part of me left for myself.

Some thinkers, and some poets, identify that inner remnant, that "me my-self" (Walt Whitman's term) or "soul in space" (Rainer Maria Rilke's), with the spirit of lyric poetry. The lyric poem, according to this argument, gives voice to just the part of a person that social life cannot display, the same part (the argument goes) that makes me "me." Millay's sonnet renders at once hol-low, and haunting, that controversial definition of a lyric poem. Almost all her sonnet says about the inner life, the secret room, is that Bluebeard keeps one, and Bluebeard needs one. There need not be anything that it displays or con-tains.

Reduced from its figurative terms into an explicit psychological argument, the poem would argue that my inner life, the parts of me that make me "me" and not a predictable creature of social statistics, consist only of my need to say that I have an inner life. Everything about me can be explained by visible facts (analogous to clothes, jewelry, food, and furniture), save only my need to feel that some part of me has remained hidden from view. Thus the empty closet in Bluebeard's home; thus, perhaps, lyric poetry, or even literature gen-erally, in human life.

Millay makes that minimal claim for poetry more attractive—and also more pathetic—by modulating from a less to a more artificial register (most of her more famous sonnets do just the reverse). The octave concludes with flat, sad words in prose order (it sounds less like Millay than like E. A. Robin-son, whom Millay would have read in her youth in Maine). The sestet begins with a flurry of inversions and omissions, distinguishing its language sharply from prose. The same sentence, in present-day spoken English, might be: "I kept for myself, out of everything in my life, this room alone, so that no one else would know everything about the real me."

The poem also flaunts allusions. "Profane" in this context suggests, and re-verses, a scene from *Romeo and Juliet*. Romeo, taking Juliet's hand for the first time, says: "If I profane with my unworthiest hand / This holy shrine, the gen-tle sin is this: / My lips, two blushing pilgrims, ready stand / To smooth that rough touch with a tender kiss." Those very famous lines also make up the first quatrain of a Shakespearean sonnet; at its conclusion, the lovers do kiss. Millay likely has in mind that first encounter as she stages this antiromantic final scene. Crossing a "threshold" like a groom lifting a bride, defiling or pro-faning a private space, the lover or spouse to whom this Bluebeard speaks seems almost (to Bluebeard) to have taken a virginity, a taking which is the opposite of a courtship, like Romeo's, and the opposite of a marriage—not the beginning of anything, but an end.

Millay's other poems, with their strong suggestions of sexual experience, challenge received notions about the high value of female virginity. This one keeps ideas of virginity (the secret of access to a woman's body) far in the background, but it may not entirely hold them off. Instead, Millay's sestet reverses conventions (some of which we still hold) about virginity, privacy, and marriage. We might expect a consummated and lasting marriage to make husband and wife "one flesh," in the words of Saint Paul, with no secrets from each other; but Millay suggests that in order to endure, a marriage requires a secret, a sense that one partner does not and cannot know everything the other partner feels.

Is Millay's Bluebeard a husband or a wife, a man or a woman? Millay does not want us to know for sure; she uses only first- and second-person pronouns. Since it is "Bluebeard" who speaks, we might expect a man's voice, and Millay does not rule that reading out. Yet the force of the sestet suggests a woman's dilemma. Many people in the America of Millay's youth expected married women, mothers and wives, to exemplify charity, to live for other people. They were thought selfish, as well as unfeminine, if they kept back anything for themselves. A series of famous writings by women from Millay's day into our own argues that women, if they are to fulfill any creative aspirations (Virginia Woolf's essay *A Room of One's Own*) or even simply to understand their own lives (Doris Lessing's story "To Room Nineteen," Rita Dove's poem "Daystar"), must control and keep private some space and some time for themselves.

To call a woman a Bluebeard merely because she keeps some space of her own is to equate such self-protection, in the case of a woman, with serial murder in the case of a man. It is to say that both shock society equally, that both do equal violence to social norms. Such an equation amounts to a caricature; marriages varied, as historians attest, and so did the wishes of individual wives and husbands (including Millay's own husband). Yet it is an equation with some historical force—an equation Millay attacks with power and grace. The fantasy of privacy which this probably-female new Bluebeard cannot sustain gives way, with the sonic self-enclosure of the last couplet, to a fantasy of departure, as if this new Bluebeard could find another place, another mansion, at least as good as the one that she abandons here.

SB

"Firelight"

EDWIN ARLINGTON ROBINSON

1921

Ten years together without yet a cloud,
They seek each other's eyes at intervals
Of gratefulness to firelight and four walls
For love's obliteration of the crowd.
Serenely and perennially endowed
And bowered as few may be, their joy recalls
No snake, no sword; and over them there falls
The blessing of what neither says aloud.

Wiser for silence, they were not so glad
Were she to read the graven tale of lines
On the wan face of one somewhere alone;
Nor were they more content could he have had
Her thoughts a moment since of one who shines
Apart, and would be hers if he had known.

BY FAR the closest American precursor—in chronology, in style, and in temperament—to the darkest, most modern aspects of Robert Frost, Robinson began to publish grim, finely turned sonnets and stanzaic poems during the 1890s, though it required more than two decades (and the approval of Theodore Roosevelt) for him to find public acclaim. Like Frost, Robinson used inherited forms and meters for homely American subjects, though without Frost's range of topic and technique. Like Frost, and like Thomas Hardy, Robinson wrote verse that tried to become at once lyric and narrative, to present at once an interior life and a set of causally related events. He spent the last years of his life writing narrative poems, including the bestseller *Tristram* in

1927. The following year, he collected all eighty-nine of his sonnets into a single volume, and wrote no more of them for the rest of his life.

Robinson's most famous sonnets stand out for single images, or for their last lines. "The Sheaves," for example, imagines its wheat harvested "As if a thousand girls with golden hair / Might rise from where they slept and go away." "Firelight," a lesser-known poem, stands out instead for the way that it uses the nuances of single words (many of them hard-to-handle abstractions), along with the structure of the Italian sonnet, in order to portray its characters. We see those characters, adults already settled in their lives, first with straightforward respect, then with irony, then with a return upon that irony, realizing (much as in Hardy's "A Church Romance," earlier in this volume) that what looks like a sad outcome might be the best any of us could do.

Robinson's octave depicts an apparently enviable couple, "ten years together" and happy to stay that way. The lines remain calm, nearly invariant in tone, and stately in their arrangement, two balanced sentences of one quatrain apiece. Husband and wife are "grateful" to the titular "firelight" not because it keeps them warm (though Robinson's Maine night may be cold), but because, by lighting up "four walls," it makes their house, their sanctuary, seem more self-contained: other people, here, at this hour, may as well not exist. The scene is timeless and plotless, a minute so fair that we too wish it would stay. Husband and wife are "perennially endowed," as if immortal, and "bowered," as if in a garden. In fact, they are a new Adam and Eve, whose sexual "joy" comes without tumult or accusation. Their bower contains "no snake," no tempter, and "no sword" like the one that God puts at the gates of Eden, to make sure that the first Adam cannot return (Genesis 3:24). If anything "falls" in this serene indoor Eden, that fall will be a "blessing."

The blessing, however, lies in what they do not know, and in what she does not say. Having depicted marital commitment amid calm, like an unclouded sky, the poet then compares it, less happily, to the silence on which it depends. This octave will stand to sestet as thesis to antithesis, as benefit stands to harm, or (more chillingly) as promise to fulfillment. Robinson looks beyond the room, and beyond the present time, beyond this warm night, into the past, and into these adults' hearts. The revelation these second looks bring will alter, and ironize, the calm delight that has come before, but will not quite cancel it out.

The irony, of course, involves a third party (if "one" refers to the same man twice) or—as Robinson's critics conclude—a third and a fourth. "One" (line 11) is a woman, now grown old, who loved the husband in vain (or, possibly, whom he seduced and abandoned, years ago); another "one" (line 13) is a man who once loved the wife, and whom she loved, though neither of them knew how the other felt, so that she married instead her second choice, the husband into whose eyes she gazes now. This wife would not be "so glad" if she knew about the long-ago other woman; this husband would not be "so glad" if he knew that his wife, as they sit by the fire together, has just been thinking of that other man. Their happiness depends (as the prelapsarian happiness of Adam and Eve depended) on a kind of ignorance. Husband and wife must neither speak, nor "read," the "tale" of lines on an absent face. These adults, seen together by firelight, now look sadder than they first appeared—more involved with loss, and with the passage of time. They look, too, like people upon whom the sun has set. Robinson's signals suggest a passing day: a cloudless sky, then the fire lit at evening, and then the star, or planet, that "shines / Apart," overhead, at night.

Published in 1921, relatively late in Robinson's life, "Firelight" might have seemed quiet and old-fashioned even then, with its almost perfectly regular meter, and its relatively ordinary, if emotionally significant, rhyme words: "glad"-"had," "walls"-"falls," "alone"-"known." It bears neither the glamour of mythological and biblical topics (such as Robinson pursued elsewhere in the same book, *The Three Taverns*), nor the up-to-date facts about life in a failing Maine town (such as Robinson depicted in the 1890s), nor the fractures and excitements of modernist techniques (which Robinson never used).

Robinson finds instead a near-dead calm appropriate to the subdued ironies of his subject. He gets his aesthetic effects from his verbal restraint, from the symmetries and ironies with which his words reflect his story. No word in the sestet has more than two syllables. Gone are the Latinisms of "obliteration" and "perennially"; gone, too, are the words reminiscent of Eden—"bower," "snake," "fall." Instead of colorful diction, instead of allusion, Robinson offers symmetries. The sonnet began with a string of present active indicatives ("they seek," "their joy recalls," "there falls"), and it ends in counterfactuals, clause after clause. One shocker, "Apart"—a literally breathtaking caesura, at an unusual place in the line—emphasizes another sort of balance: the sonnet began with "together," and ends with "apart."

And yet we should not exaggerate the sad undertones to Robinson's dimly lit room. Both husband and wife are happy, within their limits. Nothing in this sonnet suggests that she would have had a better life with another man. "Better a quivering firelight," says the critic James Barry, "than no light at all." This quiet couple are as "glad," and as "content," as adult human beings, in

Robinson's characteristic view, can hope to remain. The poem sets out at once to share its pathos and to limit our expectations. No wonder, then, that Robinson has chosen such a calm palette of words and rhymes, and no wonder that he grows quieter near the end.

Late in life, Robinson wondered whether his poetry, on the whole, "wasn't too dry, too plain." In the same way an adult, having settled down in a marriage, a family, and a career, might wonder if some less settled life would have been better, if convention could be cast aside. Here the answer is no. When the poet writes "their joy," he means it. Husband and wife will likely remain as they are until (what Robinson does not mention) illness or death intervenes. The poet therefore calls both parties "Wiser for silence": wiser not to ask, and not to tell. The events that have shaped their love lives—the romance unknown or rejected, the marriage achieved—now lie in the past. There is not much more for which they should hope: their current, chosen restraint is the best they can do.

SB

"America"

CLAUDE MCKAY

1921

Although she feeds me bread of bitterness,
And sinks into my throat her tiger's tooth,
Stealing my breath of life, I will confess
I love this cultured hell that tests my youth!
Her vigor flows like tides into my blood,
Giving me strength erect against her hate.
Her bigness sweeps my being like a flood.
Yet as a rebel fronts a king in state,
I stand within her walls with not a shred
Of terror, malice, not a word of jeer.
Darkly I gaze into the days ahead,
And see her might and granite wonders there,
Beneath the touch of time's unerring hand,
Like priceless treasures sinking in the sand.

CLAUDE MCKAY, like Countee Cullen a major writer of the Harlem Renaissance, was born in Jamaica, but moved to New York in the 1910s. In 1919 he was working as a waiter in the dining cars of the Pennsylvania Railroad. The bloody "Red Summer" of that year saw race riots in a series of American cities (two dozen of them by the end of the year). Blacks were still being lynched in the South, and subjected to systematic discrimination in the northern ghettos. Later, McKay remembered that time as a fearful, embattled one. He wrote of himself and his fellow black workers: "We stuck together, some of us armed, going from the railroad station to our quarters. We stayed in our quarters all through the dreary ominous nights, for we never knew what was going to happen."

In this volatile atmosphere, McKay stood out for his bold, defiant response to the African American predicament, expressed in a striking handful of sonnets. His most famous poem, "If We Must Die" (quoted by Winston Churchill during the Battle of Britain), ended with a call to blacks to resist: "Pressed to the wall, dying, but fighting back!" Elsewhere, in "To the White Fiends," McKay suggested he might take vengeance "with a gun" for "my black brothers murdered, burnt by you."

McKay's sonnet "America" is more ambivalent and less inflammatory than "To the White Fiends." (The poem was published in 1921 in the *Liberator,* a Communist newspaper edited by McKay's close friend Max Eastman.) McKay in his stoic pride steers a course between the twin dangers of bitterness and self-pity. He fervently confronts the America of his title, seeing it as both prison and promised land.

In the first line, America feeds the poet "bread of bitterness," perhaps an echo of the bitter herbs and unleavened bread that the Israelites eat during the Passover meal, in the Bible's book of Exodus. The bitterness is that of slavery, coupled with the consciousness that African Americans were dependent on their white owners for nourishment—and even after emancipation, still had to rely on inferior, low-wage jobs (like McKay's in the railroad's dining cars). The second and third lines are heightened by melodrama: the tiger's tooth sinks into the poet's throat, "stealing my breath of life." In the face of this assault, McKay asserts himself. He makes a surprising confession: "I love this cultured hell that tests my youth." There is a decadent, ripe flavor to the line. McKay gives in to the temptation to see himself as a young, ardent hero, tried by the fires of a hell that is nevertheless cultured and vigorous (perhaps because of the cosmopolitanism and energetic racial mixing of Harlem life).

This double nature, the hellish liveliness of America, makes for the poet's strength, as we see in the second quatrain. Here he is flooded by the waves of America's sheer "bigness," so different from the confined world of Jamaica, McKay's birthplace. Inspired by America's grand scale and its raw power, McKay poses himself "erect against her hate." (The critic Nathan Huggins compares McKay's mood to the defiance of the British poet W. E. Henley in his "Invictus," from 1875: "I thank whatever gods may be / For my unconquerable soul").

The final line of the second quatrain strikes a Shakespearean tone (as his sonnet adopts the Shakespearean rhyme scheme). McKay expands the earlier picture of his strong, erect spirit to a truly theatrical sumptuousness: he stands against America "as a rebel fronts a king in state." "In state" here means "on the throne"; the encounter is official, ceremonious. The regal imagery lifts the poet past the dangers of bitterness, of "terror, malice," and "jeer[ing]." King and rebel share the same high, dignified playing field. McKay credits himself with fiery enthusiasm in place of the near-poisonous grief and rage that he shows in other poems. Here, he plays Hotspur to America's Prince Hal.

In his last four lines, the poet strives for another kind of stature, one that will allow him to pronounce on the future of his adopted country. In his conclusion, McKay voices a prophecy. "Darkly . . . gaz[ing] into the days ahead," he sees a gleaming, abstract, and rather forbidding image of American power: "her might and granite wonders." This phrase could have formed the end of a complete sentence, leaving us with a picture of American might that was uninviting but neutral. McKay goes on, however, to pronounce judgment: "time's unerring hand" will submerge America's wonders in the sand. Like Shelley's fallen king, Ozymandias, America can boast of its treasures, its achievements, and its mastery: but all these will be leveled, sunk into the desert of oblivion. In contrast to Emma Lazarus, who gives us in "The New Colossus" an America that is welcoming, generous, and responsive to suffering, McKay sees his nation as coldly self-concerned, animated by hate and by oppressive might. (He is himself the Atlas-like colossus with the unconquerable soul, receiving tides of vigor and hatred.) The "priceless treasures" that she prides herself on trouble McKay, since they have been won at the cost of such great injustice: slavery and exploitation.

McKay's poem bears witness to a tumultuous time, and describes an America that inspires him with both love and disdain. As often in the sonnet tradition, so here: the poet explores his own responses, answering one emotion with another. McKay's final sentence on America is superior and headstrong, and forecasts his country's decline into nothingness. But this verdict asks to be set against the drama of internal feeling that his sonnet as a whole charts.

DM

"Self-Portrait"

ELINOR WYLIE

1922

A lens of crystal whose transparence calms
Queer stars to clarity, and disentangles
Fox-fires to form austere refracted angles:
A texture polished on the horny palms
Of vast equivocal creatures, beast or human:
A flint, a substance finer-grained than snow,
Graved with the Graces in intaglio
To set sarcastic sigil on the woman.

This for the mind, and for the little rest
A hollow scooped to blackness in the breast,
The simulacrum of a cloud, a feather:
Instead of stone, instead of sculptured strength,
The soul, this vanity, blown hither and thither
By trivial breath, over the whole world's length.

IN HER essay "Jewelled Bindings" (1923), Elinor Wylie described poets as "careful lapidaries" who work "in metal and glass, in substances hard and brittle." "Self-Portrait," published in 1922, pursues the idea of the poet's art as a craft, precise and hard-edged. "Self-Portrait" is an unexpectedly harrowing poem, the poet's unsparing glance at herself. Wylie's precision is no mere ornamental refinement, but a sharp and necessary discipline. In another poem, "Minotaur," Wylie advises, "distrust the exquisite"; so in "Self-Portrait," the cameo she describes is not precious, but rather cruelly self-mocking.

In Wylie's novels, her characters lead lavish, privileged lives, surrounded by crystals and precious stones. She herself was a wealthy aristocrat in Jazz Age

New York. But she experienced the pain of social ostracism: in her early twenties she eloped with a married man, causing a scandal. Married three times in her brief life (the last time in 1923), Wylie was no stranger to emotional turmoil.

"Self-Portrait" is an ekphrastic poem, like Keats's "On Seeing the Elgin Marbles," Dante Gabriel Rossetti's "For a Venetian Pastoral," and Rilke's "Archaic Torso of Apollo" (all of them in this book). These poems react to a work of art, real or imagined. Unlike Keats, Rossetti, and Rilke, Wylie describes a humanly fragile rather than a sublime and immortal artwork—and one that portrays her own face. The poet compares her portrait to a photograph (produced by a "lens of crystal") or an etched line-drawing ("intaglio" is a technique for incising an image on a surface in negative relief, sunken rather than raised). These comparisons signal the tenuousness of the self-portrait in Wylie's poem. A photograph captures the impression that a person makes, and is more strongly tied to the moment than painting or sculpture. The intaglio image is shallow and shadowy, rather than definitive like a sculpted monument.

The crystal lens, we are told, "calms / Queer stars to clarity." The basic sense of "queer" in this line is a rare one: related to "query," it suggests a baffled or puzzled yearning, a discontented questioning. (More common, but less relevant, meanings of "queer" are "odd"; "dubious, not to be trusted" (the French *louche*); and "transvestite or homosexual," a meaning that was just beginning to emerge in Wylie's era.) Wylie is a disreputable character; more important, however, she is an unquiet, searching soul. Her stars are her ruling powers (as in astrology); and they appear glimmering and unsteady, like the light of a fox-fire (the faint phosphorescent glow emitted by decaying timber). The camera turns this muted uncertainty to "clarity" and "austere refracted angles." But as it accomplishes this "disentangl[ing]," the camera also subjects the poet to naked scrutiny. The austerity here is a mark not of strength, but of stripped-down exposure. We see the core of the woman, and the slightness of her grip on existence.

The image of "horny palms" that caps the first quatrain (rhyming, disturbingly, with "calms") conveys the crude, heartless quality of the society that was Wylie's environment—a quality that paradoxically supports this society's high artifice. "Horny" means "calloused"; the image implies the figurative callousness with which the world handles the poet. Hard and "equivocal," Wylie's gossiping accusers might as easily be beast as human. Their judgments are made of "flint"—implacable, capable of hitting and hurting.

The "substance finer-grained than snow" suggests the poet's pristine, feminine appearance (apparent in existing photographs of Wylie: with her tiny mouth and porcelain-white skin, she looks like a faultless work of art). In other poems, Wylie recognizes in herself something "delicate and cold" (as she puts it in "A Lady's Countenance"). The distant, impervious character of the poet matches the world's derision; its hardness hardens her.

"Graved with the Graces in intaglio / To set sarcastic sigil on the woman": so ends Wylie's octave. A sigil is a seal or signet, often made by intaglio. The perfection of the poet's portrait seals her fate: in the high society of the 1920s, adept at flippant cruelty, sarcasm was a means of survival.

The octave, then, describes the poet's mind: austere, self-sufficient, and disdained by the equivocal creatures who so roughly apportion reward and punishment in the social world. As Graces, providers and judges of upper-class manners, they "set" the sigil "on" her, passing sentence, summing her up. But the sarcasm is also the unflinching poet's, directed at herself—a weapon turned inward.

The sestet goes on to depict the "little rest," the thing that is left out of the poem's first eight lines. The entity depicted in Wylie's sestet is elusive. It seems to be her soul or heart, or a "simulacrum," a queer, counterfeit version of soul or heart. It resides somewhere, perhaps, in the "hollow scooped to blackness in the breast"; the heart that should be there is just a suggestive, shadowy region, the discreet cleavage shown in a portrait. The grim resonance of "blackness" implies the shadow of death or oblivion, as does "vanity." A self-description such as Wylie's necessarily courts vanity (the narcissistic attachment to self), but "vain" more often means, in traditional poetic usage, "empty" or "futile." Koheleth, also known as Ecclesiastes, announces that "all is vanity"; nothing is new under the sun. Because we are always passing on and passing away, human life amounts to a series of ironic disappointments.

Instead of the proud monument to the self that Wylie wishes for in line 12, the stone-carved "sculptured strength," the poet's self-portrait is a snapshot subject to the whims of others. Her image flutters through the world, buffeted by harmful, gossiping words: "blown hither and thither / By trivial breath." The feathery *th*-sounds in these two lines serve to accentuate the lightness and triviality of the poet's soul. "Trivial" means "paltry," but also (in an older sense) "commonplace," and therefore subject to rumor. A *trivia,* in Latin, is a place where three roads meet and everyday news is exchanged.

The closing image of Wylie's sonnet asks to be juxtaposed with a famous passage by one of Wylie's favorite poets, Shelley. In his "Ode to the West

Wind," Shelley addresses the wind as the "breath of Autumn's being." He writes, "Oh, lift me as a wave, a leaf, a cloud," and later on, "Drive my dead thoughts over the universe / Like withered leaves to quicken a new birth!" Shelley's lines are a poetic prayer, even a command. He shares in the majesty of the wind, as it elevates and empowers him. For Wylie, by contrast, "trivial breath"—the chatter that decides what is fashionable and what notorious— directs the soul's fate.

In addition to her scathing adaptation of Shelley, Wylie casts a sardonic look at the Emperor Hadrian's well-known image of the soul as an "animula vagula blandula" (gentle, fluttering creature). Wylie is no brave, prophetic voice like Shelley, nor does she cherish the soul's delicacy, like Hadrian. Instead, the solitary soul she invokes proves hapless, blown through the world. No longer embattled, compact, and "polished" by tough experience as in the octave, now she is borne passively on the weightless, withering currents of drawing-room talk.

In "Self-Portrait," Wylie's image is set adrift on the winds of gossip, the "trivial breath" of the social world that persecutes her, but that she also adores. Her poem tells of a person who, despite her lapidary edge, is subject to the fleeting opinions of others, and to her own changeable desires. But the sonnet's yielding to such transience, emphasized in its conclusion, cannot conceal the poet's impulse toward lasting, unwavering expression. Wylie sees her own sonnet as a chiaroscuro evocation of the hidden soul, but also as a work of searching clarity, a gem-like piece handed over to us for inspection. Through this doubleness, she reflects as well on the image of the lyric poem: devoted to the fragile and momentary, to a glimpse of passion, lyric is also artful and permanent. Wylie grimly estimates the way such permanence seals the human image, fixing its character. More urgently, though, she sees this image—sees herself—as a defenseless outcast, driven "the whole world's length."

DM

"On Somme"

IVOR GURNEY

Written 1922; published 1982

Suddenly into the still air burst thudding
And thudding, and cold fear possessed me all,
On the gray slopes there, where Winter in sullen brooding
Hung between height and depth of the ugly fall
Of Heaven to earth; and the thudding was illness' own.
But still a hope I kept that were we there going over,
I, in the Line, I should not fail, but take recover
From others' courage, and not as coward be known.
No flame we saw, the noise and the dread alone
Was battle to us; men were enduring there such
And such things, in wire tangled, to shatters blown.

Courage kept, but ready to vanish at first touch.
Fear, but just held. Poets were luckier once
In the hot fray swallowed and some magnificence.

THE FIRST WORLD WAR changed Britain in ways that most Americans never saw. Almost a million young men from Britain, its empire, and its dominions died in four and a half years (1914–1918) of fruitless bombardment, gas attacks, machine-gun fire, and trench warfare. The Battle of the Somme, which stretched from July to November 1916, was one of the bloodiest and longest engagements, with nearly half a million Britons and half a million Germans killed or wounded, for gains often measured in inches of waste ground.

As a form both personal and occasional, a kind of poem that could be written quickly (and sent home in letters from the front), and a kind associated with Englishness, the sonnet took on a large role in the poetry of that war. Rupert Brooke celebrated the start of the conflict in five sonnets widely reprinted at the time ("If I should die, think only this of me: / That there's some corner of a foreign field / That is forever England"). Later sonnets by such war poets as Siegfried Sassoon and Wilfred Owen (both officers) recorded carnage, bitterness, and disillusion. Sassoon pictured his men "in foul dug-outs, gnawed by rats"; Owen's double sonnet "Dulce et decorum est" gave a grisly description of a chlorine gas attack.

Trained as a musician and composer, and sent to France as a private in 1916, Ivor Gurney wrote disillusioned, reportorial sonnets during his service there; one begins "Pain, pain continual . . ." Though he published those sonnets, and others, in his collections *Severn and Somme* (1917) and *War's Embers* (1919), Gurney's real achievement in verse came later, as his mental health collapsed. After a gas attack and a diagnosis of shell shock, he had a series of psychotic breaks, with delusions of persecution and attempts at suicide. In 1922 his friends had him committed to an asylum. There he wrote the strongest, and the strangest, of his war poems.

"On Somme" stands among them. Gurney does not write (as Owen and Sassoon sometimes did) with an eye to the education of civilian readers. Nor does he write out of simple disillusion: he resists the corrosive irony that other writers of the First World War, from Owen to Ernest Hemingway, display. Rather, he writes a poem that begins in reportage but concludes in introspection, and a poem whose abstractions (courage, fear, poetry, "magnificence") remain constant as the poet's own consciousness changes. His problem is not that "courage" has lost its meaning, but that he might not be able to find it in himself.

The scholar of English war poetry Tim Kendall writes that Gurney, after his commitment, relived his war years as if they were still taking place. Gurney indeed writes as if the battle had just happened, but he locates himself in a much longer history too. He is not only a poet of the Great War but a war poet coming after (and failing to measure up to) the poets of earlier wars, from Homer on. He is both a soldier and a soldier-poet; so, at least, during the war, he wanted to be. He asks whether he failed in those roles, then and now.

Seeing past as present, and the present against prior eras of war, Gurney creates an unusual temporal structure, moving from one instant (the first quatrain) to its potential future (the second quatrain), then to the next instant, then to the distant past. That temporal structure nearly matches (but does not quite match) the fourfold division of Gurney's unusual rhymes (*abab cddc cece ff*), which link the second quatrain (a moment as wrongly anticipated) to the third (the same moment as it truly took place).

Gurney begins with imitative effects: he launches the poem with jarring triple rhythms ("*Sud*-denly *in*-to the *still air*," dactyl-dactyl-spondee, as at the end of a Homeric line). He then repeats, across a strong enjambment, a word ("thudding") onomatopoetic to begin with. "I have more training in music than [in] verse," Gurney mused in a letter, "yet a sonnet comes far easier to me than a prelude or any other small form in music." That training helped Gurney build his frequently unconventional rhythms; here he begins and ends in irregular pentameters, deploying six-foot and seven-foot lines in between.

As original as his aural effects can be, Gurney's diction and syntax may seem naive, the work of a young nineteenth-century poet brought forward into modernity against his will, with inverted word order and omitted articles ("and not as coward be known"), evaluative adjectives ("ugly"), anthimeria (or the use of one part of speech as if it were another: "recover" for "recovery") and repeated abstractions ("courage"). As in most of his best poems, these devices together present the poet as self-conscious yet innocent, out of place, unguarded, sincere.

A poet attracted (as Gurney was) to nineteenth-century notions of nature and beauty could scarcely feel more out of place than he does here. The slopes are "gray" because they have been denuded of vegetation, by winter and by constant bombardment, which has killed all the trees. Between the blasted ground and the blasts from the sky, it looks and sounds as if the heavens had fallen—like a thunderstorm, but also like the fall of Lucifer (whose name means "light-bearer") from heaven. Modern war is so loud, and so "ugly," as to suggest that the divine order has collapsed: no wonder its sounds, and its lights, make soldiers ill.

Having shown the consequences for nature, for landscape, of modern ground warfare, Gurney can show the consequences in himself. The Gurney of "On Somme" does not fear death so much as he fears failure. He wants to "recover" from fear, to emulate the courage of the other, less introspective, infantrymen, and—in the kind of honesty that distinguishes the best war writing—he says that he wants not integrity for its own sake, but enough courage that the men around him will not think him worse than they.

Gurney waits in a dugout, near but behind the front line; he might at any moment be ordered to lead a charge ("going over"), which would expose him directly to enemy fire. As the sestet begins, we learn that he was not so ordered. Other soldiers died while he survived, and through no virtue of his own. "The noise and the dread alone" brought Gurney the knowledge (later confirmed by sight) that some of his comrades were now dismembered corpses, "in wire tangled, to shatters blown." Gurney (as we might expect from a composer) does more with hearing than he can with sight. He says what he could not see, and what he could not bring himself to name ("Such / And such things"), but emulates what he heard.

Gurney can then turn to introspection, and to judgment, in sentences much shorter than those before; his verdicts sound the more final for their brevity. (The stanza break, which separates reportage from judgment, slices across the rhyme—one reason his earlier editors missed it.) Gurney first evaluates himself as a soldier: How has he handled his fears? Here he may say that he passed the test, having performed as his peers expected, having shown the "courage" he needed, though not, perhaps, the greater courage he would have needed had a different order come.

Rather than condemn himself for surviving, he displaces his dissatisfaction onto the verse he writes, which does not measure up to the verse of the past. Poets were "luckier once" in that the wars they described seemed more conducive to beautiful verse. Who wouldn't rather be Homer than Wilfred Owen, sing of combat at Troy or longbows at Agincourt rather than write about gas and shells at the Somme? Does Gurney, the survivor, envy poets who died? Does he envy them because they could prove their valor in battle, a valor perhaps negated by trench warfare's grisly scale? (Proof of valor had been a theme of the early, delusively hopeful war poetry written by Brooke, and by Gurney himself in 1914–1915.) Did he have in mind, in 1922, Walt Whitman's proclamation, "To die is different from what any one supposed, and luckier"? (Gurney had been reading, and praising, Walt Whitman in 1916–1917.) Does Gurney shock himself by realizing that he wants now, or wanted then, to die?

None of those meanings exclude any of the others; all enter Gurney's last line. That line may also bring back a titular pun on "Somme" / "some" / "sum" and the French en somme ("in short," "in sum"). Gurney rarely puns, but his sonnet does try to sum up the difference between prior conflicts and this modern war. Whatever else it implies, with its strings of consonants and its muffled short vowels, this anticlimactic conclusion says that Gurney has not seen what all poets might want to see: "some magnificence," some evidence of beauty or virtue, in nature, or in heaven, or among the actions of people on earth. Avoiding, barely, a potentially fatal order, he did not feel lucky then, and does not now.

SB

"Nomad Exquisite"

WALLACE STEVENS

1923

As the immense dew of Florida
Brings forth
The big-finned palm
And green vine angering for life,

As the immense dew of Florida
Brings forth hymn and hymn
From the beholder,
Beholding all these green sides
And gold sides of green sides,

And blessed mornings,
Meet for the eye of the young alligator,
And lightning colors
So, in me, come flinging
Forms, flames, and the flakes of flames.

TRAVELING in Florida in 1919, and ravished by the lush radiance of its land-scape, the Connecticut poet and businessman Wallace Stevens scribbled "No-mad Exquisite" on a postcard. He sent it to Harriet Monroe, the editor of *Poetry* magazine. For the previous few years, Monroe had been eagerly pub-lishing Stevens's work, including his early masterpiece "Sunday Morning." Stevens's postcard to Monroe offers up a flamingo-like flourish, a cascade of bright language emanating from a sensibility suddenly set free by the tropics.

Until the 1930s, when his poetry took on a more somber tone, Stevens was often considered an aesthete or hedonist. But "Nomad Exquisite" is a demon-stration of visionary imagination, not a dandyish exercise in style. Stevens gives us not the impressionist's flash of color, but rather an intense moment issuing from an illuminated self. "Exquisite," in the title, derives from the Latin *exquisitus,* "chosen" or "selected." Stevens feels himself elected as the vehicle of poetry's "lightning colors," its rapid, galvanizing way of remaking the world in its own image.

Stevens wrote to his wife, Elsie, during his 1919 trip to Florida that "the wind blows incessantly. It gives a kind of fever to one's blood." Florida's enormous fecundity joined in Stevens's mind with the hard, clear atmosphere of wind and water, the bizarre animals (alligators, pelicans), and, above all, the proximity of the southern sun, which seemed to both afflict and harshly bless the traveler.

The scene "brings forth" life in Stevens's version of Florida, birthing itself. All is animate, on the increase. Creation generates its own substance, rather than waiting for God to start the life process. The "big-finned palm" moves forward graspingly like a giant predatory fish; the green vine is "angering for life," showing an ornery energy that seems strange and threatening. Stevens may have been remembering Milton's version of creation in Book 7 of *Paradise Lost,* where lions and stags spring from the ground, shaking off dirt and ready for action. In Milton's creation, all is "bursting with kindly rupture," and Stevens demonstrates a similar crude, energetic vitality.

Stevens's tricky stanza breaks slyly disguise the fact that "Nomad Exquisite" is a sonnet. Two quatrains make up his octave, the second one a reprise of the poem's opening line, "As the immense dew of Florida." In Stevens's second stanza, the "immense dew" brings forth hymns from the beholder. (The sestet will move from honoring nature to praising the art that bursts forth from the poet.) The phrase "immense dew" is something of an oxymoron: the adjective feels imposing; the noun, delicate. Dew is a traditional sign of God's blessing. In the Eden of Genesis, a fine mist arises and waters the ground, anointing the Creation; and Moses, in his last speech in Deuteronomy, blesses the land "for the precious things of heaven, for the dew" (Deut 33:13). Here, in contrast to the biblical sources, the dew is the mark not of God's favor, but of the landscape's own raw power. Nature itself, Stevens implies, deserves the obeisance, the praises and petitions, familiar from the Psalms of the Hebrew Bible. Stevens is (as Emerson puts it in "The American Scholar") "beholding and beholden": happily obligated to hymn what he sees.

In line 9 (the beginning of the sestet, which contains, unconventionally, a stanza break), the Floridian landscape's "green sides" slant off into "gold sides": what is natural (green) becomes artful and precious (gold), the sign of a lavish, ornate presence. Shading from green to gold in this manner, Stevens's second quatrain becomes a five-line stanza, suggesting the overflowing exuberance of the Florida landscape. Then the poem draws back into a final five-line stanza (rather than the usual six-line sestet). "Blessed mornings" refresh and renew us. Stevens considered morning the best time for poetry (as, he added, it was also the best time for prayer, the religious practice displaced by Stevens's poetic one).

The hieratic solemnity of Stevens's tableau now incorporates a playful element. The flamboyant pun on "meet" and "meat" in line 11 depicts the poet as a dapper young alligator with a carnivorous appetite for the sights and sounds around him.

In its first version, as sent to Monroe, the poem's final two lines were "so, in me, come flinging / Fruits, forms, flowers, flakes and fountains." Stevens thought better of this overlushness: his revision omits the fruits and flowers, substituting for natural abundance the glinting power of light itself. (The revised version, which we give here, appears in Stevens's landmark volume of 1923, *Harmonium.*)

"So, in me, come flinging / Forms, flames, and the flakes of flames." In these two lines, the equivalent of the traditional sonnet's couplet ending, Stevens reaches back to Walt Whitman, who writes in his "Starting from Paumanok," "I will therefore let flame from me the burning fires that were threatening to consume me"; and in "Song of Myself," "Dazzling and tremendous how quick the sun-rise would kill me, / If I could not now and always send sun-rise out of me."

Whitman in his "Paumanok" passage is speaking of "manly love" and companionship. Stevens invokes not Whitman's ideal of fellowship but nomadic solitude, for him the true home of imaginative experience. The flames of inspiration are flung not just from Stevens's nomad, but also *in* him. He bursts with light, the primal source of earthly life and the emblem of God himself ("God is light," announces the Gospel of John). Far off his coming shines; Stevens here bears the sun's potency itself. He casts himself as the successor to the young man with "flashing eyes" and "floating hair" in Coleridge's "Kubla Khan." (In his marvelous "Mrs. Alfred Uruguay," a later poem, Stevens will invoke a "lover with phosphorescent hair," "no chevalere and poorly dressed," riding energetically down the mountain of late Romantic grandeur.)

Stevens's word "flakes" derives from Edmund Spenser's "Epithalamion" (the conclusion to his *Amoretti,* excerpted in this volume). Excitedly anticipating his own wedding, Spenser describes Hymen, the god of marriage, "With his bright Tead [torch] that flames with many a flake." Stevens's own marriage would be increasingly unhappy as he struggled to coexist with an incompatible wife immune to poetry's capacities. During his trip to Florida he experienced nomadic solitude, a solitude that he would retain even after he returned to Connecticut and to Elsie, his wife. In this emotionally desolate existence Stevens strengthened himself by relying on the primal flame of imagination. In "Nomad Exquisite" Stevens is both exquisite and hearty, and we too rejoice in his unexcelled vigor.

DM

"Leda and the Swan"

WILLIAM BUTLER YEATS

1924

A sudden blow: the great wings beating still
Above the staggering girl, her thighs caressed
By the dark webs, her nape caught in his bill,
He holds her helpless breast upon his breast.

How can those terrified vague fingers push
The feathered glory from her loosening thighs?
And how can body, laid in that white rush,
But feel the strange heart beating where it lies?

A shudder in the loins engenders there
The broken wall, the burning roof and tower
And Agamemnon dead.
                                    Being so caught up,
So mastered by the brute blood of the air,
Did she put on his knowledge with his power
Before the indifferent beak could let her drop?

ONE OF Yeats's best-known poems, "Leda and the Swan" confronts the reader with shattering, visionary intensity. Yeats published "Leda" in 1924; he had composed it the previous year, convinced that mankind was heading down an extreme, even catastrophic path. The violence of the Irish troubles was spurring Yeats to disturbed, monumental poems like "Meditations in Time of Civil War." Explicating his sonnet, Yeats remarked, "Nothing is now possible but some movement, or birth from above, preceded by some violent annunciation." The comment implies an ambivalence on Yeats's part: Does he welcome or is he horrified by the prospect of this "birth from above"? "Leda" suggests that Yeats feels more horror than sympathy for the imminent violence he foresees. Yet he implies that this future, harsh and inevitable, must be embraced.

In Greek myth, Zeus, king of the gods, takes the form of a swan and ravishes Leda, a mortal woman. The god's brutal act leads to the birth of the twins Helen and Clytemnestra (among other offspring), the Trojan War (instigated by Helen's astonishing beauty), and finally Clytemnestra's revenge on the leader of the Greek expedition against Troy, her husband Agamemnon (she and her lover Aegisthus murder him on his return from Troy). Yeats depicts the ruin of Troy with panoramic intensity in "the broken wall, the burning roof and tower." He compresses into just a few words Virgil's description of the Trojan downfall in Book 2 of the *Aeneid*.

The opening words of "Leda" give a sharp shock: "A sudden blow: the great wings beating still / Above the staggering girl." Yeats's lyric starts *in medias res* ("in the middle of things," a phrase from Horace's *Ars Poetica* describing how epic poetry characteristically begins). We are thrust into the midst of the action, mercilessly subject, like Leda herself, to the god's force. By means of the colon in the first line, Yeats generates an afterimage of Zeus's momentary, irrevocable rape: it's over in an instant, but the effects reverberate through all Greek and Trojan (and, perhaps, all human) history. The girl is still staggering, the wings beating: we are caught up, like Leda herself, in a harsh initiation that will not let us go. In Yeats's hands, the swan-Zeus becomes a "white rush"—a bewildering blur, cinematic and sublime.

In the first quatrain, Leda is "helpless." The swan's "dark webs" caress her thighs. The descent of the god is not merely bestial; there is a seductive gentleness to it as well. The ambiguity is troubling. Seductiveness would imply empathy on the part of the sufferer, Leda, for the alien divinity that has overtaken her: "And how can body, laid in that white rush, / But feel the strange heart beating where it lies?" (Note how Yeats glides from the crude sexual reference of "laid" to the quiet "lies.") The mortal woman Leda's feeling for the strange and otherworldly power that masters her suggests that we welcome the same devastation we lament. For the reader as for Leda, to be "caught" is also to be "caught up": taken by violence, intrigued and involved.

Yeats has the events of his own time in mind here, as his comments on "Leda" indicate. The ideologies that bedeviled twentieth-century history, fascism and communism, both relied on terror. Yeats, who was horrified by the mass murders committed in revolutionary Russia, and by the bloody struggle in his own country, prophesies in "Leda" a career of unprecedented violence for the twentieth century. Alas, his prediction was accurate. As Yeats exclaims in "The Second Coming," "The blood-dimmed tide is loosed." Yeats told his friend and patron Lady Gregory that, as he was writing "Leda," "a bird and lady took such possession of the scene that all politics went out of it." But he began with political concern, and he later placed "Leda" in his complex prophetic book, *A Vision* (1925), giving it the force of world-historical testimony.

Metrically, Yeats's sonnet relies on a stunning syncopation. In the phrases "stággering gírl," "lóosening thíghs," and "indífferent béak," Yeats creates a rapid, breathless rhythm by blending two unstressed syllables into one (an effect called synizesis or elision: "stagg'ring," "loos'ning," "indiff'rent"). As we read, we are brought up short, overrun by the vigorous excitement of the verse. Yeats's rough annunciation picks up speed in his sestet (rhymed *efgefg*). "A shudder in the loins" clearly suggests orgasm, but also fright. Momentary ecstasy melds with the vision of disaster. Yeats becomes a full-fledged prophetic voice as he holds out his reckless premonition of war.

In "Leda," Zeus's proof of aggressive male domination is answered by an equally brutal revenge, Clytemnestra's murder of Agamemnon. Like Lady Macbeth, Clytemnestra in Aeschylus' *Agamemnon* outdoes the male of the species in bloody ruthlessness. She is Helen's twin, born with her from Leda, and she matches Helen's beauty with her rage. Zeus violently imposes the divine on the human; Clytemnestra pays him back. She provides a savage, reductive comment on Homeric heroism, the charmed and glorious interchange of gods and men. In a quick, exultant scene of slaughter, Clytemnestra cuts down her husband in his bath, relishing his vulnerability and her own ascendant strength.

The break in line 11, between "And Agamemnon dead" and "Being so caught up," makes a jarring gap: the distance between the vast sweep of the Homeric and Virgilian account (ending in the ruins of Troy and Agamemnon's corpse) and the solitary, seized figure of Leda (whose rape starts the whole dreadful process). We are made subject to the cataclysmic shift of gears between a trauma and its aftermath, the single individual and monumental history.

Yeats ends this epochal sonnet with the last of his poem's three questions. Does Leda, like Mary impregnated by the Christian God, "put on" the god's knowledge of future history as she feels his power course through her? (In the Gospel of Luke, 1:30–33, the angel of the Lord gives the pregnant Mary news of Jesus' messianic status, his endless reign on David's throne.) Perhaps, Yeats suggests, Leda is just an expendable vehicle-victim for divine lust and its consequences. She is not merely "caught up," but "mastered." Zeus's "indifferent beak" lets her drop, discards her. So, too, the millions of dead produced by the modern age are thrown aside, once history has finished with them. Yeats asks whether knowledge can be gleaned from such disaster, or whether sublime terror overwhelms knowledge and judgment. The question goes to the heart of his poetry—and of our dangerous age.

DM

"To Emily Dickinson"

HART CRANE

Written 1926; published 1933

You who desired so much—in vain to ask—
Yet fed your hunger like an endless task,
Dared dignify the labor, bless the quest—
Achieved that stillness ultimately best,

Being of all, least sought for: Emily, hear!
O sweet, dead Silencer, most suddenly clear
When singing that Eternity possessed
And plundered momently in every breast;

—Truly no flower yet withers in your hand.
The harvest you descried and understand
Needs more than wit to gather, love to bind.
Some reconcilement of remotest mind—

Leaves Ormus rubyless, and Ophir chill.
Else tears heap all within one clay-cold hill.

HART CRANE wrote this mysterious sonnet one day in November 1926, while he was trying to finish his long poem *The Bridge*. He sent it immediately to his friend Waldo Frank, calling it a "little thing I did yesterday." It is a poem of vocation, like John Keats's famous sonnet "On First Looking into Chapman's Homer," in which one poet honors another's achievement and tries to learn from it for his own work. Yet it is also a poem about spiritual and artistic failure, about obscurity, silence, and the abandonment of impossible projects, akin to Coleridge's sonnet "Work without Hope." It is Crane's achievement, in his homage to Dickinson, to write both these kinds of lyric at once. Dickinson did not write sonnets; Crane wrote only two. His "To Shake-speare" uses Shakespearean structure and rhymes. Here, though, he has ar-ranged a set of couplets as if they followed Shakespearean form. The poem is a sonnet and not one, as Dickinson's poems and Dickinson's life were (for Crane) successful failures, versions of Silence that were also eternal poetic speech.

Dickinson during Crane's lifetime was hardly canonical, but neither was she entirely obscure. Many of her poems had been available (in heavily rewrit-ten versions) since the 1890s, with a selection by the modernist poet Conrad Aiken, a new *Complete Poems,* and the first *Life and Letters* all appearing in 1924. (Crane's em-dashes, signs of urgency, probably do not emulate Dickin-son's, since he would have read her in conventionally repunctuated editions.) Dickinson's lyric gifts, her secluded life, her obvious unconventionality, and her spiritual ambition had already won her attention among other modern-ists: Crane's close friends and frequent correspondents Allen Tate and Yvor Winters both (as of 1926) recommended her work.

Though these lines flaunt words important to Dickinson, their forceful pentameters and colliding Latinisms typify not Dickinson but Crane, whose gorgeous, Orphic diction sometimes puzzled even his closest friends. The usual story of Crane's career, with *The Bridge* at its center, shows the poet as a tragic hero who could not quite reconcile the ornate language and inherited forms he cherished with his Whitmanesque embrace of gay desire and Ameri-can life. Dickinson becomes, for Crane, an alternative to Whitman (and Crane becomes one of the first memorable poets to see her this way): a poet who turned not toward imagined crowds, but toward her own solitary con-templation, who saw for herself not a public future but a private endurance, in art that could live on after her body died.

Crane's sonnet argues for Dickinson's poetic success, so intimately tied (for him as for her) to the seclusion that other people saw as worldly failure. Yet it is also a sonnet about the aesthetic and commercial failures he feared for him-self: after many delays, his first book of verse, *White Buildings,* was in press when he wrote this poem. Crane honors at once the "hunger," the "endless task," the "labor," the "quest" involved in the making of art, and the "stillness" that follows either its completion or its abandonment, whether or not it finds an audience. "In vain to ask" means either that Dickinson wanted more than she could ever get, or that we ask in vain just what she wanted (her sublime poems render her desire mysterious), or that she wanted things she could not get just by asking (things such as artistic immortality). She wanted things for which she had to work, things that even the "endless task" of poetic making, pursued in good faith, may not bring.

Dickinson is a "Silencer": her sublime strangeness intimidates later poets (as in Harold Bloom's famous model of "the anxiety of influence"), who, if they do not swerve away from her outlook, may be "silenced" by her example. Yet Crane may intend the verb "silence" intransitively (a usage the *Oxford English Dictionary* calls rare): Dickinson, her heart "possessed / And plundered" by Eternity, fell silent, communicated only with herself. The poems that resulted seem to make her immortal, yet they solicit more interpretation, more sympathy, more understanding ("more than wit") than any earthly reader could ever provide. She remains "remote," beyond the reach of interpreters, after her death, as she and her poems remained "remote" from American readers during her lifetime. Would Crane and his poems (the sonnet inquires by implication) see a similar fate?

Crane plays on terms important to Dickinson, on what he knew about her writing practice, and on contemporary debates about her. She sent some poems to correspondents with dried flowers, and her early editors gave several of her poems the title "With Flowers." Some readers saw her as a gifted naïf: Thomas Wentworth Higginson, in his introduction to Dickinson's *Poems* (1890), called them "poetry torn up by the roots, with rain and dew and earth still clinging to them." Other readers saw her as a spinster whose sexual inexperience disabled her art, as when William Carlos Williams complained in 1925 that American poetry had produced no "true woman in flower." The likeness between lyric poems and plucked flowers is traditional ("anthology" comes from the Greek for "collection of flowers"), but Dickinson herself thought that the old analogy might not suit her poems. She wrote, in one of the poems Crane could have read, "If the foolish call them 'flowers' / Need the wiser tell?" The true bounty of Dickinson's poetry, the "harvest" that Crane praises in his sestet, is at once the immortal flower of Dickinson's language (a flower that does not "wither") and something stranger than flowers, more austere ("no flower" at all).

Crane shifts his attention from botany back to Eternity, a word important to him as it was to her. In his essay "New England Culture and Emily Dickinson" (1932), Tate would single out for sustained praise the poem "Because I could not stop for Death," which ends with "the horses' heads . . . towards Eternity." The eternal reward that Dickinson's poetry merits, the more-than-human satisfaction that it gave her, seems more important to Crane, in his penultimate line, than any worldly good. The "reconcilement" her poems contain, even if intelligible only to her, makes Ormus and Ophir—ancient Near Eastern cities proverbial for their wealth—seem by comparison cold and poor (in the Book of Job, 28:16–21, wisdom "cannot be valued with the gold of Ophir . . . for the price of wisdom is above rubies," though it is also "hid from the eyes of all living").

Is Dickinson's hermetic poetry, the wisdom or "stillness" it attains, "ultimately best"? So Crane's comparisons imply. Yet those comparisons come in the next-to-last line: Crane is not finished with Dickinson, nor is he finished with his own self-doubt. What if wisdom, sublimity, and Eternity are after all the creatures of a moment, not an immortal "harvest" but a brief and all too conventional flower? Then death would be the only great truth about life, and mourning the only appropriate reaction. All life would end only under the earth, amid tears—or so Crane's last line says.

Like many of Crane's poems, the sonnet may have—in addition to its overt subjects—an occluded sexual subject too. Crane pursued a stormy love affair with the sailor Emil Oppfer, on whose name the poem begins and ends. As the Crane scholar Langdon Hammer points out, "Emily" contains "Emil," and "Ophir" is a near-homonym for "Oppfer." Dickinson's poems would not have appealed to Crane's unliterary paramour—they would have left him "chill" (if he'd read them). Crane, like Dickinson, might have to live without sexual fulfillment, having fallen in love with a man who could not grasp his "remotest mind."

Such a subtext, if there is one, drops out of the poem in its stark last line. Tate's essay of 1932 argued that Dickinson, by isolating herself from her time, became its truest poet: "When she went upstairs and closed the door, she mastered life by rejecting it." Crane's sonnet explores the same position, asking whether life—and poetry—could be mastered, could permit themselves to be comprehended, in any other, less ascetic way. Rather than settle on a single answer, it ends with unreconciled alternatives (X . . . Else Y). Crane's poem, at once a sonnet and not a sonnet, thus pursues poetic vocation and poetic frustration. It honors the achievement of Dickinson's verse, and honors (as Dickinson, more than any other American poet, honored) the silence and the "stillness" that shadow artistic achievement, as death shadows life.

SB

"At the Wailing Wall in Jerusalem"

COUNTEE CULLEN

1927

Of all the grandeur that was Solomon's
High testament of Israel's far pride,
Shedding its lustre like a sun of suns,
This feeble flicker only has not died.
This wall alone reminds a vanquished race,
This brief remembrance still retained in stone,
That sure foundations guard their given place
To rehabilitate the overthrown.

So in the battered temple of the heart,
That grief is harder on than time on stone,
Though three sides crumble, one will stand apart,
Where thought may mourn its past, remembrance groan,
And hands now bare that once were rich with rings
Rebuild upon the ancient site of things.

THIS SONNET, by the Harlem Renaissance writer Countee Cullen, stems from a trip to the Middle East that Cullen took with his adoptive father, a Methodist minister, in 1926. The poem uses one of the central monuments of Jerusalem, the ruins of the Jewish temple, as an analogy to the speaker's emotional life. Cullen also suggests a parallel between the history of the Jews and that of African Americans. Writing at the height of the African American cultural flowering of the 1920s, a decade that saw spectacular achievements by black Americans in painting, poetry, fiction, and music, Cullen was painfully aware that his people's social status and legal rights fell far short of those granted to whites.

Cullen, who studied at New York University and Harvard, wrote his senior thesis on Edna St. Vincent Millay, and Millay's hard survivor's tone is prominent in this sonnet. As Millay often does, Cullen speaks in the tough, wise voice of one who has been "overthrown" by experience (as "At the Wailing Wall" puts it). He trains himself for a new start, sadder and older, but determined to "rebuild."

Cullen begins by evoking the greatness of Solomon's kingdom: the "far pride" that stretched, according to the Bible, from the borders of Egypt to the Euphrates (though there is little or no archaeological evidence that such was the case). With overtones of extravagance and inexpressible glory, the Israelite kingdom "shed . . . its lustre like a sun of suns."

At the center of Solomon's realm was the lavish temple he built for the worship of the Israelites' God. Here was a vast space thronged with priests and pilgrims, loud with fervent hymns, full of the smoke of animal sacrifices. Near the temple's closely guarded inner sanctum (the Holy of Holies), which contained the Ark of the Covenant with its golden cherubim, was the *ner tamid,* the flame that was kept eternally lit (or, perhaps, was lighted each day). This everlasting light has now become a "feeble flicker," Cullen writes—his symbol for the slight but persistent Jewish presence in Jerusalem, which had lasted since Solomon's day (some three thousand years), and had been augmented since the 1880s by Zionist settlers.

The temple, several times destroyed and rebuilt, fell for the last time when Rome suppressed the disastrous Jewish revolt ending in 70 CE. In that year and then again during a rebellion in the next century, the Romans set Jerusalem in flames, killing perhaps as many as a million Jews. Jews were still an important presence in the Roman Empire; at their height they made up about 10 percent of the population, comparable to African Americans in the United States today. But whatever autonomy they had in Palestine had been eliminated. All that was left of Jerusalem's splendid sanctuary was the *kotel,* as it is known in Hebrew: the Wailing Wall, where Jews still lament the long-ago ruin of their temple.

After describing in his first quatrain the reduction of Solomon's kingdom to the Wailing Wall, Cullen devotes the second quatrain to the wall's significance. "Alone" and unsupported, the *kotel* "reminds a vanquished race": Cullen must be alluding to his own race, vanquished and enslaved by whites. The poet moves on from reminding to remembrance, describing the wall as "this brief remembrance still retained in stone." The value of *zakhor,* memory, is central in Jewish tradition. To retain is to hold (from Latin *retinere*), as one's past is held by memory. But the remembrance remains, as Cullen puts it, "brief." This adjective, used here (unusually) to describe an object, tells us that the Wailing Wall is small, fragmented. But this tenuousness provides strength as well, since the same word, "brief," implies that there is only a short temporal distance between Solomon's day and our own. And the sonnet form itself, a small enclosure, speaks across the ages.

The second quatrain, assisted by the firm adjectives "sure" and "given," ascends powerfully. The muscular Latinate word "rehabilitate" (here meaning "to build another habitation") lends substantial vigor to the idea that the Jews can still locate their history and their identity in the temple, however ruined— in the "given place." But the sentence leaves a syntactic ambiguity around the question of who will be doing the rebuilding: the Jews or (strangely) the wall itself. The ambiguity leads us to suppose that the power of the place itself collaborates with the Jews in their labors, upholding their tenacity.

The sonnet's sestet, acknowledging weakness, retreats from the octave's high claim. Cullen begins his third quatrain by suggesting a parallel between the Jews' temple and the "temple of the heart" (as he puts it in his sestet). The image of the heart's temple was used by the central poet-prophet of Christianity, Saint Paul, in 1 Corinthians. In Paul, the discipline of conscience and faith replaces the actual Jerusalem temple (still standing when Paul wrote his obsessive, passionate epistles). For Cullen, the "battered" temple survives within, a symbol of the self that has suffered and endures. The heart is like a temple because there is a mysterious rite at its center. It has a sacredness, or uncanny sequestered quality. The heart's grief is hard; it wears one away as time wears away stone. And the heart can, like the Jews of Roman times, be overthrown by an enemy (for example, a treacherous lover). But the sestet implies that personal grief, the loss of love or of a loved one, can be followed by recovery (as in some of Millay's sonnets).

Three of the heart's walls have crumbled—yet "one will stand apart," with the lonely autonomy of the abandoned lover, the survivor of trauma. Cullen here draws on Numbers 23:9, with its image of the Israelites as a "people that shall dwell alone," and on 2 Samuel 7:10, where God tells the prophet Nathan that he "will plant [the Israelites], that they may dwell in a place of their own, and move no more."

This stubborn permanence gives a staying power not to be denied. As so frequently in sonnets after Shakespeare, love yields to the law imposed by Time, the destroyer; but then the heart, wounded as it is, takes on law's binding strength. Mourning begins to seem the same as rebuilding (as in Jewish thinking on the destruction of the temple). In his quiet, intense final couplet, Cullen pictures a remaking that, while allowing the lament for lost wealth, knows the more direct need of the present: "And hands now bare that once were rich with rings / Rebuild upon the ancient site of things." (The hands rich with rings are perhaps those of African kings, now become the bare hands of black American ex-slaves.) Those final words, "the ancient site of things," are themselves stark, bare. They speak to Cullen's steadfastness, his coming to terms with reduced conditions that are all the more true because of the reduction. The richness of Solomon's kingdom may have been impressive, as the biblical account tells it. But this lavishness cannot match the dedication to a simple piece of the past, the Wailing Wall, that tells of a people's persistence— and of the self's unrelenting hold on life.

DM

"The Castle of Thorns"

YVOR WINTERS

1930

Through autumn evening, water whirls thin blue
From iron to iron pail—old, lined, and pure;
Beneath, the iron is indistinct, secure
In revery that cannot reach to you.
Water it was that always lay between
The mind of men and that harsh wall of thorn,
Of stone impenetrable, where the horn
Hung like the key to what it all might mean.

My goats step guardedly, with delicate
Hard flanks and forest hair, unchanged and firm,
A strong tradition that has not grown old.
Peace to the lips that bend in intricate
Old motions, that flinch not before their term!
Peace to the heart that can accept this cold!

FAMOUS AS a severe, sometimes hectoring literary critic, Yvor Winters condemned much poetry of his day. He rejected the idea of the poem as expressive process—the tracings of impulse prized in the modernism of Ezra Pound, William Carlos Williams, and others. Poetry for Winters was judgment, not creative feeling.

Like much of Winters's work from the 1930s on, "The Castle of Thorns" is tersely accomplished, modest in its lineaments, and written in strict meters. It aspires, quietly, to permanence. Many called Winters conservative, but the word gives a false impression. He did not wish to assert decorum, good manners, or the comfort of sensible opinion. Rather, he saw style as a difficult moral act—an act of will and of the thinking self. Often, as in "The Castle of Thorns," the self is poised against a forbidding darkness.

"The Castle of Thorns" begins in muted fashion, with the dreamlike picture of an "autumn evening." An ordinary action is taking place: someone pours water "from iron to iron pail." "Whirls thin" and "iron . . . lined" bear sharp, bright assonance. Winters' poem itself is "old, lined, and pure": rugged with integrity, resisting corruption, and made of iron, unbending lines. His pails are homely images—poetic metaphors, carriers of meaning.

Line 3 changes the picture. Now the iron, rather than a vehicle for the poet's sense, becomes "indistinct, secure / In revery that cannot reach to you." With "you," Winters directly addresses the reader and himself: both quest for meaning, and for life. The realm of darkness (death, forgetfulness) shadows all our actions. The dream of this other world cannot reach us, cannot animate our lives. Lodged beneath waking existence, it remains "secure"—without care (*sine cura*), profoundly unsympathetic. Winters's quester must neither surrender to the darkness, nor declare victory over it. The lapse into instinct and the rigid trumpeting of reason both avoid the struggle that Winters values.

In a footnote to his poem, Winters mentions the medieval legend of a Robber Knight, who (he writes) "commonly represents death." The Robber Knight takes his victim to a castle surrounded by a wood of thorns. On this journey, Winters remarks, the knight "must in some way cross or dive under water, which is the most ancient symbol of the barrier between the two worlds." The castle means death, nothingness, the unknowable. To reach it, we must travel over what Wallace Stevens in "Sunday Morning" calls that "wide water, without sound": the river of Lethe, or its equivalent, which separates the dead from the living. (Fairy tale aficionados may remember, as well, that Sleeping Beauty lies unconscious for a hundred years in a castle encircled by lethal thorns, until a brave prince awakens her.)

Winters's hard, stony octave inserts water between man's mind and "that harsh wall of thorn, / Of stone impenetrable." The verse thickens and drags, nearly halted by the many syllables of "impenetrable" after a decisive string of monosyllabic words. On the barrier that closes us off from the unknown hangs a horn, "like the key to what it all might mean." (The horn is prominent in stories of quest and chivalric strife, from the medieval *Song of Roland* to Robert Browning's "Childe Roland to the Dark Tower Came.") Winters's emphasis rests on "like." The horn—instrument of high song and spirit, ready to announce the inception of a hunt, or to seal a triumph—resembles the key to all meaning; but this poet remains skeptical of such myths. T. S. Eliot writes, "we think of the key, each in his prison / Thinking of the key." Winters's irony plays against Eliot's grander yearnings. For Winters, there is no definitive key—no apocalyptic response to our disquiet like the one Eliot conjures at the end of *The Waste Land*.

In his sestet, Winters moves away from the stone-bound fixation of the octave and toward a sunlit, pastoral landscape. Goats are a frequent, amiable presence in Winters's early poetry. In "The Castle of Thorns," they dot the sestet like animating spirits of proper poetic practice. The goats symbolize a constant awareness that remains responsive, refusing to harden into strategy. (So Winters distinguishes himself from those modernists who wield obscurity like a weapon against unfit audiences.)

The poet's goats "step guardedly"; in other words, he positions his verse feet nimbly, with the light touch of an expert. Across an enjambment the goats' flanks move, both "delicate" and "hard." Winters juxtaposes these two adjectives to make a point about his own poetry: it stays "unchanged and firm," yet subtle. Gesturing toward pastoral's graceful use of conventions, these lines share in "a strong tradition that has not grown old." This, the most slogan-like line in the poem, may be hard for some readers to swallow. But we should trust the style, yield to its strength. Winters offers a sound, confident assonance: the ringing tone of "strong" echoes in "not grown old." Winters comes by his aesthetic claims honestly, through clear thinking and writing. As the poet and critic David Yezzi notes, Winters espouses propriety and precision, and makes emotion answer to reason.

Claims for tradition would have little weight without a sense of the burdens that tradition can bear. The "intricate / Old motions" (another deft enjambment) are not just weavings of verse, but the bold, adept movements of the heart, present behind the mouth that speaks. These motions, bending yet resistant, "flinch not before their term"—before the mortal end that defines us. The poet now grants peace, but his blessing comes only to those who "can accept this cold." Death is the encroaching, alien presence that resists all schemes, and defeats evasion. The large myths of modernism, spurned by Winters, stand in the way of his goal: a composed, direct acceptance of our lonely and independent place in the world.

Such a vision poses a challenge. Those who fail this trial risk becoming chilly, empty practitioners, proud and false. In a 1947 poem ("An Ode on the Despoilers of Learning in an American University"), Winters passed sentence on a few of the professors of his day, "the insensate, calm / Performers of the hour, / Cold, with cold eye and palm." He judged that "these have come too far: / They stand here, coarse and lined, / And permanent as stone, / In the final light of mind." Here, the slow, drawn word "insensate" surveys the shortcoming of the ones who use knowledge to ward off weakness. They build a wall of obsessive learning, with no place for life. In a poem like "The Castle of Thorns," Winters distinguishes himself from such rigid makers. The true poet stays supple, cognizant. We defer to the measured beauty of Winters's poetry: its willingness to live within sharp limits, and find bravery and constancy there.

DM

"No Swan So Fine"

MARIANNE MOORE

1932

"No water so still as the
    dead fountains of Versailles." No swan,
with swart blind look askance
and gondoliering legs, so fine
    as the chintz china one with fawn-
brown eyes and toothed gold
collar on to show whose bird it was.

Lodged in the Louis Fifteenth
    candelabrum-tree of cockscomb-
tinted buttons, dahlias,
sea-urchins, and everlastings,
    it perches on the branching foam
of polished sculptured
flowers—at ease and tall. The king is dead.

IN 1931 Marianne Moore read an article in the *New York Times* on the ongoing restoration of Versailles. Versailles's extravagant statues and gardens reminded her of an advertisement she had seen the previous year for a Christie's auction. Among the items on sale, and shown in the advertisement, were two porcelain candelabra, each decorated with a swan wearing a golden sawtoothed collar and perching on a tree. Most recently the property of the late Lord Balfour, the swan candelabra had originally belonged to Louis XV. These peculiar relics were in Moore's mind when, in 1932, she composed "No Swan So Fine." Moore asks how she (or we) might distinguish her poetic art from the artifice of Louis's Versailles, represented by the swan sculpture. As a stylist, Moore is elegant and elaborate. She prefers the posed to the spontaneous and

lively. One would expect her, then, to find the china swan a sympathetic sub-
ject. In fact, though, she has a troubled relation to the ornate splendor that
the swan represents. Its cloying refinement contrasts with Moore's poem,
which is poised, pointed, and economical.

Moore begins by quoting, with slight alteration, a sentence from the author
of the *Times* article, Percy Phillip: "No water so still as the / dead fountains of
Versailles." The inert fountains, with their pools of water, provide the most
telling comment on Versailles, the monument of a dead social order. For a
contrast to this ominous stillness, Moore goes on to describe a living swan.
She sees it as an ingenious contraption sporting a look of haughty disapproval:
"with swart blind look askance / and gondoliering legs." The inventive wit of
this depiction (the bird's legs angle like a gondolier's pole) combines with a
strange, murky power in the "swart blind look." Here, "swart" (meaning
"dusky" or "baleful") suggests, perhaps, an uncanny, faint malignance in the
swan's eyes as it gazes at its rival, the Louis XV sculpture. The living swan is a
mere passing presence in Moore's poem. She focuses instead on the china swan
atop the candelabrum, the decorative object that outshines the actual bird.

Swans convey melancholy poignance in Romantic and post-Romantic tra-
dition. According to legend, the swan sings a beautiful song just before its
death (as depicted in Shelley's "Epipsychidion" and Tennyson's "The Dying
Swan"). Moore's artificial swan, by contrast, remains fixed in its place, perma-
nently mute—neither alive nor dead. Choosing such an emblem over the liv-
ing presence of the animal, Moore recognizes an important fact about her
poetry: its finished, intricate, somewhat stilted character. But Moore's poem,
unlike the Louis XV swan, is not heaped with ornament. Instead, it is witty
and final.

To see how Moore executes her ingenious phrases in "No Swan So Fine,"
we must turn back to her depiction of the china swan in her first stanza.
Lines 4 through 7 show a subtle pattern of sound, as they move from the
mincing, finicky *i*-sounds of "fine / as the chintz china" to the open *ow*'s, *oh*'s
and *aw*'s of "fawn- / brown," "gold / collar on," and "show." As the vowel
sounds suggest, this description begins in (over)delicacy and ends in vulgar
possession: the purpose of the fancy gold collar is "to show whose bird it was."
Whose bird is it? the reader asks. Did it belong to Lord Balfour? King Louis?
A buyer at the Christie's auction? Poetic speech, like nature itself, belongs to
no one, and to everyone (every reader or observer). The contrived charm of
the swan candelabrum, by contrast, parades the fact of its royal ownership—
via a collar like that of the deer in Wyatt's "Whoso List to Hunt" (the first
poem in this volume).

A paradoxical law takes effect with regard to the "chintz china" bird: the more extraordinary and luxurious the *objet d'art,* the more tawdry it looks. ("Chintz," meaning multi-colored, already in Moore's day had the prevalent meaning of cheap-looking, chintzy.) Kings, too, may be vulgarians. In "No Swan So Fine," Moore reveals herself as a stylistic moralist. She counterposes an efficient, graceful art form—her own—to the tasteless, piled-on extravagance of the French court. (Her implicit suspicion of lavish wealth takes on added historical meaning, since the poem was written in one of the worst years of the Great Depression.)

"No Swan So Fine" is, for a sonnet, unusual in form. It divides into two precisely mirrored halves: two stanzas of seven lines each, rather than the conventional eight and six. But it has the query-and-resolution pattern so characteristic of the sonnet. The second stanza's answer (the king is dead) exactly balances the first stanza's question (whose swan is it?). The poem is in syllabics rather than the more usual accentual-syllabic meter: that is, Moore counts the number of syllables in each line, rather than the accents. Each stanza has the following number of syllables per line: 7, 8, 6, 8, 8, 5, 9 (with "dahlias" counted as two syllables, and "flowers" as one).

Moore begins the second half of her poem by continuing the ekphrastic representation of the swan "lodged in" the candelabrum. (Does it reside there, or is it stuck?) She gives us a catalogue of decorations: "cockscomb- / tinted buttons, dahlias, / sea-urchins, and everlastings." This precipitous stream of dainties is faintly bizarre; the candelabrum resembles a Christmas tree top-heavy with glittering doodads. Among the precious junk we see a flower, the everlasting—a perennial with brilliant, and numerous, petals. The everlasting is often dried and kept for years as a souvenir. Here, its existence stretches even further, since it has been reproduced in porcelain. These "polished sculptured / flowers" form the base for the swan, which "perches" amid blossoms as if on the "branching foam" of a ceramic sea. (The "buttons" are probably button chrysanthemums, with small spherical flowers; and sea urchins resemble flowers too.)

In her last line, Moore wonders who rules in the world that succeeds the death of the king. After the doomed King Louis came the French Revolution. Poetry's critique is more subtle. Moore, instead of confronting us with political force, offers sharp-eyed reflection. In "No Swan So Fine," the china swan (worth mocking and wondering at, too) survives as an object of description. But Moore's poem, more than the swan, conveys a presence "at ease and tall"—one that, unlike the king, survives.

DM

"Single Sonnet"

LOUISE BOGAN

1937

Now, you great stanza, you heroic mould,
Bend to my will, for I must give you love:
The weight in the heart that breathes, but cannot move,
Which to endure flesh only makes so bold.

Take up, take up, as it were lead or gold
The burden; test the dreadful mass thereof.
No stone, slate, metal under or above
Earth, is so ponderous, so dull, so cold.

Too long as ocean bed bears up the ocean,
As earth's core bears the earth, have I borne this;
Too long have lovers, bending for their kiss,
Felt bitter force cohering without motion.

Staunch meter, great song, it is yours, at length,
To prove how stronger you are than my strength.

LOUISE BOGAN'S "Single Sonnet" does not reveal its secret until its third stanza: that it is a poem about disappointed eros. Until then, Bogan addresses the sonnet itself as a form, one that she has adopted and strenuously empowers (though Bogan wrote few sonnets). She wrestles with its weight, and gains strength from the struggle. The reticence of "Single Sonnet" becomes a form of strength, too, as Bogan turns at the poem's end to poetry itself, seeing in it a greater power than her own will.

The poet begins by invoking, in the second person, the "great stanza" she is writing. In Italian, "stanza" means "room"; a poetic stanza therefore offers a firm place for the poet's energies. Here, it even provides a vehicle for her heroic image of herself, a "heroic mould." Like a sculptor manipulating recalcitrant materials, Bogan orders the stanza to "bend to [her] will." She is obligated to the form, bound to infuse it with "love." In "Single Sonnet," love means both the devoted energies of the artistic creator and the amorous subject matter that Bogan finally identifies near the end of her poem.

We perceive a strong hint of the erotic distress the poet feels at the end of the first quatrain, where she depicts a suffocating burden that seems like King Lear's *hysterica passio,* the vise-like suffering clutching at his heart. (Lear cries, "O how this mother swells up toward my heart! / Hysterica passio, down, thou climbing sorrow, / Thy element's below.") "The weight in the heart that breathes, but cannot move": this passion is unbudging, a dread obstacle rather than an inspiration. Line 4 ties itself in syntactic knots, an image of the constriction the poet feels. This line, "Which to endure flesh only makes so bold," might be paraphrased as "only flesh would be so bold as to endure [the heart's weight]." Depressingly, Bogan here defines boldness as the will to bear suffering. Bogan endured a shattered marriage, and then embarked on a long, troubled affair with the poet Theodore Roethke. This poem reflects the frightening intensity of her attachments, and the sense of doom and disappointment that often accompanied them.

In the second quatrain, the poet tells herself to "take up" her burden "as it were lead or gold." When reading the poem aloud, we should pause after "lead": changing direction, the poet considers that the excruciating emotional weight she bears might be not merely leaden, but radiant and rewarding as gold. But we suspect, in the next few lines, that she performs a wishful alchemy and is merely fooling herself: her love is lead after all, or even heavier, and worse. "No stone, slate, metal under or above / Earth is so ponderous, so dull, so cold." Ponderous because unwieldy, but also because Bogan ponders it, carrying her dead passion like a stillborn child.

As the sestet begins, Bogan explores several images for her oppressive confinement under a stone-like love. She is like the ocean bed, crushed by so many tons of water; or like earth's core supporting the earth. In lines 11 and 12, she tells as much of a story as she can manage, casting her dismal situation in universal terms: "Too long have lovers, bending for their kiss, / Felt bitter force cohering without motion." This sentence recapitulates earlier images in "Single Sonnet": the bending recalls the poet stiffly making the stanza bend to her will, and the lack of motion evokes the inflexible weight in her heart (both in the first quatrain). The eros that governs these lovers is a "bitter force"—harsh and stinging, and colored by resentment, even hatred. They bend for their kiss: rather than being attracted or drawn by a seductive spell (as in so many sonnets about love, beginning with Dante's *Vita nuova*), they stand painfully ready, planted by gravity. The fact that the lovers cohere is the work not of sympathy, but of rule. They cling together as molecules do, forced into place by the laws of physics.

Bogan's "Single Sonnet" is a frustrated and austere poem. With determination, the author confirms her sense of life as hampered, weighed down, unfree. What saves the poem from bitterness, what gives it its singularity (so that it is not merely one more complaint against love) is its couplet ending. Here, Bogan turns to poetic form itself, as she did at the beginning, but now with a sense of destiny rather than imprisonment. Speaking to her sonnet, she musters the praise that she could not summon for romantic love. "Staunch meter, great song": poetic meters may not be able to stanch our emotional wounds, but they are themselves staunch, that is, solid, lasting—strong. Bogan relies on poetry, not (as is more traditional) as a vehicle of immortality, of undying fame for the poet or the poet's beloved, but rather as an exemplary case of sheer stubborn survival—which in turn gives the poet herself ironic satisfaction (since her poem has proven its superiority to her). This use of the idea of a poem's strength—its imaginative power, its memorability for future readers—may be unique. It is certainly distinguished in its gallows humor.

The poet's burden proves greater than she can bear, but she has no choice except to continue to bear it: it defines her. Go ahead, she tells the poem she has written; show how much stronger you are than I am. In the case of Bogan, as in that of any worthy poet, the song outlasts the singer. Accordingly, in her conclusion, she demonstrates an envy of her poem's imperviousness. In contrast to the author, who remains coupled unwillingly to her affection, this is a "Single Sonnet." Like all art, it stands alone, impersonal. Bogan's sonnet becomes a grim reflection on the difference between the words we craft and our own graven injuries. Perfectly scaled to its subject, it shows decisive heft.

DM

In Time of War 27

W. H. AUDEN

1939

Wandering lost upon the mountains of our choice,
Again and again we sigh for an ancient South,
For the warm nude ages of instinctive poise,
For the taste of joy in the innocent mouth.

Asleep in our huts, how we dream of a part
In the glorious balls of the future; each intricate maze
Has a plan, and the disciplined movements of the heart
Can follow for ever and ever its harmless ways.

We envy streams and houses that are sure:
But we are articled to error; we
Were never nude and calm like a great door,

And never will be perfect like the fountains;
We live in freedom by necessity,
A mountain people dwelling among mountains.

W. H. AUDEN wrote this sonnet, part of his sequence *In Time of War*, in 1938. During the previous two years, Auden had traveled to the Spanish Civil War, and then gone to China to report on the Japanese invasion of that country. *In Time of War* reflects Auden's direct experience of the hardships imposed by military action, and the fateful choices it presents. "Wandering lost" ends *In Time of War* by meditating on the interplay of choice and necessity, and the longing for innocence in a time of impending, worldwide disaster.

Auden begins with the picture of humans "wandering lost upon the mountains of our choice." Expelled from Paradise, we have been cast out into the fallen world of choice, where we are responsible for our decisions. In the notes to his long poem *New Year Letter* (1941), Auden wrote, "The *Now* we must accept, our freedom *to,* is continually changing into the *Then* we must reject, our freedom *from.* Choice is our term for expressing the continuity of this change. But there is no escape from necessity." According to Auden, we must accept our freedom; it is forced on us by the fact of change, and is therefore a form of necessity. In "Wandering lost," Auden reflects on the duties of the poet, as he sees them. Rather than providing a fantasy of youthful vigor, or promising to transform the world via the power of imagination, the poet is obligated to remind us of our mature, troubled state.

Yet Auden wishes for an antidote to this maturity, to the mountains where we wander, alone and in exile. He finds it in a southern lushness, located somewhere in a remembered or fantasized past. "Again and again we sigh for an ancient South," Auden writes; the repeated "again" expresses frustration, and implies the impossibility of the wish, since there is no road back to Eden. "Oh for a beaker full of the warm South": so Keats yearned in his "Ode to a Nightingale." In Auden's mind as in Keats's, the Mediterranean climate signifies an easier life, carefree and full of sensual enjoyment (suggested here by "nude"). The "innocent mouth" that tastes joy resembles the poet's palate in the Nightingale Ode, which delights in the bursting of the grape. This aesthete's ease, both Auden and Keats indicate, is a fantasy rather than a reality.

The first quatrain's wish for a life free from care and beautifully at ease is summed up in the phrase "instinctive poise." Taken together, these two words are something of an oxymoron. Poise is an attainment, not an inherent quality. But it seems instinctive—somehow natural, rather than studied or learned by rote. Such stylish beauty, uniting cultivation and ease, here represents a yearned-for escape from the situation implied in line 1: wandering through the dilemmas of adult life, including the terrible choices made in wartime. The charming pose assumed by innocence, Auden suggests, stands for our wish to be ignorant of life's conditions.

From the imaginary freedom evoked in the first quatrain, Auden turns, in the second, to a vision of the future. Now we are "asleep in our huts"—sheltered and dreaming, but still in the mountains (the hut is a climber's overnight lodging, the poem suggests). The fantasy described in the second quatrain proves just as unrealizable as the one in the opening lines of the poem. The phrase "glorious balls of the future" conjures up a world of lavishness and polished manners. This is a planned, "disciplined" scene, where even the heart follows a structured path. Auden here alludes to Alexander Pope's famous description of human life, in his *Essay on Man,* as "a mighty maze! but not without a plan." (Significantly, Pope's first version of the line was "a mighty maze, and all without a plan.") Life is like a dance we have learned well, whose movements we follow "for ever and ever" (a heightening of the first quatrain's "again and again," but this time sounding like a child's wistful wish, distantly, and hopefully, echoing the Lord's Prayer: "For thine is the kingdom and the power and the glory, for ever and ever, Amen"). The innocence depicted in the second quatrain is mated with grown-up discipline, in the form of a game (the dance at the ball, the labyrinth we thread carefully and successfully). If all life resembled such a game, we would be free from political evil, from the insidious plotting of war. (In Auden's later critical prose, the game—not a trivial thing but a serious and needed activity—becomes one of his favorite images for what the poet or artist creates. But he cautions that the outside world is more pressing, and far more threatening, than the playful maneuvers of artistry, however worthy, and wise, such play may be.)

The second quatrain's vision of "harmless[ness]" proves inadequate to the looming danger that Auden senses in the history of his time. And so, in the sestet (rhymed in Italianate rather than Shakespearean fashion, *efegfg*), Auden banishes the dream: he denies the octave's fantasies of "streams and houses that are sure." Human life may be located in a scene, and we may inhabit houses; but these places provide no guidance for us. (They are like huts, temporary and provisional.) We must guide ourselves. Our choices do in fact resemble mountains, which we gain strenuously and at much risk of losing our way. *Error* in Latin means "a wandering about." Our wrong turnings are not mere lostness, as in line 1, but now a sort of constitution. "We are articled to error," Auden writes—it is our basic law. To be articled is to be apprenticed; permanent students, we are still learning how to wander. ("Articled" also means "set down in articles," like a law or a creed. Newspaper articles, which trade in errors—false rumors—and convey with urgency international events, have become the obligatory scripture of the time.)

The fervent counterfactual wish for a "nude and calm" past, to be cherished and perhaps recovered, must be renounced; it is not a "great door" we can pass back through (a possible allusion to the gates of Eden in Genesis 3:24, guarded by cherubs with a flaming sword). Equally, Auden adds in his final stanza, we "never will be perfect like the fountains." The fountain's ever-flowing motion is meaningless and repetitive, perfect only in the most restricted sense. We remain, by contrast, in the midst of action, discontent.

Where do we belong? What is our proper setting? The genre of pastoral, with its "nude and calm" accord between the human and the natural, suggests a blending of innocence and experience. In pastoral, the poet (or his representative, the shepherd) can be both a sophisticated artist and a naïf. But in this poem, Auden rejects as an illusion the paradoxical consciousness of pastoral, represented by the "ancient South" of the first quatrain with its "instinctive poise." (In a later sequence, *Bucolics,* he will reach hopefully toward such consciousness.) He also denies the feasibility of the second quatrain's more urbane vision, the maze-like dance of an improved world to come. (Such a world was, in the 1930s, the dream of many progressive liberals, who were unable to grasp the fact of the coming war.)

Turning away from these optimistic dreams, Auden opts for a hard reality. In "Wandering lost," he recognizes a crucial fact about himself: that he wants an escape from the crises of mid-twentieth-century politics, from the extreme solutions, the dreadful mass movements, and the imminent war. But he knows that he can't have such a way out. This adult knowledge informs the poet's concluding lines: "We live in freedom by necessity, / A mountain people dwelling among mountains." Exploiting the double meaning of "by," Auden argues that we know, at last, where we belong: the realm of freedom that borders necessity, and is in fact necessary. In this sober awareness, Auden—perhaps the twentieth century's preeminent didactic poet—takes strength.

DM

"Never Again Would Birds' Song Be the Same"

ROBERT FROST

1942

He would declare and could himself believe
That the birds there in all the garden round
From having heard the daylong voice of Eve
Had added to their own an oversound,
Her tone of meaning but without the words.
Admittedly an eloquence so soft
Could only have had an influence on birds
When call or laughter carried it aloft.
Be that as may be, she was in their song.
Moreover her voice upon their voices crossed
Had now persisted in the woods so long
That probably it never would be lost.
Never again would birds' song be the same.
And to do that to birds was why she came.

FROST's haunting "Never Again Would Birds' Song Be the Same," written in 1942, revises the story of the Garden of Eden, familiar from Genesis and from Milton's *Paradise Lost*. Frost resists the plot of these earlier versions; he omits the traumatic ritual moment of the Fall. In "Never Again," Eden is subtly retained: the continuing influence of Eve on her surroundings, the poet writes, "probably . . . never would be lost." Eve's voice—a softness with an edge— stands for the persistence of poetry itself. The poet's song insinuates itself into our speech and into our thought, a quiet, sure undercurrent.

The sonnet begins with a mood of self-reassurance on the part of Adam (the "he" of the opening line). "He would declare and could himself believe": Adam makes his declaration experimentally, inventively, and finds that he trusts his own surmise. It is plausible to him that the birds of Eden "had added to their own an oversound," Eve's "tone of meaning but without the words." The oversound is what matters when you read a line of poetry. In a poem, what Frost called "sentence sounds," the characteristic intonations of everyday speech, are made to work toward a different sort of artfulness; we listen for the peculiar accents of an original voice. Frost's point is that such originality—the Edenic element in poetry—can be heard in the poet's stance and style, long before the careful reader stops to paraphrase the poem's argument (as I am doing here). Woven into the verse is "a tone of meaning": meaning resides in tone, in how something sounds. "No one invents new tones of voice," Frost remarked in a prose piece, "The Last Refinement of Subject Matter: Vocal Imagination." "So many and no more belong to the human throat, just as so many runs and quavers belong to the throat of the cat-bird, so many to the chickadee. . . . The imagination is no more than their summoner—the imagination of the ear."

Tone is the means for making relationships, as well—for connecting the self to its surroundings. Milton in *Paradise Lost* gives Eve sympathy with the flora of Eden, a closeness to nature's responses, whereas Adam is less intuitive, riper for analytic discussion with the visiting angel Raphael. Both Eve's way of thinking and Adam's are necessary; so too in Frost, where Adam's hypothesizing reaches out toward Eve's expressive "call" and "laughter." She sings; he interprets. These two aspects, seen together, are equal parts of the writing, and reading, of poetry.

Birds are a perennial subject for poetry, perhaps most notably in Keats's "Ode to a Nightingale." In Keats, the nightingale is the envy of the human singer, who remains oppressed by his consciousness of weakness and mortality. Keats argues that the bird is more innately melodious than we can be— that human self-awareness gets in the way of full-throated expression. (Of course, as Keats well knows, only a sophisticated consciousness would desire in this way the simple voice of nature.) Frost changes the formula. For him, nature (the birds) and the human (Eve) collaborate, but the human speaker is preferable.

Like "Mowing," then, "Never Again" calmly argues against the fantasy of escape from the Fall—from the death, guilt, and sorrow that (we often think) distinguishes man from other animals. Instead, Frost posits that Eve's voice remains "upon their [the birds'] voices crossed." Womanly speech harmonizes with birdsong, two utterances that sustain each other. Like Cordelia's in *King Lear*, Eve's voice is "gentle, sweet, and low." She guides the birds in their music; and so the difference between the human and the natural gets into nature, and persists. This is not a fall but a healthy flaw. As in Frost's "Mowing," nature seems amenable to human expression, to what that earlier poem calls "earnest love." The garden, like the field, welcomes the pressure that our heightened consciousness—our labor of meaning—gives to it. Similarly, in the pastoral tradition, the shepherd's singing may tune itself to the waters' fall, but it also rises from the nature that surrounds it—a distinctly human cry that impresses itself on the landscape. Expressing ourselves like Eve, with the wholehearted conviction of impulse, we interrupt the comforting monotony of our environment. We even, Frost suggests, converse with and alter that environment.

Frost's "Never Again" opens itself to the subject of poetic survival. The poet's eloquence is not a strident raising of the voice, not a straining for effect, but a mild wafting—like Eve's "eloquence so soft," heard at intervals and "carried . . . aloft" by our speaking. "Call or laughter" are the buoyant moments in our speech, the occasions when we communicate excitedly or rise to a bout of ecstatic gaiety. The emphasis on Eve's song-like exclamations in "Never Again" tugs against the series of hesitant qualifiers that mark Adam's analytic perspective: "admittedly," "be that as may be," "moreover," and "probably."

With his last two lines, Frost makes a compressed etiological fable. In this Shakespearean sonnet, he uses the final couplet rhyme to surprise us, and to drive home the point of the third quatrain, with its exploration of the crossing of voices. The concluding couplet is "Never again would birds' song be the same. / And to do that to birds was why she came." Frost implies that the first woman was created as an independent spirit: domestic yet uncanny, off on her own—not, as in Milton, to be a helpmeet or "other self" to Adam. Eve proves her independence in *Paradise Lost,* as well; but there the difference between her and Adam, described by a poet devoted to his heroine, proves catastrophic. Not so in "Never Again," which smoothly elides the Fall.

The dire conflicts that often occur between male and female characters in Frost's dialogue poems (most famously "Home Burial") are nowhere apparent here. In this sonnet, the man's role is to puzzle, to guess, and finally to appreciate. Eve's work is love as action: it leads to realization, and alters the face of the world. Like Eve, Frost has left his mark on our poetic listening. "Never Again" recalls a fine change in the way things are, and in the way they sound.

DM

"Epic"

PATRICK KAVANAGH

1951; first book publication 1960

I have lived in important places, times
When great events were decided: who owned
That half a rood of rock, a no-man's land
Surrounded by our pitchfork-armed claims.
I heard the Duffys shouting "Damn your soul"
And old McCabe stripped to the waist, seen
Step the plot defying blue-cast steel—
"Here is the march along those iron stones."
That was the year of the Munich bother. Which
Was more important? I inclined
To lose my faith in Ballyrush and Gortin
Till Homer's ghost came whispering to my mind.
He said: I made the *Iliad* from such
A local row. Gods make their own importance.

ONE OF the most influential poets in English to emerge from genuine rural poverty, Kavanagh belonged to the first generation of writers to grow up in Ireland after the twenty-six counties of the Irish Free State achieved de facto independence in 1922. The son of a cobbler and an illiterate mother, he came from the village of Inishkeen, County Monaghan; Ballyrush and Gortin are villages nearby. The poet left school at thirteen, learned shoemaking but did not like it, and, after his father died, acquired a small farm, which he worked himself. In 1937, having published a volume of verse, he gave up agricultural labor to write full-time, making a go of it first in London, and from 1939 on in Dublin, where he wrote poems, novels, and a great deal of occasional prose— book and movie reviews, reminiscences, personal essays, reportage on rural life, and cantankerous opinion pieces. For twenty years he enjoyed almost no esteem outside Ireland, and a controversial reputation within it. Was he a gad-fly, a crank, a curiosity, a great talent badly misused? Then came the publication, in London, of *Come Dance with Kitty Strobling* (1960), which included this sonnet, and most of his best short poems: since then, his place among Irish poets has seemed secure.

"Epic" uses "important" or "importance" three times, in the first line, in the last line, and in the poem's only question. Kavanagh asks, as William Wordsworth before him had asked, what sort of people and places make poems important; and he answers (as Wordsworth had answered) that he, at least, will make important poems from the obscure material of rural life. Kavanagh's farmers—the Duffys, "old McCabe"—are moved, like Achilles, by uncontainable wrath. Like Achilles, they make speeches about it, and like all the Greeks at Troy, they fight over land. "Epic" becomes both noun and honorific adjective. Kavanagh's transitions (from "great events" to "half a rood of rock," for example) flirt with the mode called mock-epic, which stresses the comic smallness of trivial disputes (e.g., in Pope's "The Rape of the Lock," over a severed lock of hair). How can a tiny tract of unpropitious land support great, and serious, art?

Kavanagh wants to demonstrate that it can—indeed, that for a certain kind of poet (his kind, and perhaps Homer's too) it is only from the local, the close-to-home, that important art can grow. "Rood" here means a unit of land, perhaps sixty square yards, though it varies by local convention; a "march" is a boundary, usually between nations but here between neighboring farms. These two farms—the Duffys' and McCabe's—are almost comically militarized, and Kavanagh gives them the language of war: "cast-steel," "iron," "no-man's land" (originally, "no-man's land" was the land between opposing armies in World War I, within reach of shells from either side). McCabe steps across what the Duffys take to be the boundary between their farms, asserting his ownership over disputed ground, which the Duffys have probably already ploughed (with "steel"—a pitchfork, a plough, or a spade). The poet's language likens the farmers' dispute to the Trojan War, and to the Second World War, and flirts again with the mock-epic belittlement that Kavanagh always rejects. Rather than diminish the "importance" these "great events" on an Irish farm hold, Kavanagh will show why they seem, to him, more significant—better material for poetry—than the most consequential of public events.

That demonstration begins with the sestet. Though "bother" suggests an ironized dismissal, Kavanagh expects us to know that "the Munich bother" was one of the most important steps on the road to the Second World War: in

Munich, in September 1938, France and the United Kingdom agreed to let Hitler seize part of Czechoslovakia. British prime minister Neville Chamberlain returned home boasting that he had avoided war, though in fact he had only postponed it. The agreement, and even the name "Munich," soon came to connote cowardice in foreign affairs.

Kavanagh himself spent much of 1938 in London, trying to make a literary career. He settled in Dublin in 1939, after a lawsuit torpedoed whatever chances his first novel had for commercial success. In the late 1950s and 1960s, Kavanagh sometimes said he regretted ever leaving Inishkeen, though he could also excoriate the narrow sensibilities of farm life in ways that looked back to "The Great Hunger," his famously bleak 1942 poem. Deleting his own binational, urban experience from his later sonnet about 1938, Kavanagh portrays instead a rivalry between the "real life of real folk" (his term for farm life, in a newspaper column from 1939) and an international view of "importance" that assigns it only to people, places, and conflicts already well known.

That view, for Kavanagh, is always the wrong one: any life, anywhere, provides material for great art, if the artist knows it well enough. Joyce's *Ulysses* had already made an obscure Irishman, Leopold Bloom, into ambitious modern literature with Homeric roots. Yet Joyce wrote an urban novel. Kavanagh is writing a rural lyric. He too (he says here) can make obscure Irish life important, and he can do so in ways that do not even stray much from their ancient models. Like Homeric heroes, and unlike Neville Chamberlain, these farmers will cede not an inch of pride or land.

Like most Irish poets of the twentieth century, Kavanagh had to distance himself assiduously not from Joyce, but from W. B. Yeats. "Yeats was a troubled man because he couldn't achieve peasantry," Kavanagh wrote in 1962. Kavanagh himself, by contrast, was told "from all sides that I was peasant and a ploughman to boot." "Epic" shares with Yeats the sense that Irish peasant life, relatively unchanged from preindustrial times, relatively remote from cultural centers, could preserve the sensibility of ancient heroic epic. Ireland and the Irish language had their own epics, such as the *Táin bó Cúalnge* (Cattle Raid of Cooley), and their own epic heroes, such as Cuchulain. Kavanagh, though, wants nothing to do with them here. His point is not pride in a national tradition, but attention to local material. It is not that Cuchulain's Ireland is uniquely equal to Homeric Greece, but that the O'Tooles, Ballyrush, and Gortin (placed in rhyming position, and paired with "importance") are as good as the walls of Troy.

Who are Homer's—and Kavanagh's—"gods"? They are not the Trinity: Kavanagh regains "faith in Ballyrush," not in Christ or the church. We might instead take Kavanagh to mean that poets, by elevating insignificant struggles, prove that they are inspired, even divine. Yet Homer was not a god, and never called himself one; the "local row" that became the *Iliad* involved the Achaean equivalents of McCabe and Duffy, not the poet himself. Kavanagh sees the actuating emotions of epic poetry, pride and loyalty and rage, in the breasts of his farmers. Homer saw the same emotions in his warriors—warriors whose emotions and motives, in Homeric epic, are placed there by the gods. True poetry grows out of those true and divinely inspired motives, and cares little for their scale. A fight over half an acre matters more than a fight over half a continent, if half an acre is what the poet knows.

SB

"The Illiterate"

WILLIAM MEREDITH

1958

Touching your goodness, I am like a man
Who turns a letter over in his hand
And you might think this was because the hand
Was unfamiliar but, truth is, the man
Has never had a letter from anyone;
And now he is both afraid of what it means
And ashamed because he has no other means
To find out what it says than to ask someone.

His uncle could have left the farm to him,
Or his parents died before he sent them word,
Or the dark girl changed and want him for beloved.
Afraid and letter-proud, he keeps it with him.
What would you call his feeling for the words
That keep him rich and orphaned and beloved?

Now beloved of teachers, this quietly moving sonnet offers at once a tour de force of simplicity, a poem about the reading of poetry, and a hesitant, sympathetic picture of inexperience in romantic love. Meredith keeps his diction as plain as in any serious poem of his century, using only common words in common combinations, with almost no description, no sense-details. He deploys, indeed, banal phrases, such as a man unused to reading might use ("And you might think," "truth is," "what would you call"). Meredith signals his simplicities further with the repetitive use of identical rhyme (also known by the French term *rime riche*): he fills out the Italianate scheme *(abba cddc ef-gefg)* not with rhymes, but with repeated words. One of the words, of course, is "word," or "words": the illiterate man in receipt of his first-ever letter "turns

[it] over in his hand," over and over, as if that way he could figure out what it meant, as if he did not yet want to find out.

Meredith repeats "afraid" and "letter," though neither occur in rhyming position. The illiterate man's unread letter, like any recipient's letter before it is opened, could disclose bad news (for example, the death of both parents). Yet this man's repeated apprehension might come from good news as well as from bad. Might the letter, once understood, solicit frightening action? Might it contain, for example, a marriage proposal? ("The dark girl" echoes the so-called "dark lady," the beautiful dark-haired and finally treacherous woman in Shakespeare's later sonnets.) Given all the uncertainty in the octave, we might expect the sestet to tell us "what [the letter] says." Instead, it repeats the situation of that octave (using "afraid" and "letter" again), without allowing any time to pass, or any potential events to take place. At the end of the poem, after one more unanswered question, the illiterate man, and the poet "touching your goodness," remain in the same situation as before: gently if nervously marveling at the letter's existence, at "your goodness," and at your mysterious "touch."

Once read, once decoded, the letter will come to mean what its contents mean. Before it is interpreted, though, the letter has another signification: it represents a gesture of human connection, what linguists call a "phatic" communication, which we might signal in person by a touch on the shoulder or hand. It shows that somebody cares what happens to this man, that somebody wants to tell him something. "Touching your goodness," the man holds on to that signal of human care.

We could say as much of a letter unopened, turned "over and over" by a recipient "proud" to keep it and able to read it at will. But Meredith's man could not read it alone if he tried. Moreover, he "has never had a letter from anyone"; even the experience of asking somebody to help him decode it would be new for him (and he has not yet asked). As much as he cherishes this "touch," this gesture, as much as he may be "proud" to have received it, the man seems "afraid" not only of what it might say but of asking for help, of revealing his weakness, his need. Rather than show that weakness to somebody else—rather than learn what somebody else wants from him, wants him to do, or wants him to know—Meredith's illiterate retains in himself a suitably nameless feeling, sad in part (because it reflects incapacity), but appropriate to the unrealized possibility, the fearful and wonderful news, that his letter may contain.

So far, the unread—and to this man, unreadable—letter might resemble an unread poem, or a poem admired but not quite understood. Part of its "goodness" derives from the way it allows the man to remain in the realm of surmise. Moreover—like a letter to an illiterate man—a poem may exert its full powers only when heard. Meredith's "feeling" includes some marveling at the potential in language generally: in familiar epistolary language, on the one "hand," and in poetic language (or modern lyric poetry) on the other. Like Elizabeth Barrett Browning's sonnet earlier in this volume, Meredith's sonnet depends on the similarities and differences between a familiar letter and a lyric poem. Both kinds of language can embody the inner life of the author, in ways that seem exciting, but also frightening, and perhaps difficult to sustain. The familiar letter ordinarily finds just one reader, one named recipient, and refers to his or her situation alone. A lyric poem, by contrast, has an abstract or "algebraic" element (as W. H. Auden, an important influence on Meredith, put it in the 1930s). "Feeling" in poems becomes available, interpretable, in ways that leave behind the circumstances of authors' lives and times.

But Meredith's sonnet is not only a sonnet about lyric poetry—about the mystery and the abstraction it offers, about the personality, "touch," or "feeling" disclosed and concealed by the "words" in poems. Though "touching" means "considering," "regarding," it also suggests the touch of a human hand: Meredith's sonnet is also a love poem, a poem that ends with the illiterate man imagining himself not only rich (inheriting a farm) "and orphaned" (by the death of his parents), but "beloved." And here the poem begins to acquire additional sense if we look to Meredith's own life. Admired for his poetry since the 1940s, when he won the Yale Younger Poets Prize, Meredith served in the U.S. Navy from 1941 to 1946 and again from 1952 to 1954. He was also gay. His sonnet describes a particular moment in the life of a lover and a "beloved," a moment unusually familiar, perhaps, to gay men who came to adulthood in an era especially hostile to same-sex love: the moment when an inexperienced lover believes (but cannot yet know) that he might be the beloved, the moment when the lover finds what he thinks (but cannot be sure) is an invitation, a pointed suggestion, a hint.

Such an invitation, like all flirtations, might come in the dual sense of some action, some word—in something that might look, to a stranger, innocent, until its doubled erotic sense is revealed. Meredith's doubled words (ordinary, but with dual meanings, and dual uses as rhyme-substitutes) stand for the double sense of any word, any gesture, used as a romantic hint. And such invitations can always be disavowed; indeed, an ardent or a merely awkward lover may see them where they are not meant, may take hints where no hints are given, and may (especially if these matters feel new to him) embarrass himself a great deal by reacting eagerly to invitations that nobody gave.

"The obstacle—effectively a double-bind," writes the critic Tony Tanner (he is analyzing Jane Austen's novel *Persuasion*), "seems to be that you cannot speak 'openly' and 'directly' about . . . your feelings of love, *to* the person you love, until you have achieved a certain intimacy. . . . But how do you ever manage to get intimate enough to be intimate, as it were?" As in Austen, so throughout Meredith's poem. "Touching your goodness" could mean, simply, being touched (moved) by your goodness (benevolence); it could also refer to the brush of a hand, to the discovery that, within some new friendship, there might be something physical, something more. That discovery remains merely exciting—and cannot be threatening, disappointing, embarrassing—so long as it remains merely conjectural, so long as the lover does not try to follow it up, does not try to reciprocate with his own hint.

That moment of thinking that one has received a hint, of thinking that a flirtation *might* have begun, of feeling unable to "read" the language of love, because it is by its nature never explicit, and because it feels new—that moment is the moment of Meredith's poem. His "feeling" is not apprehension merely, not fear alone and not quite joy, but rather the mixed feelings of a lover who cannot yet know whether he is beloved, a lover who does not know how to interpret a gesture that may signify love returned—who may not, indeed, know anybody he can trust enough to ask. Such feelings are familiar to many teenagers, to many heterosexual adults, and to the characters in Jane Austen, who can also respond by writing letters (where, as Tanner says, "there may always be another message in—under—the ostensible message"). Yet that sense of shameful inexperience prolonged into adulthood, of not knowing whether a message is "double" or not, and of not knowing how or whom to ask, might seem especially plangent in this poem about hints and uncertainties if we connect it to homosexuality in the white-collar America of 1958, before the word "gay" meant in public what it means now.

During the 1980s Meredith's poem became an anthology staple, a sonnet about inexperience (in reading as in love) whose tact and care inexperienced readers enjoyed. By that time, the poem had acquired more poignant dimensions, ones the poet could not have foreseen. In 1983, Meredith suffered a stroke that severely limited his ability to process language—to speak, to read, and to hear. He wrote little afterward, but could, in his last years, read movingly from his work on public occasions, when "The Illiterate" became an especially appropriate, and well-received, set piece.

SB

"Marsyas"

JAMES MERRILL

1959

I used to write in the café sometimes:
Poems on menus, read all over town
Or talked out before ever written down.
One day a girl brought in his latest book.
I opened it—stiff rhythms, gorgeous rhyme—
And made a face. Then crash! my cup upset.
Of twenty upward looks mine only met
His, that gold archaic lion's look

Wherein I saw my wiry person skinned
Of every skill it labored to acquire
And heard the plucked nerve's elemental twang.
They found me dangling where his golden wind
Inflicted so much music on the lyre
That no one could have told you what he sang.

IN GREEK myth, the satyr Marsyas found a flute (or a pan-pipe) and taught himself to play. He became (or believed himself) so good at it, and had such pride, that he challenged the god Apollo to a musical contest— satyr against god, flute (or pan-pipe) against lyre. Of course, Apollo won; the divinity punished the satyr for his presumption by flaying Marsyas alive. Ovid, in Book 6 of the *Metamorphoses,* dwells on the flaying: "Nought else he was than one whole wound," says Arthur Golding's 1567 translation, "the quivering veins without a skin . . . and in his brest the shere small strings." Tortured for arrogance, for having dared even to challenge the god of the lyre, Marsyas becomes himself a lyre, "played" by wind. Merrill may have in mind the several ancient versions of the Marsyas story, or the famous representations (Titian's, for instance) in European art. But he plays down the grisly bits that Ovid and Titian play up. Instead, Merrill thinks about Marsyas alive, about rivalry among poets, and about the role of technique in poetic art.

This Marsyas is not a satyr but a human being: the poem begins in Marsyas' own demotic and low-pressure language. Readers expecting the archaic settings of myth instead find a café; readers expecting a third-person tale instead hear the titular victim speak the whole poem. He is an amateur or unsuccessful poet, a habitué of café culture, a bit like the melancholy characters in the poetry of C. P. Cavafy, the modern Greek poet of same-sex love and dejection, whom Merrill imitates directly elsewhere. This Marsyas has his poems "read all over town," but only because he writes them on menus. Nobody else cares whether his poems survive. Some are mere "talk," and all (if they resemble the first few lines here) feel casual, like conversation: they are not, and do not sound, made to last.

Nor is Merrill's Apollo clearly a god; he is, instead, a successful poet, prolific enough that a new book is "his latest." Marsyas frowns at its "stiff rhythms, gorgeous rhymes," comparing their elaborate technique unfavorably to his own authenticity; they are not, as he thinks he is, close to everyday life. No sooner has Marsyas "made a face" at the book, alas, than Apollo arrives in person, his look "gold" and "archaic" like the disk of the sun (an Apollonian symbol). In the eighth line, Merrill's syntax grows elaborate, as if to fit Apollo's greater powers. The rhymes of the sestet are odder, more interesting, than the rhymes of the octave, since it is in the sestet that Apollo's musical gifts make themselves known. Marsyas is of course intimidated, "skinned"—reduced, in the greater writer's presence, from a lesser competitor in the same art to a victim: "elemental," wordless, pained.

As in Ovid, the lesser poet-musician becomes—with a horrible "twang"— the instrument on which the greater one plays. Merrill's Marsyas is strung up, "dangling." Since Merrill's Apollo has no supernatural powers, the sestet suggests either that Marsyas simply feels strung up, or (more likely, more literally) that Marsyas, stung by the ringing realization that he would never be much of a poet, and would never get the girl, leaves the café and commits suicide. Yet Marysas (likely from the afterlife) speaks the whole poem. From that afterlife, still able to hear earthly music, Marsyas does not recant his earlier, negative judgment on Apollo's poems; instead, he tells us that his own tortured body, and the music Apollo made from it, provide further evidence against Apollo's art.

The problem with Apollo's "golden wind," the problem with a poetry generated wholly by conscious craft and superhuman nature (the wind is nature's, but also Apollo's), is that with "so much music," such "gorgeous" patterns, the human meaning gets drowned out. Merrill was himself a poet of "gorgeous rhymes" (though not, in 1959, a famous one); hostile readers, then and for decades to come, had just such objections to Merrill's own verse. Marsyas implies, by the end, claims we might associate not with Merrill but with such casual, personable, anti-elitist poets as William Carlos Williams (though Williams honed his craft skills too): that the arts at their best and most valuable are more democratic than we we often think; and that the arts in general, and poems in particular, are not a competition among great masters, but instead just parts of a broader community of human speech. To believe otherwise is to silence, and even to torture, the poets whose skills do not seem to measure up: it is to impose an inhuman scheme on what should be a compassionate art.

But that is Marsyas speaking, not Merrill. The poem presents a view that its dramatic situation (from its mythographic title forward) complicates. Apollo, in this version, did not kill the satyr, but only looked down at him; Marsyas, intimidated, seems to have gone home and killed himself. Is his death Apollo's fault? Does technique really drive out sincerity? The inverse correlation between "gorgeous rhymes" and human meaning ("what he sang"), the notion that the more music ("so much music") the less personal the resulting poem—these are Marsyas' ideas. If the poem does not allow us to reject them, neither does it make us accept them. Rather, we have here a skillful, self-distancing poet, and one who, early in his career, must have been tempted to write a poetry of pure, elaborate, impersonal, "gorgeous" music, even as his peers urged him to say more, to become less ornate.

The best poetry is neither Apollo's nor Marsyas', neither so stiff and cruel as to resemble divine legislation, nor so casual as to seem (like a menu) fit only for practical use. The best poems incorporate both compassion and skill, and no one is tortured thereby; the best poets take care not to act god-like, to meet "upward looks" in a more generous way. Merrill uses a myth to give a shocking warning to himself, and to other poets of his temperament. He may also have been thinking about the famous older poets he met in his own youth. As an Amherst College student in the 1940s, he likely met Robert Frost, whose behavior with younger admirers could set a generous, or an intimidating, example.

As we read about the contest between two kinds of art, two versions of art's purpose, we recognize the inner struggle Merrill—like every poet—under-

goes, a struggle between two conceptions of poetry. In one view, it is all com-
munication, all expression, a higher version of "talk." In another, it is auto-
telic, all skill, wholly separate from other ways language is used, as unlike
"talk" as gold is unlike pencil lead. Neither version, on its own, can explain
why poems work, why we read them; the fully achieved poem belongs neither
to Merrill's hapless Marsyas, nor to his cold Apollo. If the "supreme fiction" of
a successful poem "must be abstract," as Wallace Stevens put it, the same poem
"must be human" nonetheless. Neither the café scribbler, nor the impersonal
sun god, could ever compose such a poem—but Merrill, who understands
both of them, could, and did.

SB

The Sonnets 44

TED BERRIGAN

1964

The withered leaves fly higher than dolls can see
A watchdog barks in the night
Joyful ants nest in the roof of my tree
There is only off-white mescalin to be had
Anne is writing poems to me and worrying about "making it"
and Ron is writing poems and worrying about "making it"
and Pat is worrying but not working on anything
and Gude is worrying about his sex life
It is 1959 and I am waiting for the mail
Who cares about Tuesday? (Jacques Louis David normalcy day)?
Boston beat New York three to one. It could have been
Carolyn. Providence is as close to Montana as Tulsa.
He buckles on his gun, the one Steve left him:
His stand-in was named Herman, but came rarely

WE MAY feel put off, at first, by such difficult modernist poets as Hart Crane and W. B. Yeats (both represented in this book), but the difficulties in their strongest poems reward minute analyses; we can ask, and discover, what each symbol means. Such poems as Ted Berrigan's may seem difficult, too, but in almost the opposite way. Though his tone seems disarming, friendly, never authoritative, his unexplained references and sudden transitions repel the sort of interpretive work many critics are trained to provide. The poem feels less like dense crystals of argument, less like strenuously executed sculpture, than like lines taken out of order from diaries, or collages made out of transcriptions of telephone calls.

Yet this poem is one of the clearer ones in *The Sonnets* (composed 1962–1963), the book that made Berrigan's name—a book that many American (and some British and Commonwealth) poets esteem as highly as anything from its era. Its casual oddities seemed, to these poets, to stand perfectly for the new freedoms of the 1960s, and for the openness to new experience that innovative art, in their view, would have to convey.

Their author had just discovered such freedoms himself. Berrigan composed the sequence soon after he moved from Tulsa to New York City, where he gathered around him a circle of writerly friends. Following the conversational, associative poetry of Frank O'Hara, whom he idolized, Berrigan wrote flighty countercultural poems that reveled in New York's promise of novelty. The sheer busyness of the city itself, in his poems, means that something exciting is always happening somewhere, even if not exactly where he is.

Berrigan, like O'Hara, learned from contemporary visual art. Like such visual artists as Jasper Johns (who put lines from *The Sonnets* into a 1967 painting), the Berrigan of *The Sonnets* is not quite abstract, not quite representational, often tongue-in-cheek, concerned as much with the process of making as with the finished result. Like Johns, like Robert Rauschenberg, Berrigan often engages in collage, placing "found objects" (quotations or self-quotations, bits of other poems, overheard conversation) into the middle of what would otherwise sound like a lyric poem. Like those visual artists, Berrigan tries to share with his friends, and with us, the act of creation in the moment of creation, with all its circumstance and its detritus intact. He invites us to compose, with him, the poem of his life.

Here that life seems full of waiting, exciting in its potential, but in practice worrisomely stalled. The first few lines, beautiful in themselves, feint toward an urban autumnal descriptive lyric that Berrigan will not write; instead, his attention wanders indoors. The poet seems to be in his apartment. His mail has not come. It's Tuesday (but nobody cares; nobody likes Tuesdays). As he waits, he thinks about his girlfriend, Pat (Mitchell), who moved to New York from Tulsa, following Ted. He thinks about what he can see and hear from his apartment, and about what drugs he can take next—probably not off-white mescaline, which would be inferior and impure. He thinks about Anne (Waldman) and Ron (Padgett), about (Lorenz or Ellen) Gude, poets and friends of his own generation, their careers barely begun. Should he worry, too, about whether his poems will "make it," whether he can find aesthetic or commercial, social or sexual satisfaction? "Making it"—an idiom introduced to American poetry at midcentury ("All around me are these cats / not making it" wrote Robert Creeley in 1958)—can bear all those meanings. Does it mean the same thing for each of Berrigan's friends?

The first eight lines describe people and things in a place; the last six describe events in time. If the first eight lines dared us to find symbols (to see, for example, joyful ants as emblems of industry), the last six undercut whatever we thought we found. They begin with the most banal of nonevents, the nonarrival (as yet) of the mail, and with an allusion to O'Hara, whose poem "The Day Lady Died" begins, "It is 12:20 in New York a Friday/three days after Bastille Day, yes/it is 1959." (Has anyone in Berrigan's sonnets died? No, not yet.) "Jacques Louis David normalcy" is less allusion than parody of allusion: David's grand historical paintings exemplify just the public, representational Importance that Berrigan spurns. The sonnet then continues with a comically inconsequential, comically underspecified news item. We do not even know whether it is baseball or hockey in which Boston defeated New York (games from fall and winter 1961 included that score for both sports). The sports report is another poke in the eye to people who think everything in a poem must become a symbol, must carry its own weight.

Berrigan does not write such poems. Instead, he names his friends and remembers his past. He remembers the cities where he has lived—Providence and Tulsa, one much closer to New York City geographically, but both as far emotionally from the atmosphere of Berrigan's Bohemia as either is from the Treasure State. The poet thinks about an heirloom gun, a relic from Tulsa, perhaps, or a prop from a Western film. Finally he thinks about Steve and Herman: whoever they are, they matter more to Berrigan than Jacques Louis David ever did. Loyal to the poet's surroundings and to his friends, the poem flits about from topic to topic, surface to surface, recollection to impression, in ways that strangers might never fully decode.

The poem thus invites, but also repels, the "personal" biographical readings that so many earlier sonnets demand. Tony Lopez (himself a writer of avant-garde sonnets, like the one in this book) explains "that though the writing is made out of life material, it is made by the fracturing and inversion of that material, cutting it with whatever comes to hand." Lopez quotes Berrigan's own notebook entry from the night that he began writing the sonnets: "Wrote (?) Made five sonnets tonight, by taking one line from each of a group of poems, at random, going from first to last poem then back again until 12 lines, then making the final couplet from any 2 poems. . . . Wrote by ear, and automatically. Very interesting results." Both the in-group references and the partly random composition might seem to make the sonnet impersonal, far from any sort of revelation, never to coalesce as speech from the self.

Yet even strangers can get, here, paradoxically, a sense of Berrigan's inner life after all—a sense of what it is like to be him. He is someone almost manically sociable, manically associative, someone whose sense of himself as a new-minted New Yorker relies on his antithetical sense, his almost campily repudiated memories, of the Oklahoma from which he came. We see how much time his consciousness devotes to his friends. Perhaps he writes for them, more than for us (Anne knows who Gude is, even if we don't).

These are devices that Berrigan learned from O'Hara: indeed, it may be that Berrigan chose the sonnet sequence partly because it was a form O'Hara had not used. With its heritage of manuscript circulation, its sixteenth-century history as a court or private form, the sonnet sequence was well positioned to receive this scrappy coterie style. Other devices are Berrigan's invention—for example, his ways of invoking drugs, under whose influence every quantum of experience seems magically related to everything else. The undermotivatedness in Berrigan's speedy transitions suggests (as almost all memoirs of Berrigan confirm) his copious amphetamine intake. Would the baseball or hockey score, given the right drugs, stand for something after all? Perhaps the ants somehow caused the sports result? (Perhaps Steve is an ant!)

Still other effects that made *The Sonnets* influential—effects that also set them apart from O'Hara, and point toward the later avant-garde sonnet (toward Lopez, for example)—occur across sonnets rather than in any one of them. Lines and parts of lines are often repeated; some sonnets rework lines from others, reversed or scrambled. Scraps of French poetry (most of all, Arthur Rimbaud's) show up in translation, or in looser imitation; the phrase "Joyful ants nest in the roof of my tree" reappears elsewhere in *The Sonnets,* as do Anne and Ron (but not Carolyn). "His stand-in . . . came rarely" first popped up in Sonnet 35, where it referred to a circus performer who "was not a midget / and preferred to be known as a stunt-man." Berrigan is a sort of stunt-man himself, making acrobatic representations of the sometimes lonely, sometimes delighted, flux of his daily life. Such representations become more memorable as we see not what they mean, but what they are: a response to the coterie tradition of sonnet sequences; a view from the start of an artistic career; an anthology of remembered quotations; a consciously Rimbaldian experiment in what that teenaged French modernist called "the derangement of all the senses"; and a set of in-jokes for Berrigan's friends. The disorientation, the wildness, is part of the point: no more organized poem would do.

SB

"To a Winter Squirrel"

GWENDOLYN BROOKS

1965

That is the way God made you.
And what is wrong with it? Why, nothing.
Except that you are cold and cannot cook.

Merdice can cook. Merdice
of murdered heart and docked sarcastic soul,
Merdice
the bolted nomad, on a winter noon
cooks guts; and sits in gas. (She has no shawl, her landlord has
    no coal.)

You out beyond the shellac of her look
and of her sill!
She envies you your furry
buffoonery
that enfolds your silver skill.
She thinks you are a mountain and a star, unbaffleable;
with sentient twitch and scurry.

BROOKS spent the first fifteen years of her career using inherited rhyming forms, including the sonnet, to describe modern urban African American life, especially on the South Side of Chicago, where she lived. In 1950 she became the first black writer to win a Pulitzer Prize. She spent the last twenty years of that same career publishing, always with black-owned presses, clear, forceful free verse in a demotic style that she believed most of her black readers preferred. In between, from about 1963 to 1971, she wrote her best, and most unsettling, poems. During these same years, the poets and critics in the Black Arts Movement (such as Brooks's friend Don L. Lee, later Haki R. Madhubuti) insisted that black poets should eschew "white" forms. Brooks responded to the controversies they created by inventing a jagged, self-complicating, and sometimes self-accusing style. She broke apart familiar Anglo-American stanzaic forms, but she continued to use the pieces, and in among them she placed the syncopations of Black English.

"To a Winter Squirrel" makes a fine example of Brooks's middle style. Its fifteen lines dismantle the sonnet form even as its complexities of address unravel the sonnet's traditions. It is both a sonnet of protest about the conditions under which many black Chicagoans lived, and a sonnet of seasonal complaint (distant kin, for example, to Hopkins's "Thou art indeed just"), in which a human being wishes she were more like animals, and in which winter seems to promise no spring.

There is the squirrel, cold outdoors and hungry too, and there is Merdice, cold indoors in her bad apartment. Both human being and squirrel seem profoundly dissatisfied, and (as Brooks explains) each envies the other. Brooks's first three lines are, as she says, "sarcastic": "That is the way God made you" appears to advise the cold squirrel to accept her bad luck—just the sort of advice that genteel white racists, helped along by obtuse white liberals, gave African American civil rights activists in the years that led up to this 1965 poem. That squirrels cannot cook, that squirrel fur retains only so much heat, really are biological facts; they are not subject to change through political means. Merdice's material conditions, though, are historical and social facts. In a more just, or less segregated, city, she might have a better apartment. Will such justice ever arrive?

As in Brooks's earlier, better-known sonnet "kitchenette building," she emphasizes the everyday inconveniences of low-income domestic life, as if to say that such hassles, hour by hour and day by day, do more to damage the souls of her Chicagoans than any single dramatic event. Merdice is a "bolted nomad" because she wants to migrate, but stays put, and because she takes care to bolt the door of her flat. She cooks guts, as other householders might cook pigs' feet or cow brains, because she cannot afford more expensive fare; and she lights burners on her gas stove when she needs heat, having no other way to keep warm. Such deprivations have made her "sarcastic" at best (when she says that "nothing" is wrong at home, she cannot mean it), "docked" at worst (meaning both "at home, in port," like a docked ship, and "abbreviated, punished, cut short," as a worker's pay, or a dog's tail, is docked). "Murdered heart" might be Merdice's own melodramatic description of her mental state. Such a phrase would be shrill at the end of a stanza, and may sound shrill even here, though Brooks follows up with facts about her deprivation. Line 8 ("cooks guts" and so on) is the longest in the poem, with sixteen syllables, and fifteen words, all but one of them monosyllabic. Supplying material causes for emotional effects, the line becomes an appropriate fulcrum for the whole poem.

Lines 1–3 show why the squirrel may envy Merdice; lines 9–15 show how and why Merdice envies the squirrel. Merdice wishes she had a taste of the freedom of the city, the freedom that city dwellers attribute to rodents and birds who share the crowded streets. Projecting Merdice's human wishes into her rodent, Brooks makes the poem an animal fable, like Aesop's. She also mimics, in virtuosic sound effects and polysyllabic rhymes, the scampering urban squirrel's swiftly irregular gait. We human beings are "baffled" by our circumstances, and baffled again as we wonder (if we have energy left to wonder) how we might change them. Squirrels, however cold, seem to Merdice "unbaffleable" because self-sufficient, always able to run away.

However un-sonnet-like the poem may seem, it could not exist without the traditions and subgenres created by prior sonnets. We might call it an exploded sonnet, its array of irregularities preserving aspects of sonnet form. Some lines are pentameters; others are not. The first half of the poem (up to "coal") comprises eight lines; that first half breaks again into subsections that approximate quatrains. The last half behaves like a sestet, reversing the octave in tone and in point of view, and it rhymes almost like a Petrarchan sestet, too: *abbaba*.

Something has gone wrong with the society that lets Merdice live this way, that permits cold-water flats in cold-weather cities, where spirited women wish they were shivering squirrels. Almost all Brooks's critics emphasize such social and political judgments; Brooks, in her interviews, emphasized them herself. Yet to see only these elements would be to ignore what makes the poem memorable, and to ignore what Merdice sees in the squirrel. As Merdice imagines the scampering animal, Brooks flaunts an unmoralized pleasure simply in putting words together ("sentient twitch") and in coining them ("unbaffleable"). The passage from indoors to outdoors after line 8, from the squirrel's Merdice to Merdice's squirrel, is also a passage from language as a record of judgment and fact to language as slippery euphony, a form of fun. Linguistic elaboration, what Auden called "the luck of verbal playing," separates people from other animals. Delight in language, and unusual skill in arranging it, separates the poets whose poems we remember—Brooks, for example—from other poets who pursue, with equal commitment, the same moral and social goals.

SB

"Paradise Saved (Another Version of the Fall)"

A. D. HOPE

1967

Adam, indignant, would not eat with Eve,
They say, and she was driven from his side.
Watching the gates close on her tears, his pride
Upheld him, though he could not help but grieve

And climbed the wall, because his loneliness
Pined for her lonely figure in the dust:
Lo, there were two! God who is more than just
Sent her a helpmeet in that wilderness.

Day after day he watched them in the waste
Grow old, breaking the harsh unfriendly ground,
Bearing their children, till at last they died;
While Adam, whose fellow God had not replaced,
Lived on immortal, young, with virtue crowned,
Sterile and impotent and justified.

THE Australian poet A. D. Hope here rewrites the story of the loss of Eden, familiar from Milton and the Bible. Paradise is still lost in his account: the poet gives us, as he puts it, "another version of the fall," rather than a reminder of what remains to us of Eden (as in Frost's "Never Again Would Birds' Song Be the Same"). Unlike most poets writing on this theme, Hope does not depict unfallen life in Paradise. He implies, though, that this life is unimaginable without the companionship of Adam and Eve (so beautifully evoked in Book 4 of Milton's *Paradise Lost*). Hope here responds to the age-old tradition of "Adam alone," the male chauvinist fantasy that Paradise would never have been lost if Eve had not been created. Andrew Marvell writes in "The Garden," "Two Paradises 'twere in one, / To live in Paradise alone." In Hope's version, a rebuttal to Marvell's poem and others like it, Adam's refusal to fall condemns him to a life of exile. Adam remains in Eden, but his heart is elsewhere. He is compelled to be a spectator of the new life that Eve enjoys with her second husband.

"Paradise Saved" begins with a characterization of the first man: "Adam, indignant." Insulted by Eve's offer of the fruit, Adam considers it beneath his dignity; but by maintaining his privilege, he isolates himself fatally. When Adam refuses the fruit, he spurns Eve's company: "he would not eat with Eve." We are reminded that the society of Adam and Eve, their sustaining of each other, is the basis of Eden. Hope sides with Eve, and sees the temptation of the fall as an offer to participate, to eat together—the necessary, and happy, implication of two people being one flesh. If the happiness has turned to the hardship of fallen life, perhaps Adam is to blame. It is not Eve who sins in Hope's story, but rather Adam, when he declines her companionship.

In line 2, "They say" signals the fictive or rumored character of the poet's tale: he offers "another version." As in the Jewish midrashic reinterpretations of biblical narratives, Hope varies the facts freely. The reinvention allows Hope to make the role of God even more puzzling and mysterious than it is in the original Genesis account. God does not appear as a character until the poem's second stanza. Instead, the poet relies on the passive voice to tell us that Eve "was driven from [Adam's] side." She is punished by loss of mutuality: no longer will she share life with her spouse. But the real punishment, it soon appears, is the one meted out to Adam. As the gates of Eden close on her departing figure, the poet juxtaposes "her tears" and "his pride." Eve mourns her failure, while Adam remains rigid and unfallen (at least, so he insists to himself). In one sense, he is "upheld" by steadfastness; he will not let himself fall. In another sense, though, "he could not help but grieve." Adam too must know loss.

Unhappy in his state, alone and standing, Adam climbs the wall surrounding the garden. He scans the landscape in search of Eve, and remains stranded on the border between Eden and the outside world—unable to enjoy the delights of paradise, but equally unable to leave it. "His loneliness / Pined for her lonely figure in the dust." On the one hand, Adam yearns desperately to be together with his lost wife; on the other (as the repetition of "loneliness" and "lonely" tells us), he reaches out for a reflection of his own solitude, hoping that Eve will be just as abandoned as he. Instead, we hear a prophetic exclamation: "Lo, there were two!" The poet here admires his own invention of a new spouse for Eve (he sees that it is good), and at the same time indicates the profound surprise that shakes Adam.

God "sent her a helpmeet in that wilderness": so says the poet, concluding his octave. "Helpmeet" is the King James translation of the Hebrew *ezer kenegdo:* a "sustainer," or "helping partner" (Genesis 2:18). Since the phrase is used elsewhere in the Bible as a description of God's role in relation to humans, it clearly has no sexist connotations in the Genesis account. Here, it is a man, Eve's second husband, who is the helpmeet to her—as she earlier was to Adam, drawn from his very body. God as creator of nourishing human companionship, best imaged in marriage, proves "more than just": his compassion surpasses his strictness.

Hope's rhyme words in his octave are pointed: "Eve" and "grieve" enfold the first quatrain, "loneliness" and "wilderness" the second. The title of his poem, "Paradise Saved," by this point reveals a bitter irony: the Eden Adam has saved for himself is just as much a wilderness as the one he gazes into, the new place where human history has begun without him.

The sestet begins with a picture of what Adam sees: Eve and her spouse engaging in something new, labor. His life, "day after day," now consists of his observation of their life. (Nathaniel Hawthorne's story "Wakefield" offers a morbid, yet oddly cheerful, variation on this theme: a man leaves his wife in order to see how she will survive without him—and she does.) George Eliot writes memorably in *Middlemarch* that marriage "is still a great beginning, as it was to Adam and Eve, who kept their honeymoon in Eden, but had their first little one among the thorns and thistles of the wilderness." In Hope's sonnet, Eve and her new Adam work among the thorns and thistles, "breaking the harsh unfriendly ground," and bear their little ones—"till at last they died." This is the bleak plot of fallen life, devoid of the consolations that Eliot goes on to remind us of, "the harvest of sweet memories in common." The image of the unfriendly ground calls to the reader's mind the first event in history, the murder that occurs when Eve's children become men: Cain will be told by God that his brother's blood cries out to him from the ground (Genesis 4:10).

The lyric poet is by reputation a solitary: thus the appeal of the "Adam alone" tradition, which reaches from the seventeenth century of Marvell to Rilke, Wallace Stevens, and beyond. But lyric often turns, in compensation, toward the pair of lover and beloved, and to the idea of marriage as the fulfillment of life. Hope's sonnet suggests that we cannot have both the virtuous isolation of Adam alone and the enjoyment of marriage: isolation ruins enjoyment, and turns one into a frustrated onlooker of others' lives. The contemplative Adam, wedded to his own integrity, corrupts himself, becoming an embittered voyeur (like Satan in Book 4 of *Paradise Lost,* gazing for the first time at the pleasures of Eden).

Adam lives on, solitary in his desperate Eden. He remains "immortal, young, with virtue crowned"—again a sardonic irony. He stands crowned with his own stubborn pride, his sense of superior fitness (if you call that virtue). Adam is, in this sonnet's triumphant final sentence, "Sterile and impotent and justified." This ascending ladder of calamities forms what rhetoricians call a tricolon crescendo, a series in which the final term tops the previous two. Adam is sterile in mind and heart, as well as loins—impotent because incapable of doing anything either for himself or for Eve. Finally, the *coup de grâce:* he is "justified," a term from Christian theology that normally implies salvation or proof of righteousness. Milton memorably announces his aim at the beginning of *Paradise Lost:* "To justify God's ways to man." But for Hope, the word implies a merely legal victory. God is not interested in justification; rather, he is more than just, a nurturer of those in the wilderness. Hope's "Paradise Saved" allies God with the ones whose tough, factual existence, their work together, moves between birth, labor, and death. The man who refuses this hard communion lives on, gifted with the prestige of immortality. But he remains on the outside, looking in.

DM

Autumn Testament 27

JAMES K. BAXTER

1971

When I stayed those three months at Macdonald Crescent
In the house of Lazarus, three tribes were living

In each of the storeys—on the ground floor, the drunks
Who came there when the White Lodge burnt down;

Above them, the boobheads; and, scattered between the first
And the second storey, the students who hoped to crack

The rock of education. The drunks are my own tribe.
One Sunday, the pubs being shut, they held a parliament

In the big front room—Lofty with his walking stick,
Phil the weeper, Taffy who never spoke much,

And one or two others—in conclave they sat, like granite
    columns
Their necks, like Tritons their faces,

Like tree-roots their bodies. Sober as Rhadamanthus
They judged the town and found it had already been judged.

In New Zealand, in 1972, James K. Baxter's death made front-page, banner-headline news. He became New Zealand's national poet not by lauding the society he knew there, but by attacking it at every turn: by the time he wrote his two great sequences, *Jerusalem Sonnets* (1969) and *Autumn Testament* (1971), he had embraced a radical left-wing Catholicism and a prophetic vocation.

Baxter twice founded, and tried to maintain, a commune for troubled youth (most of them Maori, New Zealand's indigenous people) on the site of a New Zealand village called Jerusalem, or Hiruharama (the Maori transliteration of "Jerusalem"). The commune in its first version (the one chronicled in *Jerusalem Sonnets*) failed, in part because too many people wanted to live there. After leaving Hiruharama, and before returning to try again, Baxter lived in run-down Bohemian quarters in Wellington, New Zealand's capital. That city became the epitome of the status-conscious, materialist civilization whose language he wielded expertly, but whose way of life his poems condemned.

The three-story house where Baxter stayed between his two attempts to found Jerusalem is here a "house of Lazarus": a place for beggars (like the Lazarus of Luke 16), a place for people who have come back from the dead (like the Lazarus of John 11), and a shelter for lepers ("lazar house"). In this house for the downcast, as throughout Baxter's late poetry, the rejected stone becomes the cornerstone. Baxter had belonged to Alcoholics Anonymous; by calling himself a drunk, he places himself among the rejects too, among those in need of spiritual resurrection. "Tribes" suggests the twelve tribes of Israel, but also the clans and families of Maori life, for Baxter a better model than *pakeha* (European-descended) civilization. "Boobheads," in New Zealand slang, are petty criminals who keep getting caught, especially those who want to return to jail.

Here, then, are the judges according to whose verdict the city will stand or fall. The octave switches from scene to scene, tribe to tribe, in its list of the half-dispossessed: from the drunks, whose cheaper hotel or pub burnt down, to the students who live on the landing, between stories, for whom seeking education in universities is like breaking rocks, or like trying to get water from a rock (as Moses did for Israel, Exodus 17:6, and as Poseidon, the father of Triton, did for Athens). Having stood, earlier, among the transients, these sobered-up "drunks" on Sunday, in the sestet, become permanence incarnate, like ancient carved buildings (granite) but even more like the strongest parts of the living nonhuman world (not granite but "tree-roots"). Their "conclave" suggests the judgment of God on sinners, in the Old Testament and again at the end of time, when the unrighteous will be cast down.

Yet Baxter does not himself pronounce that judgment, no more than Abraham himself damns Sodom (Genesis 18). The men in the front room, more damaged than Baxter himself, are the only ones who can say whether the capital is saved. Perhaps they do not speak at all: one of them "never spoke much," and one is known for weeping. The sestet fuses Greek myth with the Bible, the better to condemn the urban modernity that has traveled so far from both. The men look "like Tritons" (like sea gods; like the sculptures on stone fountains), and, on Sunday morning, with no pubs open, they are all "sober as Rhadamanthus," in Greek myth the judge of all the dead, entirely stern but inflexibly just.

Baxter wants not quite to condemn Wellington outright, but to declare that only these sorts of people, the drunks and boobheads, have the authority to condemn it. By their condition Wellington, and not Wellington alone, should be judged. Nor need they condemn it. The present condition of the city, its industrious futility and its rat race, seem to Baxter bad enough: the people outside this house, the citizens of Wellington beyond Macdonald Crescent, are already self-condemned, already dead. They have already come before Rhadamanthus, and they have yet to embrace resurrection in Christ. That resurrection was Baxter's hope; he would accomplish it not in such harsh flats as these, but in the Jerusalem whose rural tenderness—and whose material difficulties—gave Baxter subjects for the sonnets to come.

Like all of Baxter's late sonnets, this one uses unrhymed two-line stanzas, with a pentameter base but no regular meter. Passages resolve into strings of iambic or else of dactylic feet ("a-*bove* them, the *boob*-heads; and *scat*-tered be-*tween* the *first* / And the *sec*-ond *sto*-rey, the *stu*-dents who *hoped* to *crack*"), but such regularities rarely persist. Of the last three lines, just one is a pentameter; line twelve has three feet, line fourteen six feet. The verse has the swells and recessions, the emphases and turns, of a well-made sermon: as in sermons, there is always a religious point to be driven home. There is, though, a self-undermining irony, and a sense of emotion to which the symbols point, in excess of whatever doctrine Baxter puts into the poem.

"Christ is my peace, my terror, my joy, my sorrow, my life, my death, but not my security," Baxter wrote in 1971. "If we claim to love him we have to love our own death." The poet could not imagine a Christian mercy without imagining, also, the harshest of sentences on himself and on the Western, English-speaking civilization that had made his life, and his poetry, possible. Baxter's religious poetry, like John Donne's, presents a naturally proud, theatrical man trying to show himself what it means to be humble, and to abase himself before God. Like Donne, Baxter creates harsh, sometimes thunderous effects, sharp tonal contrasts, and a wealth of allusions, both to the Scriptures and to current events. Baxter's religious poetry also contains a wealth of embedded narratives, of which we here give only one. Most of the others describe life at Jerusalem, with its helpless hippies, its rituals of repentance, its attempts at reconciliation between Maori and *pakeha,* its paid and unpaid bills. To read Baxter's late poetry at length is to find one of the great undiscovered (at least in America) styles, and one of the more vivid casts of characters, in the English language that Americans and New Zealanders still share.

SB

"Staring at the Sea on the Day of the Death of Another"

MAY SWENSON

1972

The long body of the water fills its hollow,
slowly rolls upon its side,
and in the swaddlings of the waves,
their shadowed hollows falling forward with the tide,

like folds of Grecian garments molded to cling
around some classic immemorial marble thing,
I see the vanished bodies of friends who have died.

Each form is furled into its hollow,
white in the dark curl,
the sea a mausoleum, with countless shelves,
cradling the prone effigies of our unearthly selves,

some of the hollows empty, long niches in the tide.
One of them is mine
and gliding forward, gaping wide.

MAY SWENSON records an all-too-recognizable occasion. We know the loss of friends more and more often as we enter middle age. If we live near the ocean, we may well turn to its shoreline in times of grief. The endless, imperturbable waves seem soothing, consoling, yet at the same time chillingly indifferent. Swenson's speaker, hearing the news of a friend's death, gazes at the sea and lets her imagination work upon it. The tenacity of her vision is remarkable: she allows the sea to confront her, seeing in it the very shape of mortality.

Unusually for a sonnet, Swenson's "Staring at the Sea" is divided into two even halves: a quatrain followed by a tercet (three-line unit), then another quatrain with its own tercet in its wake. (Marianne Moore's "No Swan So Fine," earlier in our book, also breaks into two seven-line parts.) In Swenson, the two halves line up exactly. The opening image of the water's "long body" filling its "hollow" (an uncannily beautiful depiction of a wave's motion) matches the later line "each form is furled into its hollow." Snugly furled like an umbrella, a flag, or a winding sheet for a corpse, the wave then becomes a shelf in a mausoleum, ready to receive the dead. Internal rhymes, assonance, and alliteration give Swenson's poem a lulling power. "Hollow," "slowly," "rolls," "swaddlings"; "form," "furled," "hollow," "curl"): these sequences of words exert a growing, hypnotic tug, like the swell of a wave.

Swenson's association of the sea and mortality comes from Walt Whitman. In "Out of the Cradle Endlessly Rocking," Whitman reports that even when he was a child the waters of Long Island Sound lisped to him "the low and delicious word death, / And again death, death, death, / Hissing melodious." The subtle whisper or hiss of Whitman's ocean becomes, for Swenson, a soundless, spectral reminder of our mortal end. But Swenson's idea that the sea's waves are "like folds of Grecian garments molded to cling / around some classic immemorial marble thing" combats Whitman's image of the ocean as undulant and ever-changing, a rapturous source of life. In "There Was a Child Went Forth," Whitman refers to "The hurrying tumbling waves and quick-broken crests and slapping." Swenson pictures the sea as a gloomy, sculptural space rather than Whitman's shifting, rude, enlivening chaos. She turns a phenomenon normally associated with time (the repetitive yet varying waves) into a scene of hieratic poise. Here Swenson looks back at the sonnet tradition of freezing the moment (which we saw in D. G. Rossetti's "For a Venetian Pastoral"): she performs a slow-motion analysis of her wave's steady roll. In her hands the ocean has a lethal, statuesque calm.

The touch of T. S. Eliot may be detectable here. Eliot, in his "Preludes," eloquently feels himself "moved by fancies that are curled / Around these images, and cling: / The notion of some infinitely gentle / Infinitely suffering thing." Swenson shares Eliot's vocabulary of curling and clinging. But for his "infinitely suffering thing" Swenson substitutes "some classic immemorial marble thing." Unmoved by Eliot's somewhat sodden fantasy of grace, Swenson offers us a harder knowledge (perhaps akin to Eliot's own "inexplicable splendour of Ionian white and gold" in *The Waste Land*). The bright, blank perfection of marble sculpture conveys the emptiness one feels when struck by sudden grief. Swenson's is a cold pastoral indeed.

Freud, in his famous essay on *The Merchant of Venice,* "The Theme of the

Three Caskets," identifies the mother who gives us life with her seeming op-
posite, the battlefield goddess or Valkyrie who bears dead warriors from the
scene of bloody combat. English Renaissance poets obsessively rhymed
"womb" and "tomb," suggesting the compatibility of these two claustropho-
bic spaces. In keeping with this mythic tendency to align birth with death,
Swenson refers to the "swaddlings of the waves," and later to the sea "cradling
the prone effigies of our unearthly selves." Swenson here describes a ghostly
self or effigy. She shows all that is left of the dead: our memory images of
those who have gone from us. The word "effigy" derives from the Latin *effin-
gere,* "to mold" or "to shape." Swenson's sea, vaster than all of us, shapes and
unshapes our lives. And the varying pace of Swenson's lines, which contain
sometimes five, sometimes four, and sometimes three stresses, mimics the ir-
regular movement of the ocean. Her three-beat lines knock definitively, and
press her point home: "Whíte in the dárk cúrl," "Óne of thém is míne."

   "Staring at the Sea on the Day of the Death of Another" ends with a final
unlocking of the puzzle. The poet suddenly acknowledges her own death
moving toward her, open-mouthed. (George Herbert writes in "Death," "Thy
mouth was open, but thou couldst not sing.") This shock disturbs and redi-
rects the poem, suddenly recasting it, in its final moment, as a threat to the
poet's self. Shark-like, the dreadful calm of this concluding gesture asserts the
unreadiness we always experience in the face of death. Try as we might to
avoid such knowledge, the hour of our death is always arriving, inevitable as a
wave, "gliding forward, gaping wide."

                                                                    DM

"Searching"

ROBERT LOWELL

1968, revised 1973

I look back to you, and cherish what I wanted:
your flashing superiority to failure,
hair of yellow oak leaves, the arrogant
tanned brunt in the snow-starch of a loosened shirt—
your bullying half-erotic rollicking. . . .
The white bluffs rise above the old rock piers,
wrecked past insuring by two hurricanes.
As a boy I climbed those scattered blocks and left
the sultry Sunday seaside crowd behind,
seeking landsend, with my bending fishing rod
a small thread slighter than the dark arc of your eyebrow. . . .
Back at school, alone and wanting you,
I scratched my four initials, R.T.S.L.,
like a dirty word across my bare, blond desk.

WHEN Robert Lowell began, in the fall of 1967, to write one unrhymed sonnet every day, he was already famous three times over: for his stormy Miltonic poems of the 1940s, for his autobiographical poems of the late 1950s, and for the controlled, dejected political verse he wrote in the early 1960s. By the end of 1968 he had written several hundred fourteen-line poems in unrhymed, harsh, restless pentameters. Over the next six years he revised them continually, and completed perhaps a hundred more. Lowell collected these fourteen-line poems in *Notebook 1967–68*, then in the revised *Notebook* (1970), and again in the trio of 1973 collections called *History, For Lizzie and Harriet*, and *The Dolphin*. He then winnowed the mass of blank-verse sonnets into the slender sequences within *Selected Poems* (1976), among them the sequence

1930s, which included this poem. Almost all the sonnets switch quickly from topic to topic, and from scene to scene. We know how they work when we see how they fit together, how each scene illuminates the others, making a whole in Lowell's mind. Later readers praised Lowell's uneasy sonnets on public events (the 1967 March on the Pentagon, the election of Richard Nixon, the assassinations of Robert Kennedy and Martin Luther King), or else debated the ethics of the sonnets that described his divorce and remarriage. Lost in those controversies were the atypically tender sonnets about his own youth.

"Searching" recalls the weeks that the teenaged Lowell spent on the New England coast, with and without his family. (The Lowells had connections to Maine, and in the summer of 1935, Robert and two friends took a cottage on Nantucket.) Like other sonnets (several entitled "Long Summers"), this one juxtaposes Lowell's memories of Maine or Nantucket with the Atlantic villages and beaches that Lowell revisited as an adult. Present scenes and accumulated experience (signaled here by one present-tense verb, "rise") color past scenes with sweetness, and with dismay; the adult sees with wonder the lack of emotional distance—the commonality of tumultuous sentiment—between the clumsily passionate teenaged Lowell and the verbally gifted adult. Though "First Love," earlier in the sequence *1930s,* remembers a same-sex crush (on "Leon Straus, sixthgrade fullback"), Lowell as an adult pursued only women. Other sonnets observe, with nostalgia and lust, "young girls": in one poem they are "two fray-winged dragonflies, / clinging to a thistle, too clean to mate." Lowell here remembers how he pined for a girl or young woman whose almost martial, almost masculine confidence he envied, and envies still.

Encountered in summer, this girl contains both summer's fertility and the strength of autumn and winter. Oaks are symbols for the sky-god Zeus; oak-leaf crowns were given to the citizens of ancient Rome for military valor, as Lowell, a classics major, would have known. "Snow-starch" makes frankly erotic reference to the fall of her white shirt across her breasts, the whiter for her shoulders' summer tan. Consonant clusters and echoes ("arrogant / tanned brunt," "bullying . . . rollicking") suggest the physical energy of the girl's body. Whatever they did together at the piers, at the beach, perhaps in the company of friends, seemed "half-erotic," located just at the boundary between child's play and the serious courtship of sexually mature adults. That boundary for Lowell recalls the other boundary between sea and land, a boundary crossed, hazardously, by "the old rock piers," now as "wrecked" as Lowell's own teenaged hopes.

Whatever they did together, Lowell wanted more; unsatisfied, like all the young, he sought time alone. The first half of the sonnet remembers Lowell and the girl together. The second half considers the young Lowell by himself, in the summer and then again in the fall. Leaving behind the "crowd" (both children and adults), the teenaged Lowell walked off to go fishing. If he was trying to distract himself, he failed—the "bending fishing rod" seemed to him an inferior version ("slighter") of her dark eyebrow. This young lover, like the earlier lovers of Petrarchan sequences, sees his beloved in every image, every scene. He also imagines that she looks back at him, perhaps with a raised eyebrow, as if to say, "Why are you still thinking about me? What makes you think I ever wanted you?" An eyebrow the size of a fishing rod (however elegant) would fit an eye larger than any human being. "Superior" to him from the moment they met, the martial beloved here becomes almost godlike, an eye dominating the sky or the sea.

Yet she cannot see him, and he cannot see her, after the summer ends. They may well never have seen each other again. The future poet, "alone and wanting you," starts the school year with nothing but letters and words. Courtly lovers may rely on eloquence, but this schoolboy lover has only the ineloquent letters he carves into his desk, a symbol (one of many in Lowell's late work) for the ineffectuality of writing, which names the wounds it can do nothing to heal. Lowell's initials are "a dirty word" because he feels dirty: his very name denotes shame and frustration. The carved initials also make a travesty—or perhaps an all-too-faithful representation—of straight male desire, at once generic (tens of thousands of schoolboys have done as much), inevitable (he can think of nothing else to do), and narcissistic (his own name, not hers). Edmund Spenser, in his famous sonnet *Amoretti* 75, writes his beloved's name by the sea, in the sand, sees it wash away, and then promises to "immortalize" her "glorious name" in his verse. Lowell's ineffectual young lover has only his own name to conjure with on his sand-colored desk; he would not then (and does not now) share her name. Worse yet, the adult seems unable to shrug off defeats, and looks anything but superior to the "failure" of love and affection that colored his teens. The grown-up Lowell, with all his verbal skills, cannot solve problems of love, or of lust, even now.

An earlier version of the same poem, from *Notebook* (1970), made the young Lowell look even worse, and more ashamed. It showed him "held over in the hollow classroom," "sanding down . . . his four initials" as an after-school punishment. The adolescent Lowell, by his own and his schoolfriends' later reports, was moody, impulsive, unpopular, sometimes cruel: they nicknamed him "Cal," for "Caligula." We might see the schoolboy's carving as an act of revenge, possessing (by marking and damaging) something else blond (his desk), since he will never have her. Yet such a revenge seems pathetically ineffectual, more likely to get our sympathy than to deserve any further punishment. This sympathy, if we can give it, makes Lowell's conclusion in this final version not bitter so much as bittersweet. The multiple deprivations of this schoolboy's autumn—no beloved, no summer, no seashore, no sex—remain painful in adult memory, yet they seem pathetically attractive when compared to the complex, perhaps insuperable problems of adult life.

SB

"The Morning Moon"

DEREK WALCOTT

1976

Still haunted by the cycle of the moon
racing full sail
past the crouched whale's back of Morne Coco Mountain,

I gasp at her sane brightness.

It's early December,
the breeze freshens the skin of this earth,
the goose-skin of water,

and I notice the blue plunge
of shadows down Morne Coco Mountain,
December's sundial,

happy that the earth is still changing,
that the full moon can blind me with her forehead
this bright foreday morning,

and that fine sprigs of white are springing from my beard.

THIS sonnet responds both to the Caribbean landscapes and seascapes that energize so many of Derek Walcott's poems, and to the many older sonnets that liken the human lifespan to the temperate northern year. Walcott, who grew up on the small Caribbean island of St. Lucia, won the Nobel Prize for Literature in 1993. The lecture he gave on accepting the award celebrated Caribbean writing and culture and attacked that culture's bigoted detractors, who believed that St. Lucia, Trinidad, Barbados, Jamaica, and so on lacked "that seriousness that comes only out of cultures with four seasons . . . and are

therefore . . . incapable of . . . imaginative complexity." "The Morning Moon"
makes such complaints look absurd (not to mention racist), and yet it begins
as they do: with the disjunction between Caribbean experience and the liter-
ary traditions of the earth's temperate zones. Rather than trying to import
such traditions unchanged—and rather than rejecting them entirely—Wal-
cott comes up with an answer to them, making a new sonnet form out of the
old, a new, more hopeful form to better fit the archipelago of his birth.

Though it opens in nearly regular pentameter, "The Morning Moon" re-
veals an untraditional form: unrhymed lines of varying length, divided syn-
tactically into unequal parts of four and ten (not eight and six), split internally
into tercets and single lines (rather than into quatrains or couplets). Its occa-
sion, by contrast, seems traditional: the poet looks up to the moon, in a mo-
ment of sublimity, and then down, to reconsider his own life. In the best-
known English poems about such moments—Philip Sidney's *Astrophel and
Stella* 31, for example—the moon's remote progress through the night sky re-
minds the poet, by contrast, of his fallen earthly state, his dashed hopes, his
advancing age.

Walcott's morning moon instead brings hope. As it lingers, out of place in
the lit-up sky, that moon looks to the poet both fresh and durable, "sane" and
speedy, like a well-trimmed sailboat in a race. The moon seems to move be-
cause wind blows clouds around it; the same wind ruffles the "skin of this
earth," the sea. Caribbean scenes, Walcott said in a 1986 interview, hold count-
less "images of erasure . . . in the surf which continually wipes the sand clean,
in the fact that those huge clouds change so quickly." This moon, like this sea,
seems to move in December's breeze, and yet it is no weaker than before.

That moon, a model of ease and vigor, inhabits a bright sky plausible only
in the tropics, where "early December" is a time of hope and comfort, after
the hurricanes end. Walcott emphasizes the name of the month: "It's early
December," the start of the second sentence, makes a line unto itself, along
with "December's sundial" the shortest line in the poem. Everything Walcott
sees in this December stands for happy persistence, for energy amid change.
The poet partakes of that renewal: he may feel like a whale coming up for air
(such a whale would "gasp" too), as the smooth back (no hazardous jagged
peak) in his mountain suggests continuities between poet and scene, the moon
and our planet, the land and the sea. Several West Indian islands have a
"morne coco" ("coconut mountain" or "coconut hill"): the best-known Morne
Coco is Haitian, but this one may be in Trinidad, where Walcott lived for

some time in the 1970s. This West Indian sea, like this moon, seems to move in December's breeze, yet it is no weaker than before.

As with moon, so with shadows: what saddened northern poets will not sadden observers in this Antillean space. Many sundials once bore, in Latin, the motto "I count only the hours that are sunny." Walcott's "sundial," recalling that motto, also reminds us that December days, near the Equator, are no less sunny and not much shorter than days in May or June. "Foreday" is West Indian English for "early morning"; "foreday morning," though pleonastic, is accepted usage, and Walcott's "foreday morning," echoing "forehead," becomes one of many doubled words in this poem about renewal, along with "December," "Morne Coco Mountain," "full," "skin," "bright," and "spring." Repetition in change, repetition without diminishment, is just what Walcott's tropical days and seasons seem (in this good mood) to bring. Any "haunt" (a ghost, "still" here though it hails from the past) serves to introduce an improving day.

The poet who starts by watching the moon and a mountain ends by contemplating his own countenance, his forehead and his beard: the scenic description reveals a compact self-portrait. The emphatic ending makes a regular, almost jaunty iambic hexameter, the only purely iambic line in the poem (though the first line comes close). Walcott in 1976 turned forty-six; his beard, with its white sprigs, reflects his advancing years. Yet for him this December feels much like what other writers have meant by "spring." The white in his beard looks nothing like northern snow, but rather like "sprigs," shoots or twigs, which imply future growth.

Walcott has inveighed against writers who viewed Caribbean places and people only through their sanguinary past. To look back at history is to see "a forgotten, insomniac night"—so Walcott in his Nobel lecture. By contrast, "there is a force of exultation, a celebration of luck, when a writer finds himself witness to the early morning of a culture," to its "self-defining dawn." That dawn belongs, here, not only to Trinidad, or to Caribbean culture in general, but to Walcott himself, to Walcott the writer, who has said that he often writes his poems in the early morning. The word "forehead," so close to so bright a moon, also suggests the Roman poet Horace's boast (in his *Odes* 1.1) that his poetic fame would elevate him to the heavens, where his forehead would touch a star.

Walcott revises not only Sidney's English sonnet about a faraway moon ("With how sad steps, O moon, thou climbst the skies"), but also all manner of famous sonnets about British, and American, seasons: Shakespeare's Sonnet 73 ("That time of year thou mayst in me behold"), for example, as well as Coleridge's "Work without Hope," Keats's "Four seasons," Hopkins's "Thou art indeed just," Frost's "Mowing" (all in this volume). Those poems make spring a symbol for youth and renewal; fall, for adulthood or middle age; and winter (Keats's "drear-nighted December"), for old age and death. Almost tautological in northern climes, such equations are wrong for Walcott, and wrong for his islands. Rather than simply attacking them, he offers—in this representation of tropical shadow and brightness, day and night—a seasonal sonnet that fits his outlook and his place. We may feel that no self-conscious adult can remain so wholly hopeful for very long. Yet just such hope seems here, to the middle-aged Walcott, available always in this West Indian scene, distinctively traced in his tropical December, with its changeable yet undiminished moon and mountain, sea and sky.

                                                                              SB

"National Trust"

TONY HARRISON

1978

Bottomless pits. There's one in Castleton,
and stout upholders of our law and order
one day thought its depth worth wagering on
and borrowed a convict hush-hush from his warder
and winched him down; and back, flayed, grey, mad, dumb.

Not even a good flogging made him holler!

O gentlemen, a better way to plumb
the depths of Britain's dangling a scholar,
say, here at the booming shaft at Towanroath,
now National Trust, a place where they got tin,
those gentlemen who silenced the men's oath
and killed the language that they swore it in.

The dumb go down in history and disappear
and not one gentleman's been brought to book:

Mes den hep tavas a-gollas y dyr

(Cornish—)
    "the tongueless man gets his land took."

BY THE start of the 1980s Tony Harrison had become one of the most fa-
mous poets in Britain, largely on the strength of *The School of Eloquence*
(1978), a series of sonnets about social class and language, and about his own
upbringing in working-class Leeds. Harrison, like George Meredith before
him, makes sonnets of sixteen, rather than fourteen, rhymed lines. He himself

designates them as sonnets, and (as in Meredith) the poems appropriate aspects of the sonnet tradition. This sonnet, for example, uses rhyming (quasi-Shakespearean) quatrains, an emphatic turn in the middle, and two lines (though they do not rhyme with each other) whose conclusion glosses the rest of the poem.

"National Trust" in the U.K. is both a category of sites (buildings, parkland, and wilderness) that the government wants to preserve, and the name of the organization that preserves them, analogous to the National Park Service in the United States. "For ever, for everyone," the National Trust slogan says. The leap from the title to the first phrase opens up the first of Harrison's vivid, and vicious, double meanings: to trust in the British nation, or in its ruling classes, is to trust in bottomless pits. They may deserve Hell (the ultimate "bottomless pit," as in Revelation 9:2) as punishment for all they have done to the regions, such as Cornwall or Harrison's Yorkshire, that their money and privilege have reshaped, and for all they have done to the working class from which Harrison came.

The binaries up-down, high-low, apparent (on the surface or obvious) and underground (hidden or suppressed), control the rest of the sonnet. Prisoners, like miners, like workers in general, have lived so far "below" aristocrats' notice (like the bottoms of "bottomless" pits or mines) that the "gentlemen" cannot see them as human, cannot, figuratively, see them at all. Blind to morality, blind to prisoners' humanity, aristocrats moved by nothing except curiosity wager on a grotesque experiment: lowering a human being into a pit whose depth nobody knows, in hopes that, brought back up, he will tell them what he has seen. Instead, he comes back insane. His dazed muteness stands for the "gentlemen's" inability to hear, or to see, what working-class, "lower"-class, people experience. In moral terms it is the "gentlemen"—well fed, "stout," confident—who have sunk unutterably low.

In yet one more cruel irony, the "scholars" and "upholders of our law and order" ("our" becomes ironic too) would not have listened to the convict anyway. They have not listened to convicts, laborers, or Cornish tin miners—the people their companies injure, whose land they take—even when those people spoke (as many of them did) in clear and well-reasoned English. Harrison's assaultive monosyllables ("back, flayed, grey, mad, dumb") stand against, or cancel, the clichés of the earlier lines ("law and order," "worth wagering on," "hush-hush"), which go past lightly, almost without thought. The shocks in his early images attack not only the privilege the "gentlemen" retain, but the pretense to disinterested, calm inquiry their cherished institutions (such as Oxford and Cambridge) perpetuate.

Not only does the sonnet condemn past injustice; it sets up, and asks us to sympathize with, a revenge fantasy. If scholars and *haut bourgeois* administrators, the classes that benefit from capitalism, will render the working class mute and invisible, if they serve a system that buries people alive, the poet imagines that he can return the favor. Harrison's sense of himself as a working-class poet is rarely so fierce, or so effective, as it is here, though his own later life (as a "scholar" himself, well trained in "dead" languages, ancient Greek and Latin) also informs the poem.

So does the history of the Cornish landscape. Wheal Coates, Towanroath, by the sea, an active tin mine (or "pit") until 1889, is now one of several National Trust sites where tourists can learn the history of tin mining. For Harrison, such historic preservation amounts to a racket, keeping the buildings up after the workers are gone. It would be better, lines 13–14 suggest, to bring back not old buildings but a very old criminal code (perhaps the Old Testament's code, "an eye for an eye"), and then apply it to the inhuman "scholars" who gambled on a prisoner's life—to the same sort of "gentlemen," Oxford and Cambridge graduates, property owners, whom Harrison blames for the loss of the region's first language. Cornish, a Gaelic language related to Irish and to Breton, was nearly extinct (to use Harrison's metaphors, muted, buried, sunk) in the 1970s: with the support of the European Union, it has since enjoyed a revival as a language learned by adults, and it has a few thousand speakers now.

Harrison is a writer conscious of his audience, and hoping for a broad one; nothing in his English sounds recherché. The ringing, almost perfectly regular lines instead seem meant for declamation. (His later career included commissioned verse meant for television and film.) Harrison's rhymes, here as often in *The School of Eloquence,* can emphasize the accent with which he grew up (as in the disyllabic full rhymes "order" and "border," whose vowels would differ according to region and class). As in most of Harrison's sonnets, the combination of fluent meter with anti-elitist sentiment seems to defend the pentameter itself: iambic pentameter (Harrison's verse seems to prove) is *not* an imposition of foreign artifice, but a more emphasized, more ordered version of the pattern inherent in English speech. The verse forms closest to English history and tradition thus become fully accessible, fully appropriate vehicles for his anger on behalf of the dispossessed, the working classes, especially those far from London—the people left out of grand narrative history, and out of the sonnet tradition, until recently.

"National Trust," so public in its aims, so democratic in its sympathies, combines anger, frustration, and futility. It demonstrates rage about something inaccessible, about dispossessions that nobody now can fix. Harrison's close, which translates the Cornish phrase, implies that his own enterprise constitutes a form of advocacy, a way to save or win back dignity, property, "land." The poet gives "tongue" to disinherited men. Yet that enterprise will not reverse nineteenth-century depredations. Like all the best verse and prose versions of left-wing history, Harrison's poem incorporates a tension between hortatory protest (as if to say, "Speak out! Raise your voice! Save your land!") and an awareness of the often long odds. The miners did not lose their land because they ceased to speak Cornish; they lost their Cornish after they lost their land, because the economy required their descendants to use English— the language in which Harrison now writes poems. If Harrison sounds at times hopeful about his own language, he also knows how economic forces can shape history; how it came to be that he wrote in English; and how harshly, and how often, money talks.

SB

"Sonnet"

ELIZABETH BISHOP

1979

Caught—the bubble
in the spirit-level,
a creature divided;
and the compass needle
wobbling and wavering,
undecided.
Freed—the broken
thermometer's mercury
running away;
and the rainbow-bird
from the narrow bevel
of the empty mirror,
flying wherever
it feels like, gay!

ELIZABETH BISHOP'S unusual "Sonnet" is slender and minimalist. It features only two beats per line. The title indicates that Bishop intends to reflect seriously on sonnet form. So she does: she weighs the role of form as both a refuge and a snare for the poet's imagination.

Form catches, but it frees as well. Bishop's "Sonnet," with its narrow contours, holds the self—and lets it go. With amiably delusive trickery, these narrow lines capture the imagination of the person who invents the poem, and the one who reads it. Bishop draws on a series of devices: a spirit-level, a compass, a thermometer, and a mirror. Each of these objects becomes a symbol of what a poem does; they are Bishop's equivalents of the Romantics' Aeolian harp. (In Coleridge, the Aeolian harp—a stringed instrument set in a window and sounded by the wind—provides an emblem of poetry's responsiveness.)

Bishop begins with a light exclamation, "Caught"—she refers to the bubble calmly trapped in the spirit-level. The word suggests a moment in a game: I've got you, the poet says to her chosen trope. Her tool, the spirit-level, indicates whether objects are truly horizontal or not. By implication, it also tests the evenness of lines of verse. The imprisoned bubble may appear tenuous, even insignificant, but it persists, unlike most bubbles. It is also, Bishop adds, "divided." Bisected by lines, it seems an animate "creature," trying to decide which way to go. It resembles a small soul, a "spirit" searching for its proper plane. The soul fits its hollow perfectly (as John Ashbery, one of Bishop's poetic heirs, remarks in his "Self-Portrait in a Convex Mirror"), but it remains uncomfortable there, a restless being. The bubble-creature is divided and uncertain.

The bubble of the opening line rhymes with "level" (and, later, with "needle" and "bevel"). These rhyme words adroitly join together the series of small machines that Bishop describes. The spirit-level measures. Bishop's next mechanism, a compass, will provide direction: so, at least, we expect. Usually, we use a compass to aid our journey. We already know which way we want to go; the compass will point us there. But Bishop's compass is itself "undecided"—it needs direction. The "wobbling and wavering" of its needle implies a hearkening to, and yearning after, something: the marks of a faltering, yet questing, sensibility. Bishop is playing a charming game by attributing human motives to objects. The game is more than just charming, however, since it discloses a secret depth of discontent.

With the description of the compass, we have reached the end of the poem's first, lopsided half. Very unusually, Bishop organizes her sonnet as a sestet followed by an octave. The answer is more expansive than the question. This bottom-heavy structure gives a decisive thrust to the second half of "Sonnet," a force lacking in its opening images of unsteady spirit-level and compass. (Two other sonnets in our collection, Coleridge's "Work without Hope" and Frederick Tuckerman's "I look'd across the rollers of the deep," also make the octave follow the sestet.)

The seventh line of "Sonnet" breaks with the first six by countering "caught" with "freed." Instead of the precise, ambiguous efforts of spirit-level and compass, we now observe the droplets of mercury from a broken thermometer. Something has shattered the enclosed, entrapping spaces of spirit-level and compass. The giddy vision of escape gives anthropomorphic qualities to an object, as earlier in the poem. Now, swift and uncontrolled, the image of the mercury "run[s] away," disappearing almost as soon as it is invoked.

The poet has yet to settle on her favored metaphor for the soul; one more is required. The glob of metallic liquid from the thermometer yields to a final image, the bevel (the terrace-like edge of a mirror). Bishop prefers the entrancing, distorted, fleeting smear of color in the bevel to the image in the mirror itself (presumably the face of the poet). (For a contrast, think of Elinor Wylie's "Self-Portrait," earlier in this book.) The freedom implied here is that of not seeing oneself; there is no need to scrutinize, to reflect accurately. Whatever object has caused the rainbow flash in the bevel is of no concern to the poet, or to us. It has become an aesthetic effect. There is a subtle hint here, in the phrase "rainbow bird," of the reassuring signs given to Noah after the Flood: a dove and then a rainbow. The rainbow-bird is Bishop's covenant with her own spirit, her sly promise of imaginative life. Peering at the margin, she prefers whim. There is safety here, an antidote to recklessness: the comfort of a trick, the illusion at the mirror's verge. The sounds of "level" and "bevel" are echoed in "wherever"—a word that flings its line, with vigorous abandon. The *fl*-sound in "flying" expands into "feels like": Bishop's bird-soul sets its upward course.

The poem's last word unlocks its truest wish. It is impossible to ignore the sexual meaning of "gay," but it would be a mistake to overemphasize this meaning. Bishop was a lesbian; her sexual identity, however, remains mostly hidden in her poems. (When asked by friends about gay liberation and coming out, Bishop reportedly quipped, "I believe in closets, closets and more closets.") The giddy, empowered spirit she invokes in "Sonnet" has a momentary intensity that surpasses conventional definitions; it cannot be confined by social or sexual roles. Significantly, "gay" rhymes with "running away," suggesting a happy evasion of responsibility. The reader who wishes to insert gay identity into "Sonnet" risks getting in the way of its free flight.

The mood of Bishop's poetry is often experimental, tentative. The poet seems equally, and deeply, committed to both the idea of travel and the idea of home. Often, Bishop combines escapism with the wish for a snug, dreamlike place of her own, as in her poems "The End of March" and "Sleeping on the Ceiling." "Sonnet," by contrast, argues that freedom means airy flight—running away like the thermometer's mercury. But "Sonnet" hints, as well, that the frolicking expressed in its conclusion cannot abolish the questions about residence and orientation that occupy its first half. There is a somber, secretive quality in "Sonnet" that belies the expansion of feeling in its final lines. We remember that, after all, this is a flight of fancy, stemming from a slight apparition located at the corner of the eye, and at the edge of the mirror. Such illumination lives in strange, liminal shapes. The world flashes forth, a mere glimpse. Bishop's poem may seem similarly evanescent. But it is by no means superficial. We detect in it a headlong, if somewhat covert, yearning. And so we turn back to the caught bubble and the wavering compass, signs of an unquiet soul. "Sonnet" is the last poem that Bishop revised for publication, shortly before her death. Though it does not sound like a testament, it may in fact be one.

The reader senses something frantic in Bishop's conclusion, for all its exhilaration. The rainbow-bird's rapid fluttering shows how intensely the poet projects onto her chosen image. "Sonnet" ingeniously provides emblems for its author's projections of self—caught by her circumstances and her peculiar makeup, yet released into openness. It resembles a riddle with several clues, but a single answer: the poet Elizabeth Bishop.

DM

An Apology for the Revival of Christian Architecture in England 7

GEOFFREY HILL

1979

Loss and Gain

Pitched high above the shallows of the sea
lone bells in gritty belfries do not ring
but coil a far and inward echoing
out of the air that thrums. Enduringly,

fuschia-hedges fend between cliff and sky;
brown stumps of headstones tamp into the ling
the ruined and the ruinously strong.
Platonic England grasps its tenantry

where wild-eyed poppies raddle tawny farms
and wild swans root in lily-clouded lakes.
Vulnerable to each other the twin forms

of sleep and waking touch the man who wakes
to sudden light, who thinks that this becalms
even the phantoms of untold mistakes.

AMID THE work of almost any other poet, this sonnet would seem dense, ornate, ambiguous, and elaborate. For Geoffrey Hill, it shows relative calm and ease; so does the sequence of twelve sonnets in which "Loss and Gain" occurs. Together, those sonnets comprise this very learned English poet's meditations on how the beauties of English landscape—its hills and shores, its houses and cathedrals—reflect, celebrate, and perhaps render all too pretty, much of British history.

Hill takes his title *An Apology* from the nineteenth-century English Catholic architect and writer Augustus Pugin, whose eponymous book defended his Gothic Revival buildings; "apology" has its Latinate sense of "defense." Other poems in the sequence consider seventeenth-century pastoral ("Damon's Lament for His Clorinda, Yorkshire, 1654"), the Church of England and its clergy ("Vocations"), and "A Short History of British India." This sonnet echoes one of the sequence's epigraphs, "the spiritual, Platonic old England": this phrase comes from the prose of Samuel Taylor Coleridge, who used it to refer to the English literary and religious inheritance he admired, as against the newer heritage (also English, but for Coleridge distasteful) of science, business, and skeptical, empiricist thought.

"Loss and Gain" begins with landscape and seascape: the octave depicts, or imagines, an English coast, with cliffs and disused churches. (It could be the North Sea, or the Channel coast, whose most famous cliffs are at Dover.) It also begins as a poem of commemoration, of public memory, and as a poem about a nation dependent on sea power ("Britannia rules the waves"). The "belfries" (bell towers, "gritty" from age or from sand in sea-wind) likely belong to local churches, though the word can also denote the frame for a ship's bell. Hill has written at length about "pitch" as a literary term; in that sense, it usually denotes a writer's attitude toward his subject, rather than toward his audience. Beginning his first line with "Pitched," Hill refers at once to the physical position the bells hold, each high in its own tower (rather than arranged in carillons), to the musical note the bells sound, and to the attitude each bell's monotone takes toward the subjects, the topics, that it (were its sound translated into language) would take up.

About all those subjects, the bells have something to say; their sound echoes far inland, and far inside the consciousness of alert listeners. "Thrum" has many meanings, some of them nautical, but here it means "vibrate, as on a stringed musical instrument." As usual, Hill's stanzas address the English past in complicated ways. Alfred, Lord Tennyson (a poet strongly associated with empire and with the sea) put into his sequence *In Memoriam* famous lines whose Christmas bells signal new beginnings: "Ring out, wild bells, to the wild sky. . . . Ring out the old, ring in the new." Hill's bells, however, "do not ring" out, but instead echo the old; England's present cannot, and should not, turn away from its past. "Air that thrums" also suggests the Aeolian harp, a stringed instrument much like wind chimes, and a figure in earlier poets, such as Coleridge, for the purifying music of nature. Here, though, the air moves only in response to the bells: Hill cannot contemplate an English landscape without also contemplating the people who have shaped our vision of it, the living and (especially) the dead who have seen and named these cliffs, this ground.

Some of those people now lie in the coastal graveyards, whose stones are so old that they resemble tree stumps, packed down hard ("tamped") into earth overgrown with heather ("ling," a North of England word). Graves and graveyards are "ruined," as are the dead bodies within them. But who or what are "ruinously strong"? Hill gives no unambiguous solution: the cliffs are strong enough to wreck unlucky ships, the church bells are strong enough to outlive their congregations, and the British Empire perhaps found its ruin in the sources of its strength—its presumption of moral superiority, its self-assurance, its exaltation of commercial gain. (Hill's long views and mixed feelings overlap here with the left-wing sentiments Tony Harrison pursues in "National Trust," also in this volume.)

The dead people under the headstones are "tenantry," occupying a plot (a cemetery plot) of land they do not own, and reminding us of glory's transience. Looking back at older seaside poems, Hill also alludes to the so-called graveyard poetry of eighteenth-century England, especially to Thomas Gray's very famous "Elegy in a Country Churchyard" (1751), which remembers (as do Hill's lines here) the ordinary rural dead, "to fortune and to fame unknown." "Tenantry" also denotes tenant farmers; Hill himself has connected the word to economic injustice, telling the scholar John Haffenden that "the celebration of the inherited beauties of the English landscape is bound, in the texture of [*An Apology*], with an equal sense of the oppression of the tenantry." "Platonic England," the spiritual and artistic essence of Englishness, retains its melancholy beauty despite the exploitation that Hill also remembers when he looks at this land.

The same mixed memories and mixed reactions—beauty, commemoration, historical guilt—afflict the sonnet as it moves inland. "To raddle" can be "to weave" or "to interlace"; "to affix a red mark or stain," as on livestock; "to afflict"; or "to wound." Poppies do all these things to Hill's English farms, weaving a thread of affliction, a spot of red, through the calm tan colors of autumnal fertility. Poppies in Britain also recall the war dead, especially the dead of the First World War (Armistice Day in Britain is sometimes called Poppy Day). "There's been an elegiac tinge to the air of this country ever since the end of the Great War," Hill told Haffenden. That air, and that tinge, suffuse Hill's lines. The most famous wild swans in English-language verse are Irish (William Butler Yeats's "The Wild Swans at Coole"), but these swans are more

likely symbols of British hierarchy: by centuries-old law, well known if un-
enforced, all wild swans in England belong to the Crown. Hill's spiritual,
yet historical image of England thus includes the millions of war dead and
the sovereign they served; "tenantry" and aristocracy; churches and navies; a
coastal scene and an inland one.

Harrison knew how he felt about his seaside places and their history; Hill
sounds as if he were still trying to find out. If Hill's ambiguous semantics
show how hard it is for him to find the right historical perpective, his fluent
music reflects the beauty he sees. The "echoing" of "fuschia," "fend," and
"cliffs," and the other consonantal echoes ("lily-clouded lakes," "phantoms
. . . untold mistakes"), along with the chiming of repeated words ("ruin,"
"wild"), give the sonnet aural beauty to match its visual splendor. Those splen-
did descriptions set up Hill's final sentence, in which he nearly deems incom-
patible ("vulnerable to each other") his own aesthetic goals.

Seen in the light of history (and they ought not be seen apart from history),
English landscape and seascape must represent both honor and shame. How
can a poet create such a representation? How can he depict what is beautiful
in England (its churches, its flora, its history of self-sacrifice) and at the same
time give appropriate place to the exploitation, the carnage and the injustice,
that raddle the nation's past? The "sudden light" of the last lines could be ei-
ther the light of history or the countervailing light of aesthetic detachment.
To "the man who wakes," that light "becalms" (puts to rest—in Hill's English,
a full rhyme with "farms") "even the phantoms" (ghosts, as from the dead in
the ground, or the unburied dead in the sea) "of untold mistakes" (of the sins
committed in founding an seagoing empire). "Untold" can mean "countless"
(too numerous to "tell") or "unacknowledged" or "unknown." The ambigu-
ous enlightenment with which Hill ends the poem, the light of "Platonic En-
gland," of English ideals, seems to the waking man to allay the demands laid
on us by the anonymous deceased.

That man—struck by light and by "forms," envisioning Englishness—
seems like a poet; he seems much like Geoffrey Hill. Yet he is not Hill. He
"thinks" what Hill may not believe, and what Hill would not have us believe
without a great deal of anguished inquiry. What sort of enlightenment, what
vision or reason, might "becalm" the "phantoms" of history? What art, if any,
can lay those ghosts to rest, or place them within a vision of England's past
that does justice to both "loss and gain"? Hill ends other sonnets with ques-
tions, but he uses no interrogatives here. Loading his descriptive phrases with

ambiguous or far-fetched terms, and then presenting an ambiguous awakening, the poet leaves the questions to us, showing how hard they have been, and how remote from clear answers they still seem.

SB

Glanmore Sonnets I

SEAMUS HEANEY

1979; revised 1998

Vowels ploughed into other: opened ground.
The mildest February for twenty years
Is mist bands over furrows, a deep no sound
Vulnerable to distant gargling tractors.
Our road is steaming, the turned-up acres breathe.
Now the good life could be to cross a field
And art a paradigm of earth new from the lathe
Of ploughs. My lea is deeply tilled.
Old ploughsocks gorge the subsoil of each sense
And I am quickened with a redolence
Of farmland as a dark unblown rose.
Wait then . . . Breasting the mist, in sowers' aprons,
My ghosts come striding into their spring stations.
The dream grain whirls like freakish Easter snows.

IN 1972 Seamus Heaney, his wife, Marie, and their two young sons (a daughter was born in 1973) moved from Northern Ireland, where he grew up, to a cottage in verdant, isolated Glanmore, in the Republic of Ireland, thirty-three miles south of Dublin. There Heaney completed his fourth and harshest book, *North* (published 1975), whose grim, short-lined stanzaic poems reacted to Ulster's violence. Yet Heaney's move to Glanmore was in many ways a respite from that violence. It let him imagine, and begin to write, a poetry not fixed on the daily difficulties and the political demands of life in the north, a poetry not dominated, as *North* was, by fear, guilt, self-division, and self-accusation. The ten *Glanmore Sonnets,* published in *Field Work* (1979), find a style for Heaney's sense of relief.

This sonnet both introduces and epitomizes that style. Like some of its successors in *Glanmore Sonnets,* it is a lyric of celebration that includes, almost defiantly, visions of peace. Like all its successors, it demonstrates verbal plenitude, bringing up the rich associations and the overlapping resonances of Latin and Greek roots ("paradigm," "fundamental"), of foundational Anglo-Saxon ("plough," "earth"), and of Heaney's Irish English. Adapting for an Irish locale (as Patrick Kavanagh had before) a form often seen, at least since the early nineteenth century, as quintessentially English, Heaney tuned his sonnets to the landscape and the mild, wet seasons in the southern part of the island. He also drew on the tradition by which ancient poets—Virgil and Horace among them—gave sober advice and found mental refuge from civil strife by writing poems about farms.

The *Glanmore Sonnets* also become poems of recollection, bringing back to Heaney the "ghosts" of his rural childhood, his first crushes and early friends, who visit him one by one (sometimes by name) in subsequent sonnets. This first sonnet, with its fertile saturation, its "lea . . . deeply tilled," its soil gorged, opens the door to those ghostly visitations, and to the poetry of married love and sexual fulfillment that the sequence later includes. Its "opened ground" is both invitation and manifesto. Heaney proposes to himself, tries to imagine ("could be," "Wait then . . ."), a sweeter and a more patient poetry than he— or any other Irish poet writing in English—had created thus far.

The sonnet begins with "mildness," literally with peace and quiet, a "no sound / Vulnerable" only to the comic, productive, nonthreatening "gargling tractors." The acoustic environment remains softly friendly; sibilants and *th*-sounds dominate, and "hard" consonants such as *b, d, g, k,* and *t* almost never collide, except in the comical "gargling." Steam rises from the road (out of morning dew) and from the newly "turned-up" soil. We may imagine the promise of Isaiah fulfilled, the metal implements of violence replaced by tools of peace, "ploughsocks" (ploughshares). The language of farming will be, in Heaney's Glanmore, continuous with the language we use for poetry, both of which have become arts of peace.

Both kinds of language welcome unimproved nature, though they also attempt to change it. Thus "Vowels ploughed into other," a way to describe the music of poetry, describes the start of the farmer's year, the work of a plough as the first thaw opens the fields. (The Heaneys did not grow crops for a living in Glanmore, though they would have seen agriculture around them.) The first line also suggests the softer sonorities of southern Irish talk, as compared to the "staccato, consonantal" feel (as Heaney once put it) of Ulster accents, including Heaney's own. Saying that "the good life could be to cross a field" makes writing, and farming, seem surprisingly easy; the classical pastoral condition of ease, called otium, merges here with georgic labor. The line also responds, as the critic Meg Tyler points out, to Boris Pasternak's poem "Hamlet in Russia," as translated by Robert Lowell: "to live a life is not to cross a field." Life in Glanmore makes poetry seem not effortless, but less fraught than it seemed elsewhere.

Heaney's lines about ploughing bring up the ancient analogy between the back-and-forth movements of the plough and the movement—a line, then another line—of verse: "Vowels ploughed into other, opened ground, / Each verse returning like the plough turned round," he says in the couplet that concludes Sonnet 2. Only by peaceful skilled labor (like ploughing, like poetry) can the ground "breathe." The phrase "opened ground," in *North,* had stood for guilty sexual and political conquest—England over Ireland, men over women, "the big pain / That leaves you raw, like opened ground, again," he wrote then. Bringing the phrase back for two of the Glanmore sonnets, Heaney removes, permanently, its implicit violence. Glanmore, the place, and *Glanmore Sonnets,* the poems, would remain for him loci of quiet plenitude, as in the much later sonnet sequence called *Glanmore Revisited,* and in the title of his 1996 selected poems, *Opened Ground.*

Were the octave in this sonnet to stand on its own, it would describe a generous but also very deliberate sort of art. In the story the octave implies, the poet-farmer regards with deliberation, and then tills, his field in a fortunate season ("the mildest February"). Such art would seem to give the artist full command of materials drawn from conscious observation, from outside himself, and from sensory experience accessible in principle to anybody (or to anybody who visits Glanmore).

Such a notion of art, unmodified, leaves out too much of what poets do. Heaney veers from the Shakespearean pattern set in the octave *(abab cdcd),* using instead a Petrarchan sestet *(eefggf;* "years" rhymes with "tractors," "aprons" with "stations"). That sestet will alter and even invert the notion of art in the octave, without forsaking Heaney's announced commitment to an art of fertility, welcome, and peace.

Rather, that sestet will bring in what the octave occludes: the way in which poetry, for Heaney, draws on often unacknowledged memories, on mysteries and images from the depths, the "dark," the unconscious. "Gorge" as a transitive verb usually means "fill up, make full," but applied to the action of a plough it may have its rare opposite meaning, "scoop out" (*OED,* definition 5): the plough turns up long-buried bits of earth, as the writer, making verse on the page, turns over or discovers memories. Obsolete farm implements might well remind Heaney of his rural youth. A poetry of conscious art, as in the octave, can survive comic rivalry with modern technology, ploughshares versus tractors, but only the "old" and preindustrial tool comports with the archetypes of the sestet.

From an octave replete with words for sights and sounds, Heaney moves to the sense of smell, "redolence," connected with involuntary memory. From an octave in which "the good life" was something chosen, and "art" something made (as fields are tilled) by choice, the poem moves to a sestet in which art is something that happens *to* the poet, who becomes less farmer than field. He must wait for ghosts after he is filled, "quickened" (either "made pregnant" or "made alive"), by a symbol whose "dark" resonance resists (though it also invites) explication. Since a "blown" rose is a rose fully in bloom, a "dark unblown rose" is a rose not yet ripe, or a rose not yet visible, one that exists only in a vision or in the future—where roses in February likely belong. This line in 1979 read "Of the fundamental dark unblown rose," connecting the poem to the mystic roses of Christian esoteric tradition, from Dante to the Rosicrucian doctrines that fascinated the young William Butler Yeats. Heaney's revision, which makes the line less mysterious, also makes clear just what he believes he can smell. The whole of the "farmland"—the land, along with its emanation—does its work in him: he is object, not only subject, not only agent, not just a man who acts on the land.

The poet in the sestet, in other words, does justice to the unconscious parts of art, the parts that involve waiting, making oneself ready, for the promptings of "dreams," or for memories that feel like ghosts. He also moves from exterior space he can share—"Our road"—to his past, which belongs to nobody else: "My ghosts." A parade of compounded consonance—"ghosts striding," "spring stations"—says that those ghosts have arrived. They take up positions behind the plough, as "sowers," ready to put the seed into the "turned-up acres," ready, in other words, to make possible the rest of the Glanmore sonnets, and the rest of the poems of memory, fertility, and peace that Heaney hopes to write (and has gone on to write).

Yet Heaney is too honest a poet, too much aware of the fear that must follow all hopes, to leave us without some note of caution. As the sowers, the memories, the agents of poetry join the meditative Heaney and follow his plough, their "dream grain" reverses the hospitable weather with which Heaney began. The odd weather of true poetry can bring a warm winter, or a new "rose," but it may also herald a cold spring, with "snows," even on the Christian holiday that celebrates resurrection and new life. Art involves both attention to the present, peaceful labor, like the plough's, and a half-conscious readiness for memory. However peaceful his aims, however careful his methods, no true poet can ascertain in advance what tones, what ideas, what kinds of interlocutors, the next poem will bring.

SB

"The Cormorant in Its Element"

AMY CLAMPITT

1983

That bony potbellied arrow, wing-pumping along
implacably, with a ramrod's rigid adherence,
airborne, to the horizontal, discloses talents
one would never have guessed at. Plummeting

waterward, big black feet splayed for a landing
gear, slim head turning and turning, vermilion-
strapped, this way and that, with a lightning glance
over the shoulder, the cormorant astounding-

ly, in one sleek involuted arabesque, a vertical
turn on a dime, goes into that inimitable
vanishing-and-emerging-from-under-the-briny-

deep act which, unlike the works of Homo Houdini,
is performed for reasons having nothing at all
to do with ego, guilt, ambition, or even money.

LIKE THE earlier poems by Marianne Moore that it recalls, Amy Clampitt's "The Cormorant in Its Element" is a variation on an age-old genre, the beast fable. In the beast fable, familiar from Aesop's tales as well as contemporary cartoons, animals bear human traits, reflecting our own anxieties and capabilities. Clampitt compares her cormorant to a person (it becomes a kind of dancer, then a magician). But she also reminds us that the bird is different from us, with utterly foreign interests and (as she puts it) talents. The realm of nature is not, or not merely, a field for our projections. Instead, it puts human life in its place, showing that there is (as the critic Elisa New says, explicating

Moore) "some richer law than law of self." Like many of Moore's poems, Clampitt's is in carefully arranged free verse; it uses strange slant rhymes in an Italian pattern, *abba abba ccd dcd*—counting "vermilion- / s" and "glance," in lines 6–7, as a rhyme.

The cormorant, Clampitt's subject, is an intimidatingly large creature about two feet long, with the vermilion bands she mentions. (She describes the pelagic cormorant, often seen in coastal waters in the eastern United States.) The Romans called the cormorant the "sea raven" *(corvus marinus)*. Like the raven, it symbolizes greedy, intense appetite; thus our word "ravenous." The cormorant dries its wings in the open air, and the bird with its spread wings furnishes a symbol of the cross in medieval art. In Book 4 of Milton's *Paradise Lost,* Satan sits like a cormorant on Eden's tree of life. Clampitt ignores the cormorant's reputation as the bird of death, so firmly established in Milton; nor does she suggest crucifixion. For her, the bird is not a repository of cultural meanings, a bearer of human significance, but a being unto itself.

Her cormorant first appears cartoon-like, grotesque, a "bony potbellied arrow." The pot belly might suggest that this bird is a sort of gourmand, indulgent of appetite. But the boniness is more telling. Clampitt's beast has a precise, machinelike approach to the act of feeding. This "performance," which takes up so much of its time, displays the cormorant's character to us. "Wing-pumping along / implacably," this creature looks both inexorable and effortful, cloddish and fine-tuned.

The "ramrod's rigid adherence" that Clampitt attributes to her cormorant in her first quatrain suggests a military stiffness. The bird, we think, may be unready for the flexibility that artful action requires. But we are wrong: the vector-like straightness of the cormorant resembles that of an airplane, not a drilled soldier (it is a minor surprise that the ramrod extends horizontally rather than, as expected, vertically). At the end of the first quatrain, the poet promises to disclose to us, in her creature, "talents / one would never have guessed at" (a very Moore-like line in its unruffled, assured, yet somewhat diffident use of the conditional mood).

When we reach the gap between the first and second stanzas, we learn why Clampitt has separated her quatrains by the empty space of the page: this device allows her to mime the vaultings of the cormorant itself. The poet too becomes an acrobat, like her bird. Across a dizzying enjambment, we feel the cormorant "plummeting / waterward," its dive precipitous and stunning. In the second quatrain the bird is still a kind of plane, and a clownish one, with its "big black feet splayed for a landing / gear." The "slim head turning and turning" resembles a gyroscope or sophisticated compass, searching out a proper target.

Then, with a "lightning glance" cast backward, the cormorant begins its swift, agile plunge. The elaborate sideways descent of the bird is reflected in Clampitt's slide from octave to sestet in the course of one drawn-out adverb: "astounding- / ly." The cormorant is now a dancer doing one of the most dramatic moves in ballet, an arabesque; and then, in a brisk shot of slang, a speedy motorist turning "on a dime" (but, in the cormorant's case, turning vertically).

Clampitt's final implicit comparison is to a magician making himself disappear and reappear (as an image for the bird skimming the water and submerging in it to find its prey). Magicians aim to astonish their audience, but the cormorant—the poet now realizes—has no sense of audience, no guilty theatricality. It just does what it does, not trying to make an impression. True magic, perhaps, inheres in the intricate but uncontrived workings of nature, rather than in human gimmickry.

All along, the bird's precise dance has been a potential emblem for the poet's own performance; but the poet wants to dazzle readers, and so the comparison must now be abandoned. The enjambment between Clampitt's third and her final stanza (between the two halves of the sestet) marks a significant conclusion. The cormorant's predatory maneuvers, the poet acknowledges, are no mere stunt but (if we disregard the enjambment for a moment) a "deep act." Its performance testifies to an impulse more profound than the power of will or intention that animates us.

Man the maker and escape artist commits virtuoso self-aggrandizement, and proves able to defeat nearly any trap. He produces astonishing signs of himself, monuments of art and politics. These "works of Homo Houdini"— whether they be the empire-building satirized by Shelley in his "Ozymandias" or the delicate porcelain of Versailles in Moore's "No Swan So Fine" (both poems in this book)—are accomplished, Clampitt suggests, for the following list of motives: "ego, guilt, ambition, or" (last but decidedly not least) "even money." By associating these terms, the poet implies that they may contaminate one another, so that (for example) we boost our egos for guilty reasons. But beasts like the cormorant have neither ego nor guilt. The motive that trumps all others, the final term in the series, is the one most alien to the animal kingdom: money. Harry Houdini worked for pay, lots of it. The fame of

the proud magician who, like Houdini, can bring himself back from the verge
of death proves fatally linked to monetary reward, the most transitory sign of
our self-esteem.

Clampitt relies on the cormorant to present her profound doubt about our
human search for distinction. Her bird, both comic and grand, does not show
off as we do. The cormorant does not strive to distinguish itself, but rather
simply demonstrates its essence. It is in its element as we are not. (What is our
element?) As in Moore's "No Swan So Fine," the poet's wit criticizes what she
deems our characteristic fault, extravagance.

But the poet cannot turn away completely from the taint of human com-
plexity. The last line of her poem is about us, not the bird. Clampitt can go
only so far in admiring the alien being that shows us up. She praises the cor-
morant, but she also makes us savor her own Houdini-like prestidigitation as
she describes it. Sonnets usually do not make their authors much money, but
they still stand as emblems of the artful ego.

In "The Cormorant in Its Element," the author's doubts enrich her art,
rather than making her reject it in the name of a superior, and plainer, moral-
ity manifested in nature. Clampitt was not an ascetic but a marvelously lavish
poet, and this sonnet is one of her most rewarding turns.

                                                                    DM

"Man Walking to Work"

DENIS JOHNSON

1987

The dawn is a quality laid across
the freeway like the visible
memory of the ocean that kept all this
a secret for a hundred million years.
I am not moving and I am not standing still.
I am only something the wind strikes and clears,
and I feel myself fade like the sky,
the whole of Ohio a mirror gone blank.
My jacket keeps me. My zipper
bangs on my guitar. Lord God help me
out by the lake after the shift at Frigidaire
when I stop laughing and taste how wet the beer
is in my mouth, suddenly recognizing the true
wedding of passage and arrival I am invited to.

JOHNSON'S man walking to work is a rock-and-roll archetype, a plebeian fig-
ure of wisdom, a vehicle for a blue-collar epiphany. He feels oppressed, erased,
by the working week, then buoyed by his hopes for the end of the day. A hos-
tile reader might see, in him, not an archetype so much as a stereotype. It is an
accusation that the sonnet anticipates, and does much to refute, not only with
the bravado of its accelerated, and apparently celebratory, ending, but also
with the sting that the ending contains.

   This man demonstrates his transcendental discoveries in words most Amer-
icans could use. He cherishes his jacket (no doubt leather) and his guitar (he
likely plays rock or blues). He works an early shift (he walks at dawn), at a
Frigidaire factory or a warehouse, and he has to walk to work (he does not

own a car). His job is so monotonous that a day at work seems like a geological era (like the Ordovician, say, when seas covered "the whole of Ohio"). His day, and his year, and his Ohio, are redeemed, with luck, at dusk, when blue-collar style can make his life worth living after all.

So the walker imagines, as he walks to work; so the dawn, as he views it, says to him, even over the freeway. His blankness is like the blankness of the workers in Bruce Springsteen's songs (say, "The River"), and like the earlier blankness of what Wallace Stevens called, mockingly, "The American Sublime," a built environment whose emptiness offers neither nature, nor rich history: "What wine does one drink?" Stevens asked. "What bread does one eat?" So the American working week says to this man, who feels, in the octave, erased.

In the sestet, he feels, instead, redeemed. His jacket is his, no one else's; his guitar, like his zipper, belongs to him. The sestet, with its emphatic concluding couplet, its "true wedding," suggests resolution, self-confidence, happiness—or it would if the syntax did not suggest something else: "Lord God help me" places the man who is walking to work alone before the abyss. What will he do, who will he be, when beer and laughter end?

The poet and critic David Wojahn once called Johnson (now well-known for his novels) "the first significant American poet who has found in rock-and-roll music his major influence," noting particular debts to Bob Dylan, which Johnson confirms in interviews. Rock-and-roll as a genre relies on instinct, on desires cherished even when unsatisfied. Johnson's late-Romantic, middle-American demotic, rock-and-roll-inflected style relies on a sense of immediacy as well. Like most rock-and-roll, it rejects irony: we cannot suspect the walking man's motives at all, cannot say to him that we know more than he knows. Whatever we know is not important to him, cannot help him, as he contemplates his insignificance beneath the Ohio sky, and tries not to contemplate the economic constraints that send him back to his job.

What can help this man? First of all, his ability (really, of course, the poet Johnson's ability) to find, for his sense of his own unimportance, images. He feels ignored (like Ohio, by the rest of America), unseen (as beneath an ocean), or indistinct (absorbed into an empty sky), and he feels like a bowling pin too. Though a "strike" is a good move in bowling (one that fells all ten pins), the paired verbs suggest the pin-setting machine that clears away downed pins after each bowler's frame. The walking man moves neither under his own power, nor because God, or another human being, wants him to move. Rather, he feels subject to a machine, a pale thing like a bowling pin, whose posture and dignity (pins, too, stand up straight) cannot prevent it from being knocked down, picked up, and swept out of sight.

"The sonnet seems to me the most vital poetic form," Johnson said in a 1983 interview. "It's still breathing and changing, and I don't think there's anybody who can stop you and hand you the rules." "Man Walking to Work" follows familiar "rules" of proportion, logic, and closure: the sonnet splits up into octave and sestet, present and future, morning and afternoon. Rules of meter, on the other hand, go out the window: the lines that approximate iambic pentameter ("a secret for a hundred million years") are exceptions, and they do not occur at climactic points. Instead, Johnson begins with a ten-syllable line that sounds anything but regular, and ends up with lines of thirteen and fifteen syllables, a "wedding" of irregularity and excess with an informal ease. As for rhyme, "years" rhymes with "clears," "across" and "visible" with "this" and "still," but "sky" and "blank" rhyme with nothing (a pun on "blank" verse). The octave ends with expected pairings not made, "the whole of Ohio a mirror" in which the man sees nothing, certainly not himself.

For such blank vagueness, the sestet, with its brief, clear phrases, feels like a remedy. Johnson's sentences about jacket and zipper are the shortest in the poem, the only ones that end midline, the first to use a possessive pronoun. For the first time, this man has the power to keep what he owns: he feels that it "keeps him," protects him, or keeps him whole. The final couplets hammer home that feeling: "zipper," with its final r, introduces "beer" and "Frigidaire," off-rhymes that lead up to the colloquial full rhyme "true . . . to."

Yet this "true wedding" may hold terror nonetheless. The meeting of "passage and arrival," the moment when this life finds its true destination, may turn out to be not a pleasant evening outdoors, but a moment of death, the end of all work and all days. "I must work the works of him that sent me, while it is day," Jesus says (John 9:4); "the night cometh, when no man can work." If the power in heaven is not an attentive God, but a blank sky or a celestial pin-setting machine, for what end, and to what hour, should any man work?

Such questions cannot be answered within Johnson's poem, any more than the cry "Lord God help me" can find a response. The cry, as the walking man imagines it, shows neither wholly relieved exhilaration, nor complete despair; rather, it has to contain elements of both. A man on foot by a freeway in Ohio shows a defiant confidence in the face of existential uncertainty, a defiance that we might name the rock-and-roll sublime. Without his jacket, without his guitar, without the beer (surely domestic) that he opens up "by the lake," the walking man would be adrift in a universe, and in a verbal environment, with nothing but dispiriting brand names (Frigidaire, "frigid air") and vast sublimities. With these homely objects, he can have a sense of belonging despite his solitude, a membership in a notional community—defined by guitars, by the walk to work, even by beer—that does not exclude individual anger, harsh frustration, and eschatological fear.

SB

"Jacob"

EDGAR BOWERS

1990

In tangled vine and branch, high weed and scrub,
I found a tree my father planted once,
A thread-leaf maple, green and old, not tall
As I am tall, but ten-foot at the base—
Ten thousand leaves contained as of one leaf.
As though I lay wrapped in the ancestral root,
Head on the stone, awake in sleep, I knew
The unity in which earth walks the earth,
Struggles with speech until a name is said,
Is lamed and blessed. A cloudless summer day.
Years up the ladder of the sky, beyond
Air, fire, and water, a jet plane barely moved,
Marked on the blue as on the final stone—
Feather, leaf, shell, fish-print, or whitened bone.

IN THE Book of Genesis, Jacob is the archetypal striver; he wrestles with his elder brother Esau even in the womb. Aided by his mother Rebekah, Jacob becomes the most wily and resourceful of the biblical patriarchs. Edgar Bowers, though, is less concerned with the character of Jacob than with his usefulness as an emblem. In "Jacob," the title character represents the poet's struggle to create a sign of humanness: a trace of himself, inscribed on the natural world.

The sonnet's elaborate opening image shows a "thread-leaf maple, green and old" planted by the speaker's father. The tangled and imposing stretch of "vine and branch, high weed and scrub," where the speaker quests after this paternal tree stands for the mystery of origins, like Darwin's "tangled bank" in

the last paragraph of *On the Origin of Species.* "Jacob" will move from this ver-
dant confusion in its opening lines to its bare and purified couplet ending.
The poem's last lines see in an empty sky a serene and definitive sign: "the fi-
nal stone," the tombstone that seals our lives.

The octave finds its versions of poetic tradition inseparable from our knowl-
edge of death: we inherit both. In the *Iliad,* the warrior Glaukos responds to
Diomedes' question about his lineage by telling him that the generations of
men are like leaves: we are ephemeral, scattered by the winds. (Virgil, Dante,
and Milton will later adopt and vary Homer's simile.) Bowers alters Homer's
image for human ancestry by making it resolved and concentric, an emblem
of coherence rather than impermanence: "ten thousand leaves contained as of
one leaf." This massive yet supple leaf, representing our past and our future,
envelops the speaker. (Les Murray's "Strangler Fig," also in this volume, simi-
larly relies on a plant as symbol for the sonnet's own concentrated power.)

With the phrase "head on the stone, awake in sleep," Bowers considers an
episode from early in Jacob's career. Fleeing from his brother Esau's wrath, Ja-
cob stops for the night. Using a stone for his pillow, he dreams of a ladder
stretching from earth to heaven, with "the angels of God ascending and de-
scending on it." Still dreaming, he hears a prophecy from God, who stands
above the ladder and tells him (in the King James Version), "The land whereon
thou liest, to thee will I give it, and to thy seed; And thy seed shall be as the
dust of the earth."

Jacob, struck with awe, responds, "How dreadful is this place! This is none
other but the house of God, and this is the gate of heaven" (Genesis 28:11–18).
Bowers's Jacob, like the Jacob of Genesis, sees a vision of "the gate of heaven"
that is also a prophecy of earthly future. With the ascetic rigor of a late mod-
ernist, Bowers stringently insists on what Genesis also implies: God sentences
his creation to death. We are in fact "as the dust of the earth," eventually re-
turning to our material origins, clarified and reduced.

"Jacob" then evokes the more familiar biblical episode of Jacob's struggle
with the angel—with a mysterious figure who wrestles with him all night un-
til the break of dawn (Genesis 32:24–32). Losing to Jacob, the angel blesses
him by giving him his new name, Israel, but also lames him. Jacob departs
from this harrowing encounter limping, yet sanctified. Here, Bowers turns
Jacob's wrestling into an image of the poet's quest for the adequate word—his
creation of a unity that will take the form of necessity.

Bowers's sonnet lacks rhyme except for its final couplet. Its most significant
formal feature, along with this final rhyme, is the caesura in line 10. Here the

poet breaks from the vision of biblical grandeur. We move from heroic speaking (as Jacob "struggles with speech until a name is said") to an impersonal process, the small signs left on sky and stone.

In Herman Melville's poem "Art," an ancestor of Bowers's work, the struggle of Jacob is refigured as the poet's contest with his materials. Melville's bold maker creates "pulsed life"; the poet invokes "Jacob's mystic heart," his ability "to wrestle with the angel—Art." Bowers replaces Melville's wrestling Jacob, his image of vivid, human artistry, with the seeming inhumanity of jet plane and fossil. This nearly blank scene shows evidence of us, but does not allow for the robust drama that Melville emphasizes: the poet's heroic enterprise of winning through to articulation.

This later Jacob sees, instead of angels, a jet plane that "barely move[s]," etching a contrail on "the ladder of the sky." The remote, flat blue of the sky resembles "the final stone," our pillow in death. The writing on the tombstone-sky is a faint fossil remnant of our life on earth. By implication, this writing is like the work of the poet who leaves as his legacy a slightly but significantly altered surface: the not-quite-blank page. Bowers's spare conception of poetic art departs from Melville's bravado, and from the vibrant spiritual and tribal connotations of the Jacob story in Genesis.

Bowers's cloudless sky suggests the stark sublime of an American poetics that extracts imagination from alien, blank places. Bowers's immediate precursor in this respect is his teacher Yvor Winters, who, like Bowers, often depends on the clear, bright atmosphere and sharp landscape of California. (See Winters's poem "The Castle of Thorns," earlier in this volume.) In both poets, the West Coast mise-en-scène, even when sunny, transmits an inhuman chill. The concluding couplet rhyme of "Jacob" makes what is left of the flesh after death (bone) into a mark on the most ancient writing surface (stone). Bowers evokes a hard, remote expanse of time and space, and witnesses our traces left on the coldest of elements.

Bowers's "Jacob" moves from earth to sky, from the initiation of a speaker enmeshed in ancestry to the bare movements of a writing in space, and then back to earth—but an earth that does not know us. The poem's concluding fossil landscape is not fertile and full of memories, like the "tangled vine and branch" with which it begins. Instead, mere persistence distinguishes us. Bowers's bleak stance refuses heroics. Tough-minded and resilient, he accepts our marginal status in the universe.

DM

"Strangler Fig"

Les Murray

1992

I glory centennially slow-

ly in being Guugumbakh the

strangular fig bird-born to overgrow

the depths of this wasp-leafed stinging-tree

through muscling in molten stillness down

its spongy barrel crosslacing in overflow

even of myself as in time my luscious fat

leaves top out to adore the sun forest high

and my shade-coldest needs touch a level that

discovered as long yearned for transmutes

my wood into the crystal mode of roots

and I complete myself and mighty on

buttresses far up in combat embraces no

rotted traces to the fruiting rain surface I one.

IN "Strangler Fig," Les Murray praises the rough landscape of his native Australia. Writing in the tradition of D. H. Lawrence, he makes his fig plant a wild, strong symbol, crawling and sprawling over the page. Like Lawrence's

"Bavarian gentians, big and dark," Murray's strangler fig guides us to the deathly underworld, but also raises us up to fertile, yearning life.

The strangler fig is native to New South Wales, where Murray grew up in rural poverty. (The plant also occurs in other places around the world, including Florida and the West Indies.) Growing as tall as twenty feet, with heavy, cable-like branches, the strangler fig wraps itself around a host tree, smothering it until the tree is reduced to a hollow trunk, a convenient nesting site for birds and bats. Often the fig is "bird-born," as Murray remarks—the product of a chance seed dropped by a passing bird. Here, the seed has landed in the branches of a stinging tree, another Australian curiosity. The stinging tree or gympie-gympie (called by Murray, with an aboriginal growl, "Guugumbakh") is "wasp-leafed" because its leaves cause intense pain to humans, dogs, and horses (but, oddly, not to native Australian animals). With its prickly weapons, the stinging tree wards off our intrusive presence. The strangler fig, by contrast, invites all; its fruit provides food for many species, and acts as a sort of impromptu womb for the gall wasp (which lays its eggs inside the fig's fleshy fruit). Asking us to admire a parasitic plant—an unexpected, even bizarre subject for a poet—Murray shows us one of the ingenious marvels of creation.

The fig's fruit is traditionally seen as a symbol of sex, partly because of its juicy, faintly obscene appearance, but also because Adam and Eve wear fig leaves after their fall. In Murray's sonnet, the fig provides more than just clothing (as in the case of Adam and Eve) or shelter (for the animals that reside in the dead tree beneath the fig vines). The strangler fig announces an intimacy with the source of life, seen as the work of necessity. Murray has written elsewhere about the overwhelming character of sex, the way it (in his view) reduces us to "subhuman" level. His fig tree is a slow-moving factory of generation: necessarily sexual, blanketing and encasing all of us.

Murray's long, loping lines mimic the twining of his fig plant. We watch as the poet generates a single continuous, almost overpowering sentence-swath, a creature of slow muscle and lush exuberance. The gaps between the lines cleverly evoke the spacing of the fig's branches as it wreathes itself inexorably around the tree. Unlike most sonnets, "Strangler Fig" shows its eloquence in rolling force rather than measured balance of parts. Murray welds form to the primal energy of words, instead of relying on the sonnet's rules to contain this energy.

Murray begins with "I"; he will return, at the very end, to this word, which announces the essence of the fig, its relentless self-assertion. His second word is "glory"—a key term in the work of one of Murray's favorite poets, Gerard Manley Hopkins. Murray, a committed Catholic, dedicates most of his books "to the glory of God"; glory is the palpable, undeniable evidence of spreading life. "Centennially" describes the improbably long lifespan of trees: they can last longer than a hundred years, outliving humans. "Slow-/ly," curling from the first to the second line, winds itself around the reader's attention, as Murray's poem tightens its grip. Here, as elsewhere in the poem, enjambment gives cumulative force. The stationary power of the fig is also a massive movement, "muscling in molten stillness down." To muscle in is to intrude in bullying fashion; so the burly fig makes its place. But the action has magnificence too, not merely rudeness: *ow* in "slow-/ly" pours its splendor along the right-hand side of the page, from "overgrow" to "down" to "overflow," in lines 3–6.

"Crosslacing in overflow/even of myself": the fig exceeds itself, lacing its branches in layers—it seeps through all limits. "My luscious fat/leaves top out," booms the plant. Murray is a man of ample girth, and fatness appears frequently in his poetry. In his work, the fat person signifies succulent enjoyment, yet he is also freakish, marked as an outsider and subject to ridicule. The fig, however, remains exempt from such social prejudice. Through it, nature demonstrates a substantial, efficient rule: the more the better. To "overflow," to "top out," and finally to "adore": these actions (with their satisfying *oh*-sounds, round and achieved) show the ascending scope of Murray's plant, as his octave reaches its end. "Adore" strives for the summit, the "sun forest high," and conveys Murray's sense of growth-as-worship.

The sestet reverses direction, pointing downward to the root of things. "My shade-coldest needs touch a level": necessity is linked by implication to the cold shades of death. This lower realm involves a "transmut[ing]" of wood to "crystal," of trunk to roots. Murray reminds us that the mineral and the organic are of a piece. Petrified wood crystals, though they seem dead and geometrically perfect by contrast with the messiness of plant life, begin as plants. Murray here reflects on the images for poetry itself. Does it come as naturally as the leaves to a tree (in Keats's phrase), or is it a hard, gem-like structure? Like Lawrence, Murray chooses the organic over the crystalline; his poems creep, slither, and become engorged. But—as in the case of a comparable writer, the American A. R. Ammons—lazy and impulsive energies can suddenly take on strict, architectonic pattern.

We see this monolithic strength in Murray's final three lines: "and I complete myself and mighty on/buttresses far up in combat embraces no/rotted traces to the fruiting rain surface I one." Completion requires the stability of a building; the might of the fig is buttressed, its tensions braced. "Combat embraces" (rhyming internally with "no / rotted traces") refers to the fig's struggle with its tree, but it also seems to be Murray's periphrasis for sex: both combat and completeness, leading to the making of children as the fig makes its fruit. The poem ends by rising to the fruiting surface and to boisterous identity. "I one," the poem's final phrase, caps the sequence of end words that sums up the plant's independence: "on," "no," and "one" (in the final three lines). His fig emerges into stolid, secure presence.

Murray has written a poem called "The Quality of Sprawl," and his own art is indeed sprawling. But it is far from unregulated, as "Strangler Fig" demonstrates. For all its bursting, fetid potentials, the fig finally provides a shape that twines together depth and surface, appetite and design. Murray's monster fig argues for a poetics of completeness, uniting tangled vegetation and glinting rock, the sun and the cold shade.

DM

Mythologies 3

A. K. RAMANUJAN

Written before 1993

"Keep off when I worship Siva.
Touch me three times and you'll never
see me again," said Akka to her new groom
who couldn't believe his ears:

           Om, Om!
she seemed to intone in bed with every breath
and all he could think of was her round breast,
her musk, her darling navel and the rest.
So he hovered and touched her, her body death-

ly cold to mortal touch but hot for God's
first move, a caress like nothing on earth.
She fled his hand as she would a spider,

threw away her modesty, as the rods
and cones of her eyes gave the world a new birth:
She saw Him then, unborn, form of forms, the Rider,

His white Bull chewing cud in her backyard.

THIS sonnet's dramatic shifts in tone and figure—from sexual comedy to religious ecstasy, from bedroom farce to vision of Godhead, and then to the homely "backyard"—might well recommend it even to readers who know nothing of the traditions on which it draws. Akka Mahadevi, or Mahadevi-akka (twelfth century CE), was one of four great composers of the South Indian devotional sayings called vaçanas (literally, "sentences"), and the only woman among them. The vaçanas reflect the spirit of the Virasaiva religious movement, expressing—in defiance of all institutions—a radical, all-consuming, and unmediated relationship to the god Siva (or Shiva). Married against her will to a king named Kausika, who did not share her faith, Akka later abandoned his household. She then chose to roam the land, naked but covered by her long hair, declaring her total devotion to Siva, her "Lord white as jasmine." Men found her stunning, despite her commitment to chastity; "wherever she went," says one modern writer, "the dazzling beauty of her person plagued her." Her passionate vaçanas use the language of eros, of bodily yearning, to portray the attention she gave to her divine Lord. "Husband inside,/lover outside," one vaçana says (in Ramanujan's translation), "This world/and that other. . . . I cannot manage them both."

Ramanujan, in *Speaking of Siva* (1973), translated many of Mahadeviakka's vaçanas from the poetic prose of the original Kannada into English free verse. This sonnet, written about twenty years afterward, does not translate anything Akka composed; instead, it takes off from traditions about her life. One tradition has it that Akka married Kausika on three conditions: that he not interrupt her in meditation, that she could meet as she chose with other Virasaivists, and that she might continue to serve her guru. When the king had broken all three promises, Akka felt free to depart.

The octave begins by quoting Akka's warnings; we hear them as the king might have heard them, less seriously than she meant. The plain diction, with its lack of metaphor, adheres to the king's aggressively literalist frame of reference. It presents what she sees, what he hears, and what he touches, or tries to touch. According to the lore, the king broke one of her three conditions when, aroused by the sight of her, he interrupted her meditation in an attempt to have sex. Ramanujan's talky, uneven rhythms suggest a domestic misunderstanding: the husband wants sex, while the wife—too bad for him—has her mind on something else.

So King Kausika thought. He thus missed what mattered to her, what matters to any Virasaiva devotee: the centrality of Siva in her life. He missed, we might add, what matters to poetry: the ability of the imagination to turn one thing into another, to say that the literal world we can touch with our bodies may not be the only one. In the octave, with its comic, belittling language, we see both the king and the poet-saint from his uncomprehending, lustful point of view.

If that octave was a comic, almost exasperated dismissal of love between mere human beings, the sestet, or septet (six plus one), flares up with the vigor that Mahadeviakka's own works display. Akka directs her eros toward the God she envisions; she is "hot for" him, but "cold to" her "mortal" spouse. Her "vision" replaces things literally seen and heard: the world of metaphor, where people meet gods, where no thing must be just one thing, replaces the literal frame of the unsatisfying marital bed. Siva, to Akka, is no mere matter, as her body and all bodies, with their arms, legs, and "all the rest," are mere matter. Instead, he is the "form of forms," a god who can take on any and every size, infinitesimal (like an embryo) or imposing (like the traditional Rider).

By the end of the poem, we have entered Mahadeviakka's vision: Ramanujan's ringing final lines imagine how we might feel if we could see what she sees. The king, reduced earlier to a spider (insignificant beside a bull), has disappeared. So has the literalism of the octave, which belonged only to him. Spiders in Hindu tradition may also imply the web of samsara, the deceitful material world, from whose enticements believers may strive to escape. From the defiant trimeter of the first line, with its triple prohibitions, Ramanujan's lines stretch out as Akka's experience expands beyond that world. Siva arrives at last, fully present to Akka, in the triumphant, and perfectly iambic, pentameter of the fifteenth and final line.

Had the sonnet concluded at line 14, with Siva as Rider, it would end with strong closure, a regular sonnet form, and a high, dignified, celebratory conclusion—Siva, the god, arriving on his traditional mount, a bull. Instead, Siva, once established as majestic, becomes at the same time domestic, allowing the bull he rides to chew its cud. Rider and Bull are at peace. Akka envisions the domestic security, and the untroubled, inspiring closeness to Siva, that her earthly husband had tried (very much in vain) to take away. The "extra" line for Siva's incarnation (stretching out the sonnet to fifteen lines) suggests the way that divine love exceeds human passion. But the final image and the homely final word bring that divine love, so to speak, down to earth. Lord Siva, for Akka, is anything but inaccessible; indeed, he is omnipresent, his comfort is everywhere, though she must nevertheless, and unceasingly, search for him.

Rods and cones, specialized cells on the human retina, process the light that enters the eye and send the resulting signals to the optic nerve. The terms, out of place in a poem about a medieval poet-saint, remind us that Ramanujan does not celebrate exactly what Akka celebrates. She cherishes the experience of the god; he, the human imaginative powers that (from a more or less secular point of view) allow her to see what she sees and to feel as she feels.

Ramanujan would have known Western parallels for this story, among them Yeats's sonnet "Leda and the Swan" (included in this volume; note the shared rhyme on "breast"), and the Annunciation, with its story of Jesus' "new birth." To compare Ramanujan's sonnet to Yeats's is to see how much power Akka has, how much her meeting with the Godhead is just what she wants, how well she knows exactly what she sees. But the rich references here are largely South Indian, and come from the polyglot writer's own traditions. The sonnet, with its unequal binary structure and its central turn, fits the structure of Mahadeviakka's life. Ramanujan's sestet, while it presents a moment in her vision, also reminds us what she did later on: Akka "threw away her modesty," both in the sense that she opened herself to Siva fully, and in the sense that she would forgo clothing as a sign of devotion to him.

Ramanujan makes this European form reflect the Indian English that he spoke and heard. Ramanujan grew up in Karnataka, in southern India, speaking English, Kannada, and Tamil at home. For most of his adult life, he taught at the University of Chicago. (Though his literary reputation rests on his verse in English, and on his translations into English, he wrote poems and fiction in Kannada as well.) The sonnet rhymes *aabb dccd ecf ecf e* ("ears" is not a line ending); almost all the rhymes take advantage of Ramanujan's non-rhotic Indian English, in which "Siva" rhymes with "never," "groom" with "Om," "earth" with "birth," and "rods" makes a near-rhyme with "backyard." (Such rhymes would also work in some British English, but not in the American English that came into daily contact with Ramanujan's own.)

The sonnet also revivifies bits of modern English that have become unremarkable, even clichés. "Bridegroom" does not ordinarily, any longer, connote the sort of groom who tends livestock; here it does—king Kausika has in effect groomed Akka for her true Rider, who soon enough arrives. Kausika "couldn't believe his ears," because the true vision of Siva comes not as sound but as vision (into Akka's eyes). Akka has waited for Siva to make the "first move," and his touch is of course "like nothing on earth," since it comes from heaven, though Siva himself will resemble (he will not be) something on earth, a Rider for his holy Bull. Most of these reanimated clichés occur in the octave; all occur in the "earthly" part of the poem, before the "new birth" that is the vision of Siva—and no wonder. They are the ordinary, too-ordinary language that achieves its full sense only in retrospect, after Akka has embraced the divine lover who allows her to leave them behind.

SB

"Into the Black"

JOHN HOLLANDER

1993

I was brought forth abroad at night, but not
To tally stars, consider the constellations
Or make the endless, pebbled calculations
Of every point and every half-seen spot;
But, looking up toward what had once been heaven,
To number and tell the spreading fields of dark,
Unharvestable, by which I would mark
The fate of my descendants six or seven
Generations hence, when grains of light
Ablaze in the dark ground of futuring sky
No longer come to life, no longer die
In their own fruitfulness: I have been sent
To found the new house of diminishment,
My growing tribe of emptiness and night.

IN THIS sonnet, the contemporary American poet John Hollander gives us a severe, poised estimation of the future of poetry. Hollander is a Jewish-American writer, and he has drawn on Jewish themes in several of his works (such as the remarkable sequence *Spectral Emanations*). "Into the Black" relies prominently on the Hebrew Bible (and, at one point, the Christian Gospels). But its real concern is literature, rather than religion. Hollander is an amply allusive poet, and we need to understand his allusions if we are to clarify his reflection on literary inheritance.

Hollander's sonnet joins a panoply of modernist works that wonder what art's task might be now. Does tradition have a future? The new work of art may well look utterly different from anything that has gone before: it provokes, even stuns, the audience. Artistic creation must be founded anew; in this forbidding new world, every writer starts from scratch. The governing paradox of Hollander's poem is that it is familiar in form (a sonnet), yet within this tightly controlled setting, it speculates about the unprecedented destiny of writing. "Into the Black" stresses the weight of literary inheritance in order to ask whether this inheritance can still serve us.

Hollander's most prominent subtext is biblical. In Genesis 15:4, God shows Abraham the night sky and tells him that his descendents will be innumerable as the stars. "Grains of light," Hollander's kenning for stars, evokes another prominent image used for Abraham's offspring in Genesis: seeds. Hollander's fields of heaven are "unharvestable"—cryptic expanses that refuse to yield any real hope for the future. In this respect, they differ from the sight of abundant destiny given to Abraham by God. In contrast to Abraham, the poet Hollander is sent forth to found a "new house of diminishment," not a flourishing nation that will be a blessing to its neighbors (the command given to Abraham's tribe). Hollander shares with Edgar Bowers, who also relies on the Hebrew Bible in "Jacob" (earlier in this book), a feeling for reduction, the straitened circumstances of contemporary poetry. For both these writers, the spare and primitive legends of the Bible supply a hardy, desert atmosphere befitting their ascetic sense of poetry's role.

Hollander, with his talk of "tally[ing] stars," invokes the most famous ode of the Roman poet Horace (*Odes* 1.11), in which he rejects the Babylonian practice of predictive astrology based on study of the constellations. Instead, Horace pronounces, "Carpe diem": pluck the day, delicately but decisively, as one would a flower—an alternative poignantly unavailable in Hollander's poem. Hollander also gestures toward a Jewish source. The Talmud frequently refers to Gentiles as "worshipers of stars and constellations," idolaters of mere knowledge (Hollander's "endless, pebbled calculations").

With his comments on the stars, Hollander nods as well in the direction of Whitman's "When I Heard the Learn'd Astronomer." Whitman rejects the classroom knowledge offered by astronomy, instead wandering off by himself to "the mystical moist night air" and gazing up at the stars. Hollander, like Whitman, spurns the work of a desiccated science, instead choosing a bold, solitary encounter with the unknown. But Hollander's night sky is neither mystical nor moist; it does not enfold the poet as in Whitman, answering his yearning. This poet, who gazes at "what had once been heaven," will "number and tell the spreading fields of dark." He watches over increasing darkness, and refuses to cling to the constellations of the past. Yet Hollander's poem is rich with references to these precursor texts. It needs the memory of the past, "ablaze" in the sky, as it readies itself for a purer "emptiness and night."

The sestet of "Into the Black" continues the poem's allusive journey. Hollander's phrase "die in their own fruitfulness" relies on the statement that John attributes to Jesus: "Verily, verily, I say unto you, Except a corn of wheat fall into the ground and die, it abideth alone: but if it die, it bringeth forth much fruit" (John 12:24). The sentence from John promises future plenty, a harvest of meaning predicated on the mortal fate of Jesus. In the Messiah's Passion, his suffering on the Cross, the isolation of a stigmatized death becomes the scene of life-bearing glory. But Hollander turns from the comfort promised by the Gospels, foreseeing a future "six or seven / Generations hence," when the word will sputter out, dwindling into nothingness like a dwarf star. The poet snatches a pared-down aesthetics from this bleak fate. The cold emptiness of the heavens, a scene of abandonment and lack of meaning, will leave us at sixes and sevens—metaphysically on edge, alert to a new blankness. Hollander takes pride in honing such austere privation. His "growing tribe" lengthens like a shadow, telling the lateness of the day.

Hollander's closing formulation recalls the School of Night, the shadowy Elizabethan Age club formed by Sir Walter Raleigh and his fellow poets. The word "tribe," which points toward the original national context in Genesis, in Hollander's usage brings to mind the stringent, forbidding idea of poetry announced by nineteenth-century French avant-gardist Stéphane Mallarmé: to purify the language of the tribe.

With "Into the Black" Hollander gives us a wry, anxious work of late modernism. His dense allusiveness renders all the more moving the thin future he foresees for poetry. Hollander sums up the poet's prospects sternly and honestly, and leaves us with only his rigorous eloquence as consolation.

DM

"Necrophiliac"

ROSANNA WARREN

1993

More marrow to suck, more elegies
to whistle through the digestive track. So help
me God to another dollop of death,
come on strong with the gravy and black-eyed peas,
slop it all in the transcendental stew
whose vapors rise and shine in the nostrils of heaven.
Distill the belches, preserve the drool as ink:
Death, since you nourish me, I'll flatter you
inordinately. Consumers both, with claws
cocked and molars prompt at the fresh-dug grave,
reaper and elegist, we collaborate
and batten in this strictest of intimacies,
my throat an empty sepulchre, my tongue
forever groping grief forever young.

"NECROPHILIAC," by the American poet and critic Rosanna Warren, can be usefully compared to May Swenson's "Staring at the Sea on the Day of the Death of Another" (earlier in this book). Swenson depicts death as open-mouthed, "gaping wide," heading for the poet who has been brooding over the loss of a friend. In Warren the poet eats, rather than being eaten. She gobbles up grief, impatient to turn human sorrow into material for poetry. Swenson places her own death fittingly, conscious that because we are mortal, we are humbled, anonymous. She does well by the dead, and becomes one of them. In "Necrophiliac," by contrast, Warren sees herself as an unjust practitioner, a poet-parasite who, as writer of elegies, lives off the sufferings of others. (*Stained Glass,* her 1993 collection in which "Necrophiliac" appears, contains several remarkable elegies, including a poem for her father, the writer Robert Penn Warren.) Warren's poem is a pained, even frenetic self-critique, by a poet who asks severe questions of her art. She is an especially allusive poet, as "Necrophiliac" demonstrates—one with a large appetite for the literary past.

At times it seems that poets write about nothing except sex and death (or, more decorously put, love and grief). Warren begins her sonnet with a frontal attack on the elegiac propensity and, by implication, the sexual one too. The sonnet's title and the drastic phrase "more marrow to suck" cast the use of the dead as a violation, an unsavory mixing of desire and mortal nature. Many a restaurant-goer (not necessarily vegetarian) has been taken aback by the eager devourer of *osso buco,* determined to extract every hidden remnant of flesh and blood from the unlucky animal's bone. Warren charges elegy-obsessed bards with a similar rapacity. Thoreau remarked in *Walden* that his aim was to "live deep . . . to suck the marrow of life." Bone marrow is good peasant fare, and highly nutritious; but Warren, unlike Thoreau, makes eating it seem greedy and crude—the grabbing of what should remain inward, hidden. Thoreau was a particular man, with an inborn delicacy. Alluding to his phrase, Warren contrasts his aloof project with the manner of the hungry elegist, sleeves rolled up and ready to dig in.

Warren's phrase "whistle through the digestive track" (not "tract," but "track"—a railroad image) nods in the direction of the greatest elegy in English, Milton's "Lycidas." Milton depicts a flock of sheep "swoll'n with wind, and the rank mist they draw," plagued with intestinal gas because attended by bad shepherds (corrupt priests, in Milton's analogy). Milton attributes this indigestion to the bad care given by a degraded clergy, who speak foul words, windy and empty. The flock gets no substantial food.

Warren attaches Milton's denunciation to the elegist herself. Her request for a second helping goes along with a parody of oath-taking ("So help / me God to another dollop of death"). She begs for more death, and feeds off what others experience as disaster. ("The words of a dead man / Are modified in the guts of the living," Auden writes in his elegy for Yeats.) In its first five lines, Warren's sonnet moves from "help" to "dollop" to "slop," a downward trek into a morass of gluttonous consumption. (All those messy *oh*'s and *ell*'s mimic noisy eating.) The elegist's responses, Warren tells us, are from hunger. He is desperate for good, meaty material.

In this first quatrain, Warren implies a hearty southern meal ("come on strong with the gravy and black-eyed peas"). The glutinous, gloppy nature of such home cooking gives us a feeling of indiscriminate cramming, the work of a ravenous maw. Warren's rhymes—"elegies" and "peas," "stew" and "you"—deflate any pretense to nobility. The effect of the rhymes is accentuated by their rareness; only the first and last lines of the opening two quatrains, along with the concluding couplet, are rhymed.

The poem itself comes on strong at this point, as it begins its second quatrain. In line 6, Warren burlesques God's reaction to Noah's sacrifice. After exiting the ark, Noah builds an altar and offers animal sacrifices to God, who "smell[s] a sweet savour," and who then agrees not to bring another such ruin on mankind (Genesis 8:21). Here Genesis remembers Near Eastern cult practice; the Mesopotamian gods delight in the smell of sacrifices (as do the Greek deities). But the Hebrew prophets announce that the Lord cannot be bribed in this way; he delights not in sacrifices, but in the pious deed and the clean heart. Warren sides with the prophets, criticizing her own dependence on sacrificial death—the way she turns real loss into symbolic gain. Death is ineradicable; it cannot be made good by therapeutic ceremony. Like the pledge "so help me God," "rise and shine" is a cliché, jaunty and deeply inappropriate, that the poet turns against herself.

"Death, since you nourish me, I'll flatter you / inordinately": so Warren begins her sestet. She compliments death—unlike Donne, who thundered "death, thou shalt die" in his Holy Sonnets. *Tempus edax rerum,* "time the eater of things," is a common Renaissance tag. Death, time's destination, is the great omnivore. The poet keeps pace with its devouring.

The partnership between death and the poet, "reaper and elegist," is further driven home by the word "batten" (in "we collaborate / and batten in this strictest of intimacies"). Warren again invokes Milton's "Lycidas." Milton pictures himself and Lycidas (the young, recently dead poet Edward King) "battening our flocks with the fresh dews of night" (they are shepherds, feeding their sheep well—battening them). By turning against the most familiar elegy in English, Warren hints at a corruption that stains the entire genre; in her sonnet, the poet-shepherd battens herself, in collaboration with the Grim Reaper. The closeness of poetry and mortality is a "strictest of intimacies," narrow and entwined. "Strict" comes from the Latin *strictum,* whose range of meanings speaks to Warren's sense. It can signify "drawn together," "pained," or "lopped off." (The near-homonym *strictim,* also relevant here, means "superficially" or "cursorily.")

Warren's closing couplet starts out harsh and provocative, but becomes tender, searching. "My throat an open sepulchre," the poet accuses herself. She powerfully evokes Psalm 5, in which the singer (by tradition King David him-self) pleads with the Lord to destroy his enemies: "For there is no faithfulness in their mouth; their inward part is very wickedness; their throat is an open sepulchre; they flatter with their tongue." Warren casts herself as the wicked, treacherous enemy of Psalm 5 (or of Romans 3:13, where Saint Paul uses the same image). She has flattered death. Her mouth is a sepulchre or tomb, open for the remains of the departed.

But the conclusion of "Necrophiliac" yields a surprise that changes every-thing. Now, in her last line, Warren turns toward the plangent. Her tongue is "forever groping grief forever young." The phrase strikes its path via allitera-tion and echo (of Keats's "Ode on a Grecian Urn"). This groping is not merely the work of appetite, as before. Rather, the poet tries to find fit utterance. Grief itself gropes, feeling for a way out, a way to survive alone. Warren has decided not to place a comma after "grief," and this omission lends her final line a pliant ambiguity. Grief, she allows herself to say, remains forever young, just like poetic expression. Keeping sorrow fresh (as the critic Edward Snow puts it) is what poets do, but it is also the enterprise of sorrow itself. Warren ends her poem not by swearing off elegy, but by turning toward it. Her art finds in grief renewed life—and not, this time, at the cost of the grieving themselves.

DM

"Party Dress for a First Born"

RITA DOVE

1995

Headless girl, so ill at ease on the bed,
I know, if you could, what you're thinking of:
nothing. I used to think that, too,
whenever I sat down to a full plate
or unwittingly stepped on an ant.
When I ran to my mother, waiting radiant
as a cornstalk at the edge of the field,
nothing else mattered: the world stood still.

Tonight men stride like elegant scissors across the lawn
to the women arrayed there, petals waiting to loosen.
When I step out, disguised in your blushing skin,
they will nudge each other to get a peek
and I will smile, all the while wishing them dead.
Mother's calling. Stand up: it will be our secret.

ALL THE poems in Dove's *Mother Love* (1995), as her prose note to the volume explains, retell or react to the Greek myth of Demeter and Persephone. Most of those versions and reactions are sonnets, alone or in narrative sequence. In the myth—familiar from Ovid's *Metamorphoses,* and retold many times since—Persephone is the nubile, virginal daughter of Demeter, the goddess of agriculture. The god of the underworld, Hades, sees Persephone gathering flowers in a field. He kidnaps her, takes her below the surface of the earth, and makes her his bride. Demeter, overcome with grief, stops making the crops grow and looks for her daughter instead: "Pitied by the other gods for the depth of her grief," as Dove writes in her note, Demeter "refuses to accept her fate." Zeus asks Hades to give the girl back. Persephone, however, has eaten six pomegranate seeds, and "anyone who partakes of the food of the dead cannot be wholly restored to the living. So she must spend half of each year at Hades' side." That half we call fall and winter: six months when crops do not grow, because Demeter grieves.

Dove has written ably of motherhood, of mothers' lives, before, notably in her 1986 sequence *Thomas and Beulah,* which followed the lives of her grandparents in Akron. Much of *Mother Love,* including its much-discussed sequence *The Bistro Styx,* shows mothers trying to understand uncommunicative runaway daughters, girls who have tried to grow up too soon. Here, though, Dove speaks for a daughter, with an estranged irony and a half-suppressed anger at mothers, at men, and at the conditions of human existence, which require that girls grow up. That anger gives the understated, colloquial sonnet its force. It becomes a sonnet not only about how mothers lose their daughters, but about how daughters address, and resist, and resent, the compromises involved in approaching maturity.

This "first born" is old enough to wear a "party dress," to attend a grown-up party, and to fit the part of Persephone (men can see her in sexual ways), though she is not what Americans now call adult; she must be in her teens. Dove's Persephone—so it seems to her—has no human interlocutor capable of understanding her frustration. She speaks neither to her mother, Demeter, nor to girls of her own age, nor to the adults outdoors. Instead, she addresses the garment she has not yet donned. The dress becomes a "headless girl," almost a younger sister ("I used to feel that way," she tells the dress). The dress-as-younger-sister might speak to the girl as the girl often speaks to her mother. Asked, "What are you thinking of?" she will answer, "nothing." (Literally the dress cannot answer at all.)

Why must this Persephone be a "first born"? Because no older sister can serve her as ally or guide. No one in her family, and no one out of it, can mediate the conflict between innocence and experience, between the already sexual, notionally independent, young woman and the dependent girl. That conflict makes it hard for this Persephone to think about her Demeter without violently mixed feelings. In the octave lie both of the simpler relations to the mother—unqualified repudiation, and unqualified embrace—that any daughter must abandon as she grows up. When she fled from some earlier distress, Persephone in her childhood "ran to my mother, waiting radiant / as a cornstalk." At that point in her life, her mother could solve any problem, could provide all the consolation she might need. "Nothing else mattered: the world stood still." (When, later, Demeter goes in search of her daughter, the world will "stand still" in another sense: no crops will come from it.)

Dove has said of her own childhood, "I wanted to be on my own, but I wanted to be held too. It was just unseemly to be held" by a parent; "You are supposed to grow up." The mythic Persephone, girl for half the year, underworld bride for the other half, is for Dove the contemporary adolescent, neither child nor adult, uncomfortable in either world. The octave looks back to childhood, to a life inseparable from the mother; the sestet, to an uncertain adult future. The daughter who speaks in the octave to the dress she has not yet put on seems already to know (alas) what will happen to her once she meets her fated man. Her mother, who asks her to join the party, knows too. As mother to daughter, so daughter to empty dress: the dress exists both prior to experience (not yet put on) and as a body already traumatized, "headless," and—like the daughter—"ill at ease."

Getting dressed reluctantly, ambivalent about her body and about her mother, Dove's Persephone sees little good in the adult world outdoors. The men "stride like elegant scissors," the women like flowers not quite in bloom, though about to be cut (Milton in *Paradise Lost* describes Persephone picking flowers, "herself the fairest flower"). She resents their apparently undamaged adulthood ("they" and "them," in the sestet, include both "women" and "men"). In that resentment, her mother is not quite an enemy, but also no ally—since she insists that Persephone come outdoors, put on the dress, meet the men on the lawn.

A simpler, happier, less interesting poem would see in Persephone's emergence into the adult world, her decision to put on the dress, what the cultural critic Ilana Nash calls a "chrysalis moment," the girl emerging from her cocoon into happily heterosexual, available womanhood. Just that moment is what Dove's Persephone puts off, refuses, and undercuts. This Persephone lives and speaks, as the people in some of Sylvia Plath's early poems also speak, from a liminal, wary, already damaged state, at once defensive and exposed (she has yet to put the dress on), now unable to live in a world defined by childhood (a world where mothers are always there). She is also unwilling to mingle with the adults, and unsure how she might benefit from their attention; sex will lead to a captivity more constraining than her own bedroom. To be taken into, or onto, a bed is for her to be beheaded, to become like something that somebody else can wear.

That the girl will seem, to the party guests, beautiful is no consolation to her; indeed, she thinks what they admire will be her "disguise." Yet she cannot simply disobey her mother's call to go outside, to "step out," to grow up (a call that must evoke ambivalence in mothers too); she owes her mother that much. She will, however, remain in something like internal exile from the world of parties and lawns, with an inner refusal she shares only with the garment that is her alter ego, her "disguise," her second skin. The men outside will know her solely by surface, by "blushing" politesse, by manner. That inner rebellion is—in a term with overtones (but no more than overtones) of child sexual abuse—"our secret."

This inner resistance, for Dove (who also wrote two poems entitled "Adolescence"), characterizes the teen years, at least for girls. Its irony, its way of presenting one face to the world and another to its own double, characterizes the best of Dove's poetry too. Dove's preface to *Mother Love* explains, "The sonnet defends itself against the vicissitudes of fortune by its charmed structure, its beautiful bubble. All the while, though, chaos is lurking outside the gate." Not chaos but irony inhabits these frequently off-rhymed, near-metrical lines. The sonnet seems to rhyme *axxxbbxx cxcxax,* with "bed"-"dead," "ant"-"radiant," and "lawn"-"skin" the only euphonious pairs. When we look harder at Dove's lines, though, we can see a subtler pattern: most of the "unrhymed" line-endings rhyme with words a syllable or two away from the endings of other lines: "plate . . . waiting," "field . . . world," "loosen . . . blushing . . . wishing," and "peek . . . secret." These odd nonrhymes half-resist, half-embrace, the dictates of the sonnet form, as this daughter half-resists, half-embraces—literally puts on—the "skin," the costume and manner, of the grown-up woman. Dove's sonnet mingles among older, more traditional sonnets, as Persephone mingles at the party, "headless dress" fastened around her, facing the grown-ups with a blush and a smile, "all the while wishing them dead."

SB

"in winter"

MICHELE LEGGOTT

1999

she was playing in a meadow I could not see

and fell miraculously past jeopardy and speech

everything was lost   we stepped off the railway

into an extension of the great landscape preparing

to forget our existence   the world was nothing

but planes and mirrors that link and space

the sugars of its invention   of meat and drink

at that dark table she took not and now like the rose

dances with all her body because the little seeds

have not been found   *destructive dove* or

fearful one walking in the gardens of the dead

when you pick the red fruit breathless risk

darts in at the gate again   swallow swallow

the stories black about you in the rainy air

THIS evocative poem comes into focus once we see the Greek myth it de-
scribes. The New Zealand–based Leggott takes her place in a long line of po-
ets who address the story of Demeter and Persephone, featured briefly in *Par-*

adise Lost (4.269–271) and retold at length, in very different tones, by the modern American poets H.D., Louise Glück, and Rachel Zucker, as well as by Rita Dove (in the previous poem in this volume). Leggott's sonnet would make no sense without the story, yet it would be wrong to call the myth a story that the poet *retells*. Instead, she uses pieces of the story, frames and moments taken from versions of it, almost as if she were writing about film stills. Her technique, full of ambiguous syntax and without punctuation, owes something to the American modernist Louis Zukofsky, on whose truly hermetic late poems about flowers Leggott wrote a scholarly book. Yet Leggott's own poem (like her other sonnets on mythic and erotic subjects) ends up neither hermetic nor scholarly. Its slippery phrases sound, instead, almost as if the poet were describing a dream.

Dove, in "Party Dress for a First Born," spoke for Persephone; Leggott becomes a modern Demeter, relating her loss, her woe, and her later visions first to third parties (to friends, to the other gods) and then to her daughter. Persephone ("she") was playing in a meadow unseen, and then Persephone ("she") "fell miraculously" (that is, through a god's intervention), out of the daylight realm of words and sense. Leggott-Demeter sought her "lost" daughter (who meant "everything" to her) in a modern world that includes railways; she risked death (nonexistence, the forgetfulness brought on by the river Lethe) to find her. That quest lent the poet-mother new respect for the chthonic force that Hades seems to exert.

Persephone's descent was not simply a kidnapping (so Leggott implies) but a willing investigation, by a curious young woman, of whatever experience lies behind the "planes and mirrors," the thin customs and illusory surfaces, that make up the civilized world. For Leggott, poetry is itself such an investigation—one in which mothers, not only daughters, and not only men, partake. The myth of Persephone also runs throughout the works of Robin Hyde (1906–1939), the passionate late-Romantic New Zealand poet, journalist, and autobiographer whose verse Leggott has edited. Hyde fought mental illness but finally killed herself—her poems can pursue the attractions of oblivion. Hyde wrote a book called *Persephone in Winter,* and a story called "Six Pomegranate Seeds." In that story, Hyde writes, "Persephone is torn. She runs back when her mother calls her name . . . but she has eaten the six seeds in the land of the dead and wants to go under the earth again." In Leggott's own sonnet, both Demeter as mother, and Leggott as belated editor, try to imagine Persephone's choice.

Sometimes hushed and wary, sometimes eager, Leggott's phrases can sound both incantatory and uncanny, in touch with sources reason never knows. The ancient "Homeric Hymn to Demeter," which tells the Persephone story, also describes the origin of the Eleusinian Mysteries. The sense of congress with the unknown, of access to mysteries (not only the mystery of sex), becomes the other subject for Leggott's poem, the topic by which she complicates what would otherwise be a far simpler story of loss and recompense. Those mysteries involve both sex and death:; indeed, they constitute the link between them. In order to enter the adult world—in order, even, to become able to love—we must cease to be purely children, must give up our inarticulate childhood belief that we will live forever. To grow up is to sit down at the "dark table," to go into the dark. Discovered in the underworld, Persephone has become not only a flower on its stem, but ripe red fruit. She also becomes not "she" but "you," as if only after the child's fall into experience could parent and child truly converse. Persephone dances because, even once found (rescued) by the daylight gods, her sexual initiation, her fall into experience, cannot be reversed. The seeds she ate are gone for good—and part of her is glad.

What parent can truly accept a child's eventual autonomy, her freedom to take a risk? What responsible parent would not aspire—someday, if never quite today—to accept it? Leggott's Demeter speaks directly to her daughter, but the poet also speaks to herself and to her readers, trying to do justice to the "breathless risk" that sexual experience entails. The story of Persephone— so the changing verb tenses suggest—takes place over and over, is always taking place. That perpetual reenactment emphasizes not kidnapping (much less rape), but the later encounter of mother and daughter, and the difficult listening proper to each.

Yet the poem does not wholly avoid the sexual violence in its ancient sources. Leggott takes "swallow swallow" from T. S. Eliot's *The Waste Land,* and Eliot took it from Ovid, where it denotes (in the story of Philomela) a bird-cry meant to denounce a brutal assault. Some male modernists (D. H. Lawrence, for example) can postulate sexual violence as the cost (well worth it) of initiation into bodily mysteries. Leggott does not endorse such an account, but she does not dismiss it entirely either: the girl's difficulty in understanding what has happened, in accounting to her own satisfaction for the connections between desire and violence, offers another topic for this thorny poem. Leggott decouples sex from male dominance, however, by depicting only mother and daughter. Neither Hades himself, nor even a masculine pronoun, appears anywhere in this poem.

Uncertainty in the octave seemed inseparable from panic and vertigo. In the sestet the uncertainty, the sense that the lines exceed any prose meaning, reflects instead Persephone's, and Demeter's, realization that they have become part of a ritual—that they occupy, willy-nilly, sacred space. Leggott concludes this largely ametrical poem by acknowledging that sacred space. Her final line sounds like a magic spell: a balanced iambic hexameter ("the stóries bláck abóut you | ín the ráiny áir") with a rapt set of liquid consonants (*r*'s and *n*'s) and semivowels (the *y* in "you"). "About you" means both "concerning you" and "around you" (as birds fly "about," or around, buildings and grounds). The spell lies in the effect of the "stories" themselves, the stories about Persephone—about fertility and adolescence and mystery, about growing up and discovering risk and death—which have survived their first tellers by thousands of years.

So full of voids, occlusions, vague patches, and darkened air, the poem may also consider another loss. During the late 1990s, Leggott was gradually losing her eyesight to the progressive degenerative disease retinitis pigmentosa: she entitled the book that contains this sonnet *as far as I can see*. The descent of Persephone, and Demeter's quest for her, give Leggott not only a way to investigate the link between sexual adulthood and consciousness, but a way to investigate her own loss of sight. The poet sees herself going down into darkness; without macular (central) sight, she must use what remains of her peripheral vision—her waning ability to see edges, corners, margins, boundaries between light and dark. Almost every line suggests an ocular failure, from "I could not see" to "nothing / but planes and mirrors" (how "the world" looks to the visually impaired), to the air of line 14. The "air" of Leggott's poem can thus fill up not with sharply defined shapes (much less with a story's details), but with hints and shades and parts of "stories," as the failing eye gives place to the ear.

SB

Voiced Stops I

FORREST GANDER

2001

Summer's sweet theatrum! The boy lunges through

The kitchen without comment, slams the door. An

Elaborate evening drama, I lug his forlorn weight

From floor to bed. Beatific lips and gap-

Toothed. Who stayed late to mope and swim, then

Breach chimneys of lake like a hooked gar

Pressing his wet totality against me. Iridescent

Laughter and depraved. Chromatic his constant state. At

Ten childhood took off like a scorched dog. Turned

His head to see my hand wave from a window, and I too saw

The hand untouching, distant from. What fathering-

Fear slaked the impulse to embrace him? Duration:

An indefinite continuation of life. *I whirled out wings.* Going

Toward. And Lord Child claimed now, climbing loose.

THE FIRST in a series of sonnets about the poet's teenaged (here, just barely teenaged) son, this one depicts a sullen temper tantrum, and starts with an exasperated exclamation. It first deplores, and then tries hard to celebrate, the tumultuous moods and swift changes of early adolescence, which make the boy both tender and uncontrollable, wild and tame, confined and free.

Gander begins with an odd word, and an exclamation: "theatrum" (a rare Latinate word that means simply "playhouse" or "theater") introduces the theatricality of the boy's gesture as he leaves the room, as if he had slammed a stage door. The son falls asleep, every night, on the hard bedroom floor; the father enters, later, to pick him up and place him in bed. The boy who wants to grow up fast moves out of the kitchen, only to shut himself into his bedroom each night. What goes up, the poet implies, must come down. Every display of independence, at that age (perhaps twelve or thirteen), precedes a compensating proof of dependence, after the boy has exhausted his energies.

Yet Gander does not convey balance, much less stability. Instead, he shows a father trying hard to keep up. Both unrhymed quatrains revel in enjambments: lines end on articles, on prepositions, on adjectives parted from their appropriate nouns. Three lines in the octave begin a new clause on the last syllable. The boy moves through these lines unstably, and fast. Gander compares his son to a gar, a kind of pike you might catch while fishing, especially in the southeastern United States. The boy shows striking physical affection; "pressing his wet totality against me," he swims up like a caught fish, in a lake that includes underwater rock formations ("chimneys"). The son's moods, and the actions of his body, vary wildly, as the colors vary on fish scales, at one moment "iridescent" in sunlight, at the next in shadow, as if "depraved" (a word whose etymology includes the sense "crooked," "turned aside"). The octave describes and even imitates his constant physical action and his ever-shifting moods, "chromatic" because they change their figurative color (as we call moods blue, or bright, or dark). Gander also plays on a usage from music, in which "chromatic" melodies include notes that do not belong to their assigned key.

Now that father and son interact tumultuously, now that their life together involves regular moping, lunging, and perhaps a sulk, the poet seems to have set himself two tasks: first, to depict the boy's energetic and unceasing changes; second, to examine his own, newly mixed feelings about the teen who wants to put some distance, some of the time, between them. The boy moves to leave his childhood behind, even as he acknowledges the bonds of love that remain. The sestet makes as if to leave syntax behind; it flaunts grammatical omissions and "mistakes": a main verb ("Turned") lacks a grammatical subject—an error in standard English, but ordinary usage in many languages (including Spanish, from which Gander has translated many contemporary poems).

"Turned" introduces a phrase that ends with a preposition ("distant from"), the longest and the most important of the fragmentary or ungrammatical sentences. The son, departing (perhaps on a school bus, for summer camp), will turn his head to see his father wave, but will not himself wave back. To return the wave would be, for this boy, too soppy, too boyish, too much affection to show at once; it would acknowledge the dependence that the teen sometimes wants to deny. It is the kind of gesture that works on film, and Gander has tried to replicate it in the awkward, almost-mirroring, almost-chiasmatic shape of this almost-sentence ("hand . . . wave . . . window . . . saw . . . hand"). The sonnet has moved back through the recent past, from the evening incident that prompted the poem ("The boy lunges through the kitchen") to the memory of a trip to the lake, to the older memory of the wave, the moment when "childhood took off." The poet and father then tries to move forward again, to say that his son's childhood has not been abandoned so much as completed by the present, difficult season.

We know more or less where adolescence begins—with the unreturned wave goodbye. But how and when, in a current American family, does adolescence end? Gander implies that we cannot know. His son's life (like any life close to us, viewed rightly) is not so much a departure from prior joy as a "Going/Toward." Gander's italics cite, and render secular, the strongly patterned lines in which Gerard Manley Hopkins described his own back-and-forth, up-and-down, and finally exhilarating love for a Christian God: "I whirled out wings that spell/And fled with a fling of the heart to the heart of the Host" ("The Wreck of the Deutschland"). The poem, with its creative iridescences, also recalls Hopkins's "As kingfishers catch fire" (included earlier in this book), paying homage to the unique inscape, or instress, that Gander has found in his son.

No one would mistake Gander's rhythms for Hopkins's, but the contemporary American father has certainly learned from—and, in the alliteration of the sestet, imitated—the Victorian Jesuit: the outright quotation, late in the poem, gives credit where due. As Christ, in Hopkins's poem, sees himself in "just men," as Hopkins pays homage to his Christian Lord, so Gander—a father who might see himself in his child—credits the energies of his "Lord Child," dependent and independent at once. Gander's extreme syntactic fragmentation, and the jittery uncertainty (like that of a nervous parent), which the syntax suggests, renders credible what might otherwise be a too-sweet conclusion. The jitters of a parent confronting early adolescence, and the protean energies of "Lord Child" himself, are liberated into the closing emphasis of the sonnet. The teen, eager at times to escape from his father, remains the child whom this father knows as his own.

SB

Radial Symmetry 3

TONY LOPEZ

2003

It was a chill, blue-fingered hour and the gardens
Were nearly empty, as will often be true
In structured or viscous populations. After
Some agonising moments with hairpins, we
Attended to a paper on rapid changes
In the geological record. These "pages"
Were not pages at all, but information dumps
Big as Bayreuth backdrops. Such variation
May be "factored out" to reveal a new reading
Of male relationships running through the book.
Stylish, slim M, played with immense authority
Seals his grip on the party. Pools of selected
Mutant genes produce a tremendous performance
Of baffled resentment: a cow for a few beans.

THE FORM of the sonnet developed alongside, and even helped to build up, the idea that each of us has an inward self, an authentic soul, separable from social circumstance. But not all poets who write sonnets believe this idea; some wonder whether the self is a kind of illusion, and lyric sincerity a bourgeois trap. Much of the poetry we now read, these writers contend, conceals what a better-informed poetry should reveal: the impersonal, often oppressive sources and powers within the language we use. That language (they also contend) is shaped and constrained by economic inequity, by the structure of the nuclear family, and by other social, ecological, even biological constraints. A poetry that points out such constraints, that helps us notice and push back against them, ought to be difficult, demanding, dissonant, with the bracing pleasures that dissonant music brings. It ought, as well, to inculcate not trust but skepticism, to help us learn to suspect all the language we see.

The British poet and critic Tony Lopez writes just such poetry; his sets of sonnets stitch together disparate kinds of language in ways calculated to grate, startle, and jar. Lopez's confusing transitions evoke emotions that arise from his counterintuitive claims—emotions such as outrage, weariness, and disbelief. Like a composer of atonal music, Lopez makes lines whose appeal can depend on the beauties and unities that they reject. And yet, as in much atonal music, the poems keep swerving back toward just the older patterns they attack. Those swerves and approximations create the tension between humanism and antihumanism, between the illusion of a unified, speaking self and antipathy toward any such illusion, that supports so much of Lopez's work—a tension Lopez himself has described in the sonnets of Ted Berrigan. This sonnet in unrhymed pentameters, the third in his sequence *Radial Symmetry*, demonstrates Lopez's disconcerting technique, indebted to Berrigan but colder, more intellectual, and less intimate than Berrigan ever could be. Lopez's colliding phrases and registers juxtapose humanistic and quantitative disciplines, personal and impersonal ways of knowing, as if to encourage us not to trust either one.

Lopez begins in a lonely place, perhaps at twilight or daybreak, when "blue-fingered" light brings a chill—a place fit for late nineteenth-century poetry, perhaps a palace or an estate (not one garden, but "gardens"). Having presented such a traditional (one might even say "poetic") locale, Lopez then switches to an impersonal register drawn from evolutionary biology (where "viscous populations" are those that disperse slowly). The people who gather outdoors in Lopez's "gardens" may be listening to scientific papers, even while they attend a party, or wait in a garden for one to begin. These activities, like the registers of language in which Lopez presents them, do not fit well together—perhaps we cannot imagine someone doing all these things (hearing papers on population biology in an aristocrat's garden at dawn), or taking in all this information at once. Indeed, "information overload," the contemporary presence of more data and more explanations than we can handle, is one of Lopez's subjects.

Someone who has "agonising moments with hairpins" may give hairpins, or poems, or matters of art, style, and taste in general, far more power than they deserve. Someone who hears "a paper on rapid changes / In the geological record," on the other hand, attends not to moment-by-moment shifts in fashion, but to alterations in the whole earth over time. Such changes seem far more important than hairpins, but they require us to abandon our sense of human interest, and of human scale: "rapid" in geological time can mean tens of thousands of years.

Lopez thus sets up a contrast between the language of the arts, of individual experience (gardens, hairpins) and the impersonal, quantitative disciplines (evolutionary biology, geology). If the humanities are agony over hairpins, the sciences are information dumps, big sets of alienating data whose gigantism suggests (in a turn back to the arts) Wagnerian opera as performed at Bayreuth. Wagner imagined his *Ring* cycle as a "total artwork" *(Gesamtkunstwerk),* incorporating not just music but drama, costume, architecture, and other fields of design. Is a "total artwork" possible now? Would it include, or surrender to, the statistical methods that scientists use? Neither personal and humanistic, nor impersonal, scientific, statistical methods satisfy this poet, whose almost deadpan tone rejects them both.

Lopez prints this sonnet (and all his sonnets) as an unbroken fourteen-line block of verse. Its scumbled texture makes it hard to identify one volta, one central turn. We might, though, find a turn, a "variation," in his eighth line: the passage that begins there introduces, first, a "reading," then "male relationships," and then something like a character—the charismatic, perhaps malevolent "M." (The eponymous "M." of Fritz Lang's famous 1931 film was a serial killer, but nothing here identifies this M. with that one.) The party that this M. controls ("with immense authority") does not sound like much fun. Indeed, that gathering might prompt "baffled resentment." The poet has made bad use of his time and energy, made a shameful trade ("a cow for a few beans"), by choosing to attend.

So we might conclude if we seek a consistent depiction of one scene, with one speaker at its center. Lopez's sonnets, though, resist such readings. As often as they evoke an emotion ("baffled resentment," for example), they take it back, reminding us that they are made out of incompatible, preexisting discourses, trends, sets of words, and that the individual, with his or her emotions, might not be the right unit of analysis for whatever the poem ought to address.

In the tale "Jack and the Beanstalk," the odd trade turned out well. Jack planted the beans, climbed the stalk, slew the giant, and brought back gold. Is the poet "Jack," having traded the clearer satisfactions of more mellifluous poetry for a new structure that will bring new rewards? Is that tale, with its riches at the end, the right analogy for aesthetic reward, or does the analogy simply show how capitalism, money, and exchange-value have come to control our thought? In an age of sociobiology and genetic engineering, should "Jack and the Beanstalk" make us think not of money, nor of poetic justice, but of mutant beans? What to do with a sonnet that seems, at times, to portray a bad party, at other times to make no propositional sense, and finally to describe, in its flat tones of disillusion, the "bafflement" that a frustrated reader might feel?

We can find the questions, though not their answers, in the colliding discourses and dissonances that inhabit Lopez's poem. We can also find implicit emotions: expectation, small-scale "agony," attention, anticipation, restlessness (during a long "information dump"), and a curt "resentment" at last. The poet—the implied author of this poem, if not quite its implicit speaker—ends up as a Jack who has not climbed his beanstalk, who does not yet know if his trade will prove worthwhile. That trade may be the one offered by some scientists, and by some writers of literary and cultural theory, in which structures, data sets, "backdrops," rather than people, cause action. It may also be the trade made by avant-garde poets, who substitute the pleasures of disjunction, disconnection, and even bafflement for what older kinds of lyric can give. The poem ends with sounds that imply sudden resolution—emphatic monosyllables and a final spondee ("few beans"), after many inert and abstract words. Yet emotional or intellectual resolution, for the questions the poem implies, seems farther off than before the sonnet began.

It would be simplistic to praise a chaotic poem for describing a chaotic state of mind, a mess for representing a messy world. But Lopez's poem is not a mess. It is a partly nonmimetic use of language, a set of incompatible sentences that return over and over to one contrast (personal as against impersonal discourse, humanist as against scientific and quantitative explanations), to one problem (which of the two, if any, explains what we do?), and arguably even to one setting (a group of people assembled outdoors, attending to "data" that remind them of art). Unresolved binaries, and unanswered questions, have animated Lopez's challenging poem.

SB

"Flirrup"

MARY DALTON

2003

Fairy squalls on the water.
I'm marooned at the window,
Waiting for the fog man,
Sewing the old black veil.
The Walls of Troy on the floor.
There's Dickey just gone up
The road in a red shirt. He's
Sure not the fog man—
Traipsing along with the swagger
Of a swiler in the spring fat.
Not a feather out of him.
Now he'd be the one to have in
For a feed of fresh flippers,
A taste of my fine figgy cake.

LIKE MOST of the poems in Dalton's book *Merrybegot* (whose title is New-foundland English for "love child" or "bastard") the unrhymed "Flirrup" de-picts the speech of Newfoundland, its tones and attitudes, its residents and their lives, through words that the poet (herself a lifelong resident) finds both in the speech she has long heard, and in documents of Newfoundland folklore and language. The island's lore and language reflect its cold, changeable Atlan-tic weather, its Celtic heritage, its long dependence on fishing, and its geo-graphic and cultural distance from the remainder of Canada, a nation the is-land joined only in 1949. Those elements animate Dalton's curt, yet passionate, amorous poem.

Dalton draws often on the *Dictionary of Newfoundland English (DNE)*, recently made available online (www.heritage.nf.ca/dictionary). There we learn that "flirrup" = "flare-up," a torch on a wharf or on a platform built for the processing of newly caught fish. The seen, manmade fire of industry on the wharf makes a contrast with the heard, and natural or supernatural (not, anyway, industrial), "fairy squalls." Once we have tracked down the rest of Dalton's folklore, and looked up the rest of her words (a Newfoundland native would not need to track them down), we can hear, and see, in her sonnet a clear twofold scene, one whose division into indoor and outdoor, present and future, actual and imagined, matches the sonnet's familiar twofold division into octave and sestet. We can see, in that division, passion frustrated, and then passion imaginatively expressed—"another sort of flare-up," as the poet herself writes.

"The fog man" is a legendary figure who controls the weather, especially the ferocious fogs. The folklorist Barbara Reiti writes that on Newfoundland's shores, "temperatures can drop many degrees in hours, and blinding storms whip up with little notice. Even more unpredictable are the drifts of fog which, at any season, shift the landscape . . . when not obscuring it entirely." Here the fog, and the fog man, have not yet come, though squalls on the ocean suggest that they are on their way, and night (if a "flirrup" is visible) may soon fall. Dalton's speaker, looking out her window, is perhaps a widow, perhaps a woman whose husband is out at sea. While men sail, hunt seals, go out fishing, or process fish, women cook or sew, "marooned" at home. Traditional Newfoundland women also drew intricate patterns in sand on kitchen floors; one such pattern was called the "Walls of Troy." If Dalton's woman recalls Homer's Penelope, weaving all day (and undoing her weaving at night) while she hopes her seafaring husband will return, she also recalls Andromache, looking out for her doomed husband, Hector, from the walls of Homer's Troy.

Dalton's Newfoundland woman sees no ancient hero, no husband, no supernatural menace ("fog man"). Instead, she sees something, or someone, more fun: a sexy local man, Dickey, whose bright shirt sets him off against any gray portent of weatherborne harm. This strong man who walks "up / The road" (rather than going out to sea) looks as confident as a "swiler," or sealer. "The sealer," writes Dalton, "is the man who can provide for his family in the lean . . . month of March," when herds of fat seals could be brought in, with luck, from the ice. ("Not a feather out of him," Dalton also explains, is an idiom meaning "unruffled.")

This manly outdoor adventurer comes as the opposite of Dalton's indoor speaker, and seems endowed with the powers her household seems to lack. She finds him charming; she wants to invite him in. In her house, he would find a traditional Newfoundland spring feast: seal flippers and "figgy cake." Both sight and hearing yield, in the sestet, to taste, as "stage" and shore yield to kitchen (and perhaps to bed). Seal flipper, says a 1969 memoir quoted in the *DNE,* is not the paw but "the front shoulder, corresponding to a shoulder of lamb or a shoulder of pork, except that it is much tastier," "so tender that you can cut it with a fork, and of a hearty, gamy flavour like that of wild duck." Figgy cake (actually a festive cake with raisins) would complete such a hearty meal. The fire on shore, the fire of men's occupations, can no more than equal the warm delight of the woman's indoor oven, or the friendly heat of her acknowledged lust.

Dalton's last six lines compile praise—for Dickey, for the proverbial successful Newfoundland "swiler" (Dickey may not be one, but he looks like one), for this speaker's culinary gifts, for the island's foodways. That praise concludes with a fusillade of fricatives: the poem began with fire, with the *f* of "flirrup," "fairy," "fog," "floor," but carries no more than one *f*-sound per line early on. Dalton's last two lines, bringing Dickey indoors, accompany him with *f*'s so thick and fast that their puckers suggest a kiss: "feed," "fresh," "flippers," "figgy," "fine." As Dalton began her sonnet with folkloric menace and danger outdoors, she concludes with equally regional, equally characteristic figures for indoor bodily pleasure. Her celebration of dialect concludes with wish-fulfillment, with hunger—and sexual hunger—imagined as satisfied.

But the couple are not satisfied; she does not (yet) bring him to bed, they do not share her food. A sonnet that began in the indicative concludes in the realm of conjecture: "he'd be the one" (a verb phrase that carries, like much Newfoundland English, a Celtic tinge) means that he has not entered her house, has not eaten her cooking, and perhaps that he never will. Dickey may pass up the road by her window all unaware of what goes on in her house, in her heart. Dalton thus celebrates appetites even while those appetites go unmet. She celebrates, too, the culinary and decorative skills the bearer of those appetites may have, skills often neglected in favor of manlier talents, as dialect and folklore are often neglected in favor of more transferable language and art.

This unrhymed sonnet finds compromises between its insistently regional, proudly "provincial" language and the sonnet as an international, and urbane, form. The only rhyming sonnet in *Merrybegot* avoids dialect words. This unrhymed poem instead celebrates Newfoundland dialect, and revels in its triple

rhythms, as if to show that a poem of lust and longing in Newfoundland dia-
lect can rival the vigor of love poems anywhere. In pursuing sexual yearning—
in making a signal fire, an indoor song, to signify such yearning—Dalton and
her speaker do as Petrarch and Sidney, and Sidney's Astrophel, did. She makes
a lament that does not sound like a lament, a poem of isolation that concludes
with vividly imagined companionship: in fact, it concludes with a boast, as if
to say that her seal feast, her figgy cake, would keep Dickey with her, could
she once bring him inside. Such fulfillments, such fiery celebrations—of local
language and foodways, of imagination—are for Dalton and for the New-
foundlanders she depicts necessary offsets to perils of the weather, the fear of
dearth, the common lot of loneliness. Such fulfillments, on any shore, are part
of the catch that poetry can bring.

SB

"Homework. Write a Sonnet. About Love?"

ALISON BRACKENBURY

2004

There are too many sonnets about love.
First let us name, then freeze, their eager faults.
(Who is it whistles, piercingly, above?
By the dark fields, the engine shudders, halts.)
No lover ever worried about fame,
More than the pearls, which tumbled round her ears.
(It might be Russia, when the quick thaw came;
Down steel steps, with a bundle, she appears.)
Nor were they ever read without a yawn;
The one who longed for them received no word.
(Behind her fall the lights of the low town.
She leaves the tracks. She whistles like a bird.)
The sonnet has no room to make an end,
The poplars dance. She takes the sudden bend.

ALISON BRACKENBURY's witty "Homework. Write a Sonnet. About Love?" considers literary convention as a classroom assignment. The poet has been given a task: to write a sonnet, one of the most familiar literary forms, and one that often relies on predictable subject matter. As we have shown in this book, sonnets are wide-ranging in their concerns; they delve into history, politics, and social life. But the sonnet is originally associated with erotic love, and in the Petrarchan tradition, sonnet writers express their yearning for an adored, distant beloved. By questioning this tradition, Brackenbury opens a broad vista on poetry's assumptions about the world.

The poet begins with a straightforward judgment: "There are too many sonnets about love." The tradition, she says, is played out, stale and unrewarding. Brackenbury will produce a new kind of sonnet: one that points out the frequent limitations of the form, which (in her reading) offers us only a partial view of life. In line 2, she assumes the supercilious pose of a lecturer discoursing on the sonnet's drawbacks. "First let us name, then freeze, their eager faults," she writes. The speaker's cool-minded wish to catalogue the flaws of the conventional sonnet suggests a critique of the Petrarchan poet, who wants to impress us with the ardor he sets down in careful verse. To be both methodical and love crazed is, in Brackenbury's book, a fault that deserves correction. She prizes the open-ended and the unexpected, rejecting the coy mistress and sighing lover who play the lead roles in so much of poetic tradition.

Brackenbury's third line features an interruption. Here her poem begins to go off course (in a productive and deliberate way). The surprised poet listens to . . . not birdsong, nor the plaints of love, but a piercing whistle and a shuddering engine—a train stopping in "dark fields." The rather grim industrial landscape described here is an antipastoral touch on Brackenbury's part. She will take up into her imagination the train and its whistle; an incidental occurrence becomes a feature of her poem's design. In this respect Brackenbury may be thinking of an example set not by a poet but by a novelist: Virginia Woolf, whose fiction and essays often follow, with curious attachment, a seemingly trivial impression that then becomes the spur for rich fantasizing. The reader's hunch that Woolf is an implied presence in "Homework" is supported by what happens next: a series of allusions to the Russian novel, which was championed by Woolf. (In her essay "Modern Fiction," Woolf argues that the Russians convey life in all its dense, diverse details.)

"No lover ever worried about fame"—so begins the second quatrain of "Homework"—"More than the pearls, which tumbled round her ears." A telling detail, the pearls around the woman's ears, outshines the fame aimed at by the male lyric poet, who seeks to immortalize himself and his beloved in verse. Brackenbury here reflects on, and rejects, the Petrarchan blason, a description of the beloved's face in terms of predictable comparisons (often, her eyes are compared to stars, her cheeks to roses, and her teeth to pearls). Brackenbury offers us real pearls instead of metaphorical ones; she turns down the sonneteer's conventional hyperboles, and descends to real life.

This poem is about to become unfrozen, thanks to the parenthetical intrusion of a novelistic reality, the "quick thaw" of line 7. Like Kitty in *Anna Karenina,* Brackenbury's heroine descends the "steel steps" of her railroad car, carrying her luggage. An intriguing character has arrived, displacing the resistant, adored mistress and the frustrated amorous plot that Petrarchan sonnets rely on (consider the poems by Philip Sidney and Samuel Daniel in this collection). Such poetry is haunted by the static, strangely abstract image of the woman. In "Homework" she appears, by contrast, a lively, unexpected presence.

In the sestet, the poet returns to her low estimation of the love sonnet: "Nor were they ever read without a yawn." Such poems, Brackenbury charges, are misdirected. Instead of piquing the common reader's interest, they wear her out with their repetitive tropes, and they fail to communicate to the actual beloved, "the one who longed for them." In *The Defence of Poetry* (ca. 1581), Sidney writes, "Truly many of such writings, as come under the banner of unresistable love, if I were a mistress, would never persuade me they were in love: so coldly they apply fiery speeches." Conventional love poetry pretends to be a form of desire, speaking urgently to the erotic object. But what this object wants to hear, the poem cannot tell her. The Petrarchan poem's characteristic assignment of a subject and a set of tropes must be broken, so that it yields to the unpredictable. By freeing the woman from the love sonnet's game of desire, Brackenbury's poem frees itself as well.

As "Homework" moves toward its conclusion, its heroine leaves the gloomy evening and the "low town" behind—going where, we do not know. (Away from preset forms and plots, perhaps; she is a refugee from the fated tragedies of the Russian novel, as well as from the artificial conventions of lyric.) Her high spirits, with her bird-like whistling replacing the train whistle, transform the scene, earlier darkly overcast. "The poplars dance": the poet's whim, reflecting her heroine's impulsive, animated presence, is infectious. Even the landscape feels it.

With a spring in its step, "Homework" heads into its couplet ending. "The sonnet has no room to make an end," the poet tells us. Paradoxically, though sonnets pride themselves on their capacity for the conclusive (demonstrated most decisively in a final couplet), they do not command spaciousness enough to follow the fate of a character to a satisfying or sufficient end, as a novel can. "Room" here plays on the word "stanza," which means "room" in Italian, and on John Donne's remark in "The Canonization," "we'll make in sonnets pretty rooms." Donne's claustrophilic wish for a love sealed within the small space of poetic expression is countered, three and a half centuries later, by Brackenbury, who yearns for a new openness. The leading character in "Homework," the woman who is no longer the imprisoned beloved of tradition, has disappeared past a "sudden bend" in the road—and this unknown future looks like freedom.

DM

"Physicism"

LUCIE BROCK-BROIDO

2004

In the valley of the Euphrates, each
Of the stars had certain shepherds

To the people there. Here, in this small valley
Showered with emboli, we each have none.

Before the Babylonians, the sun was called
Old Sheep, the planets Old Sheep Stars.

There are blood sheep everywhere
But no shepherds left.
                          Only blood sisters here,
All with the color taken from their sight.

We live in black & white, material
And motherless beneath the concavity of sky.

Phenomenal in the long aortic pulse
Of equinox, a Sumerian describes his stars

Collectively as a flock and it is heavenly to him.
Here there is no heaven here.

LIKE MOST of the poems in Brock-Broido's collection *Trouble in Mind,* this unrhymed sonnet reacts to the death of the poet's mother. Its unruly lines suggest extremes of grief, impoverished in their insistent repetitions of single words ("stars," "sheep," "blood," "here), yet extravagant in their diction ("concavity," "aortic," "phenomenal"). The sonnet depicts, on the one hand, Brock-

Broido's versions of the people who lived at the start of Western civilization, "before the Babylonians," at the very invention of writing: the Sumerians of the Euphrates Valley, whose myths and beliefs are remote ancestors of our own. At the same time, it portrays, though with much less detail, present-day people who huddle together, bereft.

Some of the oldest prayers, and some of the sturdiest traditions of poetic complaint, portray sheep and their shepherds. The ancient Greek pastoral elegies of Theocritus, for example, and Milton's "Lycidas," imagine the deceased as a shepherd slain. The Sumerians were a sheep-keeping culture, and the familiar 23rd Psalm ("The Lord is my shepherd") has Sumerian and Akkadian parallels. "The people of the world, thou dost watch over," says an Akkadian prayer to Shamash, the sun god, "Thou art indeed their shepherd both above and below." The sun is Shamash or Utu, the lawgiver god, portrayed as a shepherd in some hymns (less often, he is the destroyer god Nergal or Erra). But the sun as "Old Sheep" or first among sheep, a bellwether, does not occur in any well-known ancient Near Eastern text. Neither does the link between plural shepherds and stars.

Fortified by traditions of pastoral, and of prayer, we might expect Brock-Broido to liken her modern mourners, the poet and her "blood sisters," to their ancient counterparts, who also sang and knew death. Instead, the Sumerian valley and "this small valley," where we live now, are stark opposites. Her Sumerians saw, and made sense of, an enchanted world: stars were like sheep, the sun like a bellwether, the gods like parents or like shepherds, to the stars. We mourners, we moderns, we motherless sisters, by contrast, look up at the stars and see nothing—no sheep-stars, and certainly not any shepherds. We cannot believe that gods oversee the cosmos, and so we feel even more lost than our distant predecessors could have felt when we confront the death of a parent, a human being whose care and authority organized our early life, as a shepherd organizes and cares for his flock.

The poem describes, in other words, a consequence of the premise that its title names: "Physicism," the belief that only the material, physical world is real. Confined to this earth, unable to look up at the stars and see anything we can comprehend in human terms, we may as well be unable to see the sky: "Here there is no heaven here." We may lose sleep over such a belief; we may, indeed, count sheep all night, to no avail, lying awake below our "black & white" sky.

The contrast between a religious, and happier, past and a disillusioned, regretfully secular present, is very far from being Brock-Broido's alone. Brock-

Broido's sonnet, like Joseph Blanco White's earlier in this book, asks how much the heavens, with their scattered stars, can say about the afterlife, in a time too late for religious certainties. Her lines may also recall John Hollander's "Into the Black" in the oblivion of their night sky. Brock-Broido's sonnet (to stay within this book) also resembles Longfellow's poem "The Cross of Snow," since both depict unassuaged and insomniac grief. For Longfellow the signs of Christian consolation persist in nature ironically; for Brock-Broido, even those signs are gone. All these sonnets, in turn, belong to a much larger tradition of writing about grief after the end of shared religion, when consolation (if any), in heaven or on earth, must be worked out by the mourners themselves.

Brock-Broido brings, to that tradition, discoveries of structure, figure, and tone. She finds, first, a neat correlation between her grief and her sonnet's odd form: we are reading a poem with a hole in the middle, corresponding to the lost shepherd-gods, and to the lost mother–sun–Old Sheep. Brock-Broido's sound effects emphasize that "hole": the repeated *sh*-sounds that precede it, for example, lead up to brief silence before the sibilance resumes. More scrutiny will reveal other sound effects: the out-of-place internal rhyme of "sight" and "black & white," for example, and the buildup of *ell*-sounds in the last half of the poem.

Second, Brock-Broido has found a way to represent modern disillusion without overt nostalgia for familiar religious beliefs. What she misses, what she cannot get back, is a lost archaic mother, a lost Old Sheep, and a whole Milky Way full of shepherds, not the singular Jewish or Christian Lord. Nor does the poet miss an earlier Europe: to find a society for which each star had its shepherd, a society without irrevocable collective loss, Brock-Broido has to go back to the earliest societies about which we know anything, "Before the Babylonians," to a Sumer that itself had no precursor civilization, no previous cities whose fall it could mourn. We cannot inhabit this Sumer, whose sheep are not ours; our "here" will never be "there." If this Sumer had "Old Sheep Stars," we are modern young "blood sheep," or rather "blood sisters," connected by blood relations not so much to one another—they are no flock, no collective—as to the absent mother whose "blood" they share.

The language of pastoral—of literary pastoral and of an ancient, if lightly sketched, pastoral society—belongs to Brock-Broido's Sumerians, who imagined shepherds in their skies. The contrasting, often polysyllabic, language of modern medicine denotes the bereft valley-dwellers of the present, among whom "we" belong. Rather than meteor showers (falling stars), we are "show-ered with emboli," dangerous air bubbles that can form in the blood or mi-grate to the brain. The parent mourned here might have died from an embo-lism, from a stroke, or from complications that affected the heart. "We" seem to live on, in darkness, inside her dead body. Our sky is not "heavenly," and not like a pasture; instead it is like the "concavity" in a human organ—the womb, or a chamber inside the heart. If the earth were a heart, the alternation of day and night might be its slow beat, its "long aortic pulse," evident on the equinox, when day and night are equal in length. But for Brock-Broido that heart no longer beats; its "pulse," audible to Sumerians, has stilled.

Along with the medical language, along with the figures of pasture and heart, come color words, surprising in their paucity: a poem about hearts and blood ought to be full of red. But red, like all colors, requires certain light: in the dark all cats are gray (as the saying goes), and in Brock-Broido's heavenless night no color can be discerned. The extremity of Brock-Broido's mourning seems to undo the work of the biblical Creation. Where God in Genesis sepa-rated the day from the night, the waters from the land, and called it good, where the Sumerian saw the "pulse / Of equinox" (sunrise or sunset) and called the stars "heavenly," "Here there is" only a colorless, motherless "material" vista the poet can never quite name.

A believer in physicism knows no Lord, no shepherd—no supernatural forces of any sort, and surely no life after death. Yet to say that Brock-Broido's bleak poem describes the consequences of "physicist" belief, of modern dis-illusion, is to get its emotional trajectory backward: the titular attitude is a consequence, not a cause, of the poet's grief. Having lost a parent, a shepherd, a sun from her sky, Brock-Broido and her "blood sisters" cannot believe in any supernatural guide, resurrection, or consolation, because they cannot believe in any benevolent cosmic order that would have let their mother die. The "material / And motherless" world seems to have no one in charge, no source of final consolation or appeal, once both parents are gone. Their absence may prove that no one was in charge all along.

The symmetry of the final one-line sentence, with its framing redundancy ("Here . . . here," as if she had no one to say "There, there") underscores the apprehension, the ungainly discomfort, of the phrases that came before. Un-able to protest (who, after all, would hear her?), Brock-Broido instead resigns herself, stops short: "here," for her, is really all she has. And yet "here," while modern (and medical), is never literal. Brock-Broido has not written a poem of autobiography, has not included the details of her own life. Rather, she has remained almost defiantly within her allegorical framework, within her modern valley, known mostly by contrast with its imagined Sumer: "here" and now, "motherless" in the indefinite, uncreated dark.

SB

"Zion"

DONALD REVELL

2005

Suddenly copper roses glow on the deadwood.
I am these because I see them and also see
Abolition, the white smock on a girl
Eating an apple, looking down into
The valley, a small train steaming there.
I go to the uplands to join death,
And death welcomes me, shows me a trailhead,
Foot-tracks overfilled with standing water.
Man has never owned another man here.
Aglow in the shade hang apples free for the taking.
I'm saying that death is a little girl. The apple
There in her hand is God Almighty where the skin
Breaks to her teeth and spills my freedom all over
Sunlight turning deadwood coppery rose.

"Is THERE no change of death in Paradise?" asked Wallace Stevens in his
poem "Sunday Morning." "Does ripe fruit never fall?" Stevens, whose po-
etry almost always rejects the consolations of Christian belief, concluded that
we would not experience beauty, would not appreciate even the pleasures of
Eden, if we did not know change and even death. "Death is the mother of
beauty," the same poem says. Donald Revell is now a Christian believer, a poet
of the desert West (not Stevens's Northeast), a lover of trees and horses, an
avoider of built-up cities, a partisan of immediacy over reflection, intuition
over intellect (though his poems feed the intellect too). Yet Revell's sonnet
about death and natural beauty, his poem of epiphany, mystery, and canceled
time, reaches the same conclusions as Stevens's poem. This moment of God

and Paradise on earth, the apparition in which the poem begins and ends, is a vision of resurrection and "freedom," of spiritual liberation, which—for Revell—requires that we know death.

"Zion" is one of several recent sonnets in which Revell makes an American landscape fit space to show God's presence on earth. Raised in the Bronx, the poet moved to the American Southwest in the late 1990s, when he adopted the pellucid style that marks his recent work. The title refers to the Holy Land (Israel and Palestine), considered figuratively as a symbol for heaven, as in so many sermons, spirituals, and hymns. It is also another name—in common use since the nineteenth century, especially by Mormons—for the State of Utah, whose most visited wilderness is Zion National Park. Known for its steep hikes, sublime ruddy peaks, and mazy canyons cut by the Virgin River, this Zion is by regional standards well-watered and fertile; its soil and trees supported ancient Anasazi settlements, then Paiutes, and then Mormons on their trek west. The combination of plant life, paths, and views in Zion makes possible the vision Revell describes.

Revell's sonnet begins as a tableau: he shows bright sunlight, "deadwood," stark verticality, "a girl / Eating an apple," and a train (which then chugs on out of the poem). Reanimated, brought back from death to life, like roses (or the illusion of them) on deadwood, Revell also seems to see back into the past, when steam trains (not electric or diesel models) brought pioneers west. Zion is for him, as it was for them, the Promised Land, the future, but it is also, for Revell, the innocent past—a place for a girl (not an adult man or a woman), a place of peace, a place where most of American history has not yet occurred. That history has, so to speak, been "abolished," not by a bloody national conflict (such as the U.S. Civil War), but as if by heavenly decree. "Abolition" means both the erasure of history—the American promise (so often betrayed) of a fresh start—and an end to chattel slavery (an implication on which the poem will later turn).

The poet in Utah, in Zion National Park, has gone backward to the time of miracles, in a visionary experience with an angelic messenger. The Mormon scriptures, with their latter-day angels, certainly are not part of Revell's own beliefs, though the Mormon background of Utah, where he taught, surely influenced Revell in more diffuse ways. "God Almighty" infuses every created thing (a doctrine whose technical name is panentheism; compare Hopkins's idea of "inscape," in "As kingfishers catch fire," earlier in this book). Since I am created in God's image (says the poet), everything that God created, everything that bears God's stamp, is part of me: "I am these" too.

To know that "I am these," that I participate in God's created world, is also to know death. Having become what he beheld, having had the feeling (so far mysterious) of resurrection from "copper roses" on wood, Revell can now "go to the uplands to join death." (He may have in mind, among other allusions, the death of Moses on Mount Pisgah, in Deuteronomy 34:1–2, and D. H. Lawrence, another southwestern writer, building his "Ship of Death" in the poem of that name.) Death (who takes no personal pronoun) "welcomes me." The passage out of this life is just one more trail, or so it seems to the poet in this moment of harmony with nonhuman nature, and with the faint traces that human beings have left there.

That harmony comes from the absence of history. "Man has never owned another man here" means literally that no slaveholder has ever resided in Zion National Park. It also means that in a moral sense—the sense in which I "own" only what I justly acquire—no human being has ever owned another human being anywhere. In its balanced aural self-sufficiency (one sentence coextensive with one line), in its unqualified confidence ("never"), Revell's sentence sounds like a triumphant announcement, with the force of a prophet's command. Such announcements occur throughout the poem: "I am these because I see them" is such a sentence, and so perhaps is "death welcomes me."

The poet and critic Alan Williamson argues that for twentieth- and twenty-first-century writers, the American West has restaged the grand ambitions of the so-called American Renaissance, of Ralph Waldo Emerson and Henry David Thoreau. So it is, plainly, for Revell, who quotes Thoreau elsewhere with relish, and who stakes out here, in the abundant sunlight and rare water of this public park, a clearing free of modern society, free from its collective memory and from its guilt. A hostile political critic might argue, against Revell as against Thoreau, that no American poet ought even try to forget American history; a friendly critic might respond that we will never envision a better future if we look only and always at our bloodstained past. The experience of freedom from history—the paradisal exemption Revell feels at Zion—amounts not only to an exemption from an unjust (for Thoreau, a slave-fueled) economy, but also to freedom from commerce more generally. That is what "owned" means, and that is why "Man has never owned another man here" (line 9) serves as the sonnet's turn. Thoreau claimed that at Walden he could "avoid all trade and barter, so far as my food was concerned"; "the fruits do not yield their true flavor to the purchaser of them," he wrote, "nor to him who raises them for the market." Revell's "apples free for the taking" are, like Thoreau's huckleberries, perfect because untainted by exchange. They are pure gift, from an immanent God to the "little girl" who eats them, at once bright angel and hungry human being.

Yet this girl is also a version of death on earth. (She may, or may not, have shown him the trailhead, above.) The place of perfect "freedom" becomes a place where Revell can acknowledge death, since the only death in evidence here (the "death" of an apple when eaten, the disappearance of a trail into a canyon) comes about through what we call "natural causes." Zion lacks violence—though it contains human beings. It is a western American answer to the good place, the happy fields, of ancient classical pastoral, in which—as the famous Latin tag "Et in arcadia ego" points out—death is present too. (Revell entitled his first western book *Arcady*.) Adam and Eve had to leave Eden when the fruit of the tree of the knowledge of good and evil (in most American traditions, an apple) brought with it the knowledge of death. Revell's holy site includes death and shows a "little girl" (though not a woman) biting an apple, a bite that becomes, as in the story of Eden, the central action of the poem. Yet the knowledge of death is not, for Revell, a reason (much less a command) to wander away. Rather, he stays here, contemplating the trailhead, and feels at peace, as if time has not passed.

The poem can thus end almost as it began, with sun making "coppery" rose-like patterns on deadwood. Classicists call this device, where the last line or scene resembles the first one, "ring composition." Yet Revell does not end exactly as he began: the "copper roses" of the first line become the adjectival "coppery rose" at the end, making the last line an appositive noun phrase, not a full sentence (as is line 1) nor even an independent clause. The initial roses were metaphors; another writer might call them tricks of the light. For Revell they are not tricks but revivifications, evidence of divine bounty in sunlight, quite as if the sun across the lifeless branch could make real roses grow. Metaphor becomes faith in transformation: poetic devices, arranged in the proper spirit, testify to the *poiesis* ("making") that the religious poet acknowledges in the material world, where God's creative work goes on even now.

Revell's effects of simplicity and clarity can make his literary models hard to see. The vision of timeless roses points back to a much longer, more famous work of Christian belief, T. S. Eliot's set of poems called *Four Quartets,* whose sites (three English, one American) reveal their debt to history as eagerly as Revell's Zion refuses it: "Ash on a sleeve / Is all the ash the burnt roses leave"; "the fire and the rose are one" (Eliot, "Little Gidding"). Revell takes from *Four Quartets* not only revived roses but the alternation of stressed with unstressed syllables at the ends of pentameter lines, in Eliot as in Revell's sestet a sign of the hush that attends visionary experience (Eliot said that he, in turn, was trying to copy effects of rhyme in Dante). Revell's sunlit ending alludes to James Wright's "A Blessing," another poem of American epiphany, where "last year's droppings blaze up into golden stones." Wright, like Revell, sounds clear, confident, even artless; that confidence is a hallmark of Wright's mature style. In "Zion," as in many of his recent poems, Revell picks up Wright's confident lucidity even while keeping up a conversation with older literature, a conversation that brings the Scriptures to the western American scene.

SB

"Starlings, Broad Street, Trenton, 2003"

PAUL MULDOON

2006

Indiscernible, for the most part, the welts and weals
on their two-a-penny skins,
weals got by tinkering with tin-
foil from condoms or chewing gum, welts as slow to heal

as spot-welds on steel
in a chop shop where, by dint of the din,
their calls will be no clearer than their colors till they spin
(or are spun) around to reveal

this other sphere in which their hubbub's the hubbub
of all-night revelers at reveille,
girls with shoes in hand, boys giving their all

to the sidewalk outside a club,
their gloom a gloom so distinctly shot through with glee
they might be dancing still under a disco ball.

BORN AND educated in Northern Ireland, now teaching at Princeton, Muldoon has made the sonnet one of his specialties. He has written sonnets composed wholly in half- or near-rhymes, sonnets in clipped dialogue, sonnets that tell (real or made-up) family stories, sonnets in extraordinarily long lines, sonnets in strikingly short ones, a book of sonnets *(The Prince of the Quotidian)* that records his daily life in central New Jersey, and a shaggy-dog tale of a narrative poem about gangsters in Belfast ("The More a Man Has the More a Man Wants"), told entirely in sonnet-sized units.

For all his formal explorations, though, Muldoon's sonnets—like the rest of

his poems—almost always return to the same few ideas. They praise tricki-
ness, incompletion, and ambiguity, and treasure the ways in which words,
people, and emotions escape definition. Muldoon's panoply of reversals and
doublings, his two-sided symbols and paired puns, ask us to see at least two
sides of every question, and reserve real ire for figures of authority—priests,
political leaders, and others—who tell us what to do or what to believe. This
recent sonnet from *Horse Latitudes,* the bleakest and most political of his
American books, fits Muldoon's pattern. In its one extended sentence, Mul-
doon worries about ecological damage, registers frustration with the belliger-
ence of American public culture in the first year of the Iraq War, and saves his
appreciation for the birds and the teens who keep dancing, who keep up their
"glee," despite the approach of morning, "gloom," thieves, pollution, and dis-
ease.

Starlings are—like Muldoon himself—a transatlantic import, the only
remnant of the millionaire Eugene Schiefflin's attempt in 1890 to establish in
America every bird mentioned in the works of Shakespeare. They have since
become a nuisance across the temperate zones of the United States, compet-
ing with pigeons in cities, and nesting in flocks. Muldoon's starlings are not
beneficiaries of American folly, but victims of consumer-driven civilization.
They have poisoned themselves by ingesting foil wrappers, whose chemicals
threaten their bodily integrity much as crooked mechanics in a "chop shop"
threaten the integrity of the (stolen) automobiles whose parts they use. The
starlings are casualties, like men wounded in wars; "calls" and "colors" suggest
war cries, regimental banners, national flags.

Everything in the first half of the poem, up to the main verb and the syn-
tactic spine ("their calls will be no clearer than their colors"), suggests a la-
ment—a poem of protest about the damage we inflict on our urban environ-
ment, on our animals, and on one another. Muldoon conveys one undertone
of antiwar sentiment, and another of ecological complaint. Not only did hu-
man beings introduce starlings, an invasive species, into America; now that
they are here, we poison them with gum wrappers, so that they look ugly be-
fore they die.

Yet the first half of the poem also piles up pairs: everything has a mate, an
opposite, or an association with the number two. Starling skins have two sides,
and are "two-a-penny" because boys in Britain and Ireland have for centuries
killed and sold the birds for their skins (used to make fishing lures). "Welts"
comes with its synonym "weals," and both words reappear before the first
quatrain concludes. "Tin" echoes "tinkering"; "dint" echoes "din," and "spun"

echoes "spin." Muldoon almost never puts dates or years into his titles; doing so here, he links the poem to public events. The starlings are ill, and the United States is about to enter an ill-advised war, even if the risks of the war (the wounds it will cause, as wrappers cause wounds to starlings) remain "indiscernible" to many Americans, in Trenton (the state capital) as in Washington. Muldoon's doublings prepare for a reversal, for a volta (a turn at or around line 8) that will not refute the grim octave.

Rather, Muldoon will insist that "gloom" is not the only possible response to illness, nor to ill omens, in private and public life: rightly seen, "gloom" acquires its own double, the not quite desperate inward "glee" that animates the sestet. When Muldoon looks first at the milling starlings, he compares them to damaged things—to cars inelegantly repaired, and perhaps to wounded soldiers too. When he looks again at the starlings, they have turned around—they have likely risen up into the air, turning and wheeling like the swans in W. B. Yeats's poem "The Wild Swans at Coole." Muldoon will not see any Yeatsian gesture of purposeful unanimity (Yeats's swans "all suddenly mount"). Instead, and characteristically, Muldoon notices the ragged excitement of teens who have stayed out very late, "girls" and "boys" whose celebration acknowledges no rule, no wounds, and no closing time, who dance to music by night and seek neither violence nor profit (by contrast to the "chop shop" and its "din"). Even though their nightclub has shut down in the early morning, the dancers (en masse or in pairs) will not admit that the time to dance is done.

Nor will Muldoon; nor, perhaps, should we. Like his earlier poems about the Troubles in Northern Ireland, Muldoon's poems of post-9/11 America say that if we cannot dance during wartime, we will never dance at all—that the necessary obverse, or underside, of a harsh political climate is the continuance of play, verbal and otherwise, of risky self-reinvention, of unmoralized fun. So the clubgoers suggest, though the final verb—not "will be" (as in line 7) but "might be"—gives the suggestion a wistful note. The young dancers also connect the poem to earlier Irish and English poems in which the poet regrets his distance from youth (most of all to Seamus Heaney's "The Guttural Muse"). As usual in Muldoon, any adult point of view, any distance from first impressions and from youthful lability, has value only insofar as it shows how uncertain, how two-sided, how liable to volatile reinterpretation, all experience can be.

Where first impressions—headlines, or street scenes—bespeak violence or disgust, Muldoon's second impression, his sense that all things have two sides, seems especially welcome. The last six lines include more doublings, above and beyond the rhymes: two "hubbubs," two "glooms," two instances of "all," shoes (which come in pairs), and two forms of the sound-pattern "revel" (though "revel" and "reveille" do not share an etymology). "Reveille" here means "sun-up," and by extension "closing time," the early-morning hour when nightclubs shut down. Usually, of course, it refers to soldiers' wake-up calls, with bugle and drum. Muldoon has removed the word from its martial context, or else given a faintly martial context to the dancers' all-night fun. He has done the same thing with the words "shot" and "color" and "call."

Muldoon's elegant ending, with its balanced hexameter, implies that the dancers can live as if it were night even into the morning, amid the "reveille" that calls them to go home, or go to work, or go to war. Such defiance, Muldoon hints, might be the best way to live in America in a time of wounds and war. But to find in the poem a clear moralized recommendation is to do violence to Muldoon's tone. The poet concludes on a conditional, within an extended simile; we no longer see the starlings except through the eyes of these girls and these boys. Yet the poem does not quite recommend, to us, their point of view. Instead—half playful, more than half regretful—it records a divided outlook, one that Muldoon might, or might not, call his own.

SB

"Psalm at High Tide"

MARTHA SERPAS

2007

Rain on the river's vinyl surface:
water that glitters,
water that hardly moves,
its branches witness to trees,
to fronds, leaves, crab floats, pilings,
shopping carts, appliances—
the divine earth takes everything
in its wounded side
and gives back wholeness.
It bears the huddled profane
and endures the soaking
venerated in its wild swirls—
this river fixed with wooden weirs,
radiant in misshapen glory.

"PSALM AT High Tide" appears in Martha Serpas' collection *The Dirty Side of the Storm* (2007). In other poems in that book, the Louisiana-born Serpas reacts to the failure of her government, which abandoned its own citizens during Hurricane Katrina. In "Psalm," however, Serpas focuses not on the social ramifications of the hurricane, but on the devastation itself. In disaster, she sees a divine power, and finds that power loving rather than threatening. Serpas, a committed Catholic who has also produced moving lesbian love poems, here proves herself a remarkable devotional poet. From unlikely materials, she writes a poem of confident faith.

Serpas entitles her poem a psalm, after the earliest and most influential collection of religious verse in Western tradition. Her poem is unrhymed free verse, though it has iambic resonance in its first four lines; and it is clearly identifiable as a sonnet, with a strongly marked volta in its ninth line. In the Psalms, the poet feels himself engulfed by deep water, and begs to be rescued by a caring deity. "Save me, O God, for the waters are come in unto my soul," cries the speaker of Psalm 69. Serpas has this background in mind as she writes her own poem "at high tide." Behind her use of the word "tide," rather than "flood," is the comforting implication that the waters will ebb in regular fashion. Therapeutically, she softens destruction by seeing it as a moment in a dependable cycle, part of the rhythm of creation.

Serpas excludes another religious context for the hurricane: the flood that engulfs mankind in the age of Noah. That flood is a unique, horrifying event. God decides to destroy most of humanity, and undoes his highest work. Serpas, by omitting mention of the biblical flood, eases the impact of Katrina, refusing to see it as God's threat against his world.

In her opening line the poet pictures the water as repellent and implacable, a shiny "vinyl surface." At first, we see a sheer, stagnant tableau, death-in-life. The flood surface "glitters," but it does not move. Its trancelike presence seems an unnatural phenomenon. Water, the source of life, should flow, replenishing us. Instead, it lies still. Broken branches, not whole trees, float on this tide. The word "witness" (line 4) introduces a solemn religious dimension. The poet bears witness to the compact between God, humanity and nature, to bonds that have been strained but not shattered by the hurricane.

Serpas' mention of tree branches leads to a catalogue (or poetic list), reminiscent of passages from one of her chosen influences, Elizabeth Bishop. The list moves from the natural to the manmade, from fronds and leaves to "crab floats, pilings, / shopping carts, appliances." We see, reduced to shivered flotsam and jetsam, the tools used by fishermen and crab-gatherers on the bayous; and then the apparatus of consumerism. The shopping cart has particular resonance here: seen everywhere in our tragic inner cities, it has become an urban boat, storing the paltry goods of the most desperate. Fitting, then, that shopping carts float among the remains of civilization, after the flood.

The sonnet shifts into a higher pitch near the end of its octave. Here Serpas reenvisions the scene of ruin as a sacrament. She remembers the wound made in Jesus' side by the Roman centurion (also alluded to in Herbert's "Prayer (I)," the subject of an earlier essay in this volume), and the Savior's blood pouring out as he hangs on the Cross. Christian mystics often identify this blood with nourishing milk supplied by the comforting, maternal figure of Jesus. The story of Christ's Passion recasts tragedy as embrace, acceptance, even triumph.

So, in "Psalm at High Tide," the "divine earth takes everything / in its wounded side." The spear, piercing Jesus' body, opens a place that welcomes those who respond to his sacrifice, who look to him for their own healing.

"And gives back / wholeness" is the exalted phrase that begins the sestet. Again Serpas relies on Christian overtones. The death of God on the Cross is the wound in the universe. But this loss then unites the human and the divine, since God has become man. The ensuing mention of the "huddled profane" sends us back to perhaps the most famous American sonnet, Emma Lazarus' "The New Colossus." In Lazarus' poem, the lady with the torch welcomes the "huddled masses" of other shores. Rather similarly, Serpas' divine earth carries what might seem alien to it, inanimate refuse—all that floating junk. The human is nowhere in her riverscape, but the material signs of humanity, however ragged, give paradoxical hope.

In a manner both arch and folksy, T. S. Eliot intoned (in *Four Quartets*), "I think that the river / Is a strong brown god." Serpas is far more direct. Her river, in its sacred being, sustains the profane. It "endures," but also "bears" (gives birth). The deathly-still surface of the poem's beginning has now become a pattern of "wild swirls," adorned with weirs (dams used to divert the river's flow). "Venerated" suggests staid respect, but the word derives from Venus, the source of erotic desire: a wild energy stands at its root.

Finally, the river is "radiant in misshapen glory." The humdrum detritus on its surface tells only part of the story. The river destroys, but it also saves. The waters distort the face of nature, yet testify to divinity, a god-like acceptance shown even in ruin. Attentive and modest, Serpas' "Psalm" petitions a power wider than our fears—one that, she trusts, protects us from utter chaos, and returns us to the promise of creation.

DM

"Rest Stop near the Italian Border"

RAFAEL CAMPO

2007

Alps crowding in the distance, gas tank low,
we stop beneath the diesel clouds of trucks—
black radiators, ugly stars of bugs
squashed flat. You say you need to go.
A Muslim family, Algerian
perhaps, drifts by, the woman's robes
bright fluttering amidst the roar the road's
unending traffic raises. Evian,
some candy to defuse my garlic breath—
you're off, determined, and so I'm left
with just the warmth of your hand's soft,
negligible weight. A hand I held, near death,
back home—I can't recall his name,
but speeding, inescapable, was what came.

RAFAEL CAMPO'S complex identity as a gay man, a Cuban American, and a doctor frequently appears in his work. In this poem (part of a sonnet sequence, *Eighteen Days in France*), he is traveling with his male partner in Europe; he flashes back in memory to a patient who has recently died. A confluence of professional, personal, and poetic attachments animates "Rest Stop near the Italian Border," with a transitory power that turns out to be as profound as it is fleeting.

The Alps, seen in the distance in the first line of "Rest Stop," are a familiar subject for poetry, often associated with the sublime. In Milton's sonnet "On the Late Massacre in Piedmont," the mountains themselves echo the martyrs' cries to heaven. In Campo's poem, by contrast, an expansive, otherworldly voice is nowhere to be heard. The mountains themselves look undignified, "crowding in the distance," reinforcing the scene of congested road traffic at the familiar-looking filling station. This is a human, small-scale drama, one that could as easily take place in Texas or Canada as in France: on a long road trip, a stop for gas, for the bathroom, for water and breath mints. All this we are used to summing up, rather drearily, as a "rest stop"—"rest" in its lowest possible sense, a short break between tedious bouts of driving. During this dull event, a striking memory will break in—but not yet.

"Diesel clouds of trucks" squat at the center of this antipastoral landscape. The trucks are unthinking behemoths that, as they roar by, routinely immolate bugs on their windshields. These enormous vehicles stand for the work of the world, rushing past; while the poet, out of the mainstream, contemplates what lies before him (and leaves his mind open for the incursion of memory). The banal mention of urination ("you say you need to go") suggests a reduction of human life to basic bodily pressures. After these opening four lines, it is hard to believe that "Rest Stop" will spring to significant life.

But it does. The first signs of energy, in the second quatrain, are a "bright fluttering" of foreignness: the "Muslim family" that "drifts by," "Algerian / perhaps." Algeria, the scene of a devastating war fought to ensure independence from France, remains a presence on native French soil, in the form of a substantial North African population. The hint of history in the background is subtle, nearly drowned out by the "unending traffic" that relentlessly links via commerce every point on the globe with every other. But the historical note is there to tell us that certain momentous connections persist. The rhyme of "Evian" with "Algerian" that seals the second quatrain reminds us that the accords ending the Algerian war were signed in Evian, France, in 1962.

With the sestet, Campo moves from Evian to Eve. He evokes the separation scene in Milton's *Paradise Lost* (Book 9): as Eve goes off, determined to work alone, so the poet's traveling companion leaves him . . . but only for the restroom. The poet compares great things with small, introducing the heavy grandeur of epic into a seemingly trivial context. But the connection works. With the lovely half-rhyme of "left" and "soft," Campo reflects on the light warmth and weight of his partner's hand, which touched him before parting. In *Paradise Lost,* at the end of the achingly beautiful and painful scene that ends in Eve's departure (and leads to her fall), Milton writes, "from her husband's hand her hand / Soft she withdrew."

Something resonant, rather than merely "negligible," will come to the poet in his momentary isolation. The poet makes us say the word "negligible" fleetingly, since it bears only one stress (on the first syllable); it cannot take much weight. So far, the occasion described by the poem is indeed negligible. But the word calls forth the similarly multisyllabic "inescapable": the memory of the patient's death, a moment utterly unlike, and yet paired with, this every-day scene. After an abrupt caesura in line 12, an image rises. "A hand I held, near death": the leaden, emphatic phrase joins doctor and patient. As the grammar suggests, Campo the doctor is himself "near death," physically linked to the man who feels it coming.

Unlike the temporary parting of lovers, death is final. But the ephemeral circumstances of "Rest Stop" suit the character of this loss, which is seemingly incidental, anonymous: the poet "can't recall" his patient's name. Like the trucks roaring by, so death comes speeding, and erases the doomed man. Just in this way, the poet disposes of him with his breezy couplet rhyme. But the memory, which comes so suddenly, stings. The patient's death will give birth to nothing except this poem; the poet-doctor knows nothing about the man. Yet he matters because he embodies a fact most elemental: we are all equal before mortality. The character and personality of the dead man are irrelevant; it is the fact of the event that counts, his presence at the brink. Campo, as a doctor, held the hand of another person at the end of his life. As a poet, he respects such transience, and by doing so honors the dead. His sonnet itself is one moment's companion.

DM

"corydon & alexis, redux"

D. A. POWELL

2009

and yet we think that song outlasts us all: wrecked devotion
the wept face of desire, a kind of savage caring that reseeds itself
and grows in clusters

oh, you who are young, consider how quickly the body deranges
itself
how time, the cruel banker, forecloses us to snowdrifts white as
god's own ribs

what else but to linger in the slight shade of those sapling
branches
yearning for that vernal beau. for don't birds covet the seeds of
the honey locust
and doesn't that eye have a nose for wet filaree and slender oats
foraged in the meadow
kit foxes crave the blacktailed hare: how this longing grabs me by
the nape

guess I figured to be done with desire, if I could write it out
dispense with any evidence, the way one burns a pile of twigs
and brush

what was his name? I'd ask myself, that guy with the sideburns
and charming smile
the one I hoped that, as from a sip of hemlock, I'd expire with
him on my tongue

silly poet, silly man: thought I could master nature like a
   misguided preacher
as if banishing love is a fix. as if the stars go out when we shut
   our sleepy eyes

THIS LAST poem (the last of several sonnets) in Powell's book *Chronic* shows
the sonnet form at its most offhandedly colloquial, and most passionately se-
rious; at its most showily current, and most richly engaged with the past; at its
most ambitiously literary, and at its most inwardly vulnerable. The poet con-
templates his own advancing age, and his implied illness. He invokes the tra-
ditions of love poetry and elegy from ancient times to the present, including
the most famous poem in European literature about erotic love between men.
Powell remembers a time when, disappointed in love, he gave up on it; he
tried to banish erotic desire from his own life, and to see it only as something
that belongs only to the past—to his own life history or to literary tradition.
Such banishments, Powell decides, never work. Erotic desire is woven too
deeply through us, and leaves us only after our lives end.

Powell begins with a commonplace about love poetry generally. We who
desire, and we who sing, may die, he says, but "we think that song outlasts
us." Art about devotion survives "wrecked devotion." The word "devotion"
conflates erotic and religious attachment, transient and eternal objects of love.
It suggests the kind of eternal renewal that Powell's idea of "song" and love
contains. Yet it is not any particular song that "outlasts us all," but "song" in
general that survives. Love poetry is not (contra Shakespeare's Sonnet 55) an
ever-enduring monument, preserving the lover's desire, and the lover's own
image of the beloved, "in the eyes of all posterity." Rather, love poetry is like
erotic love itself, forever dying and forever renewed. "Desire," and the lan-
guage we use for it, thus resembles the wild ("savage") plants that spread pol-
len unaided except by wind—though such plants, unlike people, can repro-
duce alone.

With its reminder that we weep and die, its strewn seeds and spent clus-
ters, Powell's first stanza sounds like a lament, or a warning. Powell goes on to
put into his long lines the best-known warning in all of Western poetry: *carpe
diem,* "seize the day" (Horace, *Odes* 1.11). Enjoy love while you can; soon
enough you will die. (Powell also echoes T. S. Eliot: "O you who turn the

wheel and look to windward, / Consider Phlebas, who was once handsome and tall as you.") The poet stresses the contrast between a young, healthy audience and an implicitly old or very ill speaker: he is very nearly writing a deathbed poem. "Snowdrifts" might be mere white hair, but a figure with snow-white skin and visible ribs, somebody who looks like Christ on the Cross, has troubles far worse than white hair. He may feel that he has been turned out of his own body (as from a foreclosed house) into the snow. (Anglo-Saxon verse called the human body a "bone-house"; Powell may have that kenning in mind.)

Rather than saying we should *choose* to pursue earthly love (as the *carpe diem* tradition suggests), Powell's quatrain argues that we have no choice. Once we realize how quickly we age and die, we are compelled to pursue carnal desire: we act from instinct, as birds seek seeds, as ruminants forage for foliage, as predators hunt prey. "Filaree," also called storkbill, has lavender flowers and large conical, phallic buds; it grows in the American Southwest, including arid central and southern California, where Powell spent his teens. It is a western American plant, just as the black-tailed hare (or jackrabbit) and the kit fox are western American animals, and as Powell (so the sonnet announces) is a western American poet, who transports durable, ancient models for love poetry to California and to the present day.

The most important such model is Virgil, from whose Second Eclogue Powell takes the names in his title. Long a scandal to schoolteachers, and a delight to educated homosexual men, the Second Eclogue treats the erotic love of one male shepherd for another. (As in many pastoral poems, the shepherds and their song also represent poets and poetry.) The shepherd Corydon declares his love for Alexis, asking Alexis (who does not hear him) to share a secluded life of music making and natural plenitude. Powell has written a Virgilian sequel ("redux"); his octave alludes over and over to Virgil's poem. His procession of flowering plants recalls Corydon's, and he compares the lover, as Corydon does, both to predator and to prey. "Saplings" and "vernal" suggest the beloved's youth, also a Virgilian point of emphasis. The "oat" in Virgil and in Powell—and in John Milton's "Lycidas"—makes a familiar figure for poetry itself (the shepherds of pastoral verse blow through oats or reeds to make song). The laurel and myrtle in Virgil and Milton turn, in America, into "filaree," as the hungry wolves in Virgil inspire Powell's kit fox.

Corydon tells himself to give up Alexis, to weave his reeds and play his songs again, and to desire someone new. Powell remembers instead a wish "to be done with desire" in all its forms. The sestet finds Powell speaking not to us but to himself. He shifts from present to past tense, from "we" to "I," from slightly antique terminology ("vernal," "longing," "covet") to colloquialism ("guess I," "if I could") and to the modern language of crime scenes ("dispense with any evidence"), as if to shut the door on his own lusts. He would like (the turn in the sonnet says) to get his lust out of his body and onto the page, now that his body no longer seems healthy, attractive, or young.

But desire is not so easily tamed. Twigs burn, but the image of "that guy" remains. Powell here casts himself not as Corydon but as Socrates, an ugly wise man attracted to youth, and a condemned man who chooses the manner of his death (in Plato's *Phaedo*). "Hemlock" fuses Socrates' death by poison with the ingestion of semen, and with the figurative death of orgasm: to receive oral sex from "that guy" was, so to speak, an experience to die for (with an additional pun on "expire" = "die" and "expire" = "breathe out"). To try to expunge desire from one's memory, to dissociate oneself from the pleasures and yearnings proper to youth, is only to make those pleasures, and those yearnings, more vivid still: we may well seek them although they bring us death, and seek them till the day we die.

Having spoken to us in the timeless present of apothegm, Powell speaks at last, in retrospect, to himself: "silly poet, silly man." ("Silly" in Renaissance English can mean simply innocent, though Powell also uses the present-day sense of foolish, childish, naive.) Powell's long lines—his most recognizable invention—keep going, as Powell's desires keep going, past points where we might expect them to end. He sees himself not as a preacher, and not as nature's master, but as part of nature. Like all of us, the poet finds himself subject to the rhythms of hope and loss, lust and frustration, day and night, exertion and exhaustion. Even valediction, elegy, and palinode, even a poetry that tries "to be done with desire," Powell implies, feeds our addiction to desire and to its memory. Poems about "banishing love" will not "fix" (repair) our excited yearnings, but rather serve as a "fix" (maintenance dose of an addictive drug, such as heroin).

Such a comparison brings little consolation. (To write, to sing, to desire will not help us set it aside.) What does console Powell, even amid the flood of lamentation, is the realization that love poetry and desire will long outlast particular desires, particular poems, particular lovers: songs do not last indefinitely, but "song" does. Other people can see the stars while we sleep; other people will find lovers, and write poems of successful or unsuccessful love, even after we die, and while we sleep alone.

With its showy typography (lowercase letters, double spaces between stanzas), its sometimes exceptionally colloquial diction ("guess" for "I guess," "fix" as drug slang, "guy" for "man"), its final image reminiscent of popular song, Powell's sonnet may seem strenuously contemporary. Certainly its situation, like its language, would not be possible in any culture before our own: the openly gay, and HIV-positive, California poet writes explicitly about the joys of sex between men, even as he alludes to AIDS. Yet this most contemporary of love poets is also among our most traditional. Virgil, Milton, Shakespeare, Socrates—and the broader line of sonnets about frustrated love, poems that refuse to say farewell to desire—resonate in his long American lines.

SB

Editions Used

We have used the editions listed here to prepare the texts of the poems reprinted in this book. For many poems, including all those written during the twentieth and twenty-first centuries, we have adopted the texts below without change. For poems written earlier, especially those from before 1700, we have modernized some spelling and punctuation where the originals might confuse a present-day audience, and where the changes entail no loss of meaning. Like almost all modern editors, we have left the language of Edmund Spenser (who often used archaic spellings to create double meanings or make other points) unchanged.

Thomas Wyatt, "Whoso list to hunt," from *The Poems of Sir Thomas Wiat,* ed. A. K. Foxwell (New York: Russell and Russell, 1913).

Henry Howard, Earl of Surrey, "Norfolk sprang thee," from *The Poems of Henry Howard, Earl of Surrey,* ed. Frederick Morgan Padelford (Seattle: University of Washington Press, 1920).

George Gascoigne, "That self same tongue," from *The Complete Works of George Gascoigne,* vol. 1, ed. John W. Cunliffe (Cambridge: Cambridge University Press, 1907).

Sir Philip Sidney, *Astrophel and Stella* 45, from *Astrophel and Stella,* ed. Alfred Pollard (Chicago: A. C. McClurg and Company, 1888).

Edmund Spenser, *Ruines of Rome* 3 ("Thou stranger, which for Rome in Rome here seekest"), from *Spenser's Minor Poems,* ed. Ernest de Sélincourt (Oxford: Oxford University Press, 1910).

Samuel Daniel, *Delia* 38, from *Elizabethan Sonnet-Cycles,* ed. Martha Foote Crow (London: Kegan Paul, Trench, Trübner and Company, 1896).

Edmund Spenser, *Amoretti* 78, from *The Complete Works in Prose and Verse of Edmund Spenser,* ed. Alexander B. Grosart (London: Spenser Society, 1882).

Fulke Greville, Lord Brooke, *Caelica* 7 ("The World, that all contains"), from Greville, *Certaine Learned and Elegant Workes* (Delmar, N.Y.: Scholars Facsimiles, 1990; orig. pub. 1633).

William Shakespeare, Sonnets 2, 68, 116, from *Sonnets* (London: Thomas Thorpe, 1609). Facsimile edition (Oxford: Clarendon Press, 1905).

Lady Mary Wroth, *Pamphilia to Amphilanthus* 73, from Wroth, *The Countesse of*

Mountgomeries Urania (London: Mariott and Grismand, 1621), copy in the Folger Shakespeare Library, Washington, D.C. We have also consulted *The Poems of Lady Mary Wroth,* ed. Josephine A. Roberts (Baton Rouge: Louisiana State University Press, 1983).

John Donne, "At the round earth's imagined corners" and "Oh, to vex me, contaries meet in one," from Edmund Gosse, *Life and Letters of John Donne,* vol. 2 (New York: Dodd, Mead, and Company, 1899).

George Herbert, "Redemption" and "Prayer (I)" from *The English Works of George Herbert,* vol. 2, ed. A. B. Grosart (Boston: Houghton, Mifflin and Company, 1905).

John Milton, "On the Late Massacre in Piedmont" and "Methought I saw my late espousèd saint" from Milton, *Poems,* 2nd edition (London: Thomas Dring, 1673). John Milton, *Complete Poetical Works Reproduced in Photographic Facsimile,* ed. H. F. Fletcher (Urbana: University of Illinois Press, 1943–48).

Mary Robinson, *Sappho and Phaon* 24, from *Poetical Works,* vol. 3 (London: Richard Phillips, 1806).

Charlotte Smith, "Huge vapours brood above the cliftèd shore," from Smith, *The Young Philosopher,* vol. 3 (London: Cadell and Davies, 1798).

William Wordsworth, "London, 1802," from *The Earlier Poems of William Wordsworth,* ed. William Johnston (London: Edward Moxon, 1857).

William Wordsworth, "Surprised by Joy" from *The Poetical Works of William Wordsworth,* ed. William Angus Knight (London and New York: Macmillan, 1896).

John Keats, "On Seeing the Elgin Marbles," from *Poems of John Keats,* ed. H. B. Forman (London: Reeves and Turner, 1895).

John Keats, "Four seasons fill the measure of the year," from *Complete Poems,* ed. Jack Stillinger (Cambridge, Mass.: Harvard University Press, 1991).

Percy Bysshe Shelley, "Ozymandias," from *Poetical Works of Percy Bysshe Shelley,* ed. H. B. Forman, vol. 1 (London: Reeves and Turner, 1876).

Percy Bysshe Shelley, "England in 1819," from *Poetical Works of Percy Bysshe Shelley,* ed. Thomas Hutchinson (London: Henry Frowde / Oxford University Press, 1905).

Samuel Taylor Coleridge, "Work without Hope," from *The Poetical Works of Samuel Taylor Coleridge* (Oxford: Oxford University Press, 1912).

John Clare, "Swordy Well," manuscript in the Pforzheimer Collection, New York Public Library.

Henry Wadsworth Longfellow, "To-morrow," from *The Early Poems of Henry Wadsworth Longfellow* (Boston: Houghton, Mifflin and Company, 1884).

Leigh Hunt, "The Fish, the Man, and the Spirit," from *The Poetical Works of Leigh Hunt* (Boston: Ticknor and Fields, 1857).

Jones Very, "The Columbine," from *Poems* (Boston: Houghton, Mifflin and Company, 1883).

Matthew Arnold, "Written in Emerson's Essays," from *Poems* (London: Macmillan, 1890).

Joseph Blanco White, "Mysterious Night," from *Life of the Reverend Joseph Blanco White, Written by Himself,* vol. 3 (London: J. Chapman, 1845).

Elizabeth Barrett Browning, *Sonnets from the Portuguese* 28, from *Sonnets from the Portuguese* (Portland, Maine: Thomas Mosher, 1910).

Frederick Goddard Tuckerman, "I looked across the rollers of the deep," from *Selected Poems of Frederick Goddard Tuckerman,* ed. Ben Mazer (Cambridge, Mass.: Harvard University Press, 2010).

Charles Baudelaire, "Retreat," translated by Rachel Hadas in Hadas, *Other Worlds than This* (New Brunswick: Rutgers University Press, 1994).

George Meredith, *Modern Love* 50, from *Modern Love* (London and New York: Macmillan, 1892).

Charles Tennyson Turner, "A Dream," from Turner, *Collected Sonnets, Old and New* (London: Kegan Paul, 1880).

Henry Timrod, "I know not why, but all this weary day," from *Poems of Henry Timrod, with Memoir and Portrait* (Richmond, Va.: B. F. Johnson Publishing Company, 1901).

Alice Meynell, "Renouncement," from *Collected Poems* (New York:. Scribner, 1913).

George Eliot, *Brother and Sister* 7 and 8, from *The Works of George Eliot,* vol. 12: *Poems* (Boston: Little, Brown, 1900).

Dante Gabriel Rossetti, "For a Venetian Pastoral by Giorgione (in the Louvre)," from *The Collected Works of Dante Gabriel Rossetti* (London: Ellis and Elvey, 1887).

Dante Gabriel Rossetti, "A Superscription," from *Complete Poetical Works,* ed. William M. Rossetti (Boston: Roberts Brothers, 1887).

Henry Wadsworth Longfellow, "The Cross of Snow," from *The Sonnets of Henry Wadsworth Longfellow* (Boston: Houghton, Mifflin and Company, 1907).

Christina Rossetti, *Later Life* 17, from *Poems of Christina Rossetti* (London: Macmillan, 1904).

Emma Lazarus, "The New Colossus," from *The Poems of Emma Lazarus* (Boston: Houghton, Mifflin and Company, 1889).

Gerard Manley Hopkins, "As kingfishers catch fire, dragonflies draw flame" and "Thou art indeed just," from *Poems,* ed. Robert Bridges (London: Humphrey Milford, 1918).

Trumbull Stickney, "Mt. Lykaion," from *The Poems of Trumbull Stickney,* ed. George Cabot Lodge, William Vaughn Moody, and John Ellerton Lodge (Boston: Houghton, Mifflin and Company, 1905).

Michael Field, "Nests in Elms," from *Wild Honey from Various Thyme* (London: Fisher Unwin, 1908).

Rainer Maria Rilke, "Archaic Torso of Apollo," translated by Edward Snow, from *New Poems: A Revised Bilingual Edition* (San Francisco: North Point Press, 2001).

Thomas Hardy, "A Church Romance," from *Time's Laughingstocks and Other Verses* (London: Macmillan, 1909).

Robert Frost, "Mowing," from *A Boy's Will* (New York: Henry Holt, 1915).

Edna St. Vincent Millay, "Bluebeard," from *Renascence and Other Poems* (New York: Harper, 1917).

Edwin Arlington Robinson, "Firelight," from *Collected Poems* (New York: Macmillan, 1921).

Claude McKay, "America," from *The Liberator,* December 1921.

Elinor Wylie, "Self-Portrait," from *The New Republic,* March 1922.

Ivor Gurney, "On Somme," from *Collected Poems,* ed. P. J. Kavanagh rev. ed. (Manchester: Carcanet, 2004).

Wallace Stevens, "Nomad Exquisite," from *Harmonium* (New York: Knopf, 1923).

Countee Cullen, "At the Wailing Wall in Jerusalem," from *Copper Sun* (New York and London: Harper and Brothers, 1927).

William Butler Yeats, "Leda and the Swan," from *The Tower* (London: Macmillan, 1928).

Hart Crane, "To Emily Dickinson," from *Complete Poems* (New York: Liveright, 2000).

Yvor Winters, "The Castle of Thorns," from *The Selected Poems of Yvor Winters,* ed. R. L. Barth (Athens, Ohio: Ohio University Press / Swallow Press, 1999).

Marianne Moore, "No Swan So Fine," from *Complete Poems* (New York: Macmillan / Viking Press, 1982).

Louise Bogan, "Single Sonnet," from *The Blue Estuaries: Poems 1923–1968* (New York: Farrar, Straus and Giroux, 1968).

W. H. Auden, *In Time of War* 27 ("Wandering lost upon the mountains of our choice"), from *The English Auden: Poems, Essays and Dramatic Writings, 1927–1939,* ed. Edward Mendelson (London: Faber and Faber, 1988).

Robert Frost, "Never Again Would Birds' Song Be the Same," from *Complete Poems* (New York: Henry Holt, 1949).

Patrick Kavanagh, "Epic," from *Collected Poems,* ed. Antoinette Quinn (London: Allen Lane, 2004).

William Meredith, "The Illiterate," from *Effort at Speech* (Evanston, Ill.: Northwestern University Press, 1997).

James Merrill, "Marsyas," from *Collected Poems,* ed. J. D. McClatchy and Stephen Yenser (New York: Knopf, 2001).

Ted Berrigan, *The Sonnets* 44, from *The Sonnets,* ed. Alice Notley (New York: Penguin, 2000).

Gwendolyn Brooks, "To a Winter Squirrel," from *Blacks* (Chicago: Third World Press, 1994).

James K. Baxter, *Autumn Testament,* no. 27 ("When I stayed those three months at Macdonald Crescent"), from *Collected Poems,* ed. J. E. Weir (Oxford: Oxford University Press, 1979).

Robert Lowell, "Searching," from *Selected Poems* (New York: Farrar, Straus and Giroux, 1976).

A. D. Hope, "Paradise Saved," from *New Poems, 1965–1969* (New York: Viking Press, 1970).

May Swenson, "Staring at the Sea on the Day of the Death of Another," from *Nature: Poems Old and New,* ed. Susan Mitchell (New York: Houghton Mifflin Harcourt, 2000).

A. K. Ramanujan, *Mythologies* 3, from *The Oxford India Ramanujan* (New Delhi: Oxford University Press, 2004).

Derek Walcott, "The Morning Moon," from *Collected Poems* (New York: Farrar, Straus and Giroux, 1986).

Tony Harrison, "National Trust," from *Selected Poems,* rev. ed. (New York: Penguin, 1987).

Elizabeth Bishop, "Sonnet," from *The Complete Poems, 1927–1979* (New York: Farrar, Straus and Giroux, 1984).

Geoffrey Hill, *An Apology for the Revival of Christian Architecture in England* 7, "Loss and Gain," from *New and Collected Poems* (Boston: Houghton Mifflin, 1994).

Seamus Heaney, *Glanmore Sonnets* 1, from *Opened Ground* (New York: Farrar, Straus and Giroux, 1998).

Amy Clampitt, "The Cormorant in Its Element," from *The Collected Poems of Amy Clampitt* (New York: Knopf, 1997).

Denis Johnson, "Man Walking to Work," from *The Throne of the New Heaven of the Nations: New and Collected Poems* (New York: HarperCollins, 1995).

Edgar Bowers, "Jacob," from *Collected Poems* (New York: Knopf, 1997).

Les Murray, "Strangler Fig," from *Translations from the Natural World* (New York: Farrar, Straus and Giroux, 1993).

John Hollander, "Into the Black," from *Tesserae and Other Poems* (New York: Knopf, 1993).

Rosanna Warren, "Necrophiliac," from *Stained Glass* (New York: Norton, 1993).

Rita Dove, "Party Dress for a First Born," from *Mother Love* (New York: Norton, 1996).

Michele Leggott, "in winter," from *as far as I can see* (Auckland: Auckland University Press, 1999).

Forrest Gander, *Voiced Stops* 1, from *Torn Awake* (New York: New Directions, 2001).

Tony Lopez, *Radial Symmetry* 3, from *False Memory* (Cambridge: Salt, 2003).

Mary Dalton, "Flirrup," from *Merrybegot* (Montreal: Signal/Véhicule, 2003).

Alison Brackenbury, "Homework. Write a Sonnet. About Love?" from *Bricks and Ballads* (Manchester: Carcanet, 2004).

Lucie Brock-Broido, "Physicism," from *Trouble in Mind* (New York: Knopf, 2004).

Donald Revell, "Zion," from *Pennyweight Windows* (Farmington, Maine: Alice James, 2005).

Paul Muldoon, "Starlings, Broad Street, Trenton, 2003," from *Horse Latitudes* (New York: Farrar, Straus and Giroux, 2006).

Martha Serpas, "Psalm at High Tide." from *The Dirty Side of the Storm* (New York: Norton, 2007).

Rafael Campo, "Rest Stop near the Italian Border," from *The Enemy* (Durham, N.C.: Duke University Press, 2007).

D. A. Powell, "corydon & alexis, redux," from *Chronic* (St. Paul, Minn.: Graywolf, 2009).

Further Reading

We give here collections of sonnets, and books about sonnets, that have proven especially useful, along with selected works of modern literary criticism cited or quoted within our essays. We have consulted, and been influenced by, many more critics than we list here. We give only those critical works that a variety of readers might want to pursue. We do not list other and older primary works quoted (e.g., Jane Austen's novel *Persuasion,* Philip Sidney's *Defence of Poetry*), whose titles and dates of publication are given within the essays themselves. We list only some of the essays and articles we quote; the rest should be easy, given modern library resources, for other scholars to find.

ANTHOLOGIES

Boland, Eavan, and Edward Hirsch, eds. *The Making of a Sonnet: A Norton Anthology.* New York: Norton, 2008.

Bromwich, David, ed. *American Sonnets.* New York: Library of America, 2007.

Feldman, Paula R., and Daniel Robinson, eds. *A Century of Sonnets: The Romantic-Era Revival, 1750–1850.* New York: Oxford University Press, 1999.

Fuller, John, ed. *The Oxford Book of Sonnets.* Oxford: Oxford University Press, 2000.

Hunt, Leigh, and S. Adams Lee, eds. *The Book of the Sonnet.* Boston: Roberts Brothers, 1867.

Kallich, Martin, Jack C. Gray, and Robert M. Rodney, eds. *A Book of the Sonnet: Poems and Criticism.* New York: Twayne, 1973.

Levin, Phillis, ed. *The Penguin Book of the Sonnet.* New York: Penguin, 2001.

Paterson, Don, ed. *101 Sonnets: From Shakespeare to Heaney.* London: Faber and Faber, 1999.

Russell, Matthew, ed. *Sonnets on the Sonnet.* London: Longmans, Green, 1898.

Sharp, William, ed. *Sonnets of This Century.* London: Walter Scott, 1886.

CRITICAL BOOKS CITED

Bernstein, Michael André. *Modernity and the Imagination in Twentieth-Century German Writing.* Evanston, Ill.: Northwestern University Press, 2000.

Birkerts, Sven. "The Rilke Boom." *Threepenny Review* 35 (Autumn 1988): 15–18.

Bloom, Harold. "The Internalization of Quest-Romance." In Bloom, ed., *Romanticism and Consciousness*. New York: Norton, 1970.

Booth, Stephen. *Shakespeare's Sonnets*. New Haven: Yale University Press, 1977.

Brisman, Leslie. *Milton's Poetry of Choice and Its Romantic Heirs*. Ithaca, N.Y.: Cornell University Press, 1973.

Chandler, James. *England in 1819*. Chicago: University of Chicago Press, 1998.

Elder, John. "The Poetry of Experience." *New Literary History* 30:3 (1999): 649–659. (On Frost's "Mowing.")

Ferry, Anne. *The "Inward" Language: Sonnets of Wyatt, Sidney, Shakespeare, Donne*. Chicago: University of Chicago Press, 1983.

Ferry, David. *The Limits of Mortality: An Essay on Wordsworth's Major Poems*. Middletown, Conn.: Wesleyan University Press, 1959.

Greenblatt, Stephen. *Renaissance Self-Fashioning*. Chicago: University of Chicago Press, 1980.

Grossman, Allen. "Milton's Sonnet 'On the Late Massacre in Piemont': The Vulnerability of Persons in a Revolutionary Situation." In Grossman, *The Long Schoolroom: Lessons in the Bitter Logic of the Poetic Principle*. Ann Arbor, Mich.: University of Michigan Press, 1997.

Guss, Donald. *John Donne, Petrarchist*. Detroit: Wayne State University Press, 1966.

Hartman, Geoffrey. *Criticism in the Wilderness: The Study of Literature Today*. New Haven: Yale University Press, 1980. (On Yeats's "Leda and the Swan.")

Hollander, John. *The Gazer's Spirit: Poems Speaking to Silent Works of Art*. Chicago: University of Chicago Press, 1998.

——— ed. *The Essential Rossetti*. New York: Ecco Press, 1990.

Holmes, Richard. *Coleridge: Darker Reflections*. London: HarperCollins, 1998.

Huggins, Nathan Irvin. *Harlem Renaissance*. New York: Oxford University Press, 1973. (On McKay's "America.")

Hynes, Samuel. *The Pattern of Hardy's Poetry*. Chapel Hill, N.C.: University of North Carolina Press, 1961.

Kalstone, David. *Sidney's Poetry*. Cambridge, Mass.: Harvard University Press, 1965.

Kendall, Tim. *Modern English War Poetry*. Oxford: Oxford University Press, 2006.

Lopez, Tony. *Meaning Performance*. Cambridge: Salt, 2006.

McClatchy, J. D., ed. *Poets of the Civil War*. New York: Library of America, 2005.

Miller, Christopher. *The Invention of Evening: Perception and Time in Romantic Poetry*. Cambridge: Cambridge University Press, 2006.

Muir, Kenneth. *Introduction to Elizabethan Literature*. New York: Random House, 1967.

New, Elisa. *The Line's Eye: Poetic Experience, American Sight.* Cambridge, Mass.: Harvard University Press, 1998.

Oppenheimer, Paul. *The Birth of the Modern Mind: Self, Consciousness and the Invention of the Sonnet.* New York: Oxford University Press, 1989.

Phelan, Joseph. *The Nineteenth-Century Sonnet.* New York: Palgrave Macmillan, 2005.

Poirier, Richard. *Robert Frost: The Work of Knowing.* New York: Oxford University Press, 1977.

Ramazani, R. Jahan. *Poetry of Mourning: The Modern Elegy from Hardy to Heaney.* Chicago: University of Chicago Press, 1994.

Rebholz, A. C. *The Life of Fulke Greville.* Oxford: Clarendon Press, 1971.

Richardson, James. *Thomas Hardy: The Poetry of Necessity.* Chicago: University of Chicago Press, 1977.

Sacks, Peter. *The English Elegy.* Baltimore: Johns Hopkins University Press, 1985.

Schor, Esther. *Emma Lazarus.* New York: Nextbook/Schocken, 2006.

Sessions, William A. *Henry Howard, the Poet Earl of Surrey: A Life.* Oxford: Oxford University Press, 1999.

Spiller, Michael R. G. *The Development of the Sonnet.* London: Routledge, 1992.

Strier, Richard. *Love Known: Theology and Experience in George Herbert's Poetry.* Chicago: University of Chicago Press, 1983.

Tyler, Meg. *A Singing Contest: Conventions of Sound in the Poetry of Seamus Heaney.* New York: Routledge, 2005.

Vendler, Helen. *The Poetry of George Herbert.* Cambridge, Mass.: Harvard University Press, 1975.

———— *The Odes of John Keats.* Cambridge, Mass.: Harvard University Press, 1983.

———— *Our Secret Discipline: Yeats and Lyric Form.* Cambridge, Mass.: Harvard University Press, 2007.

Wagner, Jennifer. *A Moment's Monument: Revisionary Poetics and the Nineteenth-Century Sonnet.* Madison, N.J.: Fairleigh Dickinson University Press, 1994.

Williamson, Alan. *Westernness* (Charlottesville: University of Virginia Press, 2006.

Wojahn, David. *Strange Good Fortune: Essays on Contemporary Poetry.* Fayetteville: University of Arkansas Press, 2001.

Yezzi, David. "The Seriousness of Yvor Winters." *The New Criterion* 15 (June 1997): 26–35.

Acknowledgments

Stephen Burt gives thanks, here as at the conclusion of every project, for the sanity, kindness, and love of Jessica Bennett, and for the boundless energy and the love of Nathan Bennett Burt. David Mikics thanks Victoria Malkin, for endless cheering up and just the right amount of skepticism.

We thank our editor, John Kulka, who guided us toward completion with a strong and gentle hand; and Maria Ascher, Ian Stevenson, and Matthew Hills, who assisted the three of us at Harvard University Press. For correcting our own misapprehensions and improving our sense of how to read their work, we also thank some poets whose sonnets appear in this book: Lucie Brock-Broido, Mary Dalton, Forrest Gander, Michele Leggott, D. A. Powell, Donald Revell, and Rosanna Warren. We give thanks for the sharp eyes, the critical intelligence, the guidance, and the information brought to us, for use in this book, by Dan Albright, Isobel Armstrong, Dorothy Baker, Heather Dubrow, James Engell, Jamie Ferguson, Martin Greenup, Langdon Hammer, Tony Hoagland, Peter Howarth, Jennifer Lewin, Peter Sacks, Michael Schmidt, S. N. Sridhar, Helen Vendler, and the anonymous readers appointed by Harvard University Press; we are grateful, additionally, for practical assistance from the staff of the Harvard University English Department, and in particular (as regards this project) from Anna McDonald, Eric Thorsen, Case Kerns, and Sol Kim Bentley. Grants from Harvard's Clark Fund and the University of Houston's Houstoun Fund assisted with permissions. The librarians of the Carl H. Pforzheimer Collection at the New York Public Library kindly granted access to the manuscript of John Clare's "Swordy Well," and David Smith, also at the library, was helpful too. Steve Monte helped with Baudelaire.

Each of us seems to have found the other to be the best of collaborators: we are grateful that we have learned so much from each other, before and during our work on these hundred sonnets. All mistakes that remain are of course and only our own.

Credits

Index